Peace on a Knife's Edge

PEACE ON A KNIFE'S EDGE

THE INSIDE STORY OF ROH MOO-HYUN'S
NORTH KOREA POLICY

by **Lee Jong-seok**

translated by **Koo Se-woong**

Stanford | APARC Walter H. Shorenstein Asia-Pacific Research Center   FSI Freeman Spogli Institute for International Studies

THE WALTER H. SHORENSTEIN ASIA-PACIFIC RESEARCH CENTER
(Shorenstein APARC) is a unique Stanford University institution focused on the
interdisciplinary study of contemporary Asia. Shorenstein APARC's mission is to
produce and publish outstanding interdisciplinary, Asia-Pacific–focused research; to
educate students, scholars, and corporate and governmental affiliates; to promote
constructive interaction to influence U.S. policy toward the Asia-Pacific; and to guide
Asian nations on key issues of societal transition, development, U.S.-Asia relations, and
regional cooperation.

The Walter H. Shorenstein Asia-Pacific Research Center
Freeman Spogli Institute for International Studies
Stanford University
Encina Hall
Stanford, CA 94305-6055
tel. 650-723-9741 | fax 650-723-6530 | http://aparc.fsi.stanford.edu

Peace on a Knife's Edge: The Inside Story of Roh Moo-hyun's North Korea Policy
may be ordered from:
The Brookings Institution
c/o DFS, P.O. Box 50370, Baltimore, MD, USA
tel. 1-800-537-5487 or 410-516-6956 | fax 410-516-6998
http://www.brookings.edu/press

Walter H. Shorenstein Asia-Pacific Research Center Books, 2017.

Library of Congress Cataloging-in-Publication Data

Names: Yi, Chong-sŏk , 1958- author.
Title: Peace on a knife's edge : the inside story of Roh Moo-hyun's North
    Korea policy / Lee Jong-Seok.
Other titles: K'allal wi ŭi p'yŏnghwa:. English.
Description: Stanford, CA : The Walter H. Shorenstein Asia-Pacific Research
    Center, 2017. | Includes bibliographical references and index.
Identifiers: LCCN 2017039124 | ISBN 9781931368438 (alk. paper)
Subjects: LCSH: Korea (South)--Foreign relations--2002- | Korea
    (South)--Politics and government--2002- | National security--Korea (South)
    | Roh, Moo Hyun, 1946-2009.
Classification: LCC DS923.27 .Y52313 2017 | DDC 327.519505193--dc23
LC record available at https://lccn.loc.gov/2017039124

First published in South Korea in 2014 as *K'allal wi ŭi p'yŏnghwa*
First printing, 2017
ISBN 978-1-931368-43-8

Contents

Foreword

Of the alliances established by the United States in the post-1945 period, the U.S.–Republic of Korea alliance is one of the most enduring and successful, having evolved from its beginnings during the Korean War as a "patron-client" relationship, as many experts have argued, to one that has overcome many challenges. While the United States remains powerful, South Korea has moved beyond its status as subordinate partner, having developed its own "lens" through which to view the alliance. As I argued in my book, *One Alliance, Two Lenses*, in the post–Cold War era and during the Kim Dae-jung (1998–2003) and Roh Moo-hyun (2003–08) administrations, economically prosperous, democratizing South Korea developed a progressive lens or point of view.

While Korean progressives value the alliance with the United States, they stress the importance of reconciliation with North Korea. Thus, in dealing with the North, they seek to separate business and politics, as best illustrated by the Sunshine Policy of the Kim Dae-jung administration, which led to the creation of the Kaesong Industrial Complex, for example. And it was during the two progressive administrations that inter-Korean summits were able to take place (in 2000 and 2007). Although the progressive approach of engagement drew criticism from both Seoul and Washington, it clearly represented the new way of thinking about the continued division of South and North. But it is important to note that even a progressive like Roh Moo-hyun, who was often critical of U.S. policy toward North Korea, still ended up taking steps that strengthened the alliance, including the U.S.-Korea Free Trade Agreement (KORUS FTA).

The author of this memoir, Dr. Lee Jong-seok, is a key figure in the progressive camp of the South Korean national security community. Trained as a scholar of North Korea, he served as a senior advisor to the late president Roh in the Blue House and then as the unification minister. *Peace on a Knife's Edge* best represents South Korean progressive views of key national security issues, including how they view the alliance and inter-Korean relations. After leaving government, Dr. Lee spent one year here at the Shorenstein Asia-Pacific Research Center as a visiting fellow and it was my pleasure to have him share his views with us. Now, after two consecutive conservative governments, South Korean progressives are back in power with Moon Jae-in as the new president. Moon was a friend of Roh Moo-hyun and served in his administration as a key advisor, including as his chief of staff. As the Trump and Moon administrations struggle to deal with the North Korean nuclear and missile issues, it is imperative to understand the progressive thinking of the South Korean national security community. In this context, this publication could not be more important or timely.

Gi-Wook Shin
Stanford, California

Preface to the English Edition

This book is a translation of my memoir on the unification, foreign affairs, and national security (UFN) policies of the Republic of Korea (ROK) under the Roh Moo-hyun government (2003–08). The Korean version, published in 2014, was condensed and edited before being translated into English for Western readers.

Under the ROK's sixteenth president, Roh Moo-hyun, I served as a member of the transition committee, as deputy secretary-general of the National Security Council (NSC), and as unification minister—a total of about four years from the start of the administration. During that time, and especially during the first three years, which saw numerous challenges and problems for South Korea's foreign policy and national security, I was the de facto head of the NSC Secretariat, an institution that existed to realize the president's strategic thinking and policy.

I never planned to write a memoir about that time—my task was merely to uphold the president's thinking and directives, articulating or executing them. I had no story of my own to tell. President Roh would one day, during his retirement, write his own memoirs; I thought that I might consider writing about those events only if there were something I could add.

The situation changed when President Roh died unexpectedly in May 2009, without leaving behind a presidential memoir. There were two reasons in particular that influenced my decision to take on the duty of writing it. First, I felt an obligation to create a record of everything the Roh administration did in the UFN realm—its successes and failures, achievements, trials and errors, sources of pride and regret—along with the reasons behind those events, in their entirety, for history's sake. Second, I wanted to stress, to the many people who loved President Roh, that he was a leader to be proud of, not through a subjective interpretation but based on the objective record. By doing this, I wanted to set the record straight and correct the ideologically and emotionally charged criticisms against President Roh and his government, even if my defense of him came after his death. That is why, I dare say, this book has partly taken on the character of a memoir that looks back on the Roh Moo-hyun era from the perspective of President Roh himself.

Through this book, I strive to show that the values President Roh and his government pursued in the UFN domain were universal values based on common sense and rationality. Those values were peace, autonomy, and balance, and they are obvious in the Roh administration's national security strategy, which was founded on the pursuit of a policy for peace and prosperity, balanced practical diplomacy, cooperative autonomous defense, and comprehensive security. Peace, autonomy, and balance are common sense and offer a common good for South Koreans as a whole, both progressive and conservative. As the leader of an antagonistically divided nation that is dependent on foreign powers, President Roh wanted to protect his people from threats of war, to promote peace, and to pursue a way of life that was decided autonomously by Koreans as a national collective. He also pursued a balanced U.S.-ROK alliance that was in keeping with the Republic of Korea's elevated standing, and balanced diplomacy in acknowledgement of the new international reality exemplified by China's rise. In this way, President Roh was a progressive, but the values he pursued in the UFN realm were based on good sense and logic, transcending the labels of progressive and conservative. I wholeheartedly agreed with the president on his policy line, and did my best to serve him, however limited my abilities were.

The title of this book is *Peace on a Knife's Edge*. President Roh ardently desired peace, and he sought to keep and strengthen peace through autonomy and balance. Peace is a fundamental desire of the people of the Republic of Korea, who have lived through war and conflict; it is also a precondition for the two Koreas' mutual prosperity in the era of unification. But peace is difficult to achieve. Even when it seemed that we had peace, it was precarious and unstable. This peace, which barely stands on an agreement among entities that have yet to overcome their confrontational relationship of mistrust, has always been vulnerable to collapsing—it is as if we are standing on a knife's edge.

But the Roh administration did its utmost to keep this peace, even if balanced on a knife's edge. This was a precondition to progressing to the next level—peace on the *back* of a knife rather than the edge—and then to ultimately pursue peace on a solid foundation.

I wrote this book with the idea that I stand before the mirror of history. A significant portion of the foreign policy and national security thinking and its execution during the time of the Roh administration has not been revealed for security reasons. But in this book, I tried to record events as they really happened. Of course, some things still cannot be revealed or can be described only in a cursory fashion because of national security concerns or diplomatic considerations. And the fact that many of the characters in this book are still alive weighed on my mind. So, some events required a cautious approach.

But for national security matters that have already passed into history, or have already been disclosed in the press, I tried my best to relate events as they really happened. In particular, regarding situations that were widely misrepresented in contemporaneous media reports, I wrote in detail the full truth, given that the honor of the Roh administration was at stake. And when it was absolutely necessary for understanding President Roh and the Roh Moo-hyun era, I named the relevant figures, even when the disclosure might lead to some discomfort.

This is not a complete record of my four years in the Roh administration. I covered mainly events I could remember, that I considered important, and that could be confirmed through records. Once I started reflecting on the past and looking for relevant materials in order to write this memoir, I could not believe that so many things had happened during such a short time, and that I lived through them all. While this travel back in time covers only four years, I felt as though I spent more than a decade back in the past. As if unzipping a compressed computer file, so many stories that had been buried poured out. Naturally, I could not write about all of them. Some of my former colleagues might feel slighted because there isn't even a mention of the work they were responsible for. I can only say that I am very sorry.

I wrote this book as a historical record, and for the honor of the Roh administration. But my other intention was to provide researchers studying South Korea's UFN policy with a detailed primary source. I also hope that the book could be a kind of a lesson for future administrations to reflect on and draw from.

Many have helped to bring the English edition of this book to publication. First of all, I want to thank Dr. Gi-wook Shin at Stanford University. He read the Korean edition and actively encouraged me to publish an English version, saying that Americans, too, should read this book. He also allowed me a chance to publish it through the Shorenstein Asia-Pacific Research Center at Stanford University. I also want to thank Dr. Koo Se-Woong, who accepted my request without hesitation and carried out the difficult task of translating the book into English with the mindset of a co-author. It was my luck to meet this young intellectual in possession of superb translation skills and affection for the Roh administration. I also want to express my gratitude to George Krompacky at Shorenstein APARC for taking charge of publishing the English edition and seeing the project to its completion.

Finally, I want to thank my NSC and unification ministry colleagues who carried out the Roh administration's UFN policy together with me and contributed to a presidential administration worthy of recording in history. I respectfully dedicate this book to the late President Roh.

Lee Jong-seok
November 2017

Translator's Note

When *New York Times* Seoul bureau chief Choe Sang-hun asked me in the spring of 2015 whether I would be willing to translate a memoir, I thought he was speaking half in jest. Then I found out that the author was none other than Dr. Lee Jong-seok, and I immediately knew I would be taking on the project.

Dr. Lee is one of South Korea's foremost experts on North Korea, inter-Korean relations, and Korea-China relations. His tenure at the helm of South Korea's national security policy under President Roh Moo-hyun in the 2000s is well known. Dr. Lee's memoir from that time is significant not only because it offers an insider's view of South Korean progressives' thinking about North Korea and about the United States, an important ally, but because President Roh tragically died not long after his retirement from politics in 2008, without penning his own memoir. While South Korea's current president Moon Jae-in, both a friend and chief of staff to President Roh, has written at length about their relationship and Roh's personal character, Dr. Lee, as one of President Roh's closest aides, has produced an important account of national security and foreign policy under the Participatory Government (a nickname given to the Roh administration) that is unmatched by most sources in knowledge and intimacy.

I have no background in politics or international diplomacy, so translating this book has been in itself a lesson on South Korean history and governance. In translating, my primary goal was to maximize readability for others like me. This is not an academic translation, so in many cases I eschewed literal conversion of Korean into English and opted to highlight nuances and simplify the prose so that even non-specialist readers could find it engaging as well as informative.

Many characters populate this book, and I romanized their names according to the most common renditions found in English-language sources. When no preexisting English rendition could be found, I relied on the Revised Romanization of Korean, the standard system used in South Korea, except in a small number of cases involving book titles.

Korean, Chinese, and Japanese names are given according to East Asian order, with surnames first.

Finishing this translation has taken more than two years, and I want to thank Dr. Lee for the infinite patience and trust he has shown me during this long period. My gratitude also goes to George Krompacky, publications manager at Shorenstein Asia-Pacific Research Center, and to proofreader Fayre Makeig for working with me to smooth out my convoluted sentences and catch my numerous mistakes. Without their help, this project would not have been possible. And of course, any errors that may remain are entirely mine.

Koo Se-woong
November 2017

List of Names

Those from North Korea are noted as DPRK; all others are
South Koreans who appear in the text several times.

Ban Ki-moon	Foreign affairs advisor; foreign minister
Cha Young-gu	Director of policy, Defense Ministry
Cho Young-kil	Defense minister
Choi Seung-chul	Deputy director, United Front Department (DPRK)
Chung Dong-young	Unification minister (2004–05)
Chung Mong-joon	Leader of the National Unity 21 Party
Jang Song-thaek	First division deputy-chief, Administrative Department, Workers' Party of Korea (DPRK)
Lim Dong-ok	First deputy director, United Front Department (DPRK)
Kim Dae-jung	President, South Korea (1998–2003)
Kim Kye-gwan	Vice foreign minister (DPRK)
Kim Hee-sang	Defense advisor
Kim Jin-hyang	Member, NSC Secretariat
Kim Sook	Director-general, North American Affairs Bureau, Foreign Ministry
Kim Yong-nam	President, Supreme People's Assembly (DPRK)
Kim Yong-sun	Secretary for South Korean Affairs and head of the United Front Department (DPRK)
Kim Young-sam	President, South Korea (1993–98)
Lee Hae-chan	Prime minister, South Korea (2004–06)
Lee Hoi-chang	Grand National Party candidate
Lee Jong-seok	(Author) Deputy secretary-general, NSC; unification minister
Lee Soo-hyuk	Deputy foreign minister
Lim Dong-won	Senior secretary of foreign affairs and national security under Kim Dae-jung; unification minister
Moon Hee-sang	Blue House chief of staff
Park Chung-hee	President, South Korea (1963–79)

Park Sun-won	Senior official, National Security Council
Ra Jong-yil	National Security Advisor
Roh Moo-hyun	President, South Korea (2003–08)
Roh Tae-woo	President, South Korea (1988–93)
Ryu Hee-in	NSC Secretariat; head of the NSC's Center for Risk Management
Seo Dong-man	Professor, Sangji University; UFN advisory team leader
Seo Joo-seok	Researcher, National Defense Research Institute; UFN advisory team; NSC director of strategic planning
Song Min-soon	Deputy foreign minister; Blue House director of UFN policy
Suh Hoon	Deputy director, National Intelligence Service
Yoon Kwang-woong	Defense minister (beginning July 2004)
Yoon Young-kwan	Professor, Seoul National University; member, UFN advisory team; foreign minister

Abbreviations

APEC	Asia-Pacific Economic Cooperation
ASEAN	Association of Southeast Asian Nations
BDA	Banco Delta Asia
CFC	Combined Forces Command
CONPLAN	conceptual plan
DMZ	Demilitarized Zone
DOD	Department of Defense (U.S.)
DPRK	Democratic Peoples' Republic of Korea
FOTA	Future of the Alliance
GDP	gross domestic product
GPR	Global Defense Review
HEU	highly enriched uranium
IAEA	International Atomic Energy Agency
KBS	Korean Broadcasting System
KEDO	Korean Peninsula Energy Development Organization
KEPCO	Korea Electric Power Corporation
KIDA	Korea Institute for Defense Analyses
KOTRA	Korea Trade Promotion Corporation
LWR	light-water reactor
MD	missile defense
NEAACD	Northeast Asia Cooperation Dialogue
NIS	National Intelligence Service
NLL	Northern Limit Line
NPT	non-proliferation treaty

NSC	National Security Council
OPLAN	operation plan
POW	prisoner of war
PSI	Proliferation Security Initiative
PSPD	People's Solidarity for Participatory Democracy
ROK	Republic of Korea
SCM	Security Consultative Meeting
SOC	social overhead capital
SPI	Security Policy Initiative
SPT	Six-Party Talk
UFN	unification, foreign affairs, and national security
USFK	U.S. Forces Korea
UNC	United Nations Command

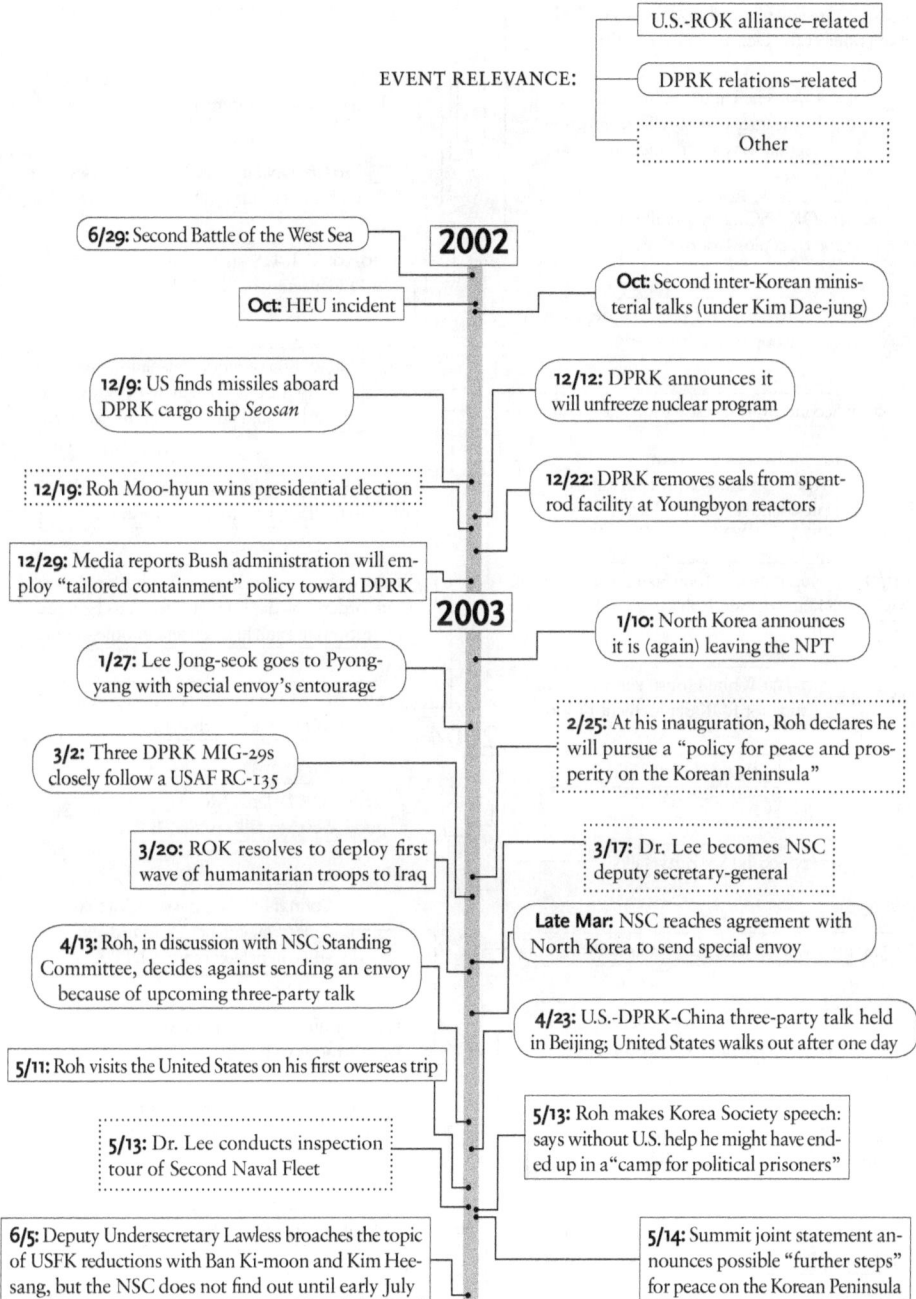

Timeline of Select Events Mentioned in the Text

EVENT RELEVANCE:
- U.S.-ROK alliance–related
- DPRK relations–related
- Other

2002

6/29: Second Battle of the West Sea

Oct: HEU incident

Oct: Second inter-Korean ministerial talks (under Kim Dae-jung)

12/9: US finds missiles aboard DPRK cargo ship *Seosan*

12/12: DPRK announces it will unfreeze nuclear program

12/19: Roh Moo-hyun wins presidential election

12/22: DPRK removes seals from spent-rod facility at Youngbyon reactors

12/29: Media reports Bush administration will employ "tailored containment" policy toward DPRK

2003

1/10: North Korea announces it is (again) leaving the NPT

1/27: Lee Jong-seok goes to Pyongyang with special envoy's entourage

2/25: At his inauguration, Roh declares he will pursue a "policy for peace and prosperity on the Korean Peninsula"

3/2: Three DPRK MIG-29s closely follow a USAF RC-135

3/17: Dr. Lee becomes NSC deputy secretary-general

3/20: ROK resolves to deploy first wave of humanitarian troops to Iraq

Late Mar: NSC reaches agreement with North Korea to send special envoy

4/13: Roh, in discussion with NSC Standing Committee, decides against sending an envoy because of upcoming three-party talk

4/23: U.S.-DPRK-China three-party talk held in Beijing; United States walks out after one day

5/11: Roh visits the United States on his first overseas trip

5/13: Roh makes Korea Society speech: says without U.S. help he might have ended up in a "camp for political prisoners"

5/13: Dr. Lee conducts inspection tour of Second Naval Fleet

6/5: Deputy Undersecretary Lawless broaches the topic of USFK reductions with Ban Ki-moon and Kim Hee-sang, but the NSC does not find out until early July

5/14: Summit joint statement announces possible "further steps" for peace on the Korean Peninsula

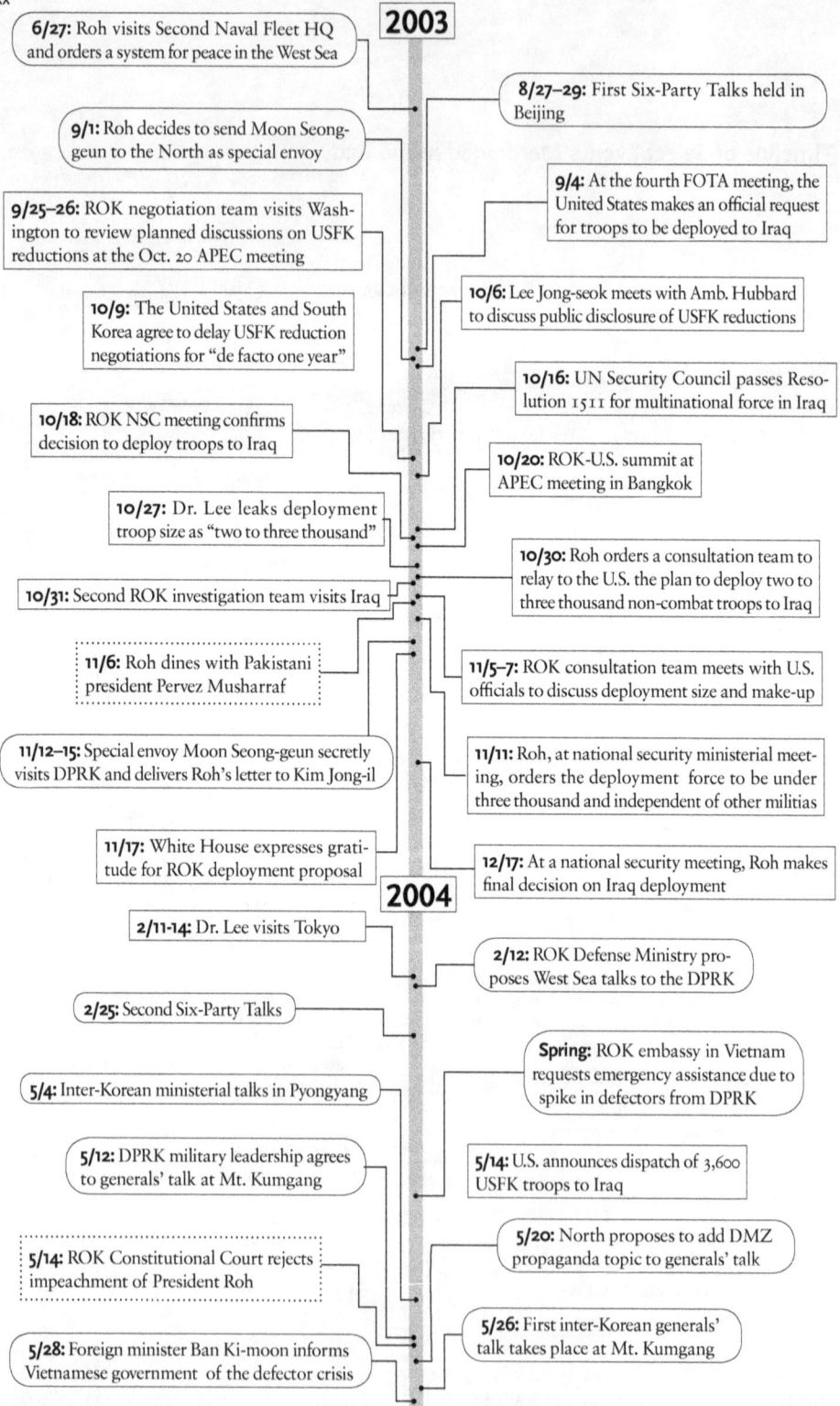

xx

2003

6/27: Roh visits Second Naval Fleet HQ and orders a system for peace in the West Sea

8/27–29: First Six-Party Talks held in Beijing

9/1: Roh decides to send Moon Seong-geun to the North as special envoy

9/4: At the fourth FOTA meeting, the United States makes an official request for troops to be deployed to Iraq

9/25–26: ROK negotiation team visits Washington to review planned discussions on USFK reductions at the Oct. 20 APEC meeting

10/6: Lee Jong-seok meets with Amb. Hubbard to discuss public disclosure of USFK reductions

10/9: The United States and South Korea agree to delay USFK reduction negotiations for "de facto one year"

10/16: UN Security Council passes Resolution 1511 for multinational force in Iraq

10/18: ROK NSC meeting confirms decision to deploy troops to Iraq

10/20: ROK-U.S. summit at APEC meeting in Bangkok

10/27: Dr. Lee leaks deployment troop size as "two to three thousand"

10/30: Roh orders a consultation team to relay to the U.S. the plan to deploy two to three thousand non-combat troops to Iraq

10/31: Second ROK investigation team visits Iraq

11/6: Roh dines with Pakistani president Pervez Musharraf

11/5-7: ROK consultation team meets with U.S. officials to discuss deployment size and make-up

11/12–15: Special envoy Moon Seong-geun secretly visits DPRK and delivers Roh's letter to Kim Jong-il

11/11: Roh, at national security ministerial meeting, orders the deployment force to be under three thousand and independent of other militias

11/17: White House expresses gratitude for ROK deployment proposal

12/17: At a national security meeting, Roh makes final decision on Iraq deployment

2004

2/11-14: Dr. Lee visits Tokyo

2/12: ROK Defense Ministry proposes West Sea talks to the DPRK

2/25: Second Six-Party Talks

Spring: ROK embassy in Vietnam requests emergency assistance due to spike in defectors from DPRK

5/4: Inter-Korean ministerial talks in Pyongyang

5/12: DPRK military leadership agrees to generals' talk at Mt. Kumgang

5/14: U.S. announces dispatch of 3,600 USFK troops to Iraq

5/14: ROK Constitutional Court rejects impeachment of President Roh

5/20: North proposes to add DMZ propaganda topic to generals' talk

5/28: Foreign minister Ban Ki-moon informs Vietnamese government of the defector crisis

5/26: First inter-Korean generals' talk takes place at Mt. Kumgang

2004

Early summer: Tongil Maji group requests permission to pay respects on tenth anniversary of Kim Il Sung's death

6/3–4: Second inter-Korean generals' talk takes place at Mt. Seorak in South Korea.

6/3–4: Ninth inter-Korean economic cooperation committee meets and makes rice shipments conditional on a West Sea system

6/23–26: Third Six-Party Talks held

6/15: Propaganda equipment along DMZ begins to be dismantled

6/27–28: 468 DPRK defectors removed from Vietnam by charter plane, although plan was leaked to press; inter-Korean dialogue comes to a halt until May 2005

7/14: DPRK patrol boat repelled after crossing the NLL; ROK military fails to report being in communication with the North's ship

7/16: NSC Standing Committee holds emergency meeting on discrepancies regarding report of the NLL incursion

7/19: Military investigative team reports on NLL incursion to president. Roh orders another investigation focusing on the inaccuracy of initial military reports.

7/21: At a press conference, President Roh suggests Seoul would not raise the "history issue" with Japan during his administration

7/23: Second investigation into NLL incursion concludes

7/28: Roh fires defense minister Cho Young-kil

Aug: Zaytun Division arrives in Arbil, Iraq

Early Sept: ROK tests of nuclear material disclosed: the "nuclear materials incident"

Oct: North Korea Human Rights Act passed in United States

11/5: Dr. Lee presents "Plan to Make Progress..." to President Roh

11/13: Roh makes anti-hardline speech in Los Angeles

11/20: ROK-U.S. summit during APEC meeting in Santiago, Chile

Dec: Roh's letter to Hu Jintao is delivered

12/2: Roh visits Britain and talks to Tony Blair

12/8: Roh visits the Zaytun Division in Arbil, Iraq

2005

1/13: North Korean Red Cross sends first of seven requests for fertilizer aid to its Southern counterpart

1/17: Roh invites newly appointed assistant undersecretary for Asian-Pacific affairs, Christopher Hill, to talk

1/18: At her confirmation hearings, Condoleezza Rice calls North Korea an "outpost of tyranny"

2/10: Pyongyang announces suspension of the Six-Party Talks and its possession of nuclear arms

2/19: Chinese special envoy Wang Jiarui visits North Korea

2/19: Dr. Lee briefs President Roh on the secret plan to directly provide North Korea with electricity

3/2: North Korean Foreign Ministry expresses conditional interest in restarting the Six-Party Talks

2005

Mar-Apr: President Roh begins to articulate the "Northeast Asia balancer theory"

3/8: In a speech to the Korea Air Force Academy, Roh asserts that South Korea will not be drawn into a Northeast Asian conflict against its will

6/10: At ROK-U.S. summit, President Bush refers to "Mr." Kim Jong-il at the press conference

5/16: Inter-Korean dialogue resumed after almost a year with vice ministers' talks in Kaesong; fertilizer shipment is sent to the North

6/17: Chung Dong-young meets with Kim Jong-il as special envoy

7/9: Following a meeting in Beijing between Christopher Hill and DPRK vice foreign minister Kim Kye-gwan, the fourth Six-Party Talks are announced for the week of July 15

7/12: At ROK-U.S. foreign ministers' meeting in Seoul, U.S. secretary of state Rice proposes discussing the establishment of a peace regime on the Korean Peninsula, contingent on the DPRK abandoning nuclear weapons

7/26-8/1: First-phase conference of the fourth SPTs takes place

8/15: DPRK delegation visits South Korea and discusses possible second inter-Korea summit

9/13: Second-phase conference of the SPTs

9/13–16: Inter-Korean ministers' conference held in Pyongyang

9/17: South Korea learns U.S. Treasury is investigating possible DPRK money laundering at Banco Delta Asia (BDA)

9/16: Roh attends the UN General Assembly and speaks at the Korea Society

9/17: ROK-U.S. foreign ministers' conference in New York

9/19: Joint Statement is concluded

Nov 9-11: First-phase conference of the fifth Six-Party Talks in Beijing

11/16: ROK-China summit in Busan

12/8: First working group meeting on a peace regime in the Korean Peninsula held in Seoul

11/17: U.S.-South Korea summit in Gyeongju, South Korea

12/13: ROK embassy receives Chinese report on BDA investigation that concludes "nothing illegal"

12/18: President Roh informs Dr. Lee he will be the new unification minister

2006

4/21-24: 18th inter-Korean ministers' meeting in Pyongyang

2/10: Dr. Lee becomes unification minister

5/16: Inter-Korean meeting at Mt. Kumgang to discuss visit of former president Kim Dae-jung to the North

5/31: Light-water reactor project officially ended

10/9: North Korea carries out nuclear test

10/24: Roh accepts Dr. Lee's resignation from his post as unification minister

2007

2/13: The so-called 2.13 agreement comes out of the Six-Party Talks

10/4: Roh Moo-hyun and Kim Jong-il sign joint declaration at second inter-Korean summit

Peace on a Knife's Edge: The Inside Story
of Roh Moo-hyun's North Korea Policy

I

Stepping Onto
History's Stage

1

A Momentous Occasion and a New Mission

The Night Before the Election:
"Will History Change Because of Bad Luck?"

It was December 18, 2002, the night before the Republic of Korea's six-teenth presidential election. Unification, foreign affairs, and national security (UFN) advisors to Roh Moo-hyun, the Millennium Democratic Party's candidate, gathered inside what is now the K-hotel (formerly the Education and Culture Hall) in Yangjae-dong, Seoul.

The meeting included Seo Dong-man, Yoon Young-kwan, Seo Joo-seok, and me, as well as Bae Ki-chan, who was in charge of the campaign.[1] We had booked a room there to work during the two days leading up to election day.

Although Roh had an advisory panel, consisting of university professors, we made up a separate team specializing in UFN matters, under the leadership of Seo Dong-man. We were there to do two things in anticipation of Roh's winning the election: to create a plan of action detailing the most urgent foreign policy and national security tasks, and to draft a report laying out the policy position of the president-elect on

---

1 Seo Dong-man was a professor at Sangji University; Yoon Young-kwan, a professor at Seoul National University; and Seo Joo-seok, a senior researcher at the National Defense Research Institute.

significant current issues. We had already met several times since early December and had, through lengthy debates, decided on the key points of the report. Our first collaborative draft was ready. I had also written an outline of a final version, based on this draft, so it seemed that we had only minor adjustments to make before we were done.

One thorny issue remained: recommending a role for Chung Mong-joon, the leader of the National Unity 21 Party, who had abandoned his own presidential ambitions to back Roh. If Roh were to win the election, he would have to mull over how best to divide executive responsibilities with Chung; ultimately, the task would fall to the state affairs team. But we, not the state affairs team, had to be prepared: If there were going to be a de facto unity government involving the two parties, it was likely that Chung would ask to be in charge of UFN matters. (Our team had reached this conclusion without consulting Roh or his state affairs team.)

Given the contribution Chung had made to what appeared at the time to be Roh's certain electoral victory, we felt it was inevitable that Chung would assume a role in the government. And with Chung's history and his future presidential aspirations, he was certain to want to participate in UFN-related areas. But these three policy areas are all inextricably linked to the authority and duty of the president. Our team then had to assume that president-elect Roh would accommodate Chung's demand, given the contributions Chung had made to the electoral campaign. We felt there had to be a way to uphold Roh's own standing as the leader of the nation, even while acceding to Roh's wishes.

We began reviewing the existing draft of the report. Although it had been debated many times already, the discussion continued late into the night of December 18. We were nearing our conclusion when Yoon's phone suddenly rang—maybe it was around 11:00 p.m. At first I paid little attention because I thought it must be a personal call, but I saw Yoon's expression harden and recognized this as an inauspicious sign. The call was from Yoon's younger brother, Yoon Young-chan, who worked as a reporter at the *Donga Ilbo*, one of the three major dailies in South Korea. The news was that Chung Mong-joon had suddenly withdrawn his support for Roh. It would later be dubbed the "Chung Mong-joon bomb."

The official statement had come at 10:30 p.m., just ninety minutes before election day. Chung's withdrawal of support had been triggered by a statement Roh had allegedly made earlier in the day while jointly campaigning in Seoul's busy Myeong-dong area. Chung claimed that

Roh had said, "If the United States and North Korea fight, we must stop it." (What Roh had actually said was, "If the United States and North Korea fight, we should position ourselves in the middle and take on an active role in resolving the situation.") Chung's stance was that since the United States is our ally, Roh's words were "extremely inappropriate" and "went against the spirit of policy cooperation between the Democratic Party and National Unity 21." At a time when tensions on the Korean Peninsula were growing and U.S.–North Korean relations were deteriorating amid the North Korean nuclear crisis, I personally could not understand why emphasizing the need for South Korea to play an active role constituted grounds for Chung's withdrawal of support.

Meanwhile, rumor was that the real reason for Chung's anger was a different statement made by Roh, who, upon seeing some Chung supporters waving picket signs that read "The Next President is Chung Mong-joon," blurted out, "There are also people like Choo Mi-ae and Chung Dong-young in the Democratic Party." This, it seems, had enraged Chung Mong-joon.

The news was simply ludicrous. Silence suddenly engulfed the room and everyone looked crestfallen. I sighed loudly: "Will history change because of bad luck?" No one in particular was to blame, but still I resented the circumstances in which we found ourselves. I had thought the outcome of the election was a sure thing—Roh was going to win. Now I had no desire to continue the discussion, though at the very least we had to finish our work. Although this unforeseen development considerably dampened the atmosphere, no one there wanted to call it quits. Fortunately, the only remaining matter was Chung's share of state affairs, and with him officially out, there was no longer any point in discussing that. We removed from the report the part that pertained to Chung's potential role and made the final edits. The Chung Mong-joon bomb had considerably reduced the certainty of Roh's election, but should he still be elected, our team leader, Seo Dong-man, would deliver the report to the president-elect. It was just after midnight when we left the Education and Culture Hall.

The morning of December 19, I was still in bed at well past 10:00 a.m. I was awake but didn't want to open my eyes. Like most people, I thought Roh's defeat was all but certain given Chung's change of heart. My heart ached. Although I did not become an advisor to Roh under the assumption he was going to be elected—he was polling at only 1 percent when I joined the campaign—I thought a new political movement with someone like Roh at its heart was sorely needed in South Korea. But I must have become greedy after Roh became the main opposition candidate. I could not calm myself down: I felt victory had been snatched away right before our eyes. My daughter, still in elementary school, came over and whispered into my ear, "Daddy, I heard some guy betrayed Mr. Roh!"

I spent the afternoon running small errands to distract myself and went to cast my vote around lunchtime. I was floored when the results came in. That night, once the votes had been counted, Roh won with a margin of 570,000 votes. It was like a dream. Many, including myself, had predicted that the Grand National Party candidate Lee Hoi-chang would win, but the people's choice turned out to be different. It was shocking. Once Roh's victory was confirmed, I chided myself for being small-minded, and savored the feeling of incredible happiness. I was ashamed of resenting how Roh, when he visited Chung the previous night after the bombshell announcement, had not stayed around long enough to attempt to sway Chung's mind. I was embarrassed, not by my wrong prediction, but because I had not trusted the decision of a leader who tried to stay on the right path, based on his faith in the electorate. This was how the two days surrounding the presidential election passed for me.

Entrusted with an Important Mission on Christmas Eve

Now president-elect, Roh spent December 21 and 22 on Jeju Island to take a break and recover from campaign fatigue. The report we had drafted had been delivered to him and our job was officially over. We disbanded with the understanding that all future communication with the president-elect would take place through Seo Dong-man. But on December 23, I unexpectedly received word from Seo that Roh had summoned us.

While the country was in the grip of Christmas Eve excitement, Roh called the four of us, as well as Professor Moon Chung-in of Yonsei University, to his private residence, where he was temporarily conducting affairs. The meeting concerned the North Korean nuclear crisis.

Two months earlier in October, U.S. assistant secretary of state James Kelly had paid a visit to Pyongyang, whereupon a controversy erupted over North Korea's development of highly enriched uranium (HEU). Because of this turn of events, the threat of the North's nuclear weapons loomed large over the entire course of the presidential campaign. In November, the George W. Bush administration declared that North Korea's pursuit of HEU had violated the Agreed Framework, signed in Geneva by the

Democratic People's Republic of Korea (DPRK) and the United States in 1994. The Bush administration then announced its decision in December to stop its supply of crude oil to North Korea as detailed in the agreement. Despite North Korea's denials, the United States maintained that the North had admitted its development of HEU to the Kelly entourage. In the midst of this, a North Korean cargo vessel, the *Seosan*, was forcibly captured by the Spanish navy in international waters near Yemen on December 9, 2002. U.S. government agents boarded the ship and discovered components for fifteen Scud missiles that North Korea was exporting to Yemen. North Korea asserted that the cargo was legal trade; Yemen, too, protested that the capture of a ship in international waters amounted to a violation of international maritime law. The *Seosan* was released just one day after capture, but this incident served as a catalyst for a worsening climate on the Korean Peninsula. On December 12, North Korea announced, in a special statement delivered by a Ministry of Foreign Affairs spokesperson, that it was unfreezing its nuclear program to counter the pressure being imposed on it by the United States. All this was taking place merely a week before South Korea's presidential election. As campaigning entered its final phase, the tension ratcheted up to a point where Roh had to appeal to the public to choose between war and peace. Things were that desperate.

The North Korean nuclear crisis, which sidelined all other national security concerns, did not show any signs of abating, even after the election. Making the situation even worse, on December 22 North Korea removed the seals from the spent fuel rod storage facility at the Youngbyon reactors and disabled security cameras installed by the International Atomic Energy Agency.

It was under this threatening atmosphere that Roh summoned us. He had decided that it was necessary to address the nuclear crisis promptly, before organizing the transition committee that would prepare for his inauguration. He asked the five of us to form a task force and use our wisdom to find a permanent solution to the North Korean nuclear problem. Roh's position had always been clear, even when he was running for the presidency: South Korea must play a strong role in facilitating a rational exchange of demands between the North and the United States. He was unequivocal that North Korea had to abandon its nuclear ambitions, but in return the United States had to create a climate under which the North's explicit demand for regime security could be accommodated. He hoped that our task force would come up with a way to bring the United States and North Korea to the table for a dialogue. We also discussed the possibility of sending special envoys to both countries.

Just a few days after the task force began its work, the makeup of the presidential transition committee was announced. The committee, consisting of twenty-five members, was to be launched in January 2013. Four people were appointed to the subcommittee on unification, foreign affairs, and national security: Yoon Young-kwan, Seo Dong-man, Seo Joo-seok, and me. We were surprised that Roh chose to retain the same four people who had banded together in January 2002 to form his advisory team on foreign affairs and national security, and were moved by the trust he showed in appointing us not only to the North Korean nuclear task force, but also to this transitional subcommittee. All of us had inwardly hoped that we could remain in his service, but we were certainly not the only people who shared the president-elect's philosophy on UFN-related issues. After all, apart from team leader Seo Dong-man, we were unknown to the outside world and had been serving in an unofficial capacity until then. I felt immense happiness, as well as a heavy burden.

The nuclear task force had essentially been absorbed into the transitional subcommittee (with the exception of Moon Chung-in). But before the committee officially began its work, the task force submitted a report to Roh in late December detailing the basic principles for dealing with the North Korean nuclear crisis and dispatching any special envoy. The report emphasized that the entity in charge of handling the nuclear crisis was still the current administration, in power until February 25; before the official handover of power, Roh would closely cooperate with the government to monitor the unfolding situation, develop solutions based on facts, and perform those duties he could, in his capacity as president-elect. The report further recommended that as a president-elect facing a nuclear crisis, Roh should embrace "Three Principles for Resolving the North Korean Nuclear Crisis": the North must not be allowed to unfreeze and develop its nuclear program, the situation must be peacefully resolved through dialogue, and South Korea must have an active role in the process.

In early January 2003, the presidential transition committee was officially launched, with the subcommittee on foreign policy and national security being responsible for four ministries and related governmental offices: unification, foreign affairs, national defense, and the National Intelligence Service (the NIS, South Korea's largest spy agency). We divided our tasks so that each of the four subcommittee members was responsible for one ministry and also served as a second-in-command in handling another ministry.

The head of each subcommittee functioned as a bridge between his subcommittee and the president-elect. Our subcommittee's head was Yoon Young-kwan, who also had the critical task of personally tutoring the president-elect on foreign policy and national security matters. In addition to his duties as the head of the subcommittee, Dr. Yoon also had to attend all foreign affairs and national security meetings that the president-elect participated in, so he was an extremely busy man. As the transition committee entered its final phase, Yoon was chosen as the incoming foreign affairs minister and seemed even busier—this meant that other subcommittee members had to carry extra weight. Seo Dong-man poured his blood and sweat into creating a proposal for reforming the National Intelligence Service and also focused attention on the possibility of reforming the Ministry of Foreign Affairs. Seo Joo-seok, the only national security expert on the subcommittee, focused his energy on linking Roh's philosophy of self-reliant national defense to the work of the Defense Ministry and tried to establish a direction for the future reform of South Korea's national defense. I was responsible for the Ministry of Unification, which, unlike other ministries, offered little reason for reform, so I spent much of my time coming up with the foundation of a new inter-Korean policy framework and writing a proposal for expanding the National Security Council.

One of the most important responsibilities that fell to our subcommittee on foreign affairs and national security was to establish the objectives and foundations of unification and foreign policy for the incoming administration. To facilitate this, in early January 2003 the transition committee identified ten main assignments and organized a task force for each. One assignment, as proposed by our subcommittee, was the establishment of a "peace regime on the Korean Peninsula." To accomplish this great task, we suggested (1) systemizing peace through the improvement of North-South relations, on the inter-Korean front; (2) creating an international environment for the establishment of peace on the Korean Peninsula on the foreign policy front; and (3) strengthening defense to guarantee peace, on the national defense front.

From the viewpoint of our subcommittee, it was inevitable that the ongoing North Korean nuclear issue would become the greatest national security headache for the new administration. It was thus deemed necessary that if Roh were called upon to clarify his position on the matter during the transition period, he should be in agreement with the administration still in power. Though president-elect Roh was reserved in speaking on other policy matters, from time to time he expressed his opinion on the North Korean nuclear issue. Our team believed that the greatest problem was the lack of dialogue between the United States and North Korea—an irony, given that everyone spoke of finding a "peaceful solution." To solve this problem, it was imperative that we bring the United States and the North to a single table for a bilateral talk and create negotiation guidelines satisfactory to both parties. But the United States remained adamantly opposed to a bilateral talk with no conditions attached; it maintained that the North's destruction of its nuclear program was a prerequisite to any talks. North Korea, meanwhile, held firm that there would be no disarmament unless its regime security were guaranteed. Under these circumstances, it was difficult to say just what the South Korean government could do to help resolve the North Korean nuclear issue. But it simply had to do all it could.

The first task for our subcommittee was to clarify its position on the U.S. policy of "tailored containment." In late December 2002, major American news outlets reported that the Bush administration was contemplating tailored containment in response to North Korea's nuclear arms development. Tailored containment, as defined in media reports citing unnamed American officials, would—should the North refuse to give up its nuclear program—refuse a dialogue with the North and would mobilize countries around the Korean Peninsula to completely isolate North Korea, such that the Pyongyang regime would suffer an economic collapse before it came into possession of a nuclear arsenal. CNN reported that President George W. Bush had already approved the strategy and that it was already being executed. The cable channel also cited unnamed American officials as saying that if the current standoff did not end, the United States was considering the possibility of asking the South Korean government to cease all cooperation with North Korea.

This report gave us a considerable headache. If true, it meant that any U.S.–North Korean dialogue would become even more difficult, and that U.S. policy was in complete opposition to that of the president-elect, who had argued for peaceful resolution through dialogue. In addition, tailored containment undermined our plan to separate inter-Korean relations as a whole from North Korea's nuclear development and to pursue the two matters separately but simultaneously. If tailored containment became a reality, there could be neither peace nor diplomacy on the Korean

Peninsula. Tensions would rise as pressure on the North built up, and the whole region would be plunged into a state of high alert. War might even break out. Seoul would lack policy independence and its only path would be to join the U.S. pressure tactics against Pyongyang.

From our perspective, it appeared as though the United States were saying it would let North Korea survive only if it completely surrendered. This was an ill-advised move by Washington—it underestimated North Korea and only worsened the situation. Our subcommittee was convinced, based on our collective experience and knowledge, that Pyongyang would not surrender under Western sanctions and pressure, and that it would certainly not collapse. If North Korea were threatened, China would not sit idle. And if somehow North Korea were to indeed fall, it would be a major catastrophe for South Korea, which was not (and to this day still is not) prepared for a North Korean collapse.

The North further heightened the sense of danger by declaring on January 10 that it was leaving the non-proliferation treaty, as it had already done once before, on March 12, 1993. But North Korea's provocative action in response to the aggressive U.S. maneuver only swayed the mood in the West in favor of the Bush administration. At that point, the United States announced that Assistant Secretary Kelly would visit South Korea as President Bush's special envoy. Before fully deploying its new strategy, Washington wanted to assess the South Korean government's stance. Our subcommittee on foreign affairs and national security prepared a response. Above all, we had to be unequivocal in stating our position during the opportunity provided by Kelly's visit, in order to prevent the United States from officially proposing its policy of tailored containment to the incoming administration.

Roh's hope was that the members of our transition subcommittee would clearly convey to the Kelly entourage the president-elect's understanding of and plan for the North Korean nuclear issue. Several days before the meeting with Kelly, Roh instructed us, "You are all slated to return to academia and will not enter the new government, so please clearly state our position and freely converse with the Kelly entourage to the fullest extent that your conscience will allow."

On January 13, the members of the subcommittee on foreign policy and national security met with the Kelly entourage and vigorously exchanged opinions on the North Korean nuclear issue and U.S.–South Korean relations. Our side, headed by Yoon Young-kwan, raised the tailored containment policy and stated, "We cannot agree on a policy with such great potential to push the people of the Republic of Korea into war when no dialogue has taken place, as it is with the case at present." We added, "We also cannot agree on a policy that presents dialogue as a reward, suggesting that North Korea must abandon nuclear development before any talks can take place." We requested that Washington and Pyongyang enter into a direct dialogue together. I cannot remember every detail of how the Kelly entourage responded, but I think that they were quite shaken by what must have seemed a very provocative statement from our side. Kelly, though, calmly explained the U.S. position and denied media reports that tailored containment was now the U.S. strategy toward North Korea. I myself argued that, while the issue of North Korean human rights was important, it was more important at the time to focus on the pressing nuclear issue. I contended that if we were to try to simultaneously solve the nuclear and human rights issues, addressing Pyongyang's nuclear development would be even more difficult. But Kelly responded—while uncharacteristically looking at his notebook—that both issues were equally important. To our suggestion that all other North Korean issues should be pursued only to the extent that they did not have a harmful effect on the nuclear issue, he responded in the negative and implied a desire to pursue all issues simultaneously. Kelly's words seemed logically flawless, while causing considerable concern from a strategic point of view.

When I saw that he was consulting his notebook as he spoke—this was rather unusual—I got the impression that he had received clear instructions from above on this point. I sensed that the way forward in solving the North Korean nuclear issue would be even more arduous.

In the end, the U.S. tailored containment policy was not immediately implemented amid opposition from countries such as South Korea and China. But the United States nonetheless consistently demanded that the governments of South Korea and surrounding countries adjust the pace of their relations and economic cooperation with the North. Washington also advanced its Proliferation Security Initiative as a way of applying the specifics of tailored containment to *realpolitik*.

The Problem of Naming North-South Policy

The transition subcommittee on foreign policy and national security embarked on the project of building a peace regime on the Korean Peninsula, and came up with a framework for inter-Korean relations that the incoming administration would pursue. We also tried to give this project a suitable symbolic meaning. I had to oversee these two tasks. Roh promised during the campaign that he would inherit and build on the existing "Sunshine Policy" when it came to dealing with the North, so there was no need to significantly shift the framework in that regard. But in consideration of the changing circumstances on the Korean Peninsula, there was certainly a need to augment and improve the existing policy. This meant that we had to come up with a new name for it.

But what would it be? I thought long and hard about this. President Kim Dae-jung pulled off the June 15 joint declaration by North and South Korea through his steadfast adherence to the Sunshine Policy. He created a historical precedent upon which inter-Korean relations, mired in hostility and competition, could transform into a relationship based on reconciliation and cooperation. The Sunshine Policy moved inter-Korean relations toward reconciliation under the Kim administration over the course of five years, despite all the difficulties the effort faced. How would President Roh then further improve inter-Korean relations? And how would peace further prosper on the Korean Peninsula?

Our team decided that while we would take as our point of departure the continued need to promote reconciliation and cooperation between the two Koreas, we would go one step further and promote peace and prosperity on the Korean Peninsula. Our conception of inter-Korean relations under Roh then demanded a concrete strategy that would transform the Korean Peninsula from the land of recurrent North Korean nuclear crisis and conflict into a region of peace and prosperity. We also took into consideration the fact that we had moved into an age that required pursuing both security (peace) and a thriving economy (prosperity). Furthermore, we saw that it was important to move beyond traditional inter-Korean relations that merely articulated the South's position toward the North and to imagine a relationship that could bring peace and prosperity to the entire region. We decided to expand our policy perspective to go beyond the Korean Peninsula and include the whole of East Asia.

According to this logic, we named the new policy toward North Korea the "Policy for Peace and Prosperity." We defined it as "President Roh Moo-hyun's strategic conception of establishing peace on the Korean Peninsula and pursuing common prosperity between the two Koreas in order to build a foundation of peaceful unification and development into a nation at the center of the East Asian economy." We further suggested four main principles for the policy: dialogue-based problem resolution, prioritization of mutual trust and reciprocity, international cooperation centered on the involvement of the two Koreas, and policymaking together with the people. Toward the end of my activities on the transition committee, I created an eponymous report on this policy and conveyed it to the president-elect.

Our subcommittee had the grand idea of articulating a comprehensive UFN policy that focused on North Korea and calling it the "Roh Moo-hyun Doctrine." For that reason, we titled my report "Roh Moo-hyun's Conception of Peace Development on the Korean Peninsula" and subtitled it "Policy for Peace and Prosperity." In the report itself we explained our terminology and referred to the policy as the Policy for Peace and Prosperity (a.k.a. the Roh Moo-hyun Doctrine). I informed the president-elect that while the policy had an official name, we wanted to try and get everyone to eventually call it the Roh Moo-hyun Doctrine. On hearing this, Roh unhesitatingly directed me to remove his name from the report and to cease referring to it as such, as it was embarrassing to see his name used in this way. This was in keeping with his personality of shying away from self-aggrandizement.

Roh was satisfied with the contents of my report as I briefed him, but he was less than happy with the title "Policy for Peace and Prosperity." He found it uninspiring and said it would not strike the electorate as fresh, either. He asked if I had any alternatives. Others around the table also chimed in and voiced that they, too, thought the name did not deliver enough impact. I was chagrined because I had come up with it. In looking for expressions that could symbolize the new administration's North Korea policy, I sought advice from many quarters and held several internal meetings within the transition subcommittee, but to no avail. No one had a particularly great idea. After much thinking, we settled on this title because it had a clear meaning and accurately reflected our policy aims. Other members of the subcommittee understood my predicament and agreed with the decision. But I did not stop looking for a better title. I still remember to this day how I kept asking the team leader in charge of policymaking at the Ministry of Unification, Chun Hae-sung, whether he had a better idea, the whole time he helped me write the policy report.

Despite Roh's misgivings, there was no apparent solution. His stance on North Korea was under intense media scrutiny and the presidential inauguration ceremony was imminent. It was customary to showcase the administration's new policies on this day and it was unimaginable that we would delay reporting the new policy on North Korea simply because the name was not satisfactory. The name was not inaccurate; it just lacked impact. I kept thinking of an alternative name even after I briefed Roh, but could not come up with anything better. I gave up in the end and, before returning to my position south of Seoul at the Sejong Institute, handed my final report over to the people who would be part of the new government. When I listened to Roh's inauguration speech on February 25, he declared that he would pursue his "policy for peace and prosperity with the goal of nurturing peace and common prosperity on the Korean Peninsula." It seemed that even the president had not been able to come up with an alternative name. The "Policy for Peace and Prosperity" became the official name of the Participatory Government's North Korea policy.[2]

Yet the president complained on several occasions early in his term that the name was not fresh enough. Every time, I felt profound unease, but at that juncture it was not possible to change a name that had already been announced to the public. I took away a measure of relief from the knowledge that even Roh, who was known for his ability to come up with great names, could not think of something better. I would eventually be vindicated years later, after I quit my ministerial post when, on October 4, 2007, the president met with Chairman Kim Jong-il of North Korea and jointly signed a historic inter-Korean summit declaration. Its title was the "Declaration for Improvement of Inter-Korean Relations, Peace, and Prosperity." That North Korea agreed on this title for the joint declaration, despite being fully aware that our North Korea policy was called the Policy for Peace and Prosperity, showed that this phrase had been widely accepted as words that symbolized a new era on the Korean Peninsula. I could finally stand tall and be proud that I had been the one to name the policy.

---

2   [The "Participatory Government," a term coined by the Roh administration to imply the peoples' participation in the functioning of the government, is still used to refer to his administration.]

2

A Visit to Pyongyang and a Message from President-elect Roh

An Unexpected Request to Accompany a Special Envoy

On January 23, 2003, busy with my duties on the transition committee, I got a call from the designated Blue House chief of staff, Moon Hee-sang, as soon as I arrived at work. He told me quite unexpectedly that the current administration had reached an agreement with the North to send an envoy to Pyongyang. The administration wanted someone from Roh's camp to join the special envoy's entourage, and Roh had selected me as his representative. We would depart on January 27, in just four days.

This unanticipated call left me more befuddled than pleased. More than anything, I was shocked by the fact that my subcommittee had not known about the administration's attempts to send an envoy to the North during the presidential transition. Then again, the issue of sending an envoy to Pyongyang must have been handled in utmost secrecy by the National Intelligence Service (NIS), so disclosing the plan to the presidential transition committee as a whole would have been problematic.

However, even though both the outgoing and incoming administrations shared a philosophical stance on inter-Korean policies, the transition subcommittee on foreign policy and national security was conflicted over whether it was truly appropriate for a government with only a month left in its term to send an envoy to North Korea. As a matter of fact, the subcommittee itself had considered sending a special envoy on behalf of the president-elect while its members were running the North Korean nuclear task force in December, but by late January that plan had come to naught, given questions over its effectiveness and feasibility. In any event, I met with a member of the special envoy's entourage, and it appeared unclear whether it would be even possible to meet with Kim Jong-il, the North's national defense chairman and supreme leader. It was uncertain whether sending a special envoy would achieve anything with regard to the North Korean nuclear problem. In addition, during the process that resulted in my selection as a member of the special envoy's entourage, there had been no discussion or consultation with the transition subcommittee. Therefore, there was a certain unease surrounding the dispatch of the special envoy and my participation in the entourage.

I myself felt uncomfortable at being chosen over all the talented and more experienced figures on the transition committee. I heard a report that the current administration itself had recommended me as the prime candidate to the president-elect. If there had been any hope of a tangible outcome, I might have felt more composed, but the thought that there was no reason to expect any results from the trip unsettled me.

I had a special connection to the government and its inter-Korean policy, given that I had participated in the inter-Korean summit of June 2002 as a member of President Kim Dae-jung's entourage, albeit in a nonofficial capacity. That is why it brought me even more pain to see the way in which Kim and Lim Dong-won—his special advisor on unification, foreign affairs, and national security—were trying, until the very end of the Kim administration, to do something for peace on the Korean Peninsula. It would be nice to have a successful visit, but if the special envoy returned empty-handed, the ensuing criticism would make the outgoing government look even more pathetic. But the issue of sending a special envoy had already been decided and I had no chance or authority to change that decision. And I was representing the president-elect—that meant that I had to keep a certain distance from the government in the media even as I accompanied the government's special envoy. It was cold political calculation, but I knew this well without being told by anyone.

I must admit that accompanying the special envoy as the representative of the incoming administration was not only personally glorious, but also a tremendous opportunity for me to make use of my academic specialization as a longtime scholar of North Korea. But many things weighed heavily on my mind, and the Pyongyang trip was a source of more pressure than pleasure. At least it was of some comfort to know that Special Advisor Lim Dong-won, whom I had considered for a long time to be my mentor, had been named the special envoy.

The press naturally paid a great deal of attention to me as someone from the president-elect's camp. But I cautioned them against interpreting my presence beyond what the word "accompany" implied. In responding to reporters who asked for the significance of the Pyongyang visit, I simply answered, "I understand it is the desire of the president-elect to show support for the current administration, which is trying hard to bring about a peaceful solution to the North Korean nuclear problem." In reality, I did not carry a written message from the president-elect. Since I was merely accompanying the current administration's special envoy, I resolved to orally convey the president-elect's message to Kim Jong-il. In some quarters there was an opinion that representatives from North Korea should be invited to the inauguration ceremony, but seeing as how it would be difficult to realize, it was concluded that such matters should be unofficially proposed. So that was what I would do during my visit.

No matter what the transition committee thought, President Kim Dae-jung earnestly tried through the end of his term to make progress in resolving the North Korean nuclear problem, to reduce the burden on the incoming administration. Since the nuclear development issue fundamentally arose from the antagonistic relationship between Pyongyang and Washington, the South Korean government was extremely limited in what it could do at a time when tensions between North Korea and America were at a fever pitch. But President Kim still tried to persuade Chairman Kim by sending Lim. For this mission to have any chance of success, however, it was imperative that the George W. Bush administration show a clear resolve toward a U.S.–North Korean dialogue. Presidential Secretary for Foreign Affairs and National Security Yim Sung-joon had visited America in early January and had met with Secretary of State Colin Powell, but did not return with any assurances that would persuade North Korea. Yim said that his idea, in agreement with Secretary Powell, was to first have the North Korean minister of foreign affairs write a letter to Powell explaining Pyongyang's plan for its highly enriched uranium (HEU), assuring him that Pyongyang had no plan to develop nuclear weapons, and requesting a resumption of dialogue. Powell would, in return, reinitiate dialogue while confirming that the United States had no hostile intention toward the North and guaranteeing there would be no invasion. But given the political climate of the day, North Korea—which demanded a "simultaneous solution" whereby North Korea would give up nuclear arms and the United States would offer regime security and financial aid—would in no way accept a demand that it take the first step. In other words, the special envoy was going to Pyongyang with a proposal that would most certainly be rejected. I left Seoul with a heavy heart.

A Sudden Obstacle: President-elect Roh's CNN Interview

It was January 27, 2003. A cold front of the severest kind swept across the Korean Peninsula. When I told my wife I was heading to Pyongyang, she spent the exorbitant sum of $1,000 on a heavy coat. It was the first long coat I had ever worn. I left the house with a slight feeling of excitement. At the Seoul airport, I joined Special Advisor Lim Dong-won; Presidential Secretary Yim Sung-joon; Suh Hoon, from the NIS; and Kim Chun-shik from the Ministry of Unification. We took off for the North. The weather wasn't too bad when we left Seoul, but as soon as we landed at Soonan Airport in Pyongyang, we were struck by incredibly cold winds, evocative of the Siberian fields. As we posed for a commemorative photo after getting off the plane, the cold wind burrowed into my whole body despite the thick coat. It was minus 17 degrees Celsius. The strong northern wind swirled all around, leaving me shaking all the way down to my shins. I cannot recall a time I felt as cold as I did that day.

Choi Seung-chul, the deputy director of the United Front Department, came to greet us, and General Manager Won Dong-yeon of the Institute for Research into National Reunification, whom I had met before, welcomed me as my personal guide. But the attitude of the North was unexpectedly cold toward everyone in our entourage, including me. In the car heading into Pyongyang, I was able to hear the whole story from Won. Just one week before, President-elect Roh had said during a CNN interview that "responsibility for crackdowns on human rights in North Korea, as well as the painful situation faced by North Korean people, lies with Chairman Kim Jong-il." Pyongyang had taken exception to that statement. This had not been completely unanticipated, but I never thought that North Korea would block the discussion from the very beginning over this issue. Thinking that North Korea would repeatedly raise this problem during the talks, I thought up a logical response during the ride to our accommodations, the Baekhwawon State Guesthouse.

We unpacked our bags at the guesthouse and attended a luncheon with Secretary for South Korean Affairs Kim Yong-sun (also head of the United Front Department); Lim Dong-ok, the first deputy director of the United Front Department; and others. At 3:45 p.m. there was a talk involving ten people, five from each side. Representatives of the North included Kim Yong-sun, Lim Dong-ok, and Choi Seung-chul.

As expected, Kim Yong-sun, after perfunctory comments about how he wished this visit from the special envoy would further inter-Korean relations to the benefit of all Koreans, North and South alike, raised in his preliminary remarks the CNN interview as an "extremely unpleasant matter." He quoted from a January 22 report by MBC[1] and railed against us. "This is simply unacceptable. I cannot help but ask for its true meaning." He added, "This comment almost led us to decide not to welcome the special envoy." His voice rose even higher. "There must be an explanation for this problem." I replied:

> This is the first time I have heard of this. I reviewed the president-elect's answers prior to the CNN interview. There was nothing of this sort in CNN's prior list of questions or in our prepared answers. I will clarify the situation after returning to Seoul and see if this was a translation problem or if he actually said it. If there are things to be explained, I will do so through the official channels. . . . The North surely knows our president-elect's position on North Korea? He wouldn't have suffered all those accusations over his ideological leanings if, while campaigning, he had made a remark of the sort you find problematic. It is the belief of the president-elect that he should refrain from remarks that will unnecessarily worsen inter-Korean relations.

Kim Yong-sun again demanded an official explanation, but I once again countered by saying, "Let us deal with it."

As I faced off against Kim Yong-sun, I got the feeling the North Koreans were not simply raising this issue to gain an upper hand during the negotiations. They seemed to really believe that the next president of South Korea had personally attacked Kim Jong-il, the supreme leader of their one-party system, and they did not seem willing to simply let it slide. I began to worry that this development might have an impact on the special envoy's mission.

---

1   [The Munhwa Broadcasting Corporation is a leading South Korean public television and radio network.]

Once my risky exchange with Kim Yong-sun came to an end, Lim Dong-won presented President Kim Dae-jung's personal letter, addressed to Chairman Kim Jong-il. Lim emphasized the necessity of a dialogue with the United States to resolve the nuclear situation and the importance of a project to connect the two Koreas via railways and roads. He then concluded his remarks on how to improve inter-Korean relations.

It was my turn to speak. Although the atmosphere had been dampened by the confrontation and my heart also had cooled, I could not allow how I felt on the inside to ruin this very important moment. I composed my thoughts and started reading aloud from "Greetings from President-elect Roh Moo-hyun to National Defense Chairman Kim Jong-il," which I had written out in advance, paragraph by paragraph, numbered one to six, on a piece of A4-sized paper:

1. The South, represented by President-elect Roh Moo-hyun, who has been elected as the sixteenth president of the Republic of Korea, has asked me, a member of the presidential transition committee, to convey a special greeting to Mr. Chairman.

2. The president-elect holds in the highest regard the achievements of President Kim Dae-jung and Chairman Kim Jong-il toward peace and cooperation between the two Koreas. The president-elect says that the new government will build on them with the national defense chairman. He says that he wholeheartedly supported the historic June 15 joint declaration in particular, and that the contents of that declaration must be expanded and developed.

3. The president-elect says that the two Koreas must not return to a period of hostility and conflict even if the political climate worsens, and that it is necessary to have open discussions and cooperate with the chairman in order to build peace on the Korean Peninsula and throw open the doors to an age of common prosperity for all Koreans.

4. The president-elect has promised the people of South Korea since the time of his candidacy that, if elected to the presidency, he would bring about prosperity for all Koreans through inter-Korean cooperation. He has plans to greatly vitalize inter-Korean economic cooperation for this purpose. But since the nuclear problem occurred, he is extremely worried that the execution of such plans could become difficult. The president-elect wishes to convey to the chairman that he hopes the nuclear problem will be quickly resolved

so that the South and North can further advance reconciliation and cooperation on many fronts and actively discuss the issue of peace.

The president-elect is, however, deeply concerned over the conflict between the North and the United States precipitated by the emergence of the nuclear problem. And he emphasizes a peaceful solution through dialogue to this problem and strives in every way for it. After his election, he has strongly urged the Bush administration to solve the problem through dialogue. To this end, the president-elect has asked me to say without fail to the chairman that the president-elect believes that this moment, when all world citizens who love peace are focused on the nuclear problem, is the right time for solving this problem.

5. The president-elect believes that it is important for the top leaders of the two Koreas to exchange opinions and cooperate to solve the nuclear problem of the day and improve inter-Korean relations in the coming days. He says that he hopes he will meet the chairman in person not long after his presidential inauguration.

6. Finally, the president-elect asks me to convey his wishes for the chairman's health and fortune.

Once I conveyed this message orally to the North, I explained the direction of President-elect Roh's North Korean policy point by point. But I kept my remarks brief since this was to be a meeting between the government's special envoy and the North, and it was certain that the North would arrange a separate meeting between Kim Yong-sun and me.

When we finished talking, Kim Yong-sun asked Lim Dong-won, in a rather petulant voice, "We have already stated our position on the nuclear problem. How do you propose to solve it?" Lim then explained, in his signature calm tone, the solution as conceptualized by the Kim Dae-jung administration. Kim Yong-sun, however, found it discomfiting that the South would participate in the process, saying that the nuclear issue was a "problem between the United States and North Korea" and should be solved through negotiations between the two countries. The conversation on the nuclear problem did not go any further. Since this issue was not, from Kim Yong-sun's point of view, a matter for the United Front Department to deal with, there was likely nothing more for him to say besides repeating the North's official position. He would report the South's stance to the superiors. The government on our side tried to arrange a meeting with the first vice minister of foreign affairs, Kang Sok-ju, who was in charge of the nuclear issue, but nothing came of it.

Vomiting after Sharing a "Love Shot" with Jang Song-thaek

It was not until eight o'clock when a late dinner began at Youngbin Hall on the Daedong River. It was attended by Jang Song-thaek, the first division deputy chief of the administrative department of the Workers' Party of Korea. Officially, Jang ranked below Kim Yong-sun, a member of the party secretariat, but as Kim Il-sung's brother-in-law, he ruled North Korea's power structure from inside the Workers' Party and was a force to be reckoned with. During the June 15 inter-Korean summit, it was Jang who introduced South Korean figures to Kim Jong-il at the official luncheon, and in fall 2002, he had led an economic monitoring team to South Korea, and thus was a familiar figure to South Korean officials. At that time, I, too, had exchanged greetings with him.

At the official dinner, in addition to Jang, Kim Yong-sun, Lim Dong-ok, Choi Seung-chul, and Won Dong-yeon, the members of the economic monitoring team who had visited South Korea with Jang were also present. Kim remarked that they had consistently predicted Roh's electoral victory and had cheered him silently, and that he wanted this fact to be known by the South Koreans. I was speechless. I was already fed up with the comments the North Koreans were making at every turn suggesting that they had supported and helped Roh during the campaign. When I heard this latest remark, I decided to put an end to it once and for all, knowing that I risked dampening the atmosphere at the dinner. I said a number of things but in particular I strongly pointed out, in a regretful tone, how North Korea's decision to announce its unfreezing of nuclear facilities on December 12—only a week before our presidential election—had had a detrimental effect on our candidate.

It was nonsensical for North Koreans to say this or that about whether they helped us during the presidential campaign. On top of it all, I simply could not stand their arrogant posturing that they had helped Roh, when their declaration of the unfreezing of nuclear facilities had in fact helped the Grand National Party's candidate, Lee Hoi-chang, precisely at a moment when the campaign was entering its last pivotal stage and the two candidates were neck and neck in the polls. So while the topic was on the table, I even went on to express my regret that the North's provocations, including the skirmish in the Western Sea in June

2002, had struck a serious blow to Roh, who had called for a policy of embracing and accommodating the North.

Although a special envoy is in principle a diplomatic envoy, it is customary for special envoys by nature to eschew official functions in favor of actual dialogue and negotiation. Historically, the special envoys between the two Koreas had operated in this way and even during an official dinner it was common to have relatively free conversations at length, without any regard for time restrictions. It was the same in this case. This dinner, in particular, was meant to convey the gratitude of the North Korean economic monitoring team for the welcome they had received in Seoul when they had visited South Korea in the fall of 2002. The dinner, served on a large round table, ended up lasting a staggering six hours, from eight o'clock until two in the morning.

During my conversation with the North Koreans, I stressed that if a North Korean representative were to attend President Roh's inauguration, it would serve as an important gesture toward peace on the Korean Peninsula, not least in regard to the North Korean nuclear problem. I asked whether the North would be willing to accept an invitation if we were to unofficially extend it. I disclosed that if a North Korean representative were to come, our government would be willing to create an opportunity for them to meet with a U.S. representative and discuss the nuclear issue. The North side, however, was neither for nor against the suggestion—their lack of a response meant they were not keen on it. But when I advised Jang Song-thaek to meet with President-elect Roh in the near future for the purpose of improving inter-Korean ties, he reacted relatively positively.

I have a personally unforgettable anecdote from this dinner. It is widely known that at North Korean–hosted dinners alcohol will inevitably be served, and most North Korean officials are experienced drinkers, to say the least. I am not much of a drinker, so I had in advance obtained from the NIS some sort of medicine, which I guessed to be a type of diuretic. I took it before dinner and thought myself ready for the occasion. But barely two hours after the dinner had begun, my body started to signal distress. Normally, I do not feel well after a few drinks and these same symptoms manifested at the dinner. After several rounds of drinking, which involved my accepting drinks from numerous people, my mind was completely clear but my body was in pain. Even the medicine from the NIS was no use. I pretended to be fine, but when I went to the toilet I unsuccessfully tried to vomit.

Around eleven o'clock, I was thinking I should refuse any more alcohol, but Kim Yong-sun suddenly brought up the topic of *poktanju*.[2] "Is it true that *poktanju* is quite popular in the South?" He made some jokes about it and then dexterously mixed North Korean liquor with imported whisky to manufacture *poktanju* on the spot, all the while saying, "I have never had it before." Glasses went around the table, but when it was my turn to accept, I began to refuse at the risk of causing offense. Jang Song-thaek, however, suggested a toast. "Mr. Jong-seok, why don't you do a glass with me?" It was hard enough for me to refuse a glass that Kim Yong-sun had passed around in the name of doing it "South Korean style." When Jang Song-thaek, North Korea's number two man, made a personal request to drink together, it was even more difficult to say no. I told myself, "Okay, just one more glass." Even in the midst of my personal distress I made an unusual proposition. "Since we are doing this South Korean–style, there is something called a 'love shot' in South Korea. Why don't I and Chief Jang do a love shot together in the interest of inter-Korean reconciliation and cooperation?" So Jang and I ended up crossing our right arms and doing a love shot together. But as soon as the *poktanju* went down my throat, my body rebelled. I vomited over Jang's shoulder. The room suddenly plunged into an uneasy atmosphere.

The North Koreans were most worried that I had become seriously ill and became very nervous. They saw that my face had turned as white as paper and hurriedly summoned a medical officer and a nurse, suggesting that I rest in the next room while being diagnosed. But the instant I vomited, my lucidity returned. I realized in that moment there was no way to erase my blunder, but there was still time to get my act together. First, I formally apologized to Jang and told the crowd, "I am all right. I don't deal well with alcohol to begin with. I am not sick at all, so please don't worry." After conveying my apology, I took my seat once again.

I declined an examination by the medical officer. I held myself together with the thought that I was there to represent a nation; although I had committed an unintended mistake, I should not lose my dignity. The banquet resumed and it ended only after another three hours. Once a little time had passed, I felt that my pale countenance was regaining its color. I stiffly remained in my seat as though pretending that I had not vomited a mere three hours ago. On the other side of the room, the

---

2   [*Poktanju* is a combination of two drinks, akin to the Western boilermaker.]

North Korean medical officer and nurse did not move from their spot, staring at me for the entire remainder of the banquet.

The Burgeoning Problem of Aid to the North, and a Heated Exchange with Kim Yong-sun

It was nine o'clock on the morning of January 28. Despite the long banquet that had continued until two in the morning and my vomiting incident, I now sat across from Kim Yong-sun and Lim Dong-ok, hard looks on our faces. It was time for the meeting between the North and the president-elect's representative. Pyongyang had placed particular significance on my accompanying the special envoy, going so far as to ask, "Is it permissible to refer to the person from the president-elect's camp also as a special envoy?" But even before I arrived in Pyongyang, their attitude had changed because of Roh's CNN interview. Furthermore, I was not carrying an attractive proposal to present to their chairman, since I was strictly there to accompany the special envoy and no more. The current government itself lacked any potentially persuasive new solution to the North Korean nuclear problem. I knew therefore that today's meeting would only consist of a litany of the North's endless complaints. Unlike our delivery of the president-elect's detailed vision of the inter-Korean policy and stance on the North's nuclear development, they would not have any concrete proposals.

As expected, Kim Yong-sun opened the meeting by mentioning the CNN interview. He raised his voice, "Surely you know that disrespectful comments toward the supreme leadership will not be tolerated by our people." He added, "I want to inform you that such noise can irreversibly harm inter-Korean dialogue beyond estimation."

He moved on. Saying that he was speaking as the chairman of the Asia-Pacific Peace Committee, he brought up the controversial money transfer to the North.[3] He was referring to events during the presidential election in 2002, when the opposition and some media outlets alleged that before and after the June 15 inter-Korean summit, the Blue House, the NIS, and the Hyundai Group had conspired to secretly send $500 million to North Korea. The opposition argued that the administration had essentially paid for the inter-Korean summit to happen and demanded a special investigation. A special investigation would, in fact, take place

---

3   [The Asia-Pacific Peace Committee, nominally a civilian entity albeit one still under the auspices of the United Front Department, is in charge of handling negotiations with the South.]

between April and June 2003 and would rivet South Korean society. (It would be revealed that of this amount, $400 million had been supplied to the North by the Hyundai Group as a compensation for projects, including for developing the Mount Geumgang resort, $100 million had been provided by the government, and the NIS had helped with the money transfer.)

"Much cooperation has taken place at the private-sector level between Hyundai and the Asia-Pacific Peace Committee, and there are many projects that Hyundai still needs to do, now that the infrastructural deficiencies in roads and railway connections have been resolved," Kim said. "But lately the projects of the Asia-Pacific Peace Committee have become complicated by the question of 400 billion *won*." He demanded that the Hyundai people, who were currently not allowed to leave South Korea because of their connection to the money transfer, be allowed to travel freely so that his committee and Hyundai could continue their relationship. He threatened that, if the travel restriction were maintained, inter-Korean relations would return the point of "zero." "Should you not take care so that inter-Korean relations do not worsen?" he asked, in reference to the investigation of the money transfer. He added that if this problem were to become more complicated, "inter-Korean relations will also become complicated."

Once I heard him say that an investigation into the money transfer to the North could destroy inter-Korean relations, I decided that I should not listen any longer. I stopped him from speaking and point-blank asked him, "This remark is serious enough to sway inter-Korean relations, so I need to understand you clearly. Are you saying this as a secretary of the Worker's Party of the People's Republic of Korea? Or are you speaking as the chairman of the nongovernmental institution that is the Asia-Pacific Peace Committee?" When I confronted him in such seriousness, Kim squirmed and backed down, trying to downplay his comment by saying that it had been in his capacity as the chairman of the Asia-Pacific Peace Committee.

Once Kim was done talking, I responded to his remarks and explained our position as I had prepared in advance. First, I discussed the circumstances under which I ended up accompanying the government's special envoy. I stated it was unfortunate that it might not be possible for us to meet with Chairman Kim, even though I had thought it would be possible. I took pains to say that I had already provided an explanation for the CNN interview and informed them of my plan to take steps and gather additional facts upon my return to Seoul. I expressed my regret that Kim was once more raising this same issue.

Regarding the money transfer to North Korea, I clarified my stance that this problem could not be linked to inter-Korean relations. As a member of the transition subcommittee on unification, foreign affairs, and national security, I had never participated in any discussion in connection to the money transfer, nor had I received any instructions pertaining to the matter before coming to Pyongyang. Frankly speaking, I was personally opposed to a special investigation of the money transfer in light of its possible impact on inter-Korean relations. But as the representative of the president-elect on a Pyongyang visit, I could not have any personal opinion. Furthermore, whether or not the money transfer was subject to a special investigation was South Korea's internal matter and not something that North Korea had any say over. Wasn't it true that where North Korea was involved, even things that could be achieved did not come to fruition? As a matter of fact, I had anticipated that North Korea might problematize the money transfer, so before leaving Seoul I had come up with an ideal response after a series of self-reflections.

Concluding, I responded to Kim,

> I will not report this conversation to the president-elect on my return to Seoul, because you told me to hear your remarks as coming from the chairman of a civilian organization that is the Asia-Pacific Peace Committee, not those made in your capacity as a secretary of the Worker's Party of the People's Republic of Korea. The issue of money transfer is subject to our domestic laws, so even the president-elect cannot influence it based on his personal whim. The North must know that in the South even the president-elect cannot get involved in the investigation. We must both work together to ensure that this problem does not influence inter-Korean relations in any way. It is desirable that Hyundai continue the project it has planned together with the Asia-Pacific Peace Committee, and it will continue, no matter what form it takes.

And at the end of this long answer, I once again emphasized, "I make it clear once again. I will not report this issue to the president-elect. I understood perfectly what you meant, but I tell you once again that this is a legal matter and the president-elect cannot arbitrarily involve himself."

I wanted to end the money transfer discussion in this way because I sought to prevent any influence it might have on the developing inter-Korean relations in the future, regardless of how the problem was resolved. Even if President Roh decided later on to allow a special investigation of the money transfer, I wanted it to be clear to the North that it should not be read as a negative signal for inter-Korean relations. Many people worried that the special investigation would have a very detrimental impact on inter-Korean relations. And there are still many who think that it did in fact have such an impact. I do not know how much of an effect the discussion that day in Pyongyang influenced inter-Korean relations. But while North Korea has made some references to the special investigation in conversations with the Roh administration, it never linked the investigation specifically to any particular matter or plan within the context of inter-Korean relations.

Continuing, I stressed that President-elect Roh had a concrete philosophy and vision for North Korea, namely to inherit and further develop Kim Dae-jung's policy of embracing the North. And as examples for the North to reflect on during future talks, I explained Roh's style in terms of different characteristics: he was resolute; he achieved victory through self-sacrifice; he placed importance on trust; he was practical. I illustrated each quality with an actual example; in particular, to show how he would sacrifice himself to gain victory, I used as an example Roh's reaction to Chung Mong-joon's bombshell withdrawal of support on the eve of the election. I explained that Roh was willing to use every method of persuasion, but if all failed, he would not desperately cling on and would decisively give up. I was sending an indirect message to the North about future inter-Korean talks. I argued, "Since the North brings up the chairman's personal character at every talk, the North should also understand our president-elect's personal character if there were to be meaningful negotiations." I added, "I believe that from now on, the conventions of negotiation must change in keeping with the president-elect's character."

With this I emphasized that Roh intended large-scale inter-Korean economic cooperation and aid to the North once the nuclear problem was resolved, and emphasized my desire that the president-elect's intent be conveyed accurately to Kim Jong-il. During the seventy-minute-long talk, we discussed a great many things, but I made no mention whatsoever of any detailed solution to the North Korean nuclear problem. That was the main task of the government's special envoy, so as the representative of the president-elect, I voluntarily limited my role to that of providing support from the sidelines.

Acknowledging a Difficult Future for the Korean Peninsula

Immediately after my meeting with Kim Yong-sun, the special envoy and his entourage met with president of the Supreme People's Assembly, Kim Yong-nam. This meeting was not entirely to the satisfaction of Special Envoy Lim, who had requested a meeting with Chairman Kim Jong-il himself. It was not unusual to meet with Kim Yong-nam in advance of meeting with Kim Jong-il, but in this case it just seemed like an excuse, since we had received a message that due to a provincial tour, Kim Jong-il would be unable to meet with us.

Around eight o'clock on the evening of January 28, Kim Yong-sun, in the presence of Lim Dong-ok and others, assumed a solemn look before the special envoy team and orally conveyed Kim Jong-il's message. It ran something like this:

> Received the report over the phone during a provincial tour. Saw the report and tried to meet with the South's special envoy team, but could not due to other matters. Could not meet because of more important business in the province but there will certainly be an occasion to meet in the future. Regarding the personal letter containing warm advice: in the future, personal letters will be received through envoys and will contact if there are reasons to do so. Assumed that our comrades have explained everything about the nuclear issue and other problems.

Kim Yong-sun plunged a dagger into the hearts of our team with his typically crude tone: "The KBS[4] has reported that the South considers the president of the Supreme People's Assembly to be the North's head of state. Since you have come as a special envoy and met with Chairman Kim Yong-nam, shouldn't you be satisfied?" So it was that the down-to-the-wire efforts of the ROK government to try and persuade the United States and North Korea to improve the situation came to naught; the remaining work would be the Roh administration's responsibility.

After the trip, I acutely felt that whether it was inter-Korean relations or the North Korean nuclear problem, the future of the Korean Peninsula was never going to be easy for the Participatory Government to navigate. As we had predicted, the visit did not offer much for the transition committee to evaluate. The press thought it only right that I should immediately report to the president-elect about the visit, and I myself avoided all media interviews after my return with the excuse that I had not yet briefed the president-elect. In reality, I was not able to immediately

---

4   [KBS, the Korean Broadcasting System, is South Korea's main national broadcaster.]

meet with him. Certainly, the CNN interview and the money transfer were important topics to discuss with him, but they were not enough to justify taking up his precious time. Roh was aware from media reports that the special envoy had returned essentially empty-handed, so there was no urgent reason to summon me.

I presented an official report to president-elect Roh a few days later. Regarding the CNN interview, I advised that the transition committee send the North a rather vague but comprehensive explanation through official channels, and that going forward we refrain from any negative comments about Kim Jong-il, given the nature of the North Korean regime; its officials were prone to responding like "Red Guards" and such comments invariably only worsened inter-Korean relations. I further recommended that it was necessary to firmly respond to the North's inconsiderate attitude toward the South and to develop negotiation strategies with the North that would improve its attitude. Concerning the money transfer, I reported the situation exactly as it had unfolded during the visit.

Finally, I counseled Roh that in developing a response to the North's nuclear development, a team should first travel to the United States to procure approval for the president-elect's strategy, then make initial contact with the North via a third nation—China. Or after the inauguration, the president-elect could dispatch his own special envoy to the North and propose our own plan to resolve the standoff over its nuclear development.

I ended my report and was about to stand up when Roh surprised me by suddenly saying, "I trust your judgment." This was the first time that I had met alone with the president-elect since our initial meeting in August 2001, when I gave a one-on-one lecture for several hours. Even when he was still just a candidate, I had had few chances to speak with him at length during the several advisory conferences where we both had been present. I had thought that the president-elect did not know me well. But Roh, who rarely spoke without sincerity, suddenly declared his trust in my judgment. This was a heavy burden on my shoulders. But it felt good.

3

With the National Security Council at Its New Beginning

Designing the Structure of the National Security Council

The presidential transition committee saw as one of its tasks the expansion of the National Security Council's (NSC's) functions. The members of the subcommittee on foreign policy and national security had worked for a long time on developing a plan to enlarge and restructure the NSC as a control tower for coordinating matters related to unification, foreign affairs, and national security (UFN). Roh was completely supportive of this plan, and there was also enough public support for changing the manner in which UFN-related issues were handled so as to place the NSC at the center. This meant that the ruling party and the opposition in the National Assembly just might be able to find common ground. With this in mind, right from its formation the transition committee began the project of restructuring the NSC. The initial plan was to handle the project as a team with one person serving as a coordinator. But it became clear that there was simply too much for a single coordinator to handle, and our subcommittee head, Yoon Young-kwan, could not deal with it on top of all his other duties. The rest of the subcommittee members also became preoccupied with other things, so in the end I ended up being in charge of it.

The reason the transition committee wanted to enlarge and restructure the NSC was that unification, foreign affairs, and national security were intimately connected. As can be seen with the North Korean nuclear problem, the important national security matters of today are handled by several different ministries, each with a slightly different perspective. Such transministerial tasks of national importance should not be decided by individual ministries according to their individual positions. To prevent policymaking chaos and to implement the most effective policies possible, discussion and compromise among ministries is necessary, and the ultimate policy direction must be determined by the president's point of view. To this end, we felt that there should be a UFN team within the Blue House to comprehensively coordinate and plan important tasks—a "control tower" that determined the nation's interests and engaged in policymaking while answering directly to the president.

However, relying on the existing governmental structure to plan, implement, and monitor the execution of a comprehensive national security strategy presented significant challenges. Until then, it was the office of the senior secretary of foreign affairs and national security—inside the Presidential Secretariat within the Blue House—that was responsible for handling UFN matters.

Under the senior secretary, there were several secretaries, each one handling unification, foreign affairs, national defense, international affairs, and other matters. They directly corresponded with the ministries within the executive branch and served as liaisons between the ministries and the Blue House.

But continuing to rely on those secretaries as counterparts to ministries, whereby they functioned as mere way stations conveying opinions between ministries and the president, made it difficult to impress the president's views on the whole of the government. Furthermore, the existing system lacked the ability to comprehensively manage information and failed to put in place a protocol for managing risk at the national level.

The Kim Dae-jung administration, in fact, had fully recognized this weakness. Therefore, at the beginning of the Kim administration, the senior secretary of foreign affairs and national security, Lim Dong-won, put considerable effort into replacing the existing system with the NSC. Although Lim was not able to bring about a complete transformation, he had been at least able to establish the NSC as a sort of conferencing structure. Working with the absolute trust of President Kim, Lim created the NSC Standing Committee, which brought together those ministers whose portfolios touched on unification, foreign affairs, and national security for a discussion at least once a week. Lim also began the practice of having officials of vice-ministerial rank meet once every two weeks to coordinate positions on UFN matters. This was when the Korean NSC was first shaped into a conferencing scheme. There was a problem, however. The NSC had a secretariat, but it lacked any function or power other than hosting such meetings and conveying their outcomes to the various ministries. It was merely an administrative organ for facilitating conferences. The NSC did not yet have the administrative capacity to consolidate and oversee policies in the UFN realms based on the outcomes of its conferences.

With this in mind, the transition committee obtained the president-elect's approval to abolish the office of the senior secretary of foreign affairs and national security, and instead create a new system that would enlarge and restructure the NSC Secretariat as a control tower that directly aids the president. Our reform was carried out with an eye to the American NSC, but taking into consideration the vast difference between the national security situation in the United States and that in South Korea, we conceived of an NSC system that would encompass information and risk management.

We decided to establish an office for policy coordination inside the NSC Secretariat that would replace the abolished office of the senior secretary of foreign affairs and national security. This new office would take a transministerial approach to moderating and unifying important policies. In addition, we decided it should be entrusted with the tasks once performed by the former senior secretary's office, administratively linking the president to the various ministries. And for the purpose of planning national security strategies and handing medium- to long-term matters of importance, such as North Korean nuclear development and national defense reform, we established an office of strategic planning. We also established an information management office for efficiently managing and supplying necessary state intelligence to individuals and ministries, instead of allowing that intelligence to be monopolized by a particular person or ministry. Also, in consideration of the Korean Peninsula's division and the importance of managing ever-increasing risks to national security, we established a risk management center as an office that would answer directly to the president. To enable a twenty-four-hour real-time assessment of the national security situation within and outside the country, we decided to create a national security situation room. And the head of the NSC Secretariat was to be the newly established national security advisor, a ministerial-rank position within the Presidential Secretariat, to be assisted by a deputy secretary-general at the vice-ministerial rank.

But in the process of discussing the full-scale implementation of the new NSC system, there was a controversy over the role of the NSC's risk management center. The transition subcommittee on foreign policy and national security believed that the NSC risk management center should be a comprehensive control tower, not only in the realm of national security but also for handling disasters. Yet many were opposed to this opinion. Should the Blue House host the control tower for risk management, they contested, the president would be directly responsible in the event of disasters and that burden would be too much. But president-elect Roh was firm in his stance: "No matter what major accident [might happen], the people will ultimately ask the president to accept the responsibility. It is right that the NSC risk management center, under the direct authority of the president, be in charge of handling disasters and respond responsibly." He added, "To respond to disasters and manage related matters, which implicate various ministries, the involvement of the presidential office is unavoidable."

On February 18, 2003, I sent to the president-elect my "Plan for Reforming the NSC Secretariat," a memo that explained the aim of the NSC Secretariat reform:

> By planning, moderating, and consolidating pressing matters in unification, foreign affairs, and national security policymaking at the level of national strategy and the entire government, it ensures the direction and consistency of national security policy. By improving the mechanism for preventing, addressing, and managing myriad risks ranging from major disasters to sudden crises in North Korea and military conflicts, it improves the state's risk management ability and strengthens the ability to assist the president.

The memo was accepted almost in its entirety by the incoming administration.

But after I completed my duties on the transition committee on February 22 and returned to the Sejong Institute, I saw the published structure of the Blue House Presidential Secretariat and was shocked to realize that in the UFN realm there were vice-ministerial positions of foreign affairs and defense advisors, in addition to that of national security advisor. In fact, during the transition committee discussions, this opinion—that inside the Presidential Secretariat there should be advisors on foreign affairs and defense—had been championed by career bureaucrats. But our transition subcommittee had strongly opposed the idea, because if such advisors were to become involved in a case or policy under the purview of the NSC Secretariat, the result would be chaos. The NSC, strengthened to confer greater presidential control over consolidating and moderating UFN policies, would only end up producing even greater policy confusion.

But the subcommittee members who had drafted our report had all returned to their regular jobs outside politics; only committee head Yoon Young-kwan was remaining in the administration, as foreign minister. There was no way our report was going to overrule the judgment of the numerous career bureaucrats who were the president-elect's advisors.

Thus, in the UFN policy realm, the Participatory Government would begin with a deep flaw: a strange organization that saw an expanded NSC Secretariat in uneasy coexistence with foreign affairs and defense advisors.

National Security under Threat: The Council Sidelined

When I had completed my duties on the transition committee, I hadn't even had the chance to consider pursuing a position in the government—I had been told by the president-elect to "return to academia." When reporters asked about my plans, I told them with every bit of confidence that I was returning to my old job to focus on scholarship. But on February 25, just as the Roh administration came into power, I heard news that not only was the newly enlarged and restructured NSC Secretariat failing to operate properly, but the transition to the NSC system itself was also not seeing much progress. Only a week into the new government's term, there was even talk that to establish the NSC system, someone from the transition committee would have to enter the Blue House.

In early March 2003, I received a call from Dr. Kim Jin-hyang, who had joined the NSC Secretariat at the same time the Participatory Government was launched, after serving on the transition subcommittee on foreign affairs and national security. "What on earth are you doing? It is total chaos here. If you don't come and sort things out, the NSC Secretariat reform will amount to nothing. Are you sure you can live with that?" The next day, Colonel Ryu Hee-in, who also had just started working at the NSC Secretariat alongside Dr. Kim, called, sounding out of breath.

"We are having a meeting chaired by the chief of staff. I am going in to give a report on the NSC situation. You have to come in. Only then will we have a solution."

Only ten days into the new administration and the NSC system that the Participatory Government had so ambitiously launched was malfunctioning from the start and in chaos. Already, rumors that the Blue House foreign affairs and national security team was unable to deal with the serious national security situation had traveled all the way to my office outside the capital in Pangyo. The transition committee members who had joined the NSC were making appeals to everyone that chaos would not be resolved unless a transition committee member who had designed the NSC system were put in charge of the NSC. They were simultaneously making desperate appeals to me, but I was conflicted. Even though I had indeed designed the NSC system, it was not as though the Blue House personnel office was asking me to come in and take charge of it.

At the launch of the Roh administration, South Korea's security situation was dire. The North Korean nuclear problem had completely shut down all talks between Pyongyang and Washington and tensions were sky-high. American officials were talking about the possibility of an attack on the North, and the North in turn reacted angrily. On March 2, North Korean fighter jets flew in close proximity to a U.S. Air Force surveillance plane in the Eastern Sea (Sea of Japan), heightening military tensions even further. South Korean and U.S. discussions over relocating the U.S. Forces Korea (USFK) bases fed public anxiety, and some media outlets fanned such concerns, exacerbating the situation. Foreign media were publishing premature projections that Secretary of Defense Donald Rumsfeld was considering three different possibilities: pulling all U.S. forces in South Korea back to the United States, moving them farther away from the frontline within South Korea, or basing them outside the country, in an area near South Korea.

U.S.–South Korean relations were already uncomfortable well before the launch of the Roh administration. Many people had ascribed to President Roh and his advisors an anti-American image, which was then projected onto the administration's policies toward the United States. Under such a cloud, any disagreement—whether over the relocation of USFK bases or the North Korean nuclear problem—was ascribed to the Roh administration's supposed anti-American stance, regardless of the truth of the matter or the background of any difference. Each and every incident was deemed to be a sign of deterioration in U.S.–South

Korean relations, and voices that warned of ensuing economic instability became louder. On the domestic front, the media were in an uproar over the special investigation of the above-mentioned money transfer to the North. The future of inter-Korean relations was becoming hard to predict.

The foreign affairs and national security circle within the Blue House should have been working to overcome this crisis and calm the anxiety over national security, but they were barely able to look after themselves. National Security Advisor Ra Jong-yil, who was in charge of the NSC, saw his standing in jeopardy as soon as he took office. When it was reported in early March that he had met with a high-ranking North Korean official in Beijing several days before his appointment was announced, it led to criticism that Ra had himself compromised the government's existing protocol for how to initiate communication with the North. On top of the outcry over the money transfer issue, his conduct allowed the opposition to go so far as to allege that the government was trying to make a back-room deal with Pyongyang.

I also heard that Ra was not able to adequately stabilize the nascent NSC system during this critical early stage—in fact, there was still no office space for the NSC Secretariat within the Blue House, and hiring had gone astray. Since the NSC Secretariat—which should have been advising the president and presiding over UFN matters within the Blue House—was not functioning as it should, the ministries of foreign affairs and defense were still conducting their policy briefings in the offices of foreign affairs and defense advisors, instead of at the NSC Secretariat. The transition committee plan had established that the NSC Secretariat would be responsible for advising the president and coordinating policies, but in reality nobody was in charge to ensure compliance with this rule. Thus, it was chaos and pure disorder at the heart of South Korea's foreign policy and national security management.

Kim Jin-hyang and Ryu Hee-in sought me out at this time. Frankly, at the Blue House, which is at the heart of the Republic of Korea's power, an air force colonel and a minor NSC secretary in special services who had not yet even received his formal credentials were as insignificant as grains of sand on the bank of the Han River. But they had designed the NSC expansion and restructuring plan with me, and they were doing everything they could to try and keep the NSC structure alive, an ambitiously conceived plan that had not yet been realized and was on the brink of completely disappearing.

I could not give them a satisfactory answer as to what I would do. If I were to join the NSC, my position would be that of the deputy secretary-general, since the national security advisor was already the secretary-general of the NSC. As a scholar who had studied inter-Korean relations and North Korea, I was willing to work in the government should President Roh give me a chance, but I did not want to be second-in-command, even if it were at an organization that I myself had been in charge of creating. The position of deputy secretary-general was high up in the government hierarchy, at the vice-ministerial rank, but I had no desire to play second fiddle, without any power. Against my hope there were already vice-ministerial-rank advisors on foreign affairs and national defense within the Blue House, so it was even less likely that there was anything I could do with real authority. So I told them to seek out someone who would not have an issue assisting the national security advisor formally in charge of the NSC. But Kim and Ryu would not relent and continued to insist that I join the NSC.

As I became even more torn between my sense of responsibility to the NSC and the thought that even after joining the organization I would be powerless to act with authority, the Blue House contacted me. They wanted me to attend a national security briefing chaired by the president on March 5. Other attendees would include Chief of Staff Moon Hee-sang, National Security Advisor Ra Jong-yil, Foreign Affairs Advisor Ban Ki-moon, and Defense Advisor Kim Hee-sang, all from within the Blue House; and three former members of the transition committee, excluding Foreign Minister Yoon Young-kwan. This would be the first time I would visit the Blue House after the Participatory Government had been launched.

At the March 5 meeting, President Roh said it was necessary for a UFN team to constantly monitor and manage the national security situation to reassure the public, and he was holding this meeting to discuss the NSC's expansion and its personnel problems. While he did not explicitly say so, it seemed as though he was looking to the members of his transition committee, whom he had not seen since they returned to academia, as reinforcements to support him.

Now that he was in the Blue House, the president was surrounded by foreign affairs and national security experts with bureaucratic backgrounds, unlike during the pre-inauguration transition phase. These bureaucrats counseled Roh that the answers to the problems of North Korean nuclear capacity and the possible relocation of U.S. military bases within South Korea would be found in close cooperation with the United States and a public affirmation of the U.S.–South Korean alliance; there should be no public perception of differences in opinion between the ROK government and the United States. Although their words clamored for undiluted cooperation with the Americans, in reality they were advocating for a strict dependence on the United States. Of course, they were making that argument for the country and for the president, they thought. But the president did not share their understanding.

Roh thought that the government of the Republic of Korea, more than any other entity, best understood the issues of safety and prosperity on the Korean Peninsula—we were the ones who had to proactively come up with an appropriate response to the status quo. Solving the North Korean nuclear problem would require close consultation with the United States, but the ROK government should be the party to ultimately create an independent plan of action that could simultaneously convince both North Korea and the United States. Roh likewise sought to pursue autonomous defense in lieu of the reality of dependence on the USFK, and to build U.S.–South Korean relations that were more balanced and amicable. During the presidential transition, we committee members shared the president-elect's philosophy and presented to the people a blueprint for UFN policies that embodied the presidential vision. But once the new government was launched, the atmosphere among the members of the foreign affairs and national security circle at the Blue House and the government was quite different. The president felt that his new advisors regarded his philosophy and inclinations as dangerous and sentimental, instead of accommodating them as his fundamental values. In fact, no small number of high-ranking foreign affairs and national security officials were dissatisfied with the president's decisions regarding foreign policy and national defense and did not hesitate to express dissent. At the meeting on this day, this fact was most obvious.

But the meeting yielded a frank and heated discussion of the North Korean nuclear problem and U.S.–South Korean relations. When the president openly shared his long-standing views on such issues, former members of the transition committee agreed with him, while his foreign affairs and defense advisors responded with reservation or even outright opposition. Roh normally carefully listened to opposing views during debates, but as this continued he put on a grave face, turned to them and said, "You two are my personal tutors. So shouldn't you be on my side in front of other people? Why are you so keen on opposing me?"

The most important and contentious topic that day was the operation of the NSC Secretariat; in particular, the role of the national security advisor within that organization was debated. The main issue was that the national security advisor was simply too overextended to oversee the NSC Secretariat, so there had to be another way to ensure that the NSC Secretariat would find its footing quickly and operate successfully. Following from this topic, there was also discussion over the exact roles of the foreign affairs and defense advisors. The transition committee members, including myself, had argued that the two advisors should not be involved in policymaking and should limit themselves to advising the president; otherwise, there would be confusion over the parameters of the NSC Secretariat's work, and the overhauled organization's effectiveness as a control tower within the administration would be shackled. After a long debate, the president finally issued his determination: someone other than the national security advisor would preside over the NSC Secretariat. This new NSC secretary would have complete authority over the organization's operation; the national security advisor would only advise the president and assist at diplomatic functions. As for the foreign affairs and defense advisors, he decreed that they should not participate in policymaking and only advise the president, render assistance at related events, and carry out special tasks as asked by the president.

Through this meeting we realized that the president was going to entrust the NSC Secretariat to an academic from the transition committee. As I was leaving the Blue House, I advised Seo Dong-man, who had been the leader of the advisory committee before the election, to take charge of the NSC Secretariat. But Seo's reaction was negative. He said he had an inkling that he would instead be heading to the NIS to reform that institution. I was flummoxed. If Seo did not assume the command post of the NSC Secretariat, the next candidate was me. While there was yet another member of the transition committee—Dr. Seo Joo-seok—who could also be nominated, rumors and the interest of the Blue House suggested that we were not being given equal consideration.

"The Architect of the NSC Should Take Over"

On my way home after the meeting, I thought that my appointment to the NSC Secretariat was more or less set in stone. Kim Jin-hyang and Ryu Hee-in, by influencing Chief of Staff Moon Hee-sang, had been directly responsible for making this meeting, chaired by the president, happen. Kim and Ryu were unlikely to leave me in peace. I took comfort in the knowledge that if I became head of the NSC Secretariat, I could do my work as I deemed fit. But the next day Kim Jin-hyang called; he had discovered that it was against the NSC rules to separate the post of national security advisor from that of NSC secretary-general, or to let the NSC Secretariat be headed by an official of the vice-ministerial rank. Kim had already informed the president of his discovery. This was an unexpected obstacle. Later I looked it up and indeed the post of NSC secretary-general was meant to be occupied by a secretary from the foreign affairs and national security part. In other words, only a presidential secretary was allowed to serve as the NSC secretary-general; other government officials at the ministerial or vice-ministerial rank were barred. My path to head the NSC Secretariat was blocked.

I sighed. The next evening Kim Jin-hyang paid me a visit at home. He said the Blue House was about to contact me, and I needed to make up my mind. Instead of answering, I excused myself, went to the bedroom and fell asleep. The next morning when I awoke Kim was gone, but it turns out he had talked with my wife until the wee hours of the morning, trying to convince her that I should enter the Blue House. In the process he had also consumed every drop of alcohol in the house before heading off to work. I was forced to think long and hard. What was I to do?

A few days later, Lee Gwang-jae, head of the Blue House situation room, asked me to meet him. He said, as I anticipated, that the president wanted me to take the position of NSC deputy secretary-general—second-in-command at the NSC. Instead of answering, I asked Lee to convey to the president a one-page letter I had written, titled "Recommendations to the President." I told him the outcome of my decision would be based on the president's answer to my recommendations. He didn't show it, but Lee was probably a little shocked on the inside. To put it bluntly, he had offered a vice-ministerial position at the Blue House to an inexperienced tenderfoot, but instead of being grateful, I had attached conditions to my appointment. In hindsight, even I consider this an astoundingly bold move on my part. The letter that I had entrusted to Lee, summarized below, contained conclusions I had reached after several days of reflection.

Recommendations by Lee Jong-seok

I am grateful for the president's trust in considering me as one of the candidates for the position of the NSC deputy secretary-general.

Upon my return to academia, I have begun my work of drumming up public support and building the theoretical foundation for the

Participatory Government's unification and national security policy, so that we can build a popular consensus. I believe this work is important for ensuring a smooth beginning and successful operation of the Participatory Government.

I am uneasy that the numerous difficulties in the process of expanding and restructuring the NSC Secretariat have rendered the issue of appointing the new deputy secretary-general important, to the point that the current chaos is starting to have a bearing on me.

It is only right that, should Mr. President order me to assume this position, I will accept that order. But given the current structure of the NSC Secretariat, it is difficult for the deputy secretary-general to play an important role beyond simply assisting the national security advisor. If this situation does not improve, I believe it would be more effective for me to assist the Participatory Government by remaining in academia, rather than as deputy secretary-general.

Therefore, at the risk of impertinence, I recommend the following: It is necessary for Mr. President to issue a special directive dividing the roles of the deputy secretary-general and the national security advisor based on the contents of the March 5 national security meeting chaired by you and attended by advisors in national security, the chief-of-staff, and the transition committee members. Only then can I assume the position of deputy secretary-general, rapidly conclude the restructuring of the NSC Secretariat, launch teams responsible for handling pressing issues such as the North Korean nuclear problem and U.S.–South Korean relations, and utilize the NSC as the center of the system.

Attached to this list of recommendations that clarified my stance, I drafted the following presidential special directive that laid out a clear division of duties between myself as the deputy secretary-general and the national security advisor:

> With regard to the division of duties of the national security advisor and the vice-ministerial-level NSC personnel, it was decided at the national security briefing on March 5, 2003, that the national security advisor shall be the presiding chairman of the NSC and a political appointee at a vice-ministerial rank shall independently serve as the NSC secretary-general. But this decision contains elements that violate the NSC Act, Section 8, Clause 3, so until the said law can be amended, it is directed as a temporary measure that duties will be divided in such a way that the national security advisor shall formally assume the position of the NSC secretary-general but the deputy secretary-general will in actuality preside over the NSC Secretariat.

Several days later Jeong Yong-chan, the presidential aide who handled personnel and appointments, asked for a meeting. My mood was mixed—it seemed that I was being summoned for a unilateral notification of my confirmation as NSC deputy secretary-general, but I had yet to hear an answer to my recommendations. I printed out a copy of the recommendations and headed to the Blue House.

It was as I had feared: Jeong informed me that I was the internal candidate for NSC deputy secretary-general. "Some people on the Blue House personnel committee expressed opposition to your appointment because you are an academic and the national security advisor who serves as the secretary-general is also an academic. But in the end the president chose you." I briefly expressed thanks and pulled out the recommendations.

"Mr. Jeong, I came to the Blue House today feeling like a student who has come to school without having done his homework."

"What do you mean?" Jeong asked incredulously.

"Did the president say anything else about me?"

"He did not say anything else."

I explained the events that had preceded and handed over my recommendations to him, asking him to contact me only when he had briefed the president on them and had received an answer. It appeared that Jeong had planned to break the news of my selection as the NSC deputy secretary-general to the media that same day. I watched as he immediately canceled the plan to announce the appointment.

Several more days passed without any news. On March 17, I happened across news of my appointment as the NSC deputy secretary-general. My first thought was that it was quite unreasonable that no one had first spoken to me about it. But it was my misunderstanding to think that the Blue House had simply appointed me without considering my demands. President Roh, at a cabinet meeting on March 18, adopted the NSC Secretariat restructuring plan and clarified the division of duties between the national security advisor, i.e., the NSC secretary-general, and the second-in-command, the deputy secretary-general: "The office of national security advisor mainly advises the president and cannot easily handle internal administrative duties, so it is necessary to have a deputy secretary-general at the vice-ministerial rank who will oversee day-to-day operations and facilitate external negotiations of the NSC Secretariat." That day the Blue House spokesperson directly quoted the presidential remarks and briefed reporters posted to the Blue House about the role of the deputy secretary-general in the same way. In other words, the president, after realizing the impossibility of his earlier decision to separate the role of the NSC secretary-general from that of the national security advisor due to the NSC Act, directed that the NSC deputy secretary-general essentially take charge of the NSC Secretariat.

At the time, the press did not focus on this fact. If they had, there might have been less of a controversy later over the assertion that "the parameters of the NSC deputy secretary-general's duties infringe on those of the national security advisor, who is also the NSC secretary-general." But at that time, it was not clear how much of an impact the appointment of a vice-ministerial-rank NSC deputy secretary-general would have on the overall picture of the Participatory Government's UFN policies, so there was no reason for them to give me any second thought. But at least *Yonhap News* and *The Hankyoreh* reported this fact.

Ultimately, President Roh accepted my recommendations in the process of appointing me as the NSC deputy secretary-general, even though he never once discussed them with me. I was thankful to the president for being this way. While I served as the NSC deputy secretary-general, I never once told him that I was uncomfortable with my position or rank. But he must have felt bad to see me constantly embroiled in controversies over the issue of my "overstepping" boundaries, and thus he ordered an amendment to the law so that I could be promoted to the position of NSC secretary-general. When that also proved difficult, he even tried to outright promote me to national security advisor. The more I think back to the consideration he showed me, the more I am moved in gratitude.

In any event, I became the NSC deputy secretary-general through this extraordinary process. I was in charge of the NSC Secretariat, which replaced what was previously the office of the senior secretary of foreign affairs and national security within the Blue House. Even though I had designed the NSC and spearheaded the project of enlarging and restructuring the NSC Secretariat during my time on the transition committee, I never once imagined that I would actually end up managing an NSC system of my own design. After my appointment, I realized how much of an influence connections can have on a person's destiny. My connection to the NSC, in fact, far predated my time on the presidential transition committee.

Although I was a scholar who researched North Korea, inter-Korean relations, and Chinese–North Korean relations, I had never worked on foreign policy or national security strategies. But in spring 1998, I did happen to have an opportunity to research national security strategy and the NSC system. Lim Dong-won, the inaugural senior secretary of foreign affairs and national security at the Blue House under President Kim Dae-jung, was a strategist who knew the usefulness of the NSC system better than anyone else. At the launch of the Kim administration, Lim created the NSC Standing Committee, consisting of ministerial-rank officials and advisors at the Blue House in UFN areas. He also undertook the project of establishing a small NSC Secretariat that would manage committee-related tasks. Although Lim failed to replace the president's foreign affairs and national security advising structure with the NSC system, Lim was a pioneer who tried for the first time in South Korea to gradually insert the NSC system into the domain of foreign affairs and national security.

Senior Secretary Lim simultaneously conceived of publishing a "national security strategy directive" for the purpose of the strategic and systematic operation of national security. In spring 1998 Lim met with Han Bae-ho, head of the Sejong Institute, and asked that the institute undertake, at the civilian level, research into various nations' national security structures and draft a tentatively titled "National Strategy" to serve as the foundation of his national security strategy directive. He singled me out at the institute as the person to take charge of this task. Thanks to him, I became the main coordinator of the national strategy research team at the Sejong Institute in the first half of 1998 and threw myself day and night into the task of producing the "National Strategy," including conducting expert interviews, research discussions, and surveys. I also received preliminary drafts of field-specific strategies from relevant government ministries, and asked researchers at the Sejong Institute to examine the structure of the NSC in the United States, not to mention in Israel, Taiwan, and Japan, and to submit research outcome reports. I consolidated the research results and applied them toward our report. While I was not completely satisfied with the results, since they had been reached in the absence of any prior research materials, yet I was proud that this was the first-ever comprehensive study of the NSC in South Korea. Kim Dae-jung consulted this research before advancing subsequent projects with the aim of creating a simple national security strategy directive, but that work was not completed for various reasons and its result did not see the light of day.

Ultimately this project ended prematurely under the Kim Dae-jung administration. But having participated in this project as an ordinary citizen, I learned a great deal about the national security strategy and the NSC system. Back then I put a lot of thought into the objectives, the strategic foundations, and the direction of the ROK's UFN policies. I also developed an interest in developing an organic, comprehensive national security system that was modeled on the American NSC but tailored to the realities of South Korea.

Was this all a matter of fate? At the transition committee, I ended up designing the NSC system for the Roh Moo-hyun administration, then I became the person to manage the NSC Secretariat under this very system. And this NSC Secretariat published for the first time in the history of the ROK government a national security strategy directive, titled "Peace, Prosperity, and National Security." I felt that destiny strangely bound the NSC with Lim Dong-won, who had adopted the NSC system and built my foundation of understanding the NSC, and me, who spearheaded the enlargement and restructuring of the NSC and became its chief operator.

II

A Dream of an Independent Nation

4

President Roh's Vision for the Country

The President's Conception of Autonomous Defense

According to materials exposed by Wikileaks, the U.S. embassy in Seoul reported in a secret cable to Washington on January 9, 2006, that "Roh [Moo-hyun] and Lee [Jong-seok] share the same world view, especially on North Korea." Maybe that idea came about because the opposition and certain media outlets ceaselessly accused the Roh administration of being pro-North, but the president and I never completely shared the same philosophy on North Korea.

On a public holiday in 2005, after I had briefed the president at the Blue House, we were chatting when the issue of inter-Korean relations came up. The president suddenly said, "My thinking is different from yours or Prime Minister Lee Hae-chan's. You two work toward unification, but I work toward peace." Bemused by this unexpected remark, I did not press him, nor did he offer any further explanation. But on the way down to my office, I pondered his comment and believed I understood what he meant.

Based on what I know, President Roh's highest goal was not unification but peace and mutual prosperity. He thought that our task was to end the combative relationship between the two Koreas and achieve mutual prosperity by establishing peace. He had the notion that the matter of unification was for later generations to decide.

In contrast, national unification was the ultimate goal—going beyond peace and prosperity—for people like me, who work to build the theoretical foundation of unification's legitimacy, and Lee Hae-chan, who had long argued for national reconciliation and unification. Like the president, we all wanted peace and mutual prosperity in the two Koreas, but beyond that point the philosophical difference was clear, and this is what the president was addressing. He thought of us as nationalists, while he considered himself more akin to a pacifist. Having retired in December 2006, I could not confirm whether the historic October 4, 2007, inter-Korean summit and declaration changed his philosophy.

But the president and I were in utter agreement when it came to the dream of an autonomous nation. The U.S. embassy described me this way in the Wikileaks report: "He is committed to seeing South Korea play a more active, independent role in the world and is sensitive to perceived slights to his nation." I do not know how Americans see this evaluation but I have no intention to deny it. I might even call it a compliment, since it better describes President Roh.

An autonomous nation is one that decides and takes responsibility for its own affairs. Of course, in this age of globalization there is no nation that can decide its own affairs with complete independence, but a nation must still control its own destiny if it is to be independent and autonomous. This is not old-fashioned nationalism but common sense. A nation must be ready to defend itself and to strive toward autonomy. Koreans are exceptionally mindful of the need for autonomy, given their painful memories of colonization by Japan and their reliance on the United States following independence.

President Roh craved autonomy for our people and our nation. Some Koreans may protest that we are already autonomous, but Roh thought such a claim was mere wordplay when the commander of the South Korean forces did not even have authority over six hundred thousand South Korean troops, and civic leaders were unashamed to talk about using American soldiers in South Korea as a "tripwire." This was the reality of South Korea's deeply rooted psychological dependence on the United States. Because of this abnormal situation, he judged that our ability to decide independently and act responsibly in inter-Korean relations and diplomacy was at best limited. He also thought that this dependence was a big stumbling block to rightly shifting U.S.–South

Korean relations toward mutual benefit and balance, a move necessitated by South Korea's growing power and stature. Many, including me, hoped that President Roh would be able to attain South Korea's autonomous defense and diplomacy—for many, this was an important ideal when the Participatory Government came into power.

President Roh's dream of autonomous defense had little to do with being progressive or anti-conservative, and even less to do with anti-Americanism. For him, it was only common sense to want to defend the nation with one's own strength and to make every effort toward this goal. But the problem was that South Korea's self-identified conservative forces, which had long been in power over the nation, had poisoned ideas of autonomous defense and autonomous diplomacy by equating them with being anti-American and pro-North Korea. Whereas true conservatives should raise their voices, higher than those of progressives, to argue and fight for autonomous defense, South Korea's so-called conservatives see autonomy as seditious and denounce any who argue for it as anti-American or pro-North. As a result, autonomy has come to be perceived in today's South Korea as a pet cause of progressives and a symptom of anti-Americanism. This situation is obviously irrational beyond comprehension.

Pursuing autonomous defense does not mean that we want to handle defense alone. Modern nations achieve defense through alliances and cooperation with friendly nations, not simply through their own capability to wage war. Roh and his advisors knew this even as they pursued autonomous defense.

What exactly was Roh's conception of autonomous defense? He saw its first and foremost goal as the ability to handle North Korea. The next step would be to possess a limited strategic veto power in Northeast Asia, where superpowers were butting heads. President Roh never had any intention or ability to attack another nation. But at the same time, he wanted us to have sufficient offensive capabilities, such that any nation that attacked us knew that the price of an attack would be critical damage.

A President Who Detested the Term "Tripwire"

President Roh, throughout his term, consistently conveyed his desire for autonomous defense through his words and actions. In particular, his decisions at the beginning of the presidential term regarding the relocation of the U.S. Forces Korea (USFK) and Seoul's Yongsan military garrison clearly showed his commitment to the idea of autonomous defense, as well as his consideration of the U.S. alliance.

On April 3, 2003, at an interministerial conference on national security, the Defense Ministry gave a briefing on the government's position on the relocation of the USFK. Under consideration was the U.S. Department of Defense's plan to move the USFK from its base north of the Han River to the south, and to relocate the Yongsan garrison, which included the Combined Forces Command (CFC).

The United States and South Korea had agreed, as early as October 2002 at the South Korea–U.S. Security Consultative Meeting (SCM), to hold the so-called Future of the Alliance conference and seriously study the problem of relocating both the USFK base and the Yongsan garrison. From the very beginning of the Roh administration, the U.S. Department of Defense was keen on obtaining quick agreement on and resolution of this matter as an extension of the 2002 agreement.

At the April 3 conference, the Defense Ministry shared the view that it was, realistically speaking, difficult to accept the American demand to relocate the U.S. Army's Second Infantry Division, stationed north of the Han River, to the south as soon as possible. The ministry held that moving the Yongsan garrison would need to be done in several stages over a longer period of time, rather than in the near future as the United States wanted. The ministry also reported that it would link the relocation of the CFC from Yongsan to the relocation of the ministry itself; in other words, the ministry determined that if it stayed in Seoul—specifically, Yongsan, where it was based—so should the CFC. The ministry's reasoning was that the United States' planned relocation of the USFK would deepen public anxiety over national security. But President Roh had a different take. He ordered that the Yongsan garrison be relocated as soon as possible in consideration of American wishes. He, however, agreed with the ministry when it came to the relocation of the U.S. Army's Second Infantry Division.

In reality, relocating much of the USFK to south of the Han River implied that American forces would completely withdraw from the Korean Demilitarized Zone (DMZ), including Panmunjom, and South Korean forces would take up defense of the entire DMZ. Many defense experts believed that, given the capability of South Korean forces, the gradual relocation of the USFK would not result in a national security vacuum. The president and the National Security Council (NSC) Secretariat also agreed that the defense of the DMZ could not be left to the

American soldiers forever. But the Defense Ministry, along with many media outlets and intellectuals, disagreed. They worried that a "trip-wire"—the name they gave to U.S. forces north of the Han River—was about to disappear. This worry, in turn, fed the country's concerns over national security.

A "tripwire" is a thin metal thread that triggers an explosion when touched. These South Koreans contended that if the USFK (the tripwire) were based north of the Han River and a war broke out, the USFK would immediately become a target of North Korean forces, guaranteeing U.S. involvement in the inter-Korean conflict. They thought the same about the Yongsan garrison: even if the USFK were relocated, ensuring that the CFC—under the authority of the USFK commander—remained in Yongsan would guarantee U.S. involvement in any war with the North.

President Roh was uncomfortable with this logic, even expressing contempt for it. He thought that the tripwire comparison was rooted in an extremely weak mindset that lacked even the barest, minimal desire to engage in self-defense; it was, he thought, immoral to demand the blood of allied forces before fighting for one's own security. At this meeting, early in his tenure, he did not directly express his feelings, but over time he began to strongly critique the tripwire logic in official settings. At discussions of national defense inside the Roh administration, the word "tripwire" essentially became taboo. The United States found the notion equally distasteful. On March 18, 2003, the United States revealed that the Second Infantry Division was moving south of the Han River, and expressed its dissatisfaction with the tripwire proponents, asserting that the term "tripwire" was unfair and held the deeper meaning that South Korea could not be defended without first spilling American blood.

On April 11, 2003, President Roh called me at my office about the relocation of the USFK. After much consideration, the president seemed to have concluded that the Defense Ministry's passive stance, as revealed in its own report a week earlier about how the USFK relocation was causing public concern over national security, should not be allowed to persist. He told me,

> Instead of being passively dragged, at the next NSC conference I want you to clearly articulate a commitment to using the USFK relocation toward the goal of building autonomous defense. We need to develop a clear logic to persuade the public that despite the USFK relocation, the government will have in place a system that can adequately handle national security, and in this way address any contraction in investor psychology, economic

instability, or public anxiety. Prepare to hold regular national security briefings to discuss what the logic of our response to the USFK relocation will be. Our doctrine must be finalized by August 15.

The president ordered that, rather than avoiding the issue of relocation reverberating across South Korean society, we accommodate the American proposal as much as possible and use the occasion to advance autonomous defense and ensure our preparedness in handling national security.

At the U.S.–South Korean summit in May, presidents Roh and Bush agreed to the early relocation of the Yongsan garrison. Also, they agreed that the relocation of the Second Infantry Division should be "pursued with utmost consideration for the political, economic, and national security situation on the Korean Peninsula as well as throughout Northeast Asia." In this agreement, President Roh focused his energy not on dictating the timing of the relocation but on ensuring that the United States not start to unilaterally move the USFK without first consulting South Korea. In conversation with the NSC officials on May 19, Roh addressed this agreement and the notion of autonomous defense:

> Because we inserted the language that the relocation of the Second Infantry Division will be "pursued carefully," the United States cannot unilaterally decide relocation. But since there still remains an imbalance of power in U.S.–South Korean relations, we can achieve nothing by shouting our demands. Yet there is a significant difference between the actual level of our reliance on the United States and South Koreans' level of psychological dependence on the United States. Because of this disparity, I emphasize autonomous defense, in the belief that we must overcome this psychological dependence and take charge of our national defense.
>
> In consideration of the U.S. alliance it is important to think in a balanced way, but it is just as important to play a leading role in national defense. If South Korean relations with the United States become excessively dependent, there are bound to be many diplomatic restrictions. That's why I have long thought we need to build autonomous defense in order to be able to reshape U.S.–South Korean relations. During my trip to the United States I anticipated American resistance if I were to talk about autonomous defense. But surprisingly we were quite in agreement.

President Roh's desire for autonomous defense periodically incurred resistance from the Defense Ministry and criticism from conservative forces, as did the relocation of the Yongsan garrison. The relocation was actually one of former president Roh Tae-woo's campaign promises—as a candidate, he argued for "recovering national autonomy and pride." His administration signed an agreement with the U.S. government in June 1990 to relocate the Yongsan garrison, an agreement according to which the side that had requested the relocation—namely, South Korea—would shoulder the cost of relocation. In 1992, the golf course in Yongsan became the first part of the land to be returned to South Korea, but for various reasons discussions came to a halt in June 1993. And in 2001, when controversy arose over the construction of an apartment complex for U.S. soldiers inside the Yongsan garrison, the necessity of relocating the base was once again raised. Washington, too, strongly demanded that the relocation be pursued in accordance with the bilateral agreement.

President Roh thought that we should actively cooperate with the relocation of the Yongsan garrison as long as it posed no major problem for national security. He felt that it was, frankly, inappropriate for a foreign military, even an ally, to take up a large space in the middle of Seoul. Furthermore, Yongsan had been the location used by the Japanese and Ming Chinese forces to negotiate a friendship treaty at the conclusion of Japan's invasion of Korea, in the late sixteenth century. Chinese forces under the Qing dynasty occupied those same grounds during the invasion of 1636–37, and during South Korea's colonial period (1910–45) the occupying Japanese army—the tool of Japanese domination—set up its headquarters there.

If this land could be returned to the bosom of the people a century after its loss, it would be a momentous occasion indeed.

Once made aware of President Roh's will, the Defense Ministry, which opposed the relocation, nonetheless accepted the plan. But it still argued that the CFC should remain in Yongsan, ostensibly for national security. Because of the ministry's position on the matter, and those of the foreign affairs and national security advisors at the Blue House, the government ultimately requested and reached an agreement with Washington to leave the CFC in Yongsan. All this happened before the new NSC Secretariat began its full operations.

After becoming the NSC deputy secretary-general and learning all this, I was quite displeased. The Defense Ministry discussed the move as though it presented threats to national security, but even if a war were to break out after the Yongsan garrison was relocated from the heart of Seoul, the CFC still would have overseen the operation from within the Seoul metropolitan area. My personal opinion was that moving the CFC from Yongsan would not create a national security problem. The land that the government was poised to reclaim from the USFK after the relocation was roughly 662 acres. But if the CFC were to remain in Yongsan, a significant portion of that land would have to be given back to Americans yet again, even though Seoul still had to foot the not-in-consequential bill for establishing new base facilities in Pyongtaek. All this, unfortunately, had been agreed on before I assumed my post, so I could not propose that it be reconsidered.

In the end, the United States and South Korea worked out that one thousand CFC personnel would remain in Yongsan and the South Korean government would give the USFK 134 acres to accommodate them. But then, in October 2003, the United States informed us that it needed at least 229 acres to defend the base from terror attacks. Moreover, they informed us that, should we reject this proposal, they would completely withdraw from Yongsan. They had nothing to lose—the original American plan had been to completely relocate the base, and it had been South Korea that had requested the CFC to remain in Yongsan.

However, Seoul thought it was excessive to grant the CFC more than 163 acres; it embarked on negotiations with the United States with a presidential mandate that anything more would not be possible—the basic position being to refuse American demands for anything more.

On November 14, the president asked Defense Minister Cho Young-kil, "If the Yongsan garrison were to be relocated completely, would that be a problem for national security?" Cho answered, "No, but the public will feel anxious about national security." Roh said, "Then it's okay. Let's proceed with complete relocation if that's what the United States wants. Please convince the public that they shouldn't feel ill at ease."

In keeping with the president's order, the NSC Secretariat emphasized time and again to the Defense Ministry that the official offer of 163 or fewer acres of land would not be changed. Nonetheless, the ministry came up with its own proposal: to combine the ministry's land holding in Yongsan (65 acres) with the 163 acres on offer from the government, thus creating a single base of 228 acres, as demanded by the United States. The move was clearly intended to skirt the explicit presidential limit of 163 acres. The proposal also signaled that the ministry in charge of defending the sovereign nation of the Republic of Korea wanted to share space with the USFK command (which also was the CFC command).

I thought that the ministry's response was simply pathetic, and also felt sad that it could possibly arrive at such a conclusion.

Simultaneously, the opposition Grand National Party pressured the administration: "It is only right for America to demand 229 acres!" On December 5, a declaration in opposition to the relocation of the USFK command from Yongsan, signed by 147 members of the National Assembly, including every sitting lawmaker from the Grand National Party, was submitted to that august institution.

The Defense Ministry, despite being fully aware of the president's resolute stance, nonetheless pushed back the final agreement with the United States until 2004 in order to ensure that the CFC would remain in Yongsan. On December 12, I met with the minister and urged him to change course: "This issue has already been decided, so don't postpone it until next year. Obey the presidential decree."

In the end, at the behest of the NSC, the president called in the minister on December 22 and issued a final decree:

> You must have many things to worry about now that the National Assembly is up in arms over the Yongsan garrison relocation. . . . Please resolve this matter before the year's end. . . . It will be best to get back all the land in Yongsan. Let's proceed in this way. . . . I ask that you demonstrate your will before all responsible officials within your ministry.

Finally, at the sixth Future of the Alliance meeting in Hawaii in January 2004, the two countries reached a final agreement to relocate the entire Yongsan garrison to the cities of Osan and Pyongtaek.

President Roh saw the relocation of the Yongsan garrison through to its completion, despite all the attacks from forces who had drummed up anxiety over national security. Over the ten years that have since passed, I have not once heard anyone suggest that the relocation jeopardized national security. Once the relocation began to be seriously pursued, all such talk vanished, and everyone, both progressive and conservative, threw themselves into drawing up a blueprint to best make use of this historic and precious land that we had finally regained.

While dealing with the USFK land issue, I often thought that the United States must have felt deeply frustrated, in light of all the criticism leveled at it for allegedly demanding too much from South Korea and exhibiting an imperious attitude. Since the USFK were relocating south of the Han River and giving up much land north of it, it was only common sense that the South Korean government should provide the forces with sufficient operational space, even if not at the same magnitude they once had. As long as the USFK are stationed in South Korea for the purpose of defending this country, it is the duty of the South Korean government to give the USFK an appropriate level of support in proportion with the American efforts. Yet some in civil society relentlessly questioned the provision of land and funds to the USFK during the entire process, to the point of seeming heartless.

Of course, it was the government's responsibility to buy the necessary land for relocating the Yongsan garrison and the USFK as a whole. Naturally, since the project was funded by taxes, civil society had every right to question the government's actions—this sort of public scrutiny is precisely what enables the government to stand up to the United States with alertness and meticulousness during negotiations. But civil opposition was at times a considerable burden for the Participatory Government, which aspired to build a more equitable relationship with the United States and was playing a delicate game of see-saw with Washington while dealing with the weighty matters of national security. During negotiations with the United States, it was necessary at times to yield or show magnanimity when dealing with matters of relatively less importance; only then could we gain their understanding on more important matters. But civil opposition made it difficult for the administration to yield on or be generous with even small issues, so major negotiations unsurprisingly became equally difficult to navigate.

Declaring the Intent to Pursue Autonomous Defense and the Military's Discontent

A nation's military, with the ability to operate independently, is the foundation of autonomous defense. In other words, the president—commander-in-chief of the national military—must possess command authority. President Roh's primary objective for national defense was twofold: to regain wartime operational control from the commander of the CFC (the American commander of the USFK), and to upgrade South Korea's capability to wage war. Wartime operational control over the South Korean military was signed over by President Syngman Rhee on July 14, 1950, to the American commander in charge of the United Nations forces during the Korean War.

Autonomous defense means that a nation possesses an independent scheme to carry out war, which is possible only if it can plan and command military operations. Regaining wartime operational control is thus crucial to autonomous defense. Even with the best soldiers and cutting-edge weapons, a military amounts to nothing if it lacks the ability to mobilize them.

Among all independent nations with their own militaries on this planet, South Korea is the only one to have bequeathed operational control over its military, whether in war or peace. President Roh and the NSC believed that regaining this power was essential to building autonomous defense and an autonomous state. It would also serve to help curb South Koreans' excessive psychological dependence on the United States and its military.

President Roh always felt a sense of humiliation that South Korea did not even exercise control over its own forces, despite being the twelfth-largest economy in the world, an economic powerhouse that overshadows North Korea, and a democratic nation. The president rued that too many South Koreans still suffered from the trauma of the outbreak of the Korean War on June 25, 1950, and that they felt as though somehow South Korea was inferior to North Korea. Such an imagined inferiority could be the only explanation for why some South Koreans could not even bring themselves to think about defending their own country without depending on America. The reality could not be any more different: in 2003, South Korea's economic might eclipsed that of the North by as much as thirty or forty to one, according to nominal statistics from the Bank of Korea; in reality, it was more like a hundred to one. South Korea outspent North Korea on defense by at least a factor of ten. The geopolitical situation in Northeast Asia had also changed. During the Korean War, North Korea invaded the South with Stalin's permission. When the North was overwhelmed, China entered the war and rescued it. But now there was no Soviet Union, and China had established diplomatic ties with South Korea. Trade between South Korea and China was incomparably larger than that between North Korea and China. President Roh emphasized this objective reality, methodically comparing the capabilities of the two Koreas and stressing the importance of regaining operational control.

But there remained a belief in South Korea that its forces were less capable than those of the North and that our defense must be entrusted to the USFK. This absence of desire for autonomous defense chagrined the president; it is why, as soon as he took office, he emphasized the need for autonomous defense and ordered the Defense Ministry to create a road map to this goal. Just as the drive toward autonomous defense kicked into gear, the Yongsan garrison relocation and the repositioning of the USFK came under discussion. The president then ordered that we respond to overall changes in the U.S. global military strategy, and come up with a plan of national defense predicated on the return of operational control of the South Korean forces and on military autonomy.

President Park Chung-hee, in the 1970s, was actually the first to publicly pursue the goal of autonomous defense; then, in 1987, Roh Tae-woo made a campaign promise to regain operational control of the military. Because both men had military backgrounds, the military naturally had no reason to criticize their efforts. And this was when the South Korean military was far inferior to the North's. When Roh Moo-hyun began pursuing the same goal, the difference in the strength and standing of the two Koreas was, to say the least, significantly in favor of the South. It was an ideal time to begin the work toward building autonomous defense.

The military, however, was barely able to hide its discomfort at the president's plan. The rationale for autonomous defense was difficult to challenge, so the military did not mount an explicit objection to the concept itself; instead, it strongly opposed the return of operational control to South Korea, something the president saw as being at the heart of autonomous defense. The Defense Ministry—well aware of the president's advocacy for autonomous defense—pointedly chose not to refer to it in any fashion in its January 16, 2003, briefing to the transition committee, "Training Strong Elite Soldiers for a Guaranteed Establishment of a Peace Regime."

Following his inauguration, the president made a case for autonomous defense on several occasions, using the looming relocation of the USFK as a precursor. He also ordered the Defense Ministry to draft a plan for retrieving operational control. But the ministry's May 6, 2003, report, "A Vision of Autonomous Defense," only mentioned an increase in military capability, and nothing regarding the return of operational control.

The military leadership, including the defense minister, argued that the capability of the South Korean forces was still inferior to that of the North, and that, given serious national security challenges such as Pyongyang's development of nuclear arms, it was not feasible to retrieve operational control. They went so far as to state, quite implausibly, that the CFC's possession of wartime operational control over South Korea's military did not constitute a violation of our sovereignty, since the CFC itself was structured to function as a "joint command" between the United States and South Korea.

Based on this logic, the military leadership argued that we should use terms such as "transfer" or "independent exercise," rather than "return," when it came to the issue of operational command. Some in the military not only opposed the return of operational command but even went so far as to see it as a dangerous development: they publicly argued that the government's mention of it was essentially a call for the withdrawal of the USFK. Ultimately, the military leadership convinced themselves that return of operational command would be impossible, even if building autonomous defense were to begin. They must have realized that pursuing autonomous defense without operational command was a hollow gesture—it meant that their feelings about autonomous defense were merely lukewarm.

The philosophical difference between the president and the military was as great as the difference in their practical approach. As far as the president saw it, regaining operational control was certain to reduce the U.S. military burden and lay the foundation for a healthier state of alliance. It had absolutely nothing to do with anti-Americanism. Yet those who had lived all their lives with the idea that the U.S.–South Korean military alliance was essential to South Korea's national defense did not agree; their stance on every aspect of the U.S.–South Korean military cooperation was in direct contrast to the president's.

President Roh promised on several occasions that, as part of the plan for autonomous defense, he would increase the defense budget, despite the difficulties an increase would pose. On July 30, 2003, he told the writers of his August 15 commemorative speech:

> If we are to be treated as an autonomous state, we must discard the idea that we should entrust the core part of our national defense to the United States. It is a contradiction to talk about autonomous defense while saying no to increasing the defense budget. It is a contradiction to talk about defensive capability while refraining from purchasing weapons.

Of course, it was essential that the existing defense system's effectiveness first be assessed and reviewed. But the remark showed that the president was absolutely determined to achieve autonomous defense and he was willing to back up his resolve with action. I myself could not understand how South Korean soldiers, defenders of the nation's sovereignty, could so underestimate their own abilities, oppose autonomous defense, and express alarm at the prospect of regaining operational control. In a normal country, it would be the soldiers themselves who would demand autonomous defense, while the civilian sector might hold various opinions. But in South Korea this was hardly the case.

Given the situation, it was no easy feat to advise a president determined to embark on a path toward autonomous defense, all while dragging along a military so adamantly opposed to it. It was necessary to strongly express the president's will and find a way to ensure the realization of autonomous defense. Things could not be left in the hands of the Defense Ministry—I believed that the NSC must take the helm. In late May 2003 I drafted a short report for the president, titled "The Defense Ministry's View on Autonomous Defense." In it I suggested that the president direct the Defense Ministry to draft all reports related to autonomous defense and defense reform, but in collaboration with the NSC.

The president immediately took up my recommendation and put it into action. On June 1, while being briefed by the ministry on matters related to the USFK, he ordered the defense minister and military officials to funnel all reports to the president on major defense issues through the NSC. He also stated that he intended to issue a decree that would ensure that important policies would be decided through the NSC. He told them to draft their plan for building autonomous defense in discussion with the NSC and further lent his support to the NSC by saying, "The NSC is doing great things and I intend to decide things together with the NSC from now on."

President Roh on this occasion offered a specific direction for autonomous defense and issued related decrees, instructing the Defense Ministry that:

> From now on, a budget must be allocated toward building defensive capability that would supplement that of the USFK (with priority given to information warfare) and the roadmap for autonomous defense must first start from building a material foundation, then move on to supplementing the existing organizational structure, and finally end with the return of operational control. But preparations to pursue the three goals must be made at the same time.

He added that the step-by-step plan for autonomous defense should be prepared separately by the Defense Ministry and the NSC but then combined at an appropriate moment through discussion.

Then, on June 10, in conversation with instructors at the Mugunghwa Symposium (which all active-duty soldiers must attend), in the presence of the defense minister, the chairman of the Joint Chiefs of Staff, the defense advisor, and myself, President Roh emphasized that the most urgent task in that moment was to "establish a state of autonomous defense." He stressed that to make this possible there must be an increase in war capability and a reform of the military organization. The president stressed, "Even if this cannot be resolved during my term, we must prepare so that under the next presidential administration operational control can be returned for certain." He also pointed out, "The reason the exercise of 'autonomous diplomacy' is difficult for South Korea, over matters such as troop deployment to Iraq or the dispatch of envoys to the United States, is that we rely on the United States in areas such as the nuclear problem and national security." He added that in addition to South Koreans' actual reliance on the United States and the USFK, "our people's excessive psychological dependence on the United States is precipitating anxiety." He stressed that, given the opportunity presented by the discussion over relocating the USFK, we must firmly defend national security and pursue autonomous defense. Only then would we be able to recover confidence as a nation. He made an impassioned plea for all of us to see that "now we must handle our defense ourselves," if only to present a clear vision to the public and instill pride in our soldiers.

Some participants at the event bristled at the president's remarks. In hearing the order that "a plan for reclaiming operational control be established in an honest and confident discussion with the United States when later the conditions allow for it," one went so far as to express worry that regaining operational control would mean the disbandment of the CFC and soon, the withdrawal of the USFK. The president countered that autonomous defense would coexist with the U.S.–South Korean alliance, and that regaining operational control did not mean the departure of the USFK. But another participant spoke out, suggesting that even the concept of "recovering operational control" was inappropriate, since the CFC was structured as a joint command between South Korea and the United States. The president flatly disagreed: "People do not think like that. And legally speaking, it is half, and practically speaking, more than half [of the CFC] that is supported by the United States." Finally, the president urged everyone:

> Our entire discussion today should be effectively communicated at the Mugunghwa Symposium before all the generals, so that the minister, the chairman of the Joint Chiefs of Staff, not to mention the entire South Korean military, will learn about this. During my term I will support the forces to the furthest extent possible by increasing defense

expenditures and through other means. The military, too, must share
in the determination to achieve autonomous defense.

This was the first practical step the Roh administration took toward
the realization of autonomous defense.

Increase in Defense Expenditures
and the Military's Inferiority Complex

The Defense Ministry reported that achieving autonomous defense
would require South Korea's annual defense expenditures to amount to
3.2 percent of its gross domestic product (GDP), a 0.5 percent increase
from the 2.7 percent of the GDP it took in 2003. The NSC did not agree
with the ministry's estimate but made no special objections.

To estimate the expenditures required for an autonomous defense
capable of standing up to North Korea, the two Koreas' military capabilities needed to be carefully compared. The South Korean military
had long estimated its own capability at 70 to 80 percent of the North's.
But some civilian experts, including Kyungnam University professor
Ham Taek-young, an authority on North-South comparative military
capabilities, presented detailed data that argued that the South Korean
military's capability to wage war far exceeded that of the North. With
such an argument from the civilian sector, the Defense Ministry should
have presented compelling evidence in favor of its stand, but it did not.
I, for one, could see that the information the ministry conveyed to the
Blue House was far too simplistic, and that its conclusion was neither
scientifically based nor objective. In short, the ministry's argument was
shoddy enough to be challenged even by nonexperts.

But in the summer of 2003, the NSC did not use analyses by civilian
experts to question the military's budget and capability assessments;
nor did the president.

As the commander-in-chief, Roh believed that the military's life force
was its chain of command, its hierarchy, and its morale. He felt it would
have been inappropriate for the commander-in-chief, at the start of his
term as president, to express distrust of the military's reports using
civilian arguments. Furthermore, it was necessary to move the military
to sincerely believe the president's philosophy of national defense and
join in the pursuit of autonomous defense. To make that happen, it was
imperative that the president show trust for the military and appear
open to its concerns.

It was in this context that the NSC unambiguously advanced the presidential agenda of recalibrating the U.S.–South Korean alliance: autonomous defense, the Yongsan garrison relocation, and the bilateral agreement on the USFK reduction. But in other areas we wholeheartedly championed the Defense Ministry's positions and I advised the president to do likewise. The reality in South Korea was that entrenched interests were strong and the national security situation was dire; there was no way to kill two birds with one stone—that is, to reduce or freeze the defense budget and achieve autonomous defense at the same time.

That is why I thought, despite the difficulties, we should try to retrieve operational control and realize autonomous defense, even at the cost of increased defense spending. Only then could we overcome the excessive psychological dependence of both the public and military on the United States and prove ourselves anew as an autonomous state. This, of course, was also the president's determination, so I advised him to play golf with members of the military leadership—to strengthen the bond between him and the military—and arranged it myself several times. I also made it my personal business to help increase the military budget.

The ministry's request for 3.2 percent of the national GDP was out of the question. And there was the total government budget to consider before we could fight for an increase in the defense budget. The Defense Ministry knew this fact all too well, and so I did not need to go through the trouble of interrogating the military's budgetary estimates.

It was no easy task to substantially increase defense spending given the tight budget, especially when the Roh administration was allocating substantial amounts for national welfare. Budgetary officials, meanwhile, were so insightful that they might as well have been top-level defense ministry officials, finding numerous flaws in the proposed defense budget. They were already lukewarm toward increasing defense expenditures to begin with, so it was hard work trying to convince them to change their minds. I sought out the finance minister, the minister of planning and budget, and the budget director, in a bid to gain their cooperation. In the end the Roh administration decided, despite difficult financial circumstances, to increase defense spending by 8.1 percent, even as the overall government budget increased by only 2.1 percent. And the government further increased the defense budget by more than 8 percent every subsequent year—the biggest increase in defense expenditures since the 1980s.

Once the Roh administration's agenda of building autonomous defense found its footing and the NSC's role as the control tower for defense policy was set, the project to obtain more objective information about the two Koreas' military capabilities began in earnest. This was in the summer of 2004, one year after the president had first proclaimed his autonomous defense agenda in his Independence Day speech.

I met with Hwang Dong-joon, the president of the Korea Institute for Defense Analyses (KIDA), to commission a study. One day Hwang came to me and lamented that the military was criticizing him for undertaking this study, because it misunderstood our intentions and believed we were looking for excuses to slash the defense budget. I had to explain to the Defense Ministry and military leaders that this study aimed to do nothing of the sort. I emphasized that there would be absolutely no decrease in military expenditures, considering that it was impossible to give the military the increase it sought. I stressed that the NSC was championing an annual increase in defense expenditures, despite criticisms from the administration's supporters. And even if our military capability was found to be superior to the North's, the national defense policy of the Roh administration was such that defense expenditures could not be reduced, as the government's plans included the strengthening of strategic planning, enhanced information gathering, and the acquisition of a strategic veto power, however limited, over Northeast Asian affairs—and all of this would entail additional costs. The military, however, never fully let go of its suspicions.

It came to my attention that the Defense Ministry had examined the preliminary figures issued by KIDA even before the report was submitted to the president, and was demanding changes to the figures on the grounds that there were problems in the calculation methods and the North's capability had been underestimated. In other words, if the comparison of the two countries' capabilities had been rendered as ninety (South Korea) to one hundred (North Korea), the ministry was asking for an estimate of eighty-five to one hundred on the grounds that our ability had been overstated. Hearing this left a bitter taste in my mouth; the ministry was acting like a student asking for a lower grade because he had done too well on a test. Despite their concerns about a possible reduction in military spending, should not the military have been overjoyed that a national defense research institute had rated its capability to be almost on par with that of the North? How could I even begin to understand the mentality of a military that spent at least 2.5 times North Korea's GDP but was still satisfied with considering itself inferior to North Korean forces?

After many such episodes, KIDA ultimately submitted its report to the president at the Blue House on August 16, 2004. Military leaders and the civilian expert, Dr. Ham Taek-young, also attended. KIDA's report concluded that the South Korean army and navy were inferior to those of the North's, with 80 and 90 percent of their Northern counterparts' capabilities, respectively, while the air force was slightly superior to the North's, at 103 percent. When the presentation ended, the president applauded, saying, "In accordance with the presidential mandate, today's report used a new approach." It did not mean that he completely trusted the figures in the report, but he at least valued the effort made to approach the problem scientifically: "Since becoming president all the reports I have received on the comparative capabilities of the two Koreas were no more detailed than what was printed in the newspapers—and this includes Defense Ministry reports."

As I saw it, the inferiority of our forces to North Korea's had been a firmly held conclusion, but the way that conclusion had been reached was unreliable. Once, in May 2004, U.S. and South Korean military intelligence offices attempted a joint, comprehensive assessment of South Korea's national security situation. The U.S. Defense Intelligence Agency sent us an independently compiled evaluation that determined that "South Korea's conventional military capability is now superior to that of North Korea."

The Defense Ministry, however, objected to the U.S. evaluation and provided its own appraisal: "Although the North's conventional military capability is superior to that of the South, it is possible to contain the North if the combined U.S.–South Korean forces maintain their present capability." The ministry insisted on having this passage included in the final joint report. It was nothing less than cheap comedy: the U.S. Defense Department was saying our military capability was superior to that of the North while our own Defense Ministry was doing its utmost to deny this. The ministry could have taken pride in the American assessment and asked the U.S. Defense Intelligence Agency for a joint investigation to ascertain the facts (since our own evaluation had showed South Korea to be at a disadvantage). It was untoward to jump to a denial and immediately demand a correction from the United States. I was at a loss for words. Did the ministry behave like this because it was so deeply committed to national security, or did it fear the reduction of the USFK so much, or was it a deeply ingrained psychological dependence on the United States?

The reality perceived by the Blue House was fundamentally different from that perceived by our defense officials. The president's desire for and philosophy of autonomous statehood could only encounter obstacles, not only within the government, but also outside. The ensuing controversy surrounding the reduction of the USFK clearly demonstrated that conflict and disagreement.

5

Obstacles on the Path toward Autonomy

The Americans Give Official Notice of Their Plan to Reduce U.S. Forces Korea

In the first half of 2003, there was an endless stream of talk from Washington and beyond about reducing the size of U.S. Forces Korea (USFK). This contradicted official discussions between the two countries' governments. On March 7, 2003, the Defense Ministry gave a presentation at a meeting, chaired by the president, of ministers whose portfolios were related to national security. The topic was the future of the U.S.–South Korean alliance. The ministry was adamant: "There is no plan to reduce American ground forces." Then, at the U.S.–South Korean summit in May, the topic was not discussed. However, rumors of a reduction continued to abound. In June, the American press reported on these, citing U.S. officials. Then, on June 26, U.S. Eighth Army Commander Charles C. Campbell publicly commented, "Pursuant to the agreement between South Korea and the United States to relocate the Yongsan garrison and the Second Infantry Division, there will be partial reductions of the USFK."

I was in a difficult spot. There were many things to deal with in relation to the USFK, including the relocations of both the Yongsan garrison and American forces in South Korea as a whole, and now this talk of reducing the forces loomed over me. The national security situation was already unstable because of the North's nuclear threat, and the domestic press were constantly reporting that the U.S.–South Korean alliance was suffering. If the United States went ahead with the reduction in the current climate, the South Korean public's unease over national security would reach new heights. The political opposition and the press were already making it seem as though national security was being threatened by the relocation of the USFK; if the plan for reductions were announced, the political opposition would deem it a sign that the alliance was falling apart, fanning the flames of anxiety even more. We needed to prepare and glean precise information to calm the situation.

The atmosphere in the media was unstable. Something was going on. When I asked the foreign and defense ministries if they had received any word from the United States about a reduction, the answer was negative. But I could not just sit idly by. The National Security Council (NSC) Standing Committee assigned a task to Defense Minister Cho Young-kil: during Cho's scheduled visit to the United States in June, his job was to ascertain the exact U.S. position on the rumored partial withdrawal of the USFK when he met with U.S. secretary of defense Donald Rumsfeld. We also reached a decision to create the necessary contingency plans for such an event.

But in early July, NSC director of strategic planning Seo Joo-seok stormed into my office, clearly alarmed. He had just met with Cha Young-gu, the director of policy at the Defense Ministry, who had returned from accompanying Minister Cho to his June 27 meeting with Rumsfeld in Washington. What Seo revealed was shocking: Cho did not ask Rumsfeld about plans to reduce the USFK, in spite of the NSC Standing Committee assigning that duty to him. Fortunately, Cha and Deputy Undersecretary Richard Lawless had met for a discussion, and Lawless had revealed,

> [that he] had visited the Blue House on June 5 with officials from the U.S. State Department and the U.S. embassy in Seoul. They were met by Foreign Affairs Advisor Ban Ki-moon and Defense Advisor Kim Hee-sang, and [had] conveyed the plan to progressively reduce the 37,500-strong USFK, beginning with a reduction of one thousand in 2004, up to a reduction of twelve thousand by 2006.[1] Lawless considered this to be an official notification to the South Korean government and understood that

---

1   Later the exact number of reductions was confirmed as 1,000 in 2004, 6,000 in 2005, 5,500 in 2006, for a total reduction of 12,500 soldiers.

it had been conveyed all the way to the president. He hoped that there could be a detailed agreement before the Republic of Korea (ROK)–U.S. Security Consultative Meeting (SCM) in October.

I was shocked—not at the plan itself but at the fact that the NSC had been completely unaware of this apparent notification of the Blue House a month prior. I felt a pang of remorse and asked myself, "What am I doing here, in this job?" My urgent task was to promptly investigate the situation and devise a plan, but there were many questions. Why did the foreign affairs and defense advisors not inform the NSC of this important development? Why did the president say nothing about it for the past month? Why did he not say anything on June 10, when he made important remarks about autonomous defense and the retrieval of operational control? Had he perhaps not received any report? Why had the defense minister failed to bring up the topic with Rumsfeld, even after the NSC Standing Committee had entrusted him with the task?

But with no time to look for the answers, I pushed them aside for the time being and focused on reporting to the president and quickly coming up with a solution—right now, it was unimportant to ascertain whether or not the president was aware of the fact. The NSC quickly compiled a report about what had transpired and what the government should do next. On Saturday, July 5, two days before the president's China visit, Seo Joo-seok and I went to his office for an emergency briefing.

As I watched the president's face during my briefing, it seemed that he had not been aware of the situation. But since he said nothing about Ban and Kim, whom Lawless had notified of the reduction, I suspected that he had received some form of report from them.[2] When the briefing ended, the president looked serious, but not flustered; it seemed like he had anticipated this. The president instinctively understood that the recalibration of the U.S.–South Korean alliance would not end with the relocation of the USFK or the Yongsan garrison, but would encompass the reduction issue as well. I did not know this at the time, but during the presidential transition period Secretary Rumsfeld had already told the South Korean special envoy about the possibility of reducing the number of American soldiers stationed in South Korea. The envoy must have reported this to the president-elect; there was also the matter of

---

2   I will go into this in detail later, but it turned out the president had been informed by the defense advisor that this was not an official U.S. notification, but rather Lawless's personal opinion.

the American press routinely publishing articles about the possibility of reducing the USFK.

President Roh ordered me to come up with a way to prevent economic instability and political and social repercussions, and said that there should be negotiations over the reduction. But he emphasized that this must be for the purpose of developing the alliance in a healthy direction, without worsening the national security situation or weakening our ability to counter the North. He said he wanted "to proactively create our own counteroffers before entering negotiations, taking into consideration our own national security capacity, as well as the need to soothe popular anxiety."

But we needed time if we were to review the U.S. reduction proposal and embark on negotiations. The president thought that his one-on-one meeting with President Bush at the Asia-Pacific Economic Cooperation (APEC) summit on October 20 would serve as an appropriate venue for negotiating with Washington; until then there should be no negotiations over the practical aspects of troop reduction, contrary to the U.S. proposal. Instead, we would formulate our own reduction plan and negotiate directly with Bush in October. We chose to convey Roh's thoughts to President Bush via a personal letter. It had been almost a month since the United States had informed the Blue House of the plan to reduce the USFK, yet the topic was deemed taboo enough that even the necessary information was not being circulated. There was no way we could trust the Defense Ministry, which in theory should handle such matters. If somehow the information were to be misrepresented or exaggerated and leaked to the press during the process of conveying the president's thoughts to Washington, it would only create further chaos. The president had National Security Advisor Ra Jong-yil deliver the letter.

The NSC drafted the letter in both Korean and English and Roh reviewed the draft after his return from China on July 10. The NSC was able to finish the letter and get the president's signature on it within a week of that first official briefing on the reduction of the USFK. Here is an excerpt of that letter:

Mr. President,

Last May we agreed that the relocation of the U.S. Forces Korea (USFK) should be pursued, taking careful account of the situation on the Korean Peninsula. I fully trust the U.S. government's explanation that the relocation of the USFK is a necessary part in the overall change of the U.S. global strategy, a change which will, in effect, enhance the capability of the USFK. Accordingly, I have come to bear in mind the possibility that in the long run, this may lead to the adjustment of the size of the troops. I thoroughly understand the strategy of the United States, and have therefore taken steps to prepare for the changes to come.

I have agreed to relocate the Yongsan garrison at an early date, as well as to cooperate closely with your government regarding the realignment of the USFK. I have also instructed our military to prepare a blueprint for the future which includes an expanded role for the ROK military in national defense. To this end, I have publicly announced my intention to increase the defense budget. My decisions were made after long and hard deliberation in [the] face of conflicting domestic public opinion, with the aim of building a national consensus for effective policy measures.

Mr. President,

I have recently been briefed by my staff, however, that the U.S. government has informed us of plans to implement the relocation of the USFK bases in a much shorter time frame than we anticipated, and to pursue an early reduction of troops. I have also learned that the U.S. government has publicly requested a large increase in the ROK defense budget. The planned reduction of troops, in particular, would be the biggest in scale since the withdrawal of the Seventh Infantry Division in 1971, which, if carried out in haste, will cause a great shock to our people.

I have thus far made the most sincere efforts to implement our agreement, while doing my utmost to resolve the North Korean nuclear problem that we face. Under such circumstances, should the content of what your government informed us be unilaterally made public or executed earlier than expected, thereby causing great political contention domestically, it could considerably undermine my initiative and political leadership in dealing with these issues effectively.

Early relocation or reduction of USFK will heighten anxiety about the security of the Korean Peninsula and consequently deal a blow to the Korean economy, resulting in the drop in our sovereign credit rating among others. [The] U.S. request for the increase in defense budget may also blew wrongful impression [sic] among the Korean public that my initiative was influenced by U.S. pressure, causing emotional resistance to such [a] plan. I am concerned that smooth and orderly implementation of our original agreements, such as the early relocation [of] the Yongsan garrison, would be hampered as the result.

Once again, I would like to point out that I am in full agreement with the broad framework of your government's initiatives regarding the key military issues between our two countries mentioned above. Nevertheless, in consideration of the negative repercussions that could result from their early implementation, I cannot emphasize enough that more time is needed for better preparation. In order for these initiatives to be successful and to contribute to the development of the ROK-U.S. alliance, close cooperation between the two countries, as well as efforts to gain the understanding of the Korean public and the National Assembly are indispensable.

I ask for your kind understanding of my particular situation, and hope that these issues can be discussed with you in person. I look forward to an opportunity to hold [a] deep and meaningful [exchange] of views with you either at the APEC Leader's Meeting or in the event of your visit to Korea, if [you] would kindly consider our invitation which was delivered to your Secretary of State by our Foreign Minister.

Delivery of the Presidential Letter, a Telephone Call between the Two Leaders, and the Communication Mishap in Hindsight

On July 13, 2003, National Security Advisor Ra Jong-yil was about to leave for Washington with the presidential letter, when a call came from Foreign Minister Yoon Young-kwan. Having heard about the planned delivery of the letter, he asked me to request the president to delay Ra's departure. Yoon said that Lawless had not officially informed our government of the reduction plan; it was possible that he was trying to get a sense of what we were thinking, or simply offering his personal view without even consulting President Bush beforehand. The minister said that he would ask the American ambassador about the situation and then we should decide whether Ra should go or not. In all honesty, despite handling this in secrecy, I ought to have informed and consulted with the minister. But between the president's China visit and the minister's own busy schedule there simply had been no time. On top of it, the Defense Ministry, which was actually responsible for this issue, was avoiding it, and the defense and foreign affairs advisors themselves had dragged us into this predicament by not sharing information with us. It had been difficult to talk about this with anyone. I told Yoon:

> The NSC believes Lawless's notification to be an official one from the U.S. government. Given all the information, it seems clear that the plan to reduce the USFK has received President Bush's approval. Ordinarily, it would be appropriate for you to consult with Ambassador Hubbard, and if the NSC's judgment had been wrong, for us to report to the president and change the plan to deliver the letter. But since the meeting between U.S. National Security Advisor Condoleezza Rice and Ra has already been fixed, it is impossible to delay his departure.

The next evening Yoon called again. He had called Hubbard about the situation. The ambassador hinted at feeling slighted for not being consulted in advance by the foreign ministry, but did confirm that "Defense Secretary Rumsfeld first proposed the plan and received President Bush's approval." Rumsfeld had argued for the U.S. plan to be announced during President Roh's U.S. visit, but the State Department and others had pushed for a delay in order to make the summit a successful one. That is why Lawless came to South Korea after the summit to personally convey the plan.

While the NSC's judgement had been correct, after Yoon's call I felt bitter rather than reassured. Whether or not there would be a real impact on South Korea's national security, a reduction of 12,500 soldiers from the USFK would be a major topic for South Korean citizens and a potent political issue. The U.S. government, fully aware of this, had unilaterally decided to proceed with the reduction, weighing when the timing would be most politically advantageous for themselves! Despite all the accusations of "compromising national security" from the opposition and the conservative press, the Roh administration had, from the very beginning, accommodated the American demand to relocate the Yongsan garrison and realign the USFK. On top of that, the South Korean government had even decided to deploy the first wave of troops to Iraq. It all meant that Bush's summit declaration two months prior, stating that the USFK realignment would be carefully pursued in consideration of the Korean Peninsula security situation, had been nothing but a farce, since all the while he had been concealing the plan to reduce the size of the USFK.

The image of a chess pawn came to mind. I once again resolved that this could not continue. I thought, "The current state of ROK-U.S. relations cannot be allowed to stand. This one-sided relationship must change, no matter the cost. We should not show ourselves to be vulnerable to being dragged around like this. We must move toward an equal relationship based on negotiation!"

On July 24 there was a call from President Bush. He said that he found President Roh's letter to be thoughtful and hoped that the issue of troop reduction would be resolved through a mutually satisfactory agreement, and that bilateral relations and security could be improved. He also expressed his desire to put President Roh more at ease and to strengthen his standing. He said he accepted Roh's proposal; he would ensure that no practical discussions of troop reductions took place and would negotiate directly with President Roh at the APEC summit in October. The diplomacy by letter had been a success.

Once the presidential letter had been delivered, I thought back to the questions raised by Seo Joo-seok's report in early July. I chose not to ask the two presidential advisors about their failure to inform the NSC about Lawless's visit, nor about how exactly the matter had been reported to the president. They were far older than me and capable of independent decision making as presidential advisors; I did not want to subject them to an apparent interrogation, since learning their reasoning now would not change anything. We had obvious differences of opinion about the troop reduction. I also did not ask Defense Minister Cho Young-kil why he had not discussed the matter with Rumsfeld, for the same reasons. But I could guess why all three had acted as they had.

The two advisors were probably quite surprised that Lawless had notified them of the reductions. They probably tried to persuade Lawless to cancel the troop reductions, perhaps by arguing that the plan was unacceptable to the South Korean government.

When our negotiation team visited Washington to hold a preliminary discussion of the troop reduction on September 25, 2003, Lawless explained why he had notified the two presidential advisors of the plan, saying that the reduction was "a sensitive matter" and he had "wanted to have a thoughtful negotiation with the South Korean side." What he had delivered was "not the final decision, but a plan." He had delivered the news through the Blue House channel because he "hoped that the Blue House would have an internal conversation about it after hearing the American position and at some point permit the Defense Ministry to hold a more detailed negotiation." This meant that Lawless had implied a degree of flexibility in his explanation of the plan, which in turn made the two advisors think that they could persuade the U.S. Department of Defense (DOD) to abort or delay it. They must have thought that informing the NSC would only make the matter all the more official.

It appears that it was Defense Advisor Kim Hee-sang who had informed President Roh about the notification of reductions—downplaying it as the position of the U.S. DOD or even Lawless's own private opinion and not an official communication. Otherwise, the president would most certainly have ordered the NSC to come up with a plan of action. In fact, at the August 19 national security inter-ministerial meeting, the president gave this rationale for sending his letter about troop reductions to President Bush: "We were not officially notified, but there continued to be talks, and there have been incidents—for example, a relevant [American] official met with the defense advisor and expressed a personal view—so I thought it was necessary to put a stop to this." But if our defense advisor had thought that what Lawless conveyed, in the company of numerous Korea experts from various American government agencies, was merely the wish of the DOD or a private opinion, then he was most certainly wrong. Defense Minister Cho Young-kil seemed to have already been aware of the plan to reduce the USFK. He probably did not ask Rumsfeld—known for his ill-temper—about the reduction, because he thought that might only serve to make the discussion official.

Still, it was striking that not a single person among them had told me or the foreign minister what was going on. If I am to put it generously, they probably thought the reduction to be a matter of such sensitivity and importance that they dared not speak about it. And they might have worried that, had they informed the NSC, at the helm of the drive for autonomous defense since June, it would itself have demanded negotiations. But I still cannot understand to this day why the U.S. State Department did not inform the South Korean foreign ministry, even though the meeting with Lawless was also attended by officials from the State Department and the U.S. Embassy in Seoul.

It did not help matters that Lawless took up the issue with the defense and foreign affairs advisors. Granted, it was the right decision to convey such an important matter to the Blue House rather than the foreign ministry, and Lawless went to the two advisors with whom he was already acquainted. But he should have informed the national security advisor (also NSC secretary-general), or me (the deputy secretary-general), or even Seo Joo-seok (who was in charge of the NSC's day-to-day operations), because the NSC was the office that handled all matters related to unification, foreign affairs, and national security (UFN), including defense. But Lawless probably did not have a clear understanding of the new system put in place by the Roh administration when even officials at our own defense and foreign ministries remained confused. The establishment of the NSC had been delayed at the beginning of the presidential term, so, early in the presidency, foreign affairs and defense advisors sometimes overstepped their strict advisory roles and became involved in policymaking. In hindsight, all this might have originated from the fact that the NSC had still not assumed full possession of a leadership role within the government.

After this drama and confusion, I thought that the NSC should solidify its standing as the control tower for UFN matters as soon as possible. Only then could we establish a system that enabled all ministries to cooperate over their shared goals.

Roh Orders a Proactive Response to Any USFK Reduction

The phone call between the two presidents did not mean the end of the problem. There was an urgent need for a plan in anticipation of the October discussion with the United States. But this was no easy task, given the Korean government's overwhelmingly negative view of the USFK reduction. Most officials working on foreign policy and national security matters, including the Defense Ministry, considered the word "reduction" taboo. If I am to exaggerate a little, they seemed to think that to announce the reduction of the USFK by 12,500 soldiers would unleash the same level of shock and terror as a bomb explosion.

Many worried that the reduction would jeopardize South Korea's national security. Even those who did not argued—given that the opposition and media behemoths were already fanning popular anxiety over national security and the state of the ROK-U.S. alliance by talking about the North Korean nuclear issue and the USFK realignment—that the government would not be able to handle the repercussions of such an announcement. Some insisted that the reduction was unacceptable, but if it had to be carried out, at least it must be significantly delayed. They argued that if Washington were to negotiate, the South Korean government must block reductions, even if this required significant concessions. Foreign Minister Yoon Young-kwan suggested to the president that trusting the United States was critical; the two governments had had their differences in dealing with the North Korean issues, and Yoon wanted the ROK to be more accommodating in order to exact more cooperation from the United States on the reduction. Such was the fear over the reduction within foreign affairs and national security circles that the foreign minister even suggested a comprehensive package aimed at mollification.

I was worried that should the USFK reduction talks immediately take place, the government's foreign and security policy would suffer because of indiscriminate attacks from the political opposition rather than any kind of real security threat. I could not understand those who gasped at the idea of reduction talks and saw them as akin to setting off a detonator. After all, it was not as though all the American soldiers were going to withdraw from South Korea; the United States wanted to change its own global strategy and assess the appropriate size of the USFK before reducing it. Rather than simply opposing the reduction, I thought we should calculate the size of the reduction we could handle. If 12,500 soldiers out of a 37,500-strong U.S. force were relocated, how much of a negative impact would it have on South Korea's national security? There was a need for a more rational approach based on scientific assessment. If reductions did not intrinsically create a substantial national security problem, we should accept them and propose a time frame that was best for our nation.

Experience showed that we could not simply block a reduction plan pursued by the United States. Historically, USFK reductions have taken place regardless of ROK desires. In 1971, in accordance with the Nixon Doctrine, which called for the reduction of American involvement in Asia, the United States unilaterally withdrew twenty thousand soldiers of the Seventh Infantry Division under the rationale that "South Korea's defense must be South Korean"—despite the fact that a large number of South Korean soldiers were deployed in Vietnam. This was a major impetus for the Park Chung-hee administration's call for autonomous defense. In 1977, in accordance with President Jimmy Carter's campaign pledge, the United States announced a three-stage withdrawal of the USFK, but the plan was nullified (due to U.S. needs) just after the first stage, which saw a reduction of three thousand soldiers. In April 1990, the United States again announced a three-stage reduction plan and withdrew seven thousand soldiers during the first stage. Washington has in this fashion repeatedly reduced the size of the USFK, then changed its plans, or sometimes increased the size of the force by a small number. These decisions were never made based on discussions with Seoul.

I thought that the USFK reduction should take place at an appropriate level as determined through negotiations; our job was to persuade the public that it would not impact national security, so we could build a healthy nation free of a psychological dependence on the United States. On this point, the president was even more strongly convinced than I was. In fact, the plan to reduce the USFK only served to confirm the legitimacy of the autonomous defense agenda that he had argued for since taking office. Some people may argue that the United States pushed for the reduction because Roh called for autonomous defense, but nothing could be further from the truth. The U.S. plan had been established as part of its global agenda, and had been put into motion before the launch of the Participatory Government. And, even if the Bush administration was known for its impulse to act unilaterally, the United States that I had come to know was not an emotionally driven country that would change the number of stationed American soldiers simply based on its like or dislike of an allied nation's government.

My assessment of the situation was clear, but I seldom expressed my feelings to others except while briefing the president during the early stages of the negotiation. Considering that the high-level foreign and defense policy officials already saw reduction as taboo, I wanted to avoid unnecessary arguments. But at a meeting presided over by the president where the decision was to be made, I did share my thoughts.

President Roh said little at the beginning so that there would be an atmosphere of free discussion among the advisors, who spoke as one in their concerns about the reduction, but he was prepared to address the counterarguments through a larger framework. The president thought that if the United States were planning to reduce the USFK, we should not be passively dragged but actively negotiate to solve the problem. He thought that this was a problem that could not—indeed, should not—be solved through vigorous opposition.

From the time when he was a presidential candidate, President Roh expressed his conviction that we should be equipped, at the minimum, with an independent defensive capability to protect ourselves from North Korea. As president-elect, on December 30, 2002, he visited Gyeryong-dae, the home of the Joint Chiefs of Staff, to ask whether the military leaders had a plan in preparation for a possible reduction or withdrawal of the USFK. The leadership perhaps thought this indicated Roh was anti-American, but the question was asked from the perspective of a strictly practical rationalist. Later it was revealed that, at the same time he was asking this question, the DOD was in fact planning to reduce its globally stationed forces, including those in South Korea.

After long consideration, the president ultimately issued the following guidelines to the NSC:

- At a time when various national security issues are arising simultaneously to create a chaotic situation, it does not help that various pronouncements about the USFK reduction are haphazardly leaking from the U.S. government and the nonofficial sector. This only fans public anxiety over national security and does not help ROK-U.S. relations. A request shall be made to the U.S. government to ensure that there are no more press leaks leading up to the ROK-U.S. summit at the APEC meeting on October 20, 2003.

- The feasibility of the reduction plan proposed by the United States must be reviewed, given the reality of our national security; in preparation for negotiations, we must formulate a plan to determine a timetable for reduction that will not negatively affect our security.
- In the event we hold negotiations on the reduction, given the importance of this matter, news of the beginning of negotiations must be transparently conveyed to the public.
- Autonomous defense must be even more vigorously pursued in conjunction with setting the reduction timetable.
- All changes in the national security situation must be actively addressed and the political will and policies toward building autonomous defense shall be proclaimed during the Independence Day commemorative speech (August 15).

I believed that these guidelines contained a rational strategy for navigating the reduction issue, but advisors who felt that the U.S. plan should be nullified or significantly delayed viewed them with a great deal of skepticism. Defense Advisor Kim Hee-sang and others still believed that Lawless's notification had not been an official one, despite the confirmation from Ambassador Hubbard and the phone conversation between the two heads of state. Therefore, they argued that the president should not say anything that called for a strategy based on the assumption that the USFK reduction was a *fait accompli*. But that view was based on a subjective hope, clung to by those who considered the reduction a catastrophe. I myself was overwhelmed with major national security issues that emerged at the beginning of the presidency and certainly did not welcome adding the reduction issue to my plate. But regardless of our own feelings, this was a real challenge before us.

Unfortunately, the atmosphere influenced the president, who himself furthered confusion over whether the American proposal to negotiate troop reduction was an official one from the U.S. government, or more like just an idea floated by the U.S. DOD. For example, he ordered that the topic be taken up for discussion if the United States raised it at any joint military conference on practical affairs leading up to the APEC summit. I felt uneasy. Washington already thought the official notification had been issued—there was no chance it would raise the topic before the summit. The president's own misunderstanding—despite the NSC briefing—indicated he had been given inaccurate assessments and bad advice by those in the foreign and national security policy circles.

The NSC and foreign policy and security advisors thought that the president's intention was to publicly disclose the reduction negotiations after an agreement had been reached at the coming APEC meeting bilateral summit. But they were wrong. At an August 19 interministerial national security meeting, Roh made a major decision. He ordered that Washington's troop reduction plan be confirmed and then transparently disclosed to the public prior to the APEC meeting. He meant for the issue to be put to a public debate before the actual summit in October. As he had described in the July letter to President Bush, he believed this was necessary as part of an "effort to gain the understanding of the people and the National Assembly," and that holding negotiations without first informing the public would be inappropriate. Roh noted:

> The reduction proposal is bound to arrive, and once it is publicly disclosed, it is expected that there will be domestic furor over it. It is a miscalculation to think that we can avoid it. . . . The writing of the text detailing the agreement and anything else must be done honestly and transparently. . . . From now on, each time there is an official proposal it must be immediately disclosed to the public, and we must state, "This is how we will respond." Our response should match what the public is told. It must all be transparent.

Drawing a Road Map for Autonomous Defense

The issue of the USFK reduction only strengthened the president's determination to pursue autonomous defense. President Roh knew that a major task like building autonomous defense, which required changing the military mindset and the national defense structure, as well as significantly increasing defense spending, had to be initiated in the early stages of a presidency, when the president's power was strongest. Therefore, in July and August the NSC and the Defense Ministry jointly drafted a national defense program that connected autonomous defense with the realignment and reduction of the USFK. This plan was to be confirmed when the president presided over a national security interministerial meeting in early September. We decided, at the president's behest, to emphasize the determination to achieve autonomous defense in his Independence Day speech.

After unofficially informing the president of its "Plan for Autonomous Defense" on July 31, the Defense Ministry built on the plan and added it to the agenda of the August 19 national security briefing for relevant ministers. It marked the public unveiling of autonomous defense, albeit only within the government. The ministry reported that it would augment those areas that relied on the USFK with significant South Korean forces in order to fully attain the capacity to contain North Korea by 2010. Among the areas that required significant buttressing, the ministry singled out early detection and alarm, command and control, mobile strikes, and defense. But the ministry did not directly address the essential condition of autonomous defense: the return of operational control. Instead it used the rather vague phrase—"development of the joint command structure"—and said, "This would be pursued in relation to the timetable for building autonomous defense capability and the plan to realign the USFK." President Roh pointed out that the ministry's report made it seem as though the very concept of autonomous defense had come into being in response to U.S. troop realignment, and ordered the ministry to stipulate as a basic principle that autonomous defense would be continuously pursued through a ten-year plan, regardless of changes to U.S. strategic planning. He stressed, "Autonomous defense is being pursued in keeping with the demands of the time, not out of unavoidable necessity to conform to changes in U.S. strategic thinking."

At the fifty-eighth anniversary of the nation's independence on August 15, President Roh forcefully proclaimed his autonomous defense agenda. Although he could not yet openly talk about the need to prepare for USFK reductions, he hinted at the possibility in a number of places in his speech. He also indirectly declared his intention to reclaim operational control by pointing out how our military still did not possess independent operational capability and authority. Here are some important excerpts from his speech:

> . . . Public opinion is divided on the matter of the USFK. On one side, there is opposition to the realignment on the grounds that a partial reduction of the USFK or its relocation can threaten national security. On the other side, though limited, there is an argument that the USFK threatens the sovereignty of the nation and must withdraw. . . .
>
> During the Korean War, the U.S. military sacrificed countless young lives to defend our freedom. And to this day, it protects freedom and peace on this land. In the future it will continue to contribute toward the maintenance of peace and stability in Northeast Asia. We have reached today's success on this foundation of peace, and we will continue to do so.

But it is not right to think that we can always rely on the USFK for our national security. An independent and autonomous nation must be able to defend itself with its own defense capability. Our military has continually grown since the Korean War and is large enough to ably defend the nation. Still, it has yet to possess an ability and authority to execute independent operation.

U.S. security strategy is constantly changing. We should not face the chaos of an unstable defense policy and turbulent public opinion each time American strategy changes. It does not do to simply call for the withdrawal of the U.S. military without any measures in place. It is time to accept the changes imposed by reality. I want to prepare the foundation on which our military can gain the ability for autonomous defense during my term and over the next ten years. To this end, I will reinforce intelligence gathering and operation planning abilities and also reform our defense spending and defense structure. . . .

It has been fifty-five years since the government was established. We now have the twelfth-largest economy in the world. It is time to take responsibility to defend our own nation. . . .

The vast majority of the public showed support for the president's declaration of autonomous defense. But the opposition and conservative media criticized him on the grounds that the declaration of autonomous defense destabilized the ROK-U.S. alliance and gave people a false sense of security. They argued that while the idea of autonomous defense might appeal to the public, it was nothing new; they expressed concern that "autonomy" meant autonomy from the USFK or from the alliance itself; and they complained that discussing U.S. military realignment during the Independence Day speech would undermine public awareness of the security threat.

Even rational experts criticized the emphasis on autonomous defense. If they had known that Washington had proposed reducing the USFK, they might have refrained from such criticism. But this could not yet be disclosed, so it was unavoidable.

The president had hoped to use his Independence Day speech to publicize the reduction and lend greater legitimacy to his autonomous defense agenda; in fact, his original speech opened with the issue of the reduction but he later deleted it, because he had already agreed with President Bush in his letter and by phone that the reduction would be kept secret and not be discussed between the two governments till the October summit meeting. That proposal had come from our side, no less.

Reduction Negotiations: "Proceed after Full Public Disclosure"

The fourth Future of the Alliance (FOTA) meeting took place in Seoul September 3–4, 2003. As expected, the United States did not raise the issue of reducing the USFK, meaning there was no change to the American plan. Instead it requested that our government deploy a large number of troops to Iraq. This complicated matters even more. We now had to deal simultaneously with two problems: on the surface, the hugely important issue of sending troops to Iraq at America's request; and below the surface, the potentially explosive U.S. proposal of troop reductions.

Following the FOTA meeting, Foreign Affairs Advisor Ban Ki-moon met with the entourage of deputy undersecretary Lawless for lunch on September 5 and discussed the reductions. Ban explained that the reduction of the USFK had great significance for domestic politics and so it was necessary to proceed with utmost caution. If reductions were to be pursued at the same time as USFK realignment and autonomous defense, the negative repercussions could be immense. Ban asked whether there was a possibility that Washington could reconsider the plan. Lawless replied that the second-stage relocation of the USFK Second Infantry Division—scheduled to be completed by 2008—was 80 percent related to troop reductions, so both had to be pursued in conjunction.

On September 9, 2003, the NSC and the Defense Ministry briefed the president on pressing defense matters. The NSC presentation, "USFK Realignment and a Comprehensive Strategic Plan for Autonomous Defense," had been compiled through discussions with the Defense Ministry; its goal was to organically and complementarily link various issues, including the realignment and reduction of the USFK and autonomous defense. The Defense Ministry presentation, "Autonomous Defense and the USFK Action Plan," detailed what they deemed to be the level of troop reduction that South Korea could accommodate. It articulated the goals of acquiring defensive capability against the North and completing an independent battle execution structure so that operational capability could be retrieved and a new war command structure be put in place by 2010. As for the USFK reduction, we advised the president to make a counteroffer, revising the U.S.-proposed reduction figure of 12,500 by 2008, to a total of 8,000.

Every move by South Korea and the United States regarding the troop reduction was reported to the president practically in real time. On September 9, the NSC informed him that it would make a plan to publicly disclose the initiation of reduction discussions in anticipation of the upcoming summit at the APEC meeting. Public disclosure and transparency were Roh's consistent principles. He believed public disclosure and discussion would be inevitable if the American side refused to delay reductions. His idea of public disclosure was to first disclose Washington's proposal and then formulate our counterproposal, and to negotiate on that basis.

At the briefing, President Roh said that the question of reduction should not be abruptly dealt with at the summit and only then brought to the public's attention, meaning that a matter of such significance for the security of the Korean Peninsula had to be brought to the public's attention prior to an agreement with President Bush. He had asked President Bush not to discuss practical aspects until after the APEC meeting because of the need for a public debate to reach a consensus. Roh was considering two possibilities for the timing and manner of the disclosure: announcing it himself on Armed Forces' Day (October 1), or having the Defense Ministry announce it. He ordered a discussion of this with the United States and directed that any announcement of the reductions be made at the same time the autonomous defense agenda was publicized. He emphasized, "There may be a controversy, but we must make the announcement before the fact and overcome the controversy. We should proceed with the reduction even as we try to delay it. Public disclosure must happen before that. Otherwise, people will not be convinced."

When Roh heard the Defense Ministry's plan to delay the start of USFK reductions until 2009—in opposition to the American position that it be completed by 2008—he said, "I find it doubtful that this is a realistic counteroffer the United States will accept." He then ordered another study that would take into consideration the American plan and work in conjunction with the relocation of the USFK's Second Infantry Division.

Most of those who attended the September 9 meeting expressed great reservations concerning public disclosure as it would create insurmountable anxiety among South Koreans over the state of national security and the economy. They argued for forcing the United States to abandon or delay the plan; failing that, they argued, the reduction negotiations should never be revealed. Some argued that the issue should be linked to troop deployment to Iraq.

However, even as they begged him to reconsider, no one was able to propose a solution capable of changing the president's mind. Above all, they could not counter the president's assessment that changing the U.S.

decision on reductions would be difficult. The argument for unofficial negotiations could only be interpreted as a call to place the needs of Washington over those of Seoul. If reduction talks were to take place unofficially and the word later got out, the opposition and the press would undoubtedly mount fierce attacks and accuse the government of hiding critical security matters—it would be regarded as an inexcusable attempt to deceive the nation.

Despite strong opposition, the president did not relent and also argued against linking the deployment of troops to Iraq and the reduction on the grounds that this would only complicate matters and cloud judgment: He said, "Deployment is a problem of today, but reduction is a problem of tomorrow," adding that, "It would not be right to deploy soldiers only to slow down the speed of the reduction." But he suggested that, because the North Korean nuclear issue had great bearing on our national security, it might be advantageous to link progress in resolving it to the troop reductions. Unsure of to what degree the two issues could be linked, he ordered a review of how best to connect them.

I frankly thought that once we received the U.S. request to deploy additional troops to Iraq, a public disclosure of the reduction negotiations was all the more inevitable. Deciding to deploy troops but secretly negotiating USFK troop reductions was not only immoral—should the back-room dealings become public, the consequences would be disastrous. The South Korean government had no choice but to disclose that the negotiations would commence before deciding whether to deploy troops to Iraq.

Collision between a Clear Command and Ambivalence during Negotiations

On September 19, 2003, the NSC Secretariat briefed the president on the plan to advance negotiations with the United States in the reduction of the USFK in anticipation of the APEC ROK-U.S. summit only one month away. We received additional instructions from him and on that basis drafted negotiation guidelines on September 23, conveying them to the team that would hammer out the practical points.

The guidelines called for first confirming any change in the U.S. position. If the United States were to cancel the plan, there was no need for additional discussion; but if the United States wished to postpone the bilateral discussion, the team was to attach the condition that the reduction "not be proposed again until 2006, when at least the relocation of the Yongsan garrison is to be completed" or "after the North Korean nuclear situation calms down." We instructed them, in the words of the president, to be ready for any possibility and leave nothing ambiguous. However, if there were no change in the U.S. plan, our team was to listen to the Americans and then make our counterproposal, which was to time the reductions alongside the relocation of the U.S. Second Infantry Division to south of the Han River, when the second phase of the relocation-related facility construction was to be completed, sometime between 2006 and 2008. Our desired reduction size was eight thousand troops.

Another important task for the negotiation team was to explain to the United States the domestic steps we would be taking. The NSC Secretariat, in particular, wanted the negotiation team to clearly explain to the U.S. side our need to hold a public debate on the issue. The NSC Secretariat therefore drafted the following talking points, showing why publicizing the reductions would be in Washington's interests:

- If the U.S. plan for USFK reductions were not significantly delayed and the reduction issue itself were leaked to the media, our government would be criticized for hiding an important national security matter from the public.
- If the reduction plan were revealed when domestic opinion is divided over the U.S. request for ROK troop deployment to Iraq, the ensuing charges of U.S. pressure on South Korea and the administration's alleged irresponsible behavior would make the government's position more difficult and damage its political leadership.
- The point of holding a public debate on the reductions is not to lead the public opinion in any certain direction and create difficulties for the U.S. side, but to proactively address the issue.
- Our government plans to inform and persuade the public at an appropriate time through appropriate means. We believe there may be chaos at first, but doing so will reduce the possibility of even greater chaos down the road.

Nowhere in the guidelines was there an order to cancel or delay Washington's reduction plan. The president's order was to measuredly convey our position, hear out the American position, and report back afterwards.

The team visited Washington and held negotiations on September 25 and 26.[3] They returned on September 28 and reported the outcome to the president:

- The United States has not changed its previously stated plan to reduce the USFK by 12,500 troops over several phases. But this is a conceptual plan only and not its final position, and the United States has conveyed its willingness to exercise discretion in terms of the final size of the adjustment.
- The United States holds that to have a detailed discussion of the reduction, there need to be negotiations between the two nations' defense ministries or a special working group. They propose that only the issue of reductions be negotiated over the next several months and that an agreement be reached over all aspects of the reduction plan by early next year. Originally, the Americans had desired that practical negotiations be allowed to proceed after their representative visited the Blue House on June 5 and informed the presidential advisors. The thinking was that a review by the Blue House would soon follow. The U.S. side explained that they had received no response from our side until President Roh's letter arrived.
- The White House NSC stated that it hoped for a discussion of political and strategic principles at the APEC ROK-U.S. summit.
- The U.S. DOD felt that the timing of public disclosure should be determined through mutual agreement, and expressed caution about early public disclosure.
- The U.S. side emphasized that the reduction plan must be treated separately from the North Korean nuclear issue or the deployment of South Korean troops to Iraq.

The briefing led to a discussion. There was still considerable objection to public disclosure and some even talked of respectfully catering to U.S. concerns. But with the U.S. reduction plan unchanged, there could be no change to our plan; the president was adamant: "Delaying disclosure is unacceptable since it amounts to deceiving the public." He asked everyone to actively engage in the issue. "The public should have complete information pertaining to national security, so the facts

---

3   The negotiation team included Cha Young-gu, the director of policy at the Defense Ministry; Seo Joo-seok, the director of strategic planning at the NSC; and Wi Sung-rak, the foreign ministry's North American affairs bureau director-general.

related to reductions should be explained to them," he said. "If there is to be additional troop deployment to Iraq, it will not be possible to disclose the reductions then as we can now. People will not accept it." The president emphasized that it would be possible to simultaneously accomplish both reductions and deployment, but publicly disclosing the negotiation process was critical.

The president ordered that when the negotiations were disclosed, the message to the public should emphasize that South Korea

> now stands shoulder to shoulder with the international community. It should no longer rely solely on the alliance, nor should it demand the sacrifice of the United States. We must mount the initial defense, and the alliance should assist us on this foundation.

He also asked the Defense Ministry to finalize a timeline for reduction of the USFK with an eye toward the autonomous defense agenda, and adjust the timetable gradually in consultation with the United States.

When it became clear that Roh was resolute on the public disclosure of the reduction, many of those opposed to it were crushed. I myself experienced mixed emotions. I, like the president, believed that public disclosure was unavoidable. Suggestions that South Korea's national security or economy would be threatened were exaggerations. After studying the reductions for the last several months, I had a certain confidence that the challenge could be overcome; the public would get past the initial shock. But the big obstacle was the deployment of South Korean soldiers to Iraq.

If the topic of deployment came up at the same time as the troop reductions, there could be negative repercussions beyond what we could handle. It was highly likely that the public would see the United States as a shameful and selfish country for reducing the size of the USFK even as it requested the deployment of additional troops to Iraq. This was precisely the scenario that the United States was most concerned about. Were it to occur, there could be no additional troop deployment, given the heightened anti-American sentiments in South Korea. And in that case, the United States would probably see our demand to publicize the troop reductions only as a ploy to increase anti-Americanism in the domestic media and decline sending additional soldiers. ROK-U.S. relations would be in shambles.

This was never something we wanted. If we decided to decline the troop deployment request, we should do so confidently, otherwise it would be like burning down the house just to catch a few lice. But there was no way we could deal with the big issue of troop deployment beforehand just for the sake of disclosing the reduction. Even if we had decided on the issue of deployment early on and then immediately disclosed the reduction in troops, it would appear that the government was utterly unable to resist U.S. demands. I felt trapped and could not fathom a way out of this predicament.

Participants at the meeting kept expressing concern over the repercussions of public disclosure. In passing, the president remarked, "If they promised that the reductions would not be discussed during Bush's term, we couldn't simply bring it up either. Barring that, not telling the public would amount to tricking the people." I had a eureka moment. "That's it! This could be our solution!" I asked the president, "Since the United States opposes public disclosure, how about we suggest that there be no reduction negotiations whatsoever until the end of 2004, given that there is a U.S. presidential election in November next year?" Since I suggested this compromise just as we were on the verge of deciding on public disclosure, many people immediately warmed up to it, regardless of its feasibility. The president did not seem keen but gave his consent.

I judged that Washington would not easily accept Seoul's public disclosure plan. But since American diplomats were eager to avoid the impression that they were interfering in South Korea's domestic affairs, they would only indirectly express their feelings. Thus, I believed there was a strong possibility that the U.S. position would change if a suitable alternative were offered. With this in mind, the NSC drafted our government's final negotiation guidelines.

But after this report was presented, I heard from within the team that the negotiation with the United States had not taken place in accordance with the established guidelines. I immediately reviewed the negotiation summary.

It was clear that there had been several problems. According to the summary, Cha Young-gu, de facto team leader, had led the conversation and conveyed our position. But while he had communicated the crucial element of the guidelines—that of public disclosure—he had also made remarks that possibly confused the U.S. team about the ROK stance. During his initial remarks, even before listening to the U.S. position, he said, "The South Korean government is worried about media criticism and concerned about national security should the USFK reductions and the Iraq deployment be simultaneously pursued," and added, "Our

people will be worried if there is a public discussion of the USFK reductions." Upon hearing that the American plan remained unchanged, he
diverged from the guidelines in the course of explaining our response
to the American plan. He said:

> If there is public disclosure, the troop deployment to Iraq will become
> extremely difficult and the public would believe that the American com-
> mitment to South Korea's defense has weakened. There will also be
> difficulties in the course of adjusting the terms of the alliance. . . . Once
> a public discussion begins, it will not be possible to maintain secrecy,
> so I think that the reduction negotiations themselves should be delayed
> until after 2006.

This personal opinion, beyond what was stipulated in the guidelines
and expressed by Cha, the lead negotiator, gave the Americans reason
to think that the ROK position—of embarking on the negotiations only
on the condition of making the proceedings public—was hypocritical.

During the negotiations, the U.S. side was clearly worried about public
disclosure, but Cha himself expressed even greater worries. I was shocked
by what I read and called in Seo Joo-seok, the NSC director of strategic
planning who had accompanied Director Cha, and demanded to know
what had happened. Seo responded with surprise. Once Cha had made
those brief remarks, Seo said, Cha asked him to explain the government's
official position to the United States, and Seo himself had read it out loud.
He said he had clearly explained the background of the government's
decision to proceed with the public disclosure. Because the document I
read was only a summary, Seo's remarks were missing. Seo acted as if he
had been wronged, since while it was true that Cha had made troubling
remarks, the South Korean government's stance had nonetheless been
clearly conveyed and there was not a shred of deception in the report.

Even so, Cha's remarks had been most inappropriate and led some
American officials to argue that South Korea was opposed to public
disclosure; rumors about the situation were even spreading to the public.
But the idea that the ROK government opposed public disclosure and
wanted to delay reduction negotiations was preposterous—it had been
Seoul that had decided that it would hold a public debate in the first place.

I felt incredibly let down by all that had happened, as I had essentially
created the guidelines and entrusted them to the negotiating team. Before
June 2003, Director Cha and the NSC Secretariat had experienced differences in opinion, but later he and my office developed a strong trust

and maintained close cooperation; it was unlikely that he had made his remarks out of some sense of rebellion against the Participatory Government's policies. Even now I do not know whether Cha's remarks at the negotiating table reflected some intention of the Defense Ministry, but it is clear that his comments reflected the tense atmosphere in South Korea's defense and foreign policy circles. A Defense Ministry official reading the summary would have assessed Cha's negotiation performance as excellent. I have no doubt that besides Cha, just about every defense official who met with Korea specialists within the American government around this time probably made similar—or even stronger—comments opposing both the reductions and public disclosure. For example, Kim Sook, the North American affairs bureau director-general at the Foreign Ministry, met with Deputy Undersecretary Lawless on May 5, 2004, to carry out a specific task entrusted by the NSC. But regarding the South Korean channel of communication for negotiations on reduction, Lawless told him, "Based on experience so far, we do not want to negotiate with the Defense Ministry, which appears to be hesitant to engage in negotiation over this matter." Even the U.S. side could see that the Defense Ministry clearly wished to avoid the very discussion of reductions, and this was the same ministry authorized to manage the negotiations with the United States. Of course, chaos ensued. There was now one path: this problem could only be solved with the strong leadership of the NSC Secretariat in foreign affairs and national security.

I said nothing to Director Cha. It was already water under the bridge and there was a great deal of work that required cooperation with the Defense Ministry. Rather than sowing seeds of contention, I thought it would be better to be encouraging and move forward together. Perhaps this incident had been unavoidable early in the presidency, given the conflict between the president's national defense philosophy and the established mindset of the Defense Ministry.

But after navigating major issues such as autonomous defense, USFK reduction, and the Iraq deployment, the Defense Ministry gradually assumed the attitude of the Roh administration. The change became even clearer once a new defense minister, Yoon Kwang-woong, took office in July 2004. The attitude of the ministry officials negotiating with the United States also changed a great deal. Ahn Gwang-chan and Kwon An-do, subsequent directors of policy at the ministry starting in 2004, always carried out the president's orders faithfully and cooperated quite closely with the NSC.

The October 10 Notification of Public Disclosure
and the Emergence of a Compromise Plan

Once the president confirmed there was no change to the U.S. reduction plan, he ordered that the issue be publicized either on October 1 (Armed Forces' Day) or October 10, but since the Americans wished to negotiate the issue of timing at the fifth FOTA meeting in Seoul (October 6–8), the NSC chose October 10 as the day of reckoning and began preparations. Reports of U.S. uneasiness about public disclosure came from all sides, but the United States did not officially oppose our plan or present an alternative as this might be construed as interference in South Korea's domestic affairs.

With all the latest developments, we had to wait for the final bilateral negotiations at the FOTA meeting. Based on the September bilateral negotiations, however, I felt that entrusting everything to the Defense Ministry would open the door to chaos on the eve of public disclosure. I decided that there was no other way to precisely and quickly conclude the negotiation with the United States in accordance with the president's order than to meet with Thomas C. Hubbard, the American ambassador.

On the morning of October 6, I escorted the presidential couple to Seoul Airport on their way to Bali, Indonesia, for the ASEAN +3 summit meeting. There I met Foreign Minister Yoon Young-kwan and Foreign Affairs Advisor Ban Ki-moon, who were accompanying the president on this trip. Both Yoon and Ban stressed to me the need to find a point of compromise with Hubbard. The two governments had had many differences on issues like North Korea policy and the Iraq deployment, but we shared a sense of desperation that, at least on the matter of reduction, we should be able to find some common ground for compromise. The responsibility for alleviating this desperation now rested on my shoulders.

That afternoon, accompanied by Park Sun-won, the senior executive officer of the NSC Secretariat, I went to the American ambassador's residence with a bottle of wine. I explained to Hubbard the reason the government was intent on public disclosure and asked for his country's understanding. The ambassador replied:

> The U.S. Department of Defense presented the South Korean side with a reduction figure it had calculated would not weaken South Korea's defense capability. It was not something President Bush had decided; he understands very well President Roh's position after the letter and the phone call, so I ask that South Korea not get ahead of the United States.

He hoped that we would not be specific about troop figures when disclosing the reduction negotiations, but rather describe the extent of the reductions in vague terms, as something that would not reduce South Korea's defense capability. Should a timeline be mentioned during the announcement, he wanted us to articulate the actual reduction was likely to take place before 2006.

Above all, the United States wanted to avoid the impression that the reduction was a one-sided decision imposed on South Korea. Hubbard hoped that the South Korean government would go on record as agreeing with the decision. "Reduction is our common project. If a decision is made to disclose the reduction negotiations, we hope for some time, even if it is only a few days, to review what would be announced." An experienced diplomat with class, Hubbard politely requested what was necessary to safeguard American interests without directly expressing how difficult public disclosure was from the American point of view.

I replied, "The South Korean government, in principle, opposes the reduction, but believes that this is a rational adjustment given the significant increase in the capability of the USFK over the last ten years. We accept this plan under the premise that the timing and size can be adjusted." I also emphasized that while the past three reductions had been unilaterally decided by the United States, this time it should be a common project, as he had stated. But I explained that if we failed to announce the specific reduction figures proposed by the Americans, it would only create suspicion and chaos. I added that, while disclosure of the negotiations might seem undesirable, the ROK government simply could not handle the repercussions of the media learning about reduction negotiations *after* the Iraq deployment. After clearly stating our position, I suggested, "If the United States really believes that public disclosure will be too difficult, how about delaying the negotiation itself until after the end of 2004?"

Hubbard, noting that the United States had never opposed a public discussion of the reduction, nonetheless showed interest in my proposal. But he expressed reservations: delaying that long would imply waiting until the end of the Bush presidency, with presidential elections in November. I countered that, even if we delayed the negotiation until next fall, there could still be an agreement. Our conversation on the topic ended here.

The reductions were not a matter to be decided by the two of us, but we did discover some common ground through this conversation. In my opinion, the White House and the State Department were likely to show interest in the compromise of delaying reductions, but the DOD would be dissatisfied. All that remained was to watch for the next move by the United States.

That evening at the Defense Ministry the Lawless entourage and our negotiating team held a discussion on the same subject. To avoid the mistake of the previous negotiations, Director Seo took matters into his own hands and laid out the position of our government. The American side asked several questions about the one-year delay that I had proposed to Ambassador Hubbard. They seemed uncomfortable with the idea that for a year, and only in South Korea, they could not discuss reductions that were part of their global military strategy. Director Cha explained, "Even if the reduction plan is unintentionally leaked to the press," we could explain convincingly to the public that "it has been delayed for one year given the burden imposed by various national security matters such as North Korea's nuclear development, the Iraq deployment, the USFK realignment, and the transfer of responsibilities." But they replied, "Even if the discussion were delayed only until *early* 2004, that explanation is still possible," and asked why the delay had to be for a year. Seo responded that the end of 2004 had been chosen to allow us to freely deal with the reduction separate from other major issues, such as the North's nuclear development and the Iraq deployment.

My proposal to Hubbard had been conditional: if the United States were uncomfortable with public disclosure, a solution could be to delay reductions for one year. But during high-level discussions the U.S. focus shifted to entirely delaying the negotiations; as a result, the delay itself became the focus of discussion, over our determination to publicly disclose negotiations. In the end, this minute difference would provide the United States with the rationale to argue that the South Korean side demanded delaying reduction negotiations, foregoing the fact that our side had informed them of our intent to publicly disclose negotiations.

In hindsight, it is rather common during diplomatic negotiations that when two sides try to save face over less-than-fundamental issues, somehow both end up winning. During negotiations it is not a bad idea— sometimes unavoidable—to leave aside a few things not fundamental to the matter at hand. But at the time, both conservatives and progressives were heavily criticizing the Roh administration's approach to negotiating with the United States, using crude phrases like "anti-American," "deceiving the public," and "autonomy in name only." So I did not have the peace of mind to absorb this important lesson about negotiations.

The Agreement on Delay and the President's Regret

A few days later the American embassy conveyed to the NSC the U.S. reaction to the idea of allowing a public debate on the USFK reduction. The United States was sufficiently aware of the political ramifications and the importance of the reduction matter in South Korea, and during an October 7 video conference with Washington, Ambassador Hubbard had strongly pushed for delaying the reduction discussion. It appeared that the consensus was moving in the direction of a delay.

Ultimately, the two nations came to an official agreement on the morning of October 9—just one day before the scheduled public announcement—to put off USFK reduction negotiations for one year and put the public disclosure on hold. It was an agreement reached between the Lawless entourage and South Korea's negotiating team. Determining the duration of the hiatus remained a challenge until the very end. We called for the end of 2004, while the United States wanted summer 2004, so there was a bit of tug-of-war, but it was ultimately agreed that the delay would be for "de facto one year."

The possibility remained, however, that the two nations might interpret the agreement differently, since the matter involved such great differences in opinion. Yet we could not ask for the drafting of an official joint statement of agreement—a feat that would require observing diplomatic protocol—over something that had not happened. From the U.S. perspective, it had informed South Korea in June 2003 of a reduction plan and requested a negotiation; in October 2003, the decision was made to delay the negotiations for a year, given feasibility problems. In this situation, however, the United States certainly held greater power and had no need for a statement of agreement.

Things were different for us. Not knowing if the United States might suddenly change its tune, it was important for us to clearly stipulate the terms of the agreement in some form. I had the NSC Secretariat draft the text of the bilateral agreement in both English and Korean. I planned to meet with Ambassador Hubbard, confirm that there were no errors, and give him a copy. That text, titled "The ROK's Understanding of the Negotiation on the USFK Reduction," ran as follows:

1. The United States and South Korea agreed to suspend any negotiation on the reduction of the USFK for (de facto) one year from the 9th of October 2003 onwards.

2. More specifically, both sides agreed to suspend consultation on the reduction issue until the summer of 2004, and to resume the talks at an appropriate point in the autumn of 2004, if necessary.

3. In accordance with the agreements of Articles 1 and 2, the South Korean side will cancel its plan to make public the contents of the negotiation on the USFK reduction which was scheduled for October 10, 2003; and both sides will jointly prepare at the earliest possible date a press guidance which aims at dealing with the possibility of a leak to the press of the negotiation on the USFK reduction plan proposed by the United States.

I met Hubbard on the afternoon of October 9 and gave him the English version of the text, asking for his confirmation. The ambassador, however, asked for two corrections. First, he wanted bilateral discussions on the reduction plan to continue within the Combined Forces Command (CFC) for the purpose of strategic operations, even if high-level discussions were suspended through summer 2004. Second, his view was that the USFK realignment and reduction were inextricably linked, so South Korean colonels inside the CFC should still be able to carry on with discussions in relation to the USFK realignment. At the risk of seeming petty, I was adamant that all negotiations must stop: "I am sorry to say this, but our position is that no one within the South Korean government can engage in a negotiation over the reduction until next summer, though the American government itself can make its own plans." As we saw it, the U.S. hope of allowing negotiations within the CFC amounted to willfully burying its head in the sand. Should the ambassador press his case, I was prepared to tell him that the reduction negotiations would be publicized the very next day. But he spoke of it no more.

Instead, he said that it would be nice to avoid mentioning the duration of delay as being either one year or until next fall. He proposed, "With elections in both countries and both sides wishing to keep this issue separate from elections, it would be nice to be vague about the exact timing." I was flummoxed; his remark shook the very foundation of the agreement. "If we are vague on the timing, we will face incredible domestic criticism that we delayed the reduction negotiations *precisely* to avoid the general election next year," I replied. "We chose to describe the restart period only by season and not by month in consideration of the U.S. position." Still, it was necessary to clarify the exact time; Hubbard was worried that the restart of the negotiations would coincide with the November 2004 U.S. presidential elections. But the agreement had been vetted by our negotiating team, who had struck it with Lawless and already reported to the president—I had no authority to exercise any flexibility. If the United States demanded something different, we would have no choice but to proceed with public disclosure. As I ended the conversation, I clearly stated, "If you take exception to or find points for change in the agreement text as we have presented, please contact us before the national security meeting for relevant ministers. . . . If you request changes in major points of the agreement, we do not have many choices. We will have to consider once again beginning the process of public disclosure." There were no further messages about this from the U.S. embassy afterwards.

A national security meeting for relevant ministers was held as scheduled on the morning of October 10, 2003. The topic had been changed to the cancellation of the public disclosure and the discussion of future plans. The consensus was that we should strongly pursue autonomous defense and actively plan for changes in the USFK configuration in preparation for bilateral negotiations in one year. I reported the process that led up to canceling the public disclosure. For the first time in a long while, the participants visibly relaxed and projected contentment—except for the president. He appeared more regretful than reassured.

Once I finished the briefing, the president evaluated the pros and cons of canceling the public disclosure and delaying the reduction negotiations by one year. He said that the delay had a positive aspect considering that the reduction issue, if publicized, would exacerbate public anxiety given the as-yet-unresolved North Korean nuclear problem and the Iraq deployment under debate. Yet he regretted losing an opportunity to have an open public debate on the reduction, reduce the public's psychological dependence on the United States, resolve anxiety over national security, and also open the door to a different kind of relationship with the United States—one based more on South Korea's identity as an autonomous nation. He said that he was positive regarding the current outcome but "given the past experience, nothing good comes of dragging one's feet." He again emphasized the need for direct action to change the people's tendency to succumb to fear and anxiety because of their dependence on the United States. In the end, my role in delaying the reduction negotiations for a year was applauded by all ministries, ministers, and advisors, but did not receive high marks from the president—it would be more accurate to say that I had disappointed him.

Every time something like this happened, the president would frequently express regret by saying, "Deputy Secretary-General Lee, why can't you be more forceful? You should have pushed harder." As I struggled to reply, he would supply the answer: "Then again, as president I can make decisions; as my advisor, you have to be cautious."

He had clearly hoped that I would be strong enough to push for a public disclosure of the reduction, regardless of the Iraq deployment. That way, the public might have suffered some shock, but it would have served as impetus for building more equitable ROK-U.S. relations. Of course, the president himself could not have been sure of our chance at victory. So while he was less than happy with the compromise plan that I had achieved, he had been positive in his practical evaluation.

Certainly, however, this compromise had only been possible thanks to the president's decisiveness on public disclosure. In the history of USFK reductions, the United States had never once changed its mind because of another party. If we had solely relied on the Americans, as advisors had urged, we would have achieved nothing. We would have been pulled into secret negotiations and faced major criticism from the whole nation. It was because of the president's decisiveness and will that we were able to achieve even this much. I am certain of this.

But even I had mixed feelings about the results. Yes, it was fortunate that we had avoided enormous repercussions by not disclosing the reductions amid the heated debate surrounding the Iraq deployment. But that was it. We had essentially given up on a chance to signal that we were striving for a more mutually beneficial and balanced relationship with the United States, all out of fear of the repercussions. We had not even tried to confirm, through a public debate, the legitimacy of the Roh administration's determination to achieve autonomous defense, nor of the presidential will to shock the public out of its psychological dependence on the United States.

"Begin the Negotiations Immediately"

On October 20, 2003, presidents Roh and Bush met at the APEC summit meeting in Bangkok. With the agreement that negotiations would be put on hold for one year, the reduction issue did not come up as a topic of conversation. But Roh did touch upon it while speaking with Bush:

> While the reduction is regrettable, we plan to cooperate out of respect
> for U.S. strategy. . . . I have always thought that it would be appropriate
> for us to take this matter into our own hands, but it was reported that

a U.S. defense official brought up the issue. I believed that it might give an impression the United States was pursuing the reduction unilaterally, so I wrote you that it would be better if South Korea were to take the lead. It was my plan to inform our public on August 15 and solicit public opinion on the reduction plan on Armed Forces' Day.

The USFK reduction discussion of 2003 thus came to a conclusion of sorts.

However, another major problem manifested in May 2004. As the situation in Iraq became urgent, Washington sent notice that it was dispatching 3,600 soldiers from a single brigade within the USFK Second Infantry Division. Ambassador Hubbard and Deputy Undersecretary of Defense Lawless informed the South Korean side on the same day from both Seoul and Washington. It happened to take place on May 14, 2004, the same day Korea's Constitutional Court rejected the National Assembly's impeachment of President Roh.

In fact, two months earlier I had heard from Lee Soo-hyuk, the deputy foreign minister who had accompanied Foreign Minister Ban Ki-moon to the United States, that the U.S. side wished to hold reduction negotiations around May. I asked Kim Sook, the foreign ministry's North American affairs bureau director-general, who would be visiting the United States in early May for a FOTA meeting, to seek confirmation. At that time in March, the president felt that since the National Assembly had approved an additional deployment of three thousand troops to Iraq "for peace and reconstruction," reduction negotiations could take place whenever the United States wished. But with Roh facing impeachment, circumstances did not allow for him to make policy decisions. Given that both heads of state were involved in the original decision to delay negotiations, I thought the United States would not ask our government to restart negotiations under the current circumstances. Making such a request to an ally's head of state at this time would be unprincipled. But we needed to ascertain the U.S. position.

Because the United States was bringing up the reduction negotiations earlier than agreed, I made sure Kim Sook carried an English copy of the agreement that I had given to Ambassador Hubbard. On May 5, Kim met with Lawless, who indicated that Washington wanted to discuss the reductions at the June FOTA meeting. Kim showed him the agreement. Lawless reviewed the contents but justified the American request, saying that when the South Korean NSC had read it to him before, he had orally corrected the phrase "de facto one-year delay" with "it is always possible

to begin the negotiations after June, should the United States wish to."
Then he added something I had not heard before: the "de facto one-year
delay" had begun the previous year on June 5, when he first notified the
two South Korean presidential advisors of the reduction plan. By this
argument, the agreed-upon one-year delay ended in just a month. I had to
some extent expected this kind of move, but there was nothing we could
do at this point. Back in October we had already written and shared with
them the text of the agreement and offered one day for the Americans to
examine all the points. The understanding had been achieved by resorting
to brinkmanship: if they wanted any changes on major points, we would
once again consider publicizing the reductions to the nation.

At the same time, I simply could not understand the constant self-ra-
tionalization. The United States could have begged for our understanding
of their critical situation and the need to hold negotiations earlier. Even
White House special assistant Michael Green, whom Director Kim had
also met with, made the absurd argument that we had agreed on delaying
the reduction to avoid the timing of our April parliamentary election, as
if to emphasize that beginning the negotiations earlier was legitimate.
Even if they had the stronger hand, this struck me as excessive. They did
not once think of how their self-rationalizations could be taken advantage
of by those Koreans who blindly trusted the United States or wanted to
underhandedly use the U.S. self-rationalizations to attack the South Korean
government. During the three years when I handled U.S. diplomacy at the
NSC, I even came to suspect that the American officials in charge of the
Korean Peninsula were, rather deviously, leaking their twisted arguments
to the South Korean press and the opposition, all for their own purposes.
Every time I experienced this kind of situation, I was once again reminded
of how difficult it is for a weaker nation within a hierarchical alliance
relationship to negotiate with a superpower over security matters.

Kim Sook reported that during his visit he sensed a certain movement
on the American side regarding the USFK reduction. His instinct had been
right: only a few days after I read his report on the U.S. visit, we obtained
intel that Washington had suddenly decided to deploy two brigades from
the USFK Second Infantry Division to Iraq.

That deployment was reported in the South Korean media on May
18, 2004, before the South Korean government could even begin to react.
Numerous rumors about the stability of the ROK-U.S. alliance, the nation's
security, and the government's incompetency were again stirred up, plunging the Roh administration into difficulty. Considering the USFK's outsized

role in South Korea's national defense, the United States should have, at the least, informed and consulted with the South Korean government in advance. No matter how urgent the situation in Iraq, there should be respect for an ally. Would the South Korean government really have objected, with the United States in a tight spot and with no choice but to deploy units from the USFK? But even as USFK troops were urgently dispatched to Iraq, the only thing on the Americans' minds was the potential damage to President Bush's political standing, as they lamely explained that it was all part of the U.S. Global Defense Posture Review (GPR).

Now the South Korean government was in a bind. Had the United States explained the USFK deployment as a result of mounting difficulties in Iraq, the South Korean public would have understood. But now it was suddenly claiming that dispatching a whole brigade away from South Korea was a readjustment (basically a reduction) of the USFK as part of its GPR. Seoul looked like a pushover; not only did it fail to notice the U.S. reduction plan, but was not even consulted on it. To put it bluntly, the United States had pushed an innocent friend into a chasm of condemnation, all just to avoid being personally insulted. Even a child could see that the USFK deployment was due to U.S. difficulties in Iraq. But when the South Korean government said as much, rumors began to fly that there was a problem with the military alliance, since the explanations from the two nations did not match. In this way, the Bush administration's unilateralism damaged the alliance.

When the domestic media, based on the one-sided U.S. explanation, began to attack the government, I proposed that—however belated—we disclose through the foreign ministry the terms the United States had agreed to the previous year. But the United States immediately expressed disapproval and opposed the disclosure.

All this was happening just as ROK-U.S. relations had reached a relatively smooth path, following difficult agreements on a number of important issues like the Yongsan garrison relocation. It also took place just as President Roh returned from facing impeachment. I thought it was most offensive of the United States to mark the president's return to duty in such a manner, and conveyed this sentiment to the United States through several channels.

Back at work, President Roh presided over a national security meeting for relevant ministers on May 20. The president had been receiving related reports since the day he returned to duty, but the main topic at this meeting was still the USFK deployment to Iraq.

The president asked Defense Minister Cho Young-kil, "If 3,600 soldiers are dispatched, is it necessary to make changes to the organization of the South Korean forces in response?" Cho replied, "I believe that there is no need for any change at the moment." After a rather long back-and-forth with the minister, the president told him, "In any case, be firm in saying 'The defense capability of the Republic of Korea is not so weak as to be shaken by this.' And say that the combined military capabilities of South Korea and the United States remain strong regardless."

The United States' unilateral decision to dispatch USFK troops to Iraq greatly undermined the voices of those government figures who had been passive about autonomous defense and had treated talk of reductions as taboo. The views of the two presidential advisors at the Blue House, who had dismissed the reduction plan as the private opinion of Lawless, were revealed as unrealistic, as was the argument that the U.S. reduction plan should be altered and any negotiations be indefinitely delayed. If we had conducted national security policy in deference to their views, the situation would have been very difficult. President Roh—who had pushed for autonomous defense and insisted that the United States could at will reduce the size of the USFK—was vindicated by this development.

The emerging reality was reflected in the atmosphere at the May 20 meeting. The president ordered the immediate start of reduction negotiations and their public disclosure. Just as he had done on October 10, 2003, he again emphasized that nothing would change by delaying the timing of the negotiations. The NSC, too, was emboldened—now it was possible to pursue autonomous defense with even greater determination. I made certain that the Defense Ministry would not respond to the U.S.-proposed reduction figure with a vague counterfigure; if a reduction of 12,500 were unacceptable, they had to give an objective explanation why. Otherwise, we would accommodate such a reduction, and only adjust its timing.

The NSC decided that it would not fight the size of troop reduction, but instead would have the Defense Ministry negotiate the reduction timeline with the United States to better fit our own plan for building autonomous defense. In June 2004, as the negotiations began, the United States had expressed its wish that it wanted to execute its plan ahead of schedule and reduce the USFK by 11,500 army personnel and 1,000 airmen by 2005, including the soldiers who were already being dispatched to Iraq. But from our point of view, this plan did not take our own preparations into consideration. Therefore, there were several rounds of negotiation over this matter. In late September, just before an agreement was imminent, our proposal for sequential reduction was 5,000 in 2004, 2,000 in 2005, 2,500 in 2006, and 3,000 in 2007. Then the final agreement in October 2004 was to reduce the USFK by 5,000 in 2004 (the first stage), 5,000 between 2005 and 2006 (the second stage), and 2,500 between 2007 and 2008 (the third stage)—for a total reduction of 12,500 soldiers over five years.

On the last day of the negotiations there was, of course, a small incident. In the evening, I received a call from Ahn Gwang-chan, director of policy at the Defense Ministry, who had been engaged in the final stages of the negotiations with Lawless in early October. Ahn, who was on his way to meet Lawless, said in an alarmed voice, "We have a big problem. Lawless says if our side doesn't accept their plan in its entirety, they will by next year pull all troops marked for withdrawal as they had stipulated in their original proposal." He was saying that we should accept the revised U.S. proposal since their position was adamant. I did not hesitate: "Then tell them to withdraw however they wish. What's the point of negotiating? Why do we negotiate? Tell them that this is what I said. Why do they negotiate with us? Just pull everything out by next year."

Back in May 2003 (this will be discussed in further detail later), as we were polishing a draft of the joint declaration at the ROK-U.S. summit, I received an urgent call from NSC Secretariat senior executive officer Park Sun-won, who was in Washington at the time; he reported that the United States was pushing up until the last minute to include in the text the phrase, "All options are on the table," in regards to the North Korean nuclear issue. I told him to just return then. So when I got this call from Ahn, it was my second experience receiving a U.S. ultimatum along the lines of, "Let's call it quits if you don't like it." So I knew that at times I had to play the villain from behind the scenes and hold the line to get things done.

The next morning, Ahn called. He sounded like he was in a fantastic mood. The ROK-U.S. reduction negotiations had concluded as our side had proposed. I conveyed my heartfelt congratulations and gratitude to him; he had actively conducted the negotiations with Lawless, one of the U.S. government's best Korea experts, and had brought the whole thing to a successful end.

The United States will always be able to carry out USFK reductions, regardless of South Korean needs. This is the truth we learned from Washington's USFK reduction proposal, the debate surrounding the public disclosure of that proposal, and ultimately the deployment of USFK troops to Iraq. It showed that President Roh's determination to achieve autonomous defense and free ourselves from U.S. dependence was all the more right. Now few could question the president's philosophy of autonomous defense and we could at last call for a resolute negotiation with the United States.

Cooperative Autonomous Defense and the Path to Reclaiming Wartime Operational Control

On November 17, 2003, U.S. secretary of defense Donald Rumsfeld visited the Blue House and expressed his support for President Roh's autonomous defense agenda, saying, "Among what the president has said, there are things that I have read and agree on. He said that he wishes to realize autonomous defense within ten years, and there is no question that this is an achievable goal." Rumsfeld said that while independent defense is impossible given today's complex international environment, President Roh's effort to achieve autonomous defense was headed in the right direction. He vowed, "The United States will cooperate to this end."

The term "autonomous defense" does not refer to purely independent national defense, which, as Rumsfeld noted, is impossible; thus, it goes without saying that the Participatory Government's autonomous defense policy did not imply a *completely* autonomous national defense. Thus, the Participatory Government could never use just "autonomous defense" in its policy formulation. In March 2004 the NSC Standing Committee had published "Peace, Prosperity and National Security," its national security strategy guidelines, which proclaimed "cooperative autonomous defense" as one of the four cornerstones of the government's strategy. The NSC defined the concept as a "parallel development of the ROK-U.S. alliance and autonomous defense," and explained the reason for using the term:

> Traditionally, autonomous defense has been thought of as an effort to defend oneself through one's own strength. But today it is impossible to completely guarantee a nation's survival and its people's safety through independent national defense; cooperation with allies and friendly nations is extremely important.

"Autonomous defense" does not imply slighting the ROK-U.S. alliance or refusing to cooperate with an ally. In other words, there is no reason to qualify it as "*cooperative* autonomous defense"; it is enough to say that we simultaneously pursue autonomous defense and the ROK-U.S.

alliance. But our military worried that the president's autonomous defense agenda would create a fissure in the relationship with the USFK or weaken the alliance, and the opposition and media behemoths exacerbated that view. That development in South Korean discourse influenced the U.S. government, which began to wonder about our government's aims—which is why Rumsfeld said that he believed "independent defense is not possible in today's complex international environment." No matter how much the president emphasized the importance of the ROK-U.S. alliance every time he mentioned the pursuit of autonomous defense, the attempts to portray the agenda as evidence of anti-Americanism continued. Thus, the NSC Secretariat, under my authority, came up with the pathetic phrase "cooperative autonomous defense," which shows deference to the limitations imposed by the political realities of our time.

While the president accepted the NSC concerns and approved the use of the phrase for the administration's security strategy, it did not sit easy with him, as he expressed at an April 2005 defense ministry briefing:

> People worry that something might happen to our relations with the United States if we spoke of autonomous defense, so the NSC called it "cooperative autonomous defense." But this is a pathetic form of autonomous defense. That language was used because there exist less than objective mindsets both within and outside South Korea. But we must be able to both maintain the ROK-U.S. alliance and pursue autonomous defense. . . . While physical capabilities are important, we must also cultivate a national mindset that is willing to risk danger if such capabilities are to be of any value. The mental conviction that one must defend oneself, centered on self-esteem, must be present.

In my view, those who considered the Roh administration's autonomous defense agenda seditious, even dangerous, were either anachronistic or opportunistic. President Park Chung-hee called for autonomous defense in the 1970s, at a time when the South was militarily far inferior to the North, and the national strengths of the two Koreas were also comparable. Should not those who viewed with suspicion the Roh administration's autonomous defense drive consider Park Chung-hee's policy even more dangerous? But was there anyone in our military or reservists who opposed or openly criticized President Park's call for autonomous defense? Those who were high-ranking generals or young officers at the time and failed to oppose or openly criticize Park's call now stood on the frontline in attacking President Roh's autonomous defense policy. Is this not a contradiction?

Fortunately, after Yoon Kwang-woong took office as defense minister in July 2004, the autonomous defense agenda began to sink in, and cooperation between the NSC Secretariat and the ministry became far easier. General Yoon was a military leader with an exceptional strategic mind and expansive military knowledge. Originally a naval operations commander, he enjoyed debates, possessed a warm personality, and was enthusiastic about national defense reform and autonomous defense. When I was on the transition committee, Dr. Seo Joo-seok said Yoon was the best person to become the defense minister. But Yoon was not selected as the administration's inaugural defense minister, and we thought he had suffered reverse discrimination for having attended the same school as the president—Busan Vocational High School.[4]

Retrieving operational control was the essence of autonomous defense. Our military's operational control authority was divided in two. Peacetime operational control had been regained from the CFC in December 1994, but it was a hollow achievement—what a nation needs to defend itself is *wartime* operational control. The division came about because, in August 1987, Roh Tae-woo, the Democratic Justice Party presidential candidate, made a campaign pledge to reclaim operational control. Once elected, he had to fulfill that pledge; in consultation and as a compromise with the U.S. DOD, operational control was split into two: peacetime and wartime. Thus, in South Korea today people speak of regaining wartime operational control.

President Roh Moo-hyun strongly pushed for the return of operational control because it was an essential step toward establishing a state that had all the capabilities of a sovereign nation. South Korea is the only country in the world that maintains a CFC with a foreign army and has entrusted its operational control to another country. Even the leaders of small countries, ones with armies having fewer than ten thousand soldiers, wield operational control of their own forces. Other American allies such as Britain, Japan, and Australia all possess their own operational control. Regaining operational control is a natural part of the process of normalizing the ROK-U.S. alliance into a balanced and friendly relationship.

For Roh, an alliance was not a relationship subject to one-sided demands, but one of mutual understanding that called for rational

---

4   [The implication is that Yoon might have been excluded from consideration for the post because Roh would expose himself to charges of favoritism if he appointed a graduate of his own alma mater.]

compromise to benefit each other's interests, and required wisdom and deference to precedents. He considered the alliance to be very important for South Korea—not a goal in itself, but rather the means to achieving South Korea's national objectives.

The political opposition criticized the argument for retrieving wartime operational control as anti-American, and claimed it was a means to force USFK withdrawal and disrupt the ROK-U.S. alliance. But if they really felt this way, they ought to have issued such criticism during the Roh Tae-woo administration, which had promised the nation the return of operational control, and even at the representative conservative media outlets that had supported retrieval through the subsequent Kim Young-sam presidency. To attack Roh Moo-hyun with such ferocity for pursuing retrieval after years of delay made no sense. While I could not publicly demand it, I felt that the military leaders should go before the public in uniform to argue for the necessity of retrieving operational control—only then could we reassure the public and push ahead with our work without further obstacles. Instead, while the president and the NSC were in full drive, the vast majority of military leaders were explicitly opposed to or putting brakes on the project with their lukewarm attitude. But this project was based on the president's resolute philosophy and had sufficient justification, so the NSC did not yield even an inch and continued its work as before.

In the summer of 2003, the president asked the military what resources and how much time it needed to prepare to equip itself with the autonomous defense capabilities necessary for retrieving operational control. The military reported that it needed to strengthen its intelligence resources and various capabilities, and considering the amount of time necessary, retrieval would be appropriate around 2010. Respecting their judgment, he allotted them time for preparation beyond his term, and ordered preparation for retrieval of operational control in alignment with this timeline.

On November 6, 2004, the president received a briefing on the overall plan for pursuing cooperative autonomous defense and asked whether it was possible to finish preparation for retrieval of operational control in 2008. The chairman of the Joint Chiefs of Staff answered that it would be difficult. The president then ordered the entire military to set a clear time frame, even if it was a longer one, and later the military reported that 2012 would be the appropriate time for retrieving operational control. The president approved that plan. Thus, the president carefully allotted sufficient preparation time. In 2005, the Joint Chiefs of Staff submitted to the president a report on the "Plan for Independent Exercise of Wartime Operational Control"; they called it the "714 Plan," in reference to July 14, 1950, the day the South Korean government relinquished operational control. The military preferred words such as "transfer" or "independent exercise," rather than "retrieval" of wartime operational control. Through such a series of internal preparations, the fourth ROK-U.S. Security Policy Initiative (SPI) meeting on September 28, 2005, saw the start of discussions between the United States and South Korea over operational control. At the meeting, the South Korean government officials formally proposed to the United States a negotiation over the retrieval of wartime operational control.

As a result of negotiations between Yoon Kwang-woong and Donald Rumsfeld, the United States agreed to transfer wartime operational control to the South Korean military by November 2011, one year earlier than when our military wanted to see it happen. So after Rumsfeld was dismissed, the Defense Ministry wanted to change the timetable. While inwardly displeased with the military's interest in delaying as long as possible, I tried my best to interpret it in a positive light—it reflected their need to be well-prepared for the handover.

In late November 2006, the new defense minister, Kim Jang-soo, invited me to the ministry for dinner. By then I had already submitted my resignation from the post of unification minister, in light of the North's nuclear experiment, and was only filling the interregnum while my successor, minister-designate Lee Jae-jung, went through confirmation hearings. Minister Kim said I was his first official dinner guest since taking office. He was happy that U.S. Secretary of Defense designate Robert Gates had gladly accepted his request to delay retrieval of operational control until April 17, 2012. I liked that he had chosen April 17 (4/17) as the date of retrieval, another reference to South Korea's original ceding of operational control in 1950 on July 14 (7/14). I wanted to believe that it reflected his commitment to autonomous defense. But Kim later switched his allegiance to the Lee Myung-bak administration, which was able to delay the retrieval until 2015 by begging the United States, essentially tarnishing this symbol of autonomous defense entrusted to the Lee administration to uphold during its term. When the Park Geun-hye administration came into power, former minister Kim became its national security director, essentially taking charge of the control tower for national security. But the Park administration went one step further and indefinitely delayed the retrieval of wartime operational control, once again by making a request to the United States. As the person who had advised President Roh and spearheaded autonomous defense even at the cost of astronomically increasing defense spending, I can only feel the worst kind of misery.

6

Dilemmas of U.S.–South Korean Relations: Between Sovereignty and Alliance

Putting a Stop to the Formalization of CONPLAN 5029

In September 2004, Ryu Hee-in, the head of the National Security Council's (NSC's) Center for Risk Management, came to me and said, "I think the Combined Forces Command [CFC] and the Joint Chiefs of Staff are moving toward converting CONPLAN 5029 into an operation plan, but I cannot get a clear sense of it." This was an alarming development.

Since 1993, the U.S. government had insisted that it was necessary to draft a plan of action under the authority of the CFC in the event of a North Korean crisis. South Korea's position was that its government—so long as it was not in a state of war—must lead any attempt to resolve problems related to North Korea; thus it opposed the U.S. proposal and blocked discussion of it. However, during the two-month power vacuum between the 1997 presidential election and the inauguration of the new president, the defense ministers of the two nations came to an agreement, in December 1997, that they must draft a concrete military plan in anticipation of a peacetime emergency on the Korean Peninsula. As a result, in late 1999 the CFC came up with CONPLAN 5029. I suspect the

South Korean government reluctantly went along with this after fielding repeated U.S. requests.

A CONPLAN, or conceptual plan, is on paper only: it needs further improvement and development before it can become an operation plan (OPLAN), which, on the other hand, is a detailed plan of action that might actually be executed, depending on possible contingencies. Logically speaking, a CONPLAN is only completed with an eye toward creating a functional OPLAN; in other words, South Korea never should have agreed on the drafting of CONPLAN 5029 if it had not wanted to see OPLAN 5029 come to life.

It was truly grave that the CFC and the Joint Chiefs of Staff wanted to proceed with converting CONPLAN 5029 into an operation plan. While conceptual plans are not used during real situations, operation plans are executed precisely as written. If OPLAN 5029 were completed, the implication was that the CFC—not the South Korean government—would take charge in the event of a sudden crisis in North Korea. But I discovered that most South Korean defense officials did not grasp the significance of this development; they passively gave consent to the U.S. proposal to turn the CONPLAN into an OPLAN.

If the North were to invade and war broke out, the CFC would be in charge of responding and the U.S. Forces Korea (USFK) commander, who also commands the allied forces, would assume operational control. But a crisis in North Korea that did not involve a military conflict would be addressed through political, diplomatic, and economic means—in other words, nonmilitary—even though the military would still maintain a high level of readiness. The South Korean government would rightly be in charge of responding to such a crisis in the North; in fact, in antici-pation of potential sudden changes beyond political and social control in North Korea, it already had emergency plans in place and continued to improve them with the participation of relevant ministries. The South Korean military's own preparedness was also something the government took care to address. Of course, this was kept under a shroud of secrecy, undisclosed to the public, because it was, literally, an emergency plan.

Thus, there was no question that if a crisis broke in North Korea, the South Korean government would be in charge of handling the situation, in cooperation with the international community. Such a development would naturally present opportunities and challenges, both of which could fundamentally alter the situation on the Korean Peninsula and bring about outcomes as varied as chaos, stability, unification, or continued division. The insistence on the central role of the South Korean government in such a circumstance was not something first proposed by the Roh administration, but a stance assumed by previous administrations as well. The official position of the South Korean government is that the CFC cannot act as the deciding body if the crisis does not involve war. But the formalization of CONPLAN 5029 as an operation plan would rob South Korea of its agency.

I asked Ryu Hee-in to submit an inquiry to the Joint Chiefs of Staff and gather more precise facts. In November 2004, Ryu unofficially obtained from them parts of the OPLAN 5029 draft. The NSC office immediately convened a meeting of concerned officials from the ministries of unification and defense and the National Intelligence Service (NIS) to review the contents of the partial draft. This meeting then led me to make an official request to the Joint Chiefs of Staff to send me all information pertaining to the OPLAN. We received a preliminary report from them on December 17 and, as feared, OPLAN 5029 contained extremely serious problems from the perspective of the South Korean government. Foremost was the possibility that it infringed on South Korea's sovereignty—it called for the CFC to practically take control of matters, even during peacetime, that should remain under the control of the South Korean government. There were also other problems that I cannot publicly disclose here due to their classified nature.

But even without revealing sensitive details, it is sufficient to quote former CFC commander Leon Laporte to show how the plan infringed on ROK sovereignty. During a January 19, 2005, visit to National Security Advisor Kwon Jin-ho, Laporte defined OPLAN 5029:

> A military measure is but another arena alongside diplomacy, intelligence, and economy. . . . The objective of this plan is to assist the civilian leadership in reaching a decision with the widest possible range of options. . . . [OPLAN 5029] should be more appropriately called an interagency model rather than a model at the level of the CFC.

In other words, OPLAN 5029 was to utilize all means, ranging from diplomatic to economic to military and intelligence.

I believe General Laporte was genuinely concerned about a crisis in North Korea and thought there should be a plan of action in preparation for such a calamity. But he overlooked the fact that this was an issue under the exclusive purview of the South Korean government and he possibly, perhaps unconsciously, underestimated the preparation that the South

Korean government had made over the years. Maybe he also underestimated the South Korean government's ability to manage risks in relation to North Korea. I walked away from this meeting with the impression that he viewed the relationship between the CFC and the South Korean government through the lens of that between the feeble Iraqi government and American forces in Iraq. But South Korea is no Iraq.

The NSC standing committee ultimately concluded that OPLAN 5029 had the potential to infringe on South Korea's sovereignty and interfere with the country's domestic affairs, so we decided that it must be stopped for the time being. The president concurred. The Defense Ministry then conveyed the NSC standing committee's decision to the CFC. This all took place while maintaining the highest level of secrecy.

But that was not the end. The United States reacted angrily and the Defense Ministry likewise dissented. The Americans protested that we were suddenly putting a stop to a matter that had been agreed on by high-level military officials of both countries and was already in motion.

Given the American objection to aborting OPLAN 5029, the NSC began poring over records of past discussions. We found that, in fact, the 2003 bilateral discussion did not delve into OPLAN 5029, but was merely a rewrite of the United Nations Command (UNC)/CFC CONPLAN 5029. But somehow, in January 2004, what was meant to be a discussion of the rewrite between the Joint Chiefs of Staff and the CFC morphed into a discussion of implementing OPLAN 5029, due to a U.S. demand. The Blue House, however, never received any report of this development, nor was there ever an official agreement between the two countries to convert the CONPLAN into an OPLAN. It was clear to us that we were not backtracking on a promise made to the Americans.

The Defense Ministry initially assumed a position similar to that of the U.S. Department of Defense (DOD). It called for a process to proceed on the basis of the agreement to rewrite the existing conceptual plan. The NSC office and ministry officials had to meet several times to address this disagreement, but in the end the ministry came to share our belief that OPLAN 5029 would amount to a major problem and would conflict with our own plans for possible North Korean crises. The ministry, therefore, decided to stop pursuing OPLAN 5029, with the agreement of the United States, and was satisfied with revising CONPLAN 5029. When President Roh was informed of this outcome, he issued the following directives on June 2.

- Regardless of whether the plan is conceptual or operational, it should not infringe on or restrict the sovereignty of the Republic of Korea.
- Unless North Korea provokes and we must respond to a war, South Korea must take clear measures to ensure that the United States does not intrude on North Korea's internal affairs, as such intrusion can catalyze incredible tension in Northeast Asian geopolitics.
- These are matters of sovereignty and of a highly political nature, so they must be managed in such a way that the military cannot unilaterally come to an agreement [with the United States].

In the end, the differences between South Korea and the United States over OPLAN 5029 were resolved during the bilateral summit in Washington, D.C. on June 10. President Roh explained to President Bush the reason South Korea objected to OPLAN 5029:

> I think that in such circumstances the South Korea government possesses sufficient capability to manage the situation and it will request U.S. assistance if there are difficulties. . . . Managing political and military matters in relation to North Korea must be done primarily by the South Korean government if there is to be no tension in relations with surrounding nations. . . . The South Korean government will always render assistance if there are matters that require U.S. involvement and the United States makes a request to South Korea.

Bush indicated that he understood Roh's explanation. Therefore, after the summit meeting, the two countries agreed to abort OPLAN 5029 and instead revise CONPLAN 5029. Thus began the phase of a more detailed discussion on the exact form of CONPLAN 5029's new incarnation.

The Leaking of 5029 to the Press and the Identity of the Leaker

Regardless of whether such plans are conceptual or operational, they are top-secret documents; in fact, all plans that anticipate sudden changes in the North are classified as top secret. If made public, South Korea would inevitably face criticism that, although it publicly promises North Korea a bright future in exchange for reconciliation and cooperation, or for abandoning its nuclear program, all the while it is secretly plotting Pyongyang's demise. It is only natural for the government to prepare for all scenarios but not disclose such plans. If an administration were to make such plans public, it would only mean it is giving up on inter-Korean talks and going for political gains by deliberately worsening inter-Korean relations.

But just as the Roh administration began negotiating with the United States over the final shape of CONPLAN 5029, it faced the worst possible situation: the discussion and the circumstances surrounding it were leaked to the South Korean press. It was in mid-February 2005 when Hwang Il-do, a reporter at the monthly magazine *Sindonga*, contacted the NIS office with a list of questions concerning OPLAN 5029. Everyone, including me, was shocked: Hwang already knew every detail of 5029, even though it had only been a month since the NSC standing committee had begun its internal discussion. Hwang's level of knowledge, however, was extraordinary; it appeared that he had already done a thorough investigation and had sent us the questions only to tie up some loose ends in his reporting.

This created an emergency at the NSC and the Defense Ministry. Officials met with Hwang and explained to him the sensitive nature of the situation, hoping to deter him from publishing his article. If the article came out, it would immeasurably undermine U.S.–South Korean relations and inter-Korean relations. I also explained this to the editor-in-chief of *Sindonga* and asked for the magazine's cooperation. But the magazine went ahead with its report in the April 2005 issue, detailing CONPLAN 5029 and its possible conversion into an OPLAN, as well as the conflict between South Korea and the United States with regard to the discussion.

The situation was dire, but the NSC could not deny the contents of the report—the information in the *Sindonga* article was true. A government attempt to deny it would only amount to public deception and invite total catastrophe were other media outlets to follow up on the *Sindonga* piece. The NSC chose to address the situation head-on: it would clearly explain to the public the reason for aborting OPLAN 5029, beg the public's understanding of the government's decision, and explain the importance of the ongoing discussion to the press in the hope that no additional media report would emerge. On March 21, 2005, the NSC issued the following press statement:

> The NSC recognized that the CFC was attempting to create OPLAN 5029 and reviewed the contents of that plan. As a result, the NSC determined that the plan contained elements that were inappropriate for the South Korean and U.S. military to pursue. Several clauses within the plan were also seen as potentially infringing on the Republic of Korea's exercise of sovereignty. Therefore, the NSC standing committee determined that it

was necessary to put a stop to the pursuit of OPLAN 5029. The Defense Ministry then conveyed this fact to the CFC.

I was keen to expose the leaker in order to prevent future media coverage of 5029, but I had no idea who it could be. I could not even understand *how* the contents of the 5029 could have been leaked. We had foolproof security and even within the Defense Ministry only a small minority knew about it; since 2004 there had been almost no leaks of important national security matters from the NSC office or the Defense Ministry. I ordered an internal investigation but we could not find any evidence connected to the leak, but it had to have originated from somewhere within the South Korean government, since the South Korean press had published the leak.

The aftershocks of the *Sindonga* article were enormous: North Korea lashed out and the American government issued a strong protest. The United States reasoned that media reports would have a negative impact on the alliance and would suggest that the two countries were secretly fighting each other. American officials in charge of Korean affairs overtly expressed strong distrust of the South Korean government over the leak, some even harboring the suspicion that our NSC had intentionally leaked the plan and emphasized its risks to national sovereignty in a bid to elicit popular domestic support, all so that OPLAN 5029 would not come to fruition.

U.S. secretary of defense Donald Rumsfeld and Deputy Undersecretary of Defense Richard Lawless also expressed strong regrets about the leak. South Korean newspapers were dominated by reports that Lawless had mentioned, to South Korean politicians visiting Washington, the blockage and leak of 5029 and the decline of the U.S.–South Korean alliance in the same breath. President Bush had even emphasized during his June summit with President Roh that "it is important for foreign affairs and defense officials not to reveal this plan since it can be seen as an attempt to establish a plan to contain [Kim Jong-il], even though that is not the case at all." The report in *Sindonga* was a real blow to the credibility of the South Korean government, not only harming the alliance but also creating difficulties with the ongoing negotiations over the rewrite of CONPLAN 5029.

In the end, in late April 2005 I decided to fly to Washington and try to calm the situation. I first met with members of the U.S. NSC, including my American counterpart, Deputy National Security Advisor Jack Dyer Crouch, II. Then it was time for a meeting with Lawless, who was at the center of the escalating situation.

But at the evening banquet with American NSC officials, I heard something completely unexpected from Michael Green, special assistant to the president for national security and senior director for Asian affairs at the NSC. He was completely familiar with the position of the previous South Korean administrations on 5029, having been a consultant to the DOD in the 1990s. Green told me,

> The discussion over OPLAN 5029 first began during the Kim Young-sam administration, and it continued with the Kim Dae-jung administration. At that time the South Korean government detested this plan. It was due to the reason just stated by you, Dr. Lee.

I had never heard from anyone, not even in South Korea, about the position assumed by the previous South Korean administrations toward 5029. It was remarkable for me to hear from an unexpected source—an American—that my actions amounted to an effort to safeguard the values previous South Korean administrations, conservative and progressive alike, had sought to protect.

I met with Lawless on April 28. While it was not entirely appropriate for me to meet him for a direct talk, given the difference in our ranks, it was also not the time to obsess over protocol. The key to resolving the escalating standoff between the United States and South Korea lay in his hands and those of his direct superior, Rumsfeld, so it was imperative that I seek his understanding. I first brought up the *Sindonga* leak, then offered a few feeble excuses about follow-up reports that appeared later that month in *OhMyNews* and *Hankyoreh*, two left-leaning media outlets. I explained South Korea's position on 5029. In short, I argued that it was a fundamental principle of the South Korean government and within its right as a sovereign nation to take charge of handling any North Korean crisis that did not develop into a war. I added that adopting OPLAN 5029 was inappropriate and asymmetric since it amounted to an effort to respond to a peacetime affair with a military strategy.

Lawless noted that, at the moment, the alliance was being seen in a far more negative light than it should be and that there were problems with how it was being managed:

> The biggest problem is that discussions are conducted in secrecy and problems are not being solved. Without receiving any appropriate expla- nations from the South Korean side, the U.S. Department of Defense is being harassed by the South Korean media. This situation is not good for the United States, which has signed a mutual treaty of defense with

South Korea, or for the alliance between the two countries. . . . Media outlets like *Sindonga*, *Hankyoreh*, and *OhMyNews*, who make this alliance difficult, are fundamentally anti-American and composed of people who wish to harm the alliance. There is no reason to publish such detailed reports otherwise. *Sindonga* may be a monthly published by *Donga Ilbo*, which is a relatively conservative publication, but even so, it's the same [as *Hankyoreh* and *OhMyNews*]. Without it [such a motive] there is no reason to expose secret plans like 5026, 5027, and 5029 with such an unbelievable degree of precision. It is simply hard to believe.

He expressed his personal view that "whether they are progressive or conservative, the South Korean media are sensing that there is a disconnect in understanding between the South Korean and American ministries of defense and national security apparatus, and they are using this disconnect, whatever their motive may be." In other words, he insinuated that the South Korean press was producing articles about 5029 out of the perception that the U.S.–South Korean alliance was being poorly managed by the South Korean government.

He further expressed his unhappiness over the statement released to the press by the NSC office in response to the *Sindonga* report. Because the NSC officially identified 5029's "possibility of infringement on sovereignty" as the reason for putting a stop to the conversion of the CONPLAN into an OPLAN, "it gave the impression that the alliance somehow damaged South Korea's sovereignty." I was inwardly in agreement with him on this. The South Korean NSC knew very well that the United States was extremely sensitive to any possibility of their actions being perceived as infringing on South Korean sovereignty. But the situation was far more complex on our side. The people of South Korea consider the U.S.–South Korean alliance to be sacrosanct. Trying to explain the blocking of OPLAN 5029, with its deep significance for U.S.–South Korean relations, on grounds other than its potential to infringe on our national sovereignty would simply not be persuasive to the public. If the government offered another reason and avoided telling the truth, the administration would not have been able to avoid waves of criticism from the opposition and the media that it was being anti-American and was destroying the U.S.–South Korean alliance. Yet no American official in charge of Korean affairs truly understood the ROK government's predicament.

This conundrum is why the NSC had originally gone to great lengths to prevent 5029 from leaking to the media: in the event of a leak, the ROK government would be forced to cite the sovereignty issue in its attempt to diffuse the situation—the exact issue the U.S. government did not want raised. A leak, therefore, was guaranteed to damage U.S.–South Korean relations.

Nine years later, in March 2014, as I was nearing the completion of this book, I called reporter Hwang Il-do at *Sindonga*. I had questioned him several times before to no avail, but, figuring there was nothing to lose, I asked him, "It's already a long time ago. Isn't it time to tell me the truth—whom did you interview?" He hesitated at first, but eventually told me the shocking truth: his source was someone from the U.S. side. He would not reveal the name but said, "This is someone you knew quite well at the time." He had completed the article after hearing from his American source and doing additional investigation based on the source's story. A veteran reporter specializing in national security issues, Hwang said, "The U.S. side probably calculated that it should make your position difficult in order to steer the negotiations over 5029 in a favorable direction." Judging by his words, this U.S. source was most certainly an American official.

I felt I had been hit over the head with a hammer. It was both incredible and tragic that an U.S. official had leaked the information to *Sindonga* to push the South Korean government into a corner during the bilateral discussions over 5029. We had been unable to hold our heads high when the United States berated us for the "crime" of failing to keep classified information secure. I never would have gone to the United States during the 5029 negotiations if it hadn't been for the *Sindonga* exposé. But here was Hwang telling me that a U.S. official had leaked 5029 on the one side and then berated the ROK government for the leak on the other. How could someone commit an action so immoral, so damaging to the alliance?

I had to reflect once again on the relationship between the media and national interest. But I was grateful to Hwang for telling me the truth, however late it may have been. He was apologetic but I told him not to worry, knowing that no journalist would be able to pass up such an exclusive. I can only hope that officials as devious as the leaker could have existed only under the George W. Bush administration.

During the scandal, conservative political circles let loose a stream of criticism that the government was blocking OPLAN 5029 out of deference to North Korea. Some conservatives even accused the government of being pro-North because it was not preparing a plan in anticipation of sudden changes in North Korea. This was simply groundless; every government must prepare for all possible political scenarios, and the

Roh administration did just that. While the Participatory Government pursued reconciliation and cooperation with North Korea with the ultimate goal of achieving peace and prosperity on the peninsula, the government also had plans in place, albeit top-secret ones, in case a major crisis struck North Korea.

The issue of 5029 still plagues South Korea; it would be a terrible sin for any South Korean government to deal with the matter in a cavalier manner. Not agreeing on implementing OPLAN 5029 will not jeopardize the U.S.–South Korean alliance—there are other ways to appropriately cooperate with the United States. The crux of any plan in preparation for a possible crisis in North Korea must be of a political, diplomatic, and social nature; should there really be a necessity for military intervention, then the South Korean military will naturally get involved. Ultimately, the South Korean government, under the direction of the president of the republic, must stand at the heart of any effort to address a crisis in North Korea. Not only is this a constitutionally inscribed duty of the president, it is also the will of the South Korean people. Future administrations should never forget that.

Contrasting Evaluations of the Agreement on Strategic Flexibility

In May 2008, I attended a meeting of the preparation committee in charge of commemorating the eighth anniversary of the June 15 joint declaration, which was to take place at the Kim Dae-jung Peace Center. At the meeting I heard a major economist and former head of a financial institution condemn the Roh administration as if it were a government that had sold off its sovereignty. He argued that the Roh administration's recognition of USFK strategic flexibility was why we had become embroiled in the regional conflict in Northeast Asia. I did not know his grounds for making such an argument, but this man—who seemed to have little special knowledge of national defense—was full of conviction in claiming that the Yongsan garrison relocation, the USFK realignment, and the South Korean government's increase in defense expenditures were all for the sake of USFK strategic flexibility. I was shocked by his distortion. If a man of such stature would say such things, then how distorted did the agreement on USFK strategic flexibility seem to ordinary citizens?

On January 19, 2006, Foreign Minister Ban Ki-moon and U.S. secretary of state Condoleezza Rice concluded a strategic dialogue and issued a joint statement. It contained the following with regard to strategic flexibility:

1. The Republic of Korea, as an ally, fully understands the rationale for the transformation of the U.S. global military strategy, and respects the necessity for strategic flexibility of U.S. forces in the ROK.

2. In the implementation of strategic flexibility, the United States respects the ROK position that it shall not be involved in a regional conflict in Northeast Asia against the will of the Korean people.

How could these two short and concise sentences be construed to indicate that South Korea had sold off its sovereignty to the United States? If we view them in the light of actual policymaking, then they simply mean that South Korea respects the necessity of deploying the USFK overseas due to changes in U.S. military strategy, and the United States respects the position of South Korea in requiring South Korea's permission for the movement of the USFK within Northeast Asia. The first statement was at the demand of the United States, while the second had been created at South Korea's demand to preclude the possibility of its own automatic involvement in any conflict if the USFK were deployed to a conflict region within Northeast Asia. From the position of South Korea, there was no reason to stop USFK deployment to any area outside Northeast Asia, whether it be Southwest Asia, Europe, or the Middle East. But deploying the USFK to another part of Northeast Asia was another matter, and so this clause was inserted into the joint statement.

But this agreement took on the form of a political declaration, without any legally binding effect. Its purpose was to prevent any conflict with the ROK-U.S. mutual defense treaty, which had the status of law (even if the two nations disagreed in their interpretation of the role of the USFK). Our Foreign Ministry's Treaty Bureau provided the authoritative interpretation that this statement was a political declaration and that our insertion of the second clause prevented the statement from conflicting with the ROK-U.S. mutual defense treaty. Ultimately, the statement simply expressed mutual respect between the two countries for each other's needs or position.

Many South Koreans, with the so-called progressives at the center of the debate, argued that it meant South Korea had wholly accepted the strategic flexibility of the USFK. This is truly an indication of the defeatism that exists within South Korea. Why is it that people think we can keep promises made to the United States, but the Americans might not keep promises made to us—even after it has been formally announced that the two countries respect each other's position? I call this progressive *sadaejuui*.[1] President Roh himself put a stop to this kind of criticism following the agreement on strategic flexibility, saying, "There are views that our opinion may be ignored, but the government is not sitting on its hands. There is no benefit to having a defeatist attitude."

There are even some who objected to the use of "it" in the second clause of the English version of the joint statement. They pointed at the possibility of a conspiracy, deeming it a major mix-up: while Minister Ban Ki-moon, who had been in charge of the agreement on our side, had interpreted "it" as South Korea, Song Min-soon, director of unification, foreign affairs, and national security policy, understood "it" to be the USFK. But there was no secret plot—the two of them were talking in alignment. This sentence had been crafted to address concern that the USFK's involvement in a Northeast Asian conflict might lead to South Korea's automatic involvement in that conflict. As the Korean version makes clear, "it" points to South Korea. But there is no practical difference if "it" is understood to be the USFK.

The issue of strategic flexibility has caused me so much personal grief that I am reluctant even to look back at it. But it is an issue that revealed some important truths of ROK-U.S. relations.

In the context of the USFK, strategic flexibility means the freedom to deploy forces to an area other than the Korean Peninsula and from another area to the Korean Peninsula in times of need. In fact, at the time, the USFK had moved between the Korean Peninsula and other regions at will without special consultation with the South Korean government. One example was the unilateral deployment of a USFK brigade to the Iraqi front in summer 2004. The DOD explained that it had experienced difficulty in the process of inserting Europe-based American forces into the Iraq War due to objections from the governments of hosting nations, and so it wanted to reach an agreement on strategic flexibility with the South Korean government to avoid a similar situation. But it was hard for me to accept this reasoning, so I considered how the DOD had first raised this issue of strategic flexibility.

It started at the launch of the Roh administration. In late February 2003, Deputy Undersecretary Lawless proposed to the South Korean

---

1 [*Sadaejuui* can be translated as "subservience before a great power." The expression is used in a historical context to refer to Korea's relationship to China, but is increasingly deployed by the South Korean left to describe the ROK-U.S. alliance.]

Defense Ministry that the character of the alliance be changed from that of "responding to threats from North Korea" to that of stabilizing the region, for the purpose of responding to crises in and around the Korean Peninsula. In other words, his view was that the role of South Korean troops in South Korea's defense would become more substantial, while the role of the USFK would be expanded to encompass dealing with the whole region. The Roh administration responded that it could welcome the role of the USFK as a balancer who maintained peace in Northeast Asia, but it adopted a cautious stance, since it could not completely exclude the possibility that this might lead to South Korea's involvement in regional disputes.

Therefore, at the ROK-U.S. summit meeting in May 2003, the U.S. government wanted to clarify the phrase "reconsideration of the USFK's regional role" in the joint statement, but this did not happen due to our government's objections. The Americans persisted, at every bilateral conference, loudly voicing their opinion that "the USFK must be able to operate beyond the Korean Peninsula to address emergencies in the region as well as worldwide." The ROK government, based on the Treaty Bureau's interpretation that "the ROK-U.S. mutual defense treaty makes it difficult to accept the regional expansion of the USFK role," responded that this change would require other rationales and a review of the American logic. The United States, however, held that even under the ROK-U.S. mutual defense treaty it was possible for the USFK to play a greater regional role.

In November 2003, the term "strategic flexibility" was used for the first time by Lawless at a ROK-U.S. defense officials' meeting; the term essentially implied an expansion of the USFK's regional role. The South Koreans demanded that Lawless define the concept, but the Americans said that they themselves were still developing its meaning. It was not until February 2005 that Lawless provided this explanation of the concept of strategic flexibility to the South Korean government:

> The flexibility to deploy U.S. forces and logistical support to, from, or through the host nation to meet U.S. global contingency needs and training requirements, based on appropriate and timely consultations with the host government.

The South Korean NSC reviewed the process that led up to this moment and determined that strategic flexibility, as proposed by Lawless, was focused on expanding the USFK's regional role. Of course, the concept surely arose not simply to explain changes to the USFK, but also greater changes in the U.S. global military strategy to cover the globe with a smaller number of soldiers abroad. But, for South Korea, the greatest significance was that the USFK could become a source of conflict in Northeast Asia. President Roh, mindful of this possibility, emphasized at a national security meeting on July 18, 2003:

> If the U.S. military uses USFK bases to involve itself in operations beyond the Korean Peninsula, there may be a possibility that it will undermine our national interest and damage our international standing. In preparation for such possibility, there must be a legal foundation that would necessitate U.S. consultation with our government and allow our opinions to be incorporated.

He ordered preparations to such end. Therefore, the point of contention during the Roh administration's negotiations over strategic flexibility was whether South Korea, in recognizing the concept, could prevent its own involvement in regional conflicts.

But the DOD stressed that when it came to the strategic flexibility of the USFK, it could not yield on two points. First, the department was adamant that if the South Korean government did not recognize strategic flexibility, then it had no choice but to withdraw the USFK. The DOD strongly defended its position on the grounds of the ROK-U.S. mutual defense treaty that if the South Korean government refused to recognize the strategic flexibility of the USFK, then it would be the only country on earth where U.S. forces would lack strategic flexibility. Since the USFK was stationed in South Korea for the latter's benefit, they argued, an alliance that blocked this force from moving to other places to address difficulties in the home country's situation was simply inexcusable. Second, the DOD argued that since the U.S. military answered only to the American president's command, the idea of requiring ROK government approval for USFK deployment was unacceptable.

While I thought the U.S. attitude presented us with a difficult situation, it was perhaps understandable from their point of view. At issue was what we had to do. Our government needed only to decide whether it would choose to enter into negotiations with the goal of securing at minimum a system of "prior consent"—and thus oppose strategic flexibility as defined by the United States, at the risk of seeing the USFK withdraw. Putting the presence of the USFK at risk went beyond the authority granted to the Roh administration by the South Korean people. Regardless of the experts who argued that the USFK is stationed in South Korea as part of U.S. global strategy, in the mind of the average South Korean, the USFK is here for the defense of South Korea. This is our national security reality, not to mention a historical reality. Therefore, the ROK government could only enter into negotiations under the understanding that the two lines the U.S. government had drawn could not be crossed.

Regarding this matter, President Roh predicted on June 7, 2004, that "it will not be easy to unconditionally oppose USFK strategic flexibility or to demand that they receive South Korea's approval for the U.S. forces' comings and goings." And on January 25, 2006, after the agreement on strategic flexibility was reached, he pointed out, "Unless we demand the withdrawal of the USFK, isn't it unavoidable to recognize strategic flexibility? It is basically impossible for the South Korean military to control every movement of the USFK, so we should not delude ourselves into thinking that we could do so."

A Watershed Moment for Negotiation on Strategic Flexibility: The ROK-U.S. Summit

Initially, the Foreign Ministry proposed to the NSC that the strategic flexibility issue be resolved by the end of 2004 through negotiations with the United States. But the NSC Secretariat judged, after review, that this was not something to be resolved in the short term. At first, we considered introducing a system of prior consultation as in Japan, but this proved to be pointless after reviewing the operational precedents set by the United States Forces Japan (USFJ). Regarding the so-called prior consultation on USFJ overseas movement, the Japanese side believed that it possessed the right to veto, but the U.S. thinking was completely different; and in reality, prior consultations between the two sides had not been active. Therefore, there was concern that a system of prior consultation would only give the United States free license of strategic flexibility, all while failing to have our opinions considered.

We needed more time to study this problem in greater depth; furthermore, with major issues like the USFK realignment and reduction already scheduled for bilateral negotiation in 2004, adding one more issue threatened to further weaken our negotiating power. The NSC Standing Committee therefore decided in spring 2004 to postpone negotiations over strategic flexibility until after 2005, and formally proposed a delay to the United States in May 2004.

The South Korean government decided to create guidelines for nego-tiations on the topic, with the goal of entering into serious negotiations with the United States by January 2005. The USFK's strategic flexibility would be recognized in principle, but any USFK movement within North-east Asia would require prior agreement from the South Korean govern-ment. The president issued a special directive. The bilateral agreement was to be such that:

> not everything regarding the scope of activity by the USFK should be defined at this juncture and many things should be left to interpreta-tion. . . . The public will demand that everything be settled now, but we have to consider political and strategic flexibility, as well as the U.S. position, so it is difficult to ask that the USFK only protect South Korea.

He ordered that the agreement should be to some degree abstract, noting, "It is better to come to an agreement each and every time it is called for."

On February 1, 2005, the government appointed the Foreign Ministry's North American affairs bureau director-general Kim Sook as the leader of the strategic flexibility negotiating team and gave him the following charge:

> We, as an ally, articulate to the United States our understanding and empathy for the principle of strategic flexibility. We also express our concern at the potentially negative effects that might result from the possibility of involvement in conflicts in surrounding regions. Before a detailed negotiation can begin, request that the U.S. side provide a conceptual definition of strategic flexibility.

Meanwhile, civil society, some media outlets, and the political sector unceasingly voiced concern that the government's recognition of stra-tegic flexibility would open the door to USFK involvement in conflicts in Northeast Asia. Truth-distorting exposés criticizing the government along these lines were published one after another. The situation was dire enough that on December 3, 2004, I had to give a background briefing to the Foreign Ministry press corps at the ministry's request. I clarified to journalists that our task was to contain the possibility of the USFK's involvement in regional conflicts even while recognizing strategic flex-ibility. But still some sectors did not withdraw their suspicious gaze. Even amid these circumstances, the DOD would not relax its stance that requesting prior consent from the host nation was unacceptable, even if consent to dispatch forces were required only within Northeast Asia. The prospects for the negotiations were not optimistic.

Then Roh came to a decision. In his speech delivered at the Air Force Academy on March 8, 2005, he chose to explain to the public the government's basic position in embarking on the strategic flexibility negotiations. To the DOD—which acted as if it would not yield an inch—he showed, in the name of the president of the Republic of Korea, the Maginot Line the South Korean government would not allow to be crossed:

> The USFK will play an important and continuing role for the peace and security of the Korean Peninsula. But there are voices of concern from some circles surrounding the expansion of the USFK's role. It is about none other than strategic flexibility. But what is clear is that *there will never be a situation in which our people will become embroiled in a conflict in Northeast Asia against our will*. This will be the unwavering principle over which we will never yield under any circumstances. [emphasis added]

The portion of the president's speech emphasized above formed the foundation of our government's position during negotiations and ultimately was implemented as the second clause in the text of the final agreement.

But the speech, because the president had essentially shut down all roads to the most desired U.S. objective for the negotiations, resulted in a backlash from the U.S. side that was much stronger than expected. I met with U.S. ambassador Christopher Hill the evening after the president's speech. I began on a friendly note: "I have high opinions of the goodwill that has built up between South Korea and the United States since your excellency came to South Korea. Of course, there must also have been a few times you were worried because of some uncomfortable matters." Hill, however, owing to the speech, was not his usual warm self and got straight to the point. I conveyed the government's position to him:

> The negotiation on strategic flexibility was first proposed by the U.S. side. But that discussion has been delayed because the greatest focus for the last two years has been on recalibrating the terms of the alliance. The negotiation then finally began this January. But since the second half of last year there has been a misunderstanding on the part of the Democratic Labor Party and civic organizations over this concept, so the government had to clarify its position. . . . South Korea basically accepts the U.S. concept of strategic flexibility. But when there are more than two hundred nations around the world, it is difficult to accept the idea that it is necessary to deploy the USFK to a conflict in Northeast Asia. Besides that, there is no problem. In other words, it is fine if the

United States wants to exercise strategic flexibility in deploying the USFK to any of the 196 out of 200 nations around the world.

After listening, Ambassador Hill answered that strategic flexibility was "only theoretically an issue in terms of the Global Defense Posture Review." Two months earlier Hill had asked USFK commander Leon Laporte about this problem, and he replied, "This is actually nothing. It's only a theoretical matter demanded by Washington." In reality, whenever Ambassador Hill met with me to discuss strategic flexibility, he complained that Lawless had made Hill's work more difficult by creating an unnecessary concept.

Ambassador Hill explained why he thought strategic flexibility was a theoretical problem:

> Let me present you with a scenario. Let's say that South Korea and the United States had produced a text of agreement stating that the USFK can always be used to invade China. And say that at a certain point, the United States actually wanted to attack China and informed South Korea it would also use the USFK in this invasion since that was the agreement six years ago. Whether it's me or you or anyone with an IQ over fifty, we will all know that this agreement on paper is of no use whatsoever. As far as I can see, what guarantees strategic flexibility is not some agreement with no binding effect but a sound alliance that allows for a perfect understanding of each other through close consultation, whether during crisis or in peacetime. Only then can we harmoniously solve an important problem when it presents itself, because we are friends and understand each other perfectly.

I nearly applauded after hearing this. Hill was completely right. Why did the DOD torture an ally by presenting an issue that was pointlessly complex and had no bearing on our future? Hill's statement was almost completely in agreement with what President Roh's had asserted: that should there really be such a situation in the future, then a discussion of strategic flexibility should proceed in a direction agreed on by the two nations. Hill said that he had been "in the process of persuading Washington to avoid forcefully presenting the issue of strategic flexibility to the South Korean government," but his work had been "made more difficult by the president's speech today." But how could we have known about such efforts? And try as Ambassador Hill might, his rational argument would not have easily swayed Washington, where neoconservatives accustomed to unilateral action were controlling the scene.

Seeing Ambassador Hill's great disappointment at the speech and knowing that the DOD likewise had reacted sensitively to it, I was even more convinced that the ultimate objective of the DOD's pursuit of USFK strategic flexibility was so it would be able to exercise it in Northeast Asia. So, to explain why we were unwilling to grant strategic flexibility, I used as an example the scenario of USFK deployment in response to tensions in the Taiwan Strait. Director-General Kim Sook, representing the negotiation team, also met with Lawless and confessed that USFK involvement in any Taiwan-related situation was what most worried the South Korean government.

The strategic flexibility negotiations lurched along through various episodes and finally came to a watershed moment at the ROK-U.S. summit in Washington on June 10, 2005, when President Roh succeeded in convincing President Bush to see things from the South Korean point of view. At that meeting, attended by Defense Secretary Rumsfeld, President Bush stressed the need for strategic flexibility. Bush asked Roh, "What is the South Korean people's concern about strategic flexibility?" Roh replied, "It is unreasonable to ask in advance for a transfer of all authority for matters that could be dealt with through agreement as they arise. If authority is given away, South Korea cannot do anything."

President Bush said, "What South Koreans don't understand well is that the USFK is stationed not just for the Korean Peninsula but for the security of the whole region. If they can accept our position, then strategic flexibility for the USFK is obviously necessary." Bush was agreeing with Rumsfeld. But without missing a beat, Roh frankly stated the ROK government's greatest concern:

> I will give you a specific example. This is something that cannot and should not happen, but our point is that there should be prior consultation with the South Korean government if there is war between the United States and China, and the United States wants to involve the USFK in this war. Our position is that an agreement with the South Korean government would be necessary, while the United States is asking to be able to do as it pleases. . . . My position is that there can be an agreement at that time and the governments of the two nations can reach an agreement as is necessary. . . . Why does it all have to be settled in advance?

In the end President Bush nodded in understanding at President Roh's proposal and decided that the two nations would conduct future talks in this direction. A few days later Assistant Secretary of State Hill[2] conveyed a message that let us know that, immediately after the summit, Bush had told Rumsfeld that Roh's logic made "complete sense."

In keeping with the discussion between the two heads of state, the United States and South Korea came to an understanding that, while the South Korean government would recognize the USFK's strategic flexibility, the United States would seek the agreement of the South Korean government in case the USFK were moved to a conflict region within Northeast Asia. There was also to be more or less an understanding that the final text detailing the agreement would be drafted in as abstract a fashion as possible so as to allow the two countries to reach an agreement. The reason it was important to share this understanding was that the DOD could no longer draft any operation plans based on the strategy of using the South Korea–based USFK for a conflict in Northeast Asia. Should there be a conflict in Northeast Asia, employing the USFK in it would first require an agreement with the South Korean government, so logically speaking it would not be possible to create a plan in advance that assumed South Korea's permission for the United States to use South Korea as its launch base.

The results of the bilateral summit took effect immediately. At bilateral negotiations on July 15, 2005, Lawless conceded to Kim Sook,

> Our assumption in preparing for an event in relation to the Taiwan crisis was to begin the operation from South Korea. . . . Since it has been revealed that the South Korean government's position is that this is unacceptable and the U.S. government understands that position, we must change our basic assumptions in making plans in response to any situation over Taiwan.

When Director-General Kim requested information about this emergency plan involving Taiwan, Lawless refused, saying that there was no need to share with South Korea any such plans, since they had been made under assumptions that were now changing.

After receiving Director Kim's report, I let out a sigh of relief. Until then, I had regarded strategic flexibility merely as a big headache, but thanks to the discussion of the issue and the refusal of the ROK government, we had changed the DOD's existing plan, which had presupposed

---

2 [Ambassador Christopher Hill had been appointed assistant secretary of state for East Asian and Pacific Affairs since the author met with him on March 9, 2005.]

the use of South Korea as the launch base in case of conflict in Northeast Asia. Now I understood the strong U.S. reaction to President Roh's speech.

In consideration of ROK-U.S. relations over the last nine years, I did not reveal this fact, not even after I returned to academia. But now it is all history, and I have decided to reveal the truth so that the Roh administration—unfairly criticized over the issue of strategic flexibility—can reclaim its honor. In fact, once the United States could no longer execute its plan to use South Korea as the operation base for the USFK, there was actually a bilateral discussion in fall 2005 to conceptually define situations under which South Korea in fact *could* become the USFK base of operations. At that time, the DOD used this example: "An American fighter jet allocated to the Korean Peninsula conducts an operation in a conflict zone outside the Korean Peninsula, returns to South Korea for refueling, and then flies off once more."

Many argued back then that the strategic flexibility discussion would threaten South Korea's sovereignty and that China would see a problem in this. But that was not the case. The United States had long planned to make South Korea a launch base in a Northeast Asian conflict and sought to formalize this arrangement through an agreement on strategic flexibility. But the issue instead created an opportunity for the ROK government to publicly express concern over possible embroilment in a conflict in Northeast Asia, and had the unanticipated outcome of scrapping the original U.S. plan to use the Korean Peninsula as a launch base. The DOD, failing in its central objective, gained strategic flexibility only to operate in regions outside Northeast Asia—which never needed to be defined in the first place.

Once the agreement had been concluded, I met with Chinese ambassador Ning Fukui and explained its contents and background to him. Ning thanked me for the explanation and said he sufficiently understood the ROK government's position. During the three years that I served at the NSC, I never once heard that the Chinese government had filed a protest or mounted a challenge to the South Korean government over the strategic flexibility negotiations.

President Roh was satisfied with the agreement on strategic flexibility. Frankly, even I did not expect that the media and public would both rate it so cruelly. Regarding such criticism, the president told his advisors:

> The final agreement was not shaped completely by the United States, nor was it shaped entirely according to our intentions. It is a product of mutual respect for each other's reality. It is a decision based on the

other's real circumstances. We have come to this agreement with an eye toward future flexibility. Therefore, there is no need to insist on an interpretation that it is unfavorable to one side. There is also no need to engage in wasteful debates beyond what is necessary. We can use our own judgment and make our own argument.

In the end, this series of events—from blocking 5029, to President Roh's speech and his persuasion of President Bush—forced the DOD to change two major policies concerning the USFK's role.

First, the DOD had to acknowledge that the agent in charge of responding to a crisis in North Korea was not the CFC but the South Korean government; second, the existing plan to use South Korea as the USFK's base of operations in the event of a situation in Taiwan had to be discarded.

Both issues involved scenarios that were very unlikely to occur and were somewhat removed from reality. But should there be a real crisis, there is no guarantee that previous agreements would be kept or that the United States would not change its strategy and act differently. But this change in U.S. policy in 2005 was meaningful, given that Washington was promising to first and foremost respect the decision of the South Korean government as a sovereign entity if there were to be any event on the Korean Peninsula or in East Asia that could fundamentally change the destiny of the Korean people.

The United States under the Bush Administration: Is the Alliance a Source of Stress?

I think that the United States is a country that has more positive sides than negative ones. While I was advising the president and overseeing foreign affairs and national security, I was focused on advancing our national interests—this meant that there would be uncomfortable moments in ROK-U.S. relations, and that some people would label me as anti-American. But this label was nothing but a groundless political attack. Even as allies, American officials place American interests above all others. In the same way, I place South Korea's national interests above all others during diplomatic negotiations. If that is anti-American, then does that mean our negotiating partners, the U.S. officials, were anti–South Korean?

We use a particular term to describe our cooperation with the United States: "ROK-U.S mutual assistance." The expression itself reveals that, even between allies, it is possible to experience differences in opinion while seeking cooperation. If both sides always agreed, there would be no need for such a term. Just as breath from a musician's mouth strikes different facets inside a flute and produces a beautiful melody, mutual assistance between nations, too, must abide by certain inviolable boundaries and respect each other's interests within those boundaries. True cooperation with the United States should be about explaining our position and circumstances persuasively, respecting the U.S. position, and finding a point of rational compromise. In fact, I heard much about the wonderful cooperation between the Kim Dae-jung and Clinton administrations from the negotiation experts in charge at that time. I thus thought that it was possible to have cooperation between two nations that respected each other's positions and accommodated each other's interests.

The Roh administration desired horizontal ROK-U.S. relations, but it was not easy to achieve. But at the very least, we thought that when issues arise, the two should have a relationship that enables push and pull during negotiations. The administration thought this would be the state of normal ROK-U.S. relations.

I have never once thought that the policies or diplomatic conduct of the Bush administration represented the whole of U.S. foreign policy. But during the Roh administration, the U.S. partner was the Bush administration, and that was all I experienced while working in government. And even then, my experience was limited to ROK-U.S. relations in the foreign affairs and national security arena, and predated the agreement on February 13, 2007, which actually saw Bush's North Korea policy pivot 180 degrees. But, at least in my limited experience, the United States as an ally was a partner that more often offered stress than joy.

If we focus only on U.S. policies toward the Korean Peninsula, I think that in the history of ROK-U.S. relations there has been no U.S. partner so unilateral, authoritarian, and irrational as the Bush administration. In 2003, the Roh administration expressed its concern over the move toward defining North Korea's highly enriched uranium (HEU) development as evidence that the Geneva basic agreement had been voided. We warned the Americans that throwing out the Geneva basic agreement, before even ascertaining the precise shape of North Korea's HEU development, might lead to the restarting of the plutonium facility the North had previously frozen, and to the production of nuclear arms, without ever finding out the truth about the HEU. We therefore suggested that we should gather more accurate information about the North's HEU and that it would be best to resolve the issue based on this new intelligence. But the reaction of Washington was more or less, "You should just trust and follow us. Are you doubting us now?" Some even reacted as though our question ought to be directed at those who had the HEU.

The North's development of nuclear arms and nuclear experiments ultimately proved to not be through the HEU program. It restarted the plutonium facility frozen by the Geneva basic agreement and armed itself with nuclear weapons—since the Geneva basic agreement had already been considered void, why should Pyongyang have any reservations about restarting the facility? Later, on February 16, 2009, U.S. secretary of state Hillary Clinton said, "There is no debate that, once the Agreed Framework was torn up, the North Koreans began to reprocess plutonium with a vengeance, because all bets were off, and the result is that they now have nuclear weapons, which they didn't have before."

If a U.S. secretary of state would make such remarks seven years after the suspicion of HEU development first arose, then the Bush administration should have approached the problem more cautiously back in 2002.

There was considerable tension between the United States and South Korea over how to solve the North Korean nuclear problem until 2007, when the Bush administration changed its overall policy toward North Korea following the February 13 agreement. This tension was also related to three principles set forth by the South Korean government, and summarized as follows.

First, to solve a problem, there needs to be direct talks between the United States and North Korea, even within the framework of multiparty talks. But the Bush administration rejected this idea. Even within the framework of the Six-Party Talks, the United States avoided bilateral talks with the North, to the extreme of ensuring their main representative avoided contacting his North Korean counterpart on visits to South Korea, Japan, China, and Russia during conference recesses. It seemed that the United States was under the impression that North Korea, despite being a small, weak country, was making threatening remarks and trying to deceive a superpower. Nonetheless, the basic shape of negotiations is a bilateral talk. Even during war, two parties must hold talks, so despite its contempt for the North, the United States should have actively engaged in bilateral talks. The U.S. avoidance of such talks was understood by the North as the rejection of its very existence. Without U.S.–North Korea bilateral talks, Pyongyang would only view the Six-Party Talks as a U.S. pressure tactic of creating a five-to-one setting.

Second, the United States needed to pursue a North Korea policy that prioritized solving the nuclear problem over all the many problems related to North Korea. Certainly human rights, illegal drugs, and circulation of counterfeit currency are all important issues, but the nuclear problem is a matter of life and death for South Koreans—solving it must be the priority. But the Bush administration did not agree. Determining an effective way to make the Kim Jong-il regime abandon its nuclear arms is a separate issue from the fact that the Kim regime is anti-democratic and violates human rights. But the Bush administration wanted to view the nuclear issue through the lens of democracy and human rights, and thus such issues, when raised by the United States, served to frequently block progress in solving the nuclear problem, and at times, even made things dramatically worse.

Third, we should boldly guarantee regime security and provide financial rewards and assistance in the event that the North promises to abandon nuclear arms and follow through on that promise. This suggestion was reflected in the September 19 joint statement, but the Bush administration had been lukewarm about the idea before then. (I will discuss in detail the process of addressing the North Korean nuclear problem later on.)

I resolutely argued for these three principles when meeting American officials or politicians, particularly after 2005. And there was almost no one who rebutted the position of the South Korean government in my presence. But officials did not respond to my suggestions, although there were quite a few politicians and former officials who responded favorably. The Bush administration's policy toward the North was certainly going in the opposite direction of these three principles.

But in 2007, the February 13 agreement was born out of the Six-Party Talks, on the basis of bilateral talks between North Korea and the United States. The process and outcome of the negotiations reflected the three principles as advocated by South Korea for this agreement. I certainly do not think that the United States made this U-turn because it accepted our opinion—probably the direct cause was the Republican Party's defeat in the November 2006 midterm elections. But what was certain was that the U.S. policy shift was based on our position, and that the Bush administration accepted that its North Korea policy was in error and changed it. But it was far too late—North Korea had already conducted a round of nuclear experiments and the United States had adhered to its irrational policy far too long, causing its South Korean ally undue stress.

Let's not forget: Under the terms of the September 19 joint statement in 2005, North Korea had promised to give up its nuclear arms in exchange for the normalization of relations with the United States, financial aid, and expansion of economic exchanges. But around the same time, the Bush administration enacted, through the Department of the Treasury, a financial embargo on North Korea, based on suspicions that it was engaging in illegal trade. This contradictory action brought about angry protests by North Korea and provided an important impetus for the North to proceed with its nuclear experiments. The Treasury Department's measure ended with the February 13 agreement, and the United States ultimately returned the North Korean funds frozen at Banco Delta Asia (BDA). It was a lame end to a move that left many questions unanswered and only served to greatly weaken the momentum created by the historic September 19 joint declaration. In response to the risk of seeing the breakdown of the hard-won September 19 joint declaration due to the BDA fund freeze, President Roh lamented on January 25, 2006, "U.S. North Korea policy lacks consistency. . . . If they wear out an ally like this, who would want to be an ally?"

On March 4, 2005, I received a call from Jack Dyer Crouch, II, the newly appointed national security advisor in the White House NSC. Once the pleasantries were over, he got right to the point. "My normal way of doing things is direct and administrative. In that vein, let me ask you a question about one of the issues you are dealing with. It's about sending fertilizer to North Korea." I explained that we were currently at an impasse: the North was demanding an unconditional supply of fertilizer, but our government was countering that fertilizer would only be available if the North entered into an intergovernmental dialogue. Crouch asked that there be no fertilizer shipment, asserting that with the North refusing to return to the Six-Party Talks, it was not the time to reward them. He conceded that the issue involved consideration of inter-Korean relations as well as a humanitarian dimension, but said, "If we give North Korea this kind of reward at this time, I think that it will have an impact on the South or the North, or even elsewhere."

I told him that the decision to provide fertilizer was something to be decided independently by our government:

> There is something you should understand about providing the North with fertilizer. Even when the HEU problem broke out in fall 2002, and in 2003 and then in 2004, the South Korean government continued to send fertilizer on humanitarian grounds and in consideration of the special

relations between the two Koreas. Fertilizer shipments can be used as an important tool for persuading, or even strongly pressuring, the North in relation to the nuclear issue. Therefore, the South Korean government will come to a decision based on its independent assessment. I think that this decision will not have a negative impact on another country or on the North Korean nuclear issue. In addition, our government will contemplate how this issue can have a positive impact on the nuclear problem, and reach its decision while fully considering other important issues between the two Koreas. I hope that you will respect such independent decision making on our part.

The Bush administration nonetheless requested that the South Korean government stop its humanitarian assistance to the North when, on February 10, 2005, Pyongyang announced an indefinite delay to its participation in the Six-Party Talks and declared itself to be nuclear-armed. The Bush administration similarly expressed its disapproval in spring 2003, just as the South Korean government was about to officially begin construction of the Kaesong Industrial Complex, claiming that the project "sends the wrong signal to the North." The U.S. embassy in Seoul also expressed its reservations to the foreign and unification ministries, complaining that, at a time when North Korea was continuing to keep tensions high, "proceeding with the ceremony marking the construction will, at the least, provide political benefits to the North, if not immediate economic benefits." U.S. disapproval made it difficult to choose a date for the ceremony marking the beginning of construction at Kaesong. When the official schedule was confirmed, then the United States demanded that no high-ranking government official be included in the team of representatives dispatched to the ceremony, under the rationale that "North Korea could use it politically." The Roh administration pushed ahead with the ceremony in June, but scaled back the event in consideration of the American demand. It was embarrassing, but at least this much had to be yielded to overcome the strong pressure from the Bush administration to halt construction of the Kaesong Complex.

Then, in spring 2006, the United States supplied the South Korean government with a list of actions—in the form of an unofficial document called a "nonpaper"—that it hoped Seoul would take in the event of a long-range missile launch by the North. After the North conducted nuclear experiments, the United States also demanded a stop to the Geumgangsan tourism enterprise.

In this manner, whenever the North acted provocatively in reference to the nuclear issue, the Bush administration tried to put an end to South Korea's aid and economic cooperation with the North—in essence insisting that inter-Korean relations be shut down. The Bush administration all but ignored the ROK government's desire to reduce the threat to national security posed by traditional weapons by improving inter-Korean relations. Washington did not share the belief that North Korea could advance to peace and prosperity through improvements in inter-Korean relations, much less acknowledge even the possibility that the North was open to persuasion. As far as the Roh administration could see, the Bush administration only wanted the South Korean government to be a passenger in its North Korea policy vehicle, owned and operated by the United States.

In fall 2007, after I completed my official duties and returned to the Sejong Institute, I was pleased to find out that there was an influential American politician who criticized Bush's policies toward Korea as overly unilateral and disdainful of allies. It was Senator Barack Obama, a Democrat. *Foreign Affairs* published an article by Obama that articulated his views on foreign policy in summer 2007, as he embarked on the contest to become the Democratic Party's presidential candidate. In the piece, Obama criticized the Bush administration for destroying alliances and too often sending antagonistic signals to friendly nations within the international community. He presented an example for each continent, and for Asia he chose ROK-U.S. relations, saying, "We belittled South Korean efforts to improve relations with the North."

In fact, because it is overly mindful of U.S. opinion, South Korea is one of the few countries in the world that has not been able to establish diplomatic ties with Cuba. While I was at the NSC, Cuba had diplomatic ties with 182 nations around the world (as of January 2005). Even as the United States was carrying out an embargo against Cuba, it still had a large-scale office of representatives in Cuba. When the Foreign Ministry's Central and Latin American director visited the United States in July 2003, he discussed establishing diplomatic ties with Cuba. The U.S. reaction was that, while the matter fell under South Korea's authority as a sovereign nation, it was not appropriate at the time, given the human rights situation in Cuba. Despite this, the NSC Standing Committee decided on December 28, 2004, to improve ties with Cuba and establish diplomatic relations in the near future. One outcome was that a Korea Trade Promotion Corporation (KOTRA) office was established in the

Cuban capital of Havana. But even to this day South Korea has yet to open an embassy in Cuba, or vice versa.

But when the South Korean government objects to such American unilateralism and an irrational policy toward North Korea, Washington is not the first to react angrily, but rather certain media outlets and political figures within South Korea. While negotiating with the United States over foreign affairs and national security, the most difficult thing was not the negotiations themselves, but having to respond to these contrary voices that argued for U.S. interests even more strongly than the Americans themselves. These voices had a major influence on negotiations with the United States and complicated the South Korean government's efforts to both improve the alliance and advance national interests. They seemed to think, regardless of whether they were right or wrong, that any U.S. policy toward South Korea must be a good one. They shouted to ROK government representatives that the alliance must not be damaged. But ironically, their habit of distorting sensible differences that emerged during negotiations as cracks in the alliance was precisely what served to alienate these two allies from each other.

Even within successful alliances, matters big and small can impact national interests. If arguing for our own position could be construed as an act of destruction against the alliance, then what national interest could be safeguarded? An overemphasis on prioritizing the alliance during negotiations means our representatives cannot consider our own national interests and will always only yield or bend our argument.

One reality that tortured me while dealing with ROK-U.S. relations was the asymmetry between the United States and South Korea when it came to understanding an issue's importance. For example, from the viewpoint of the South Korean government, CONPLAN 5029, strategic flexibility, or the USFK reduction were all critical national security matters. For the United States these matters were important, but not so much that its existence depended on them. In other words, these matters were of crucial interest to the South Korean president and major tasks for the NSC and ministers of defense and foreign affairs in South Korea, but in the United States they were simply under the purview of the deputy undersecretary in charge of the Asia-Pacific region. For South Koreans these matters commanded undivided attention, but for Americans they were just several among many regional security issues.

Therefore, it was inevitable that the pressure faced by the president or the government over these issues would be incredibly different in the two countries. When it came to the reduction of the USFK, President Bush simply received a report from Secretary Rumsfeld about the plan and approved it. But the South Korean government, which was notified of the reduction plan, had to hold a series of meetings under the president's watch and deliberate hard in order to respond. Sometimes I even got the feeling, during my involvement in negotiations with the United States over major issues, that a proposal the South Korean government had arduously worked to produce through meetings presided over by the president could be decided by an American secretary or someone even below that rank on the U.S. side, without President Bush's approval.

I did not express it at the time, but I frequently felt bitter about the asymmetry of ROK-U.S. relations. A casual demand or an idea in relation to the North Korean nuclear issue from President Bush and his advisors meant the South Korean president spent days without sleep, worrying, reviewing, and holding several official and unofficial meetings. And finally, when we would contact the U.S. side before sending a high-ranking official from our side to Washington for an urgent consultation, we would hear back that we had to wait because President Bush was on vacation. Sometimes we even received reports that a discussion over an important matter in need of immediate consultation with the United States had to be delayed because the assistant secretary in charge had to be away for several weeks because of family problems. Even though I understand these circumstances, I cannot help but feel a certain sadness over the asymmetry in bilateral relations.

This asymmetry can produce unintended unilateralist results during negotiations. But the fact of the matter is that it exists, not just between South Korea and the United States, but everywhere. Because the United States is a superpower, there can only be structural asymmetry in its relations with just about all countries. The United States must work to compensate for this trend if it is to maintain healthy and balanced alliances.

In the case of ROK-U.S. relations, this structural problem is a sovereignty issue stemming from the presence of the USFK. What I mean is that this phenomenon occurs because South Korea's national security has long depended on the USFK. As long as this asymmetry exists, South Korea is greatly limited in its maneuvers during negotiations with the United States or in foreign affairs. I am not arguing for the withdrawal of the USFK. But I think that it is possible for us to overcome a significant part of this asymmetry, in spite of the presence of the USFK, if we achieve autonomous defense, regain wartime operation control, and pursue balanced diplomacy. And I believe that adjusting this abnormal structure and developing ROK-U.S. relations in a healthy direction will help South Korea and the United States alike.

III

Additional Troop Deployment to Iraq: Between Autonomy and Peace

7

An Individual's Conviction and a President's Duty

"War Must Be Stopped"

As president, Roh Moo-hyun desired peace and autonomy for South Korea. But he was the leader of a divided country facing threats to its national security, one that had long depended on the Republic of Korea (ROK)–U.S. alliance for security. With that limitation in mind, he still pursued a path of autonomy and peace. At a time when peace on the Korean Peninsula was facing extreme threats, Roh had to open a new era—the return of the North Korean nuclear problem meant the destiny of the Korean Peninsula was at risk of being decided in a battle between Washington and Pyongyang, irrespective of the intentions of the Republic of Korea. This was the situation facing Roh when he became president.

The fate of the Korean Peninsula should be decided by Koreans, but in reality the South Korean government had little room to speak. The North Korean nuclear problem had the potential to become a black hole, absorbing and destroying all the Roh administration's initiatives, whether the policy of peace and prosperity or the pursuit of balanced diplomacy. It was urgent to find, at any cost, a peaceful resolution to the nuclear confrontation.

Such a goal required us to both persuade the North and cooperate with the United States. But neither task was easy. Our hostile relationship with the North meant persuasion was going to be very difficult. Persuading our U.S. ally and calming the situation through cooperation with Washington was more time-sensitive. This meant that to secure American cooperation, the president at times had to face the prospect of saying things he did not wish to and making decisions he did not want to.

Early in the presidency, Roh poured all his energy into relaxing tensions precipitated by the nuclear issue. He suspected that the worsening confrontation between Pyongyang and Washington might lead to war. As the North Korean nuclear threat exploded on the eve of the presidential election, Roh went into the election flying front and center the banner "War or peace?" But the reality rapidly edged closer toward confrontation than peace. The United States demanded that the North give up its nuclear arms as a prerequisite to dialogue; the North resumed the operation of once-frozen nuclear facilities, facing off with the United States without yielding an inch.

From the start, the Roh administration focused on ROK-U.S. cooperation to solve the nuclear problem. It did not matter how great a proposal we had; if the United States did not respect it and instead moved in a different direction, the risk level on the Korean Peninsula would only rise. And it would rise if the United States were to pursue a policy that had the danger of bringing about a military conflict or was irrational from the South Korean government's perspective. We had to persuade the Americans to change course, and had no choice but to concentrate on talking to Washington, since we lacked the means to persuade the North to rethink its nuclear development.

Unfortunately, the difference between the South Korean and U.S. perspectives on the North Korean nuclear problem was simply too great. According to a Foreign Ministry report, the United States concluded that North Korea's objective was to possess nuclear arms and that it was taking a series of steps to achieve this goal. The South Korean government, however, believed that the North's nuclear program had two possible meanings: yes, it was a route to possessing nuclear arms, but it was also a bargaining chip for negotiations with the United States. Regarding how to address the North's threat, the United States decided that sanctions would be unavoidable if the North proceeded with plutonium reprocessing.

Washington's position was that no option was ruled out when it came to North Korea, meaning that military action was also on the table. On the other hand, since sanctions could severely heighten tensions on the peninsula and have a terrible effect on the North Korean economy, South Korea's position was that sanctions should be considered only after all diplomatic efforts had been exhausted. And Seoul opposed any military actions that might lead to war.

But the media ceaselessly reported rumors that the United States might attack North Korea, based on American sources both within and outside Washington. The South Korean public's anxiety deepened. The president came to a decision:

> We must prevent the possibility of war on the Korean Peninsula over the North Korean nuclear problem. A war, no matter for what reason, must be stopped because it will lead our nation[1] to mutual destruction. To achieve this, we must come to an agreement with the Bush administration on the principle of peacefully solving the North Korean nuclear problem. For this sake, ROK-U.S. relations and inter-Korean relations are both things we can worry about afterwards.

To prevent the nuclear issue from precipitating war, we had to exclude the use of military force from the range of U.S. choices in dealing with the North; we also had to send a strong message to Pyongyang to cease all provocations and take the path of dialogue. President Roh, knowing the South Korean government had clear influence over its ally but no leverage over North Korea, prioritized persuading Washington.

Roh, because he believed that there was a possibility the United States could use military force against the North, thought it necessary that he procure a promise from the Bush administration not to resort to a military option and to demand that Washington refrain from all dangerous acts that could lead to war. To achieve this, it would be effective for the president himself to take action, even if it might appear somewhat undiplomatic.

On March 2, 2003, a U.S. Air Force RC-135 surveillance aircraft was closely pursued by three North Korean air force planes in the airspace over the Eastern Sea, near North Korea. Tensions immediately rose. For twenty minutes the three MIG-29s had pursued the American surveillance plane, following within mere tens of meters. If it had led to an exchange of fire, there would have been an unimaginable crisis. The United States

---

1   [Here "nation" is a translation of *minjok*, which encompasses all Koreans, both of the North and South. That usage is apparent here.]

argued that the surveillance plane was flying some 240 kilometers from the North's coastline, while the North maintained that the event amounted to an incursion into its airspace.

Roh had the Defense Ministry announce the government's official position, warning against the danger of the North's actions and demanding that there be no recurrence. But then, during a March 5, 2003, interview with the British newspaper *The Times*, Roh himself cautioned the United States: "This kind of aerial encounter was predictable ever since the United States stepped up its aerial surveillance of the North's nuclear facilities, now back in operation. I want to urge the United States not to move too far ahead." He was warning the Americans against providing the North with any excuse to engage in military provocation.

The opposition and the press were up in arms over this interview. For them, blaming an ally for this incident was unthinkable. "It is hard to believe that this remark came from a nation's president in command of the military. This in itself is a national security threat that leaves people speechless," the opposition Grand National Party raged. "This shakes the very foundation of the ROK-U.S. military alliance." Many people dismissed the president's belief that the United States might attack the North as over-the-top or anti-American. In some circles, people even thought to link his comment to the realignment of the U.S. Forces Korea (USFK) and spread rumors that the ROK-U.S. alliance was in danger.

But later it was proven that the president's warning certainly had not been excessive, but was quite realistic and appropriate. In his 2010 memoir *Decision Points*, George W. Bush reveals that during his February 2003 meeting with Chinese president Jiang Zemin, "I told President Jiang that if we could not solve the problem diplomatically, I would have to consider a military strike against North Korea."

The U.S. invasion of Iraq demonstrated just how dangerous things could get with the United States not ruling out a military option in dealing with the North. In January 2002 President Bush publicly labeled Iran, Iraq, and North Korea as the so-called Axis of Evil. This term was the product of a religious sensibility, and a group armed with such a religious conviction was likely to act against its self-defined "Axis of Evil" in a manner far removed from rational judgment. The United States invaded Iraq under the rationale that the Saddam Hussein regime was developing weapons of mass destruction, although that fact was not even confirmed. North Korea provided the United States with a far better rationale for an attack than Iraq ever did—the suspicion of nuclear weapons had a stronger basis, and American diplomats mistrusted the North well before Bush singled it out. If South Korea were to agree with the Americans about not ruling out military options, there was a strong possibility that war would become a reality on the Korean Peninsula. It worried Roh that this was the character of the Bush administration.

President Roh's efforts yielded fruit. The United States was unhappy with the South Korean government raising the alarm and voicing opposition the minute the "military option" came up, but Washington certainly began to limit such talk. Starting in mid-March 2003, U.S. calls for a military sanction against North Korea dramatically dissipated. President Roh made diplomatic efforts to ensure that the "principle of peaceful solution through dialogue" became a public principle among all involved nations, including the United States. Foreign Minister Yoon Young-kwan made every effort to create a step-by-step road map for solving the North Korean nuclear problem and threw himself into finding common ground with various governments by visiting the United States, China, Japan, and Russia from late March onward.

President Roh had a strong profile as a strategist. As momentum for a peaceful solution to the North Korean nuclear problem built and the situation started to change for the better, he worked to create an atmosphere of friendlier cooperation with the United States so that the two nations could transcend the earlier awkwardness. Once he essentially shut down the possibility of U.S. military intervention in the North, he decided it was necessary to make up for the pressure he had placed on ROK-U.S. relations. During a March 13 phone call between the two heads of state, Bush explained the impending attack in Iraq and Roh showed his absolute support. In return, the two came to an agreement on the principle of solving the North Korean nuclear problem through peaceful means. This conversation played an important role in putting to sleep all the rumors circulating about problems with the ROK-U.S. alliance.

To peacefully solve the North Korean nuclear crisis and improve ROK-U.S. relations, President Roh made the decision to deploy the first wave of South Korean troops to Iraq. On March 20, the government held a National Security Council (NSC) meeting and expressed its support for the American attack on Iraq, deciding to send soldiers for medical and reconstruction support. On the same day Roh addressed the nation in a bid for public understanding: "In consideration of several factors, including trends within the international community, the prevention of weapons of mass destruction from spreading, and the importance of the

ROK-U.S. alliance, it is in our national interest to support the American efforts." That first deployment would not meet great opposition from the public since the United States did not request combat troops; we needed only to send soldiers for medical assistance and reconstruction—all humanitarian purposes.

But it was not as though Roh had no reservations about the American invasion of Iraq and the deployment of South Korean soldiers; he in fact believed the Iraq invasion could not be justified. When the Foreign Ministry submitted to the NSC meeting a draft of the president's March 20 speech, Roh ordered that a passage calling the war "just" be removed, saying, "I do not know if this war is really a just war." The president's support of the invasion was a token of repayment to the United States for heeding his opposition to the use of military means to resolve the nuclear crisis. Roh's support for Bush's war ironically safeguarded peace on the Korean Peninsula, where the Republic of Korea was unable to maintain peace by itself.

Beginning in late March, the North Korean nuclear problem was well into the negotiation phase. All efforts up until then had paid off. Of course, this was in no small part aided by the United States' determination and China's under-the-radar efforts. Perhaps historians will not even bother to look at the role the Republic of Korea—a substantially weaker country than the four surrounding powers—and its president played, at the risk of introducing discomfort into its alliance with the United States. But it is certain that the opposition to military options and the insistence on a peaceful resolution through dialogue—two principles that Roh alone argued for when other foreign leaders kept silent because of the Bush administration's power—provided the underlying spirit for the Six-Party Talks. At the first talk in Beijing (August 27–29), a "peaceful solution of the nuclear problem through dialogue" was the first point of agreement, as summarized by the presiding nation, China.

The ROK-U.S. Summit:
"Further Steps" and a "Camp for Political Prisoners"

On May 11, 2003, President Roh went to the United States for his first overseas trip since his inauguration. The schedule called for a six-night, seven-day stay. The visit proved to be a watershed moment for both the North Korean nuclear problem and ROK-U.S. relations. While talks of mounting military attacks on North Korea mostly disappeared in the United States, both within official circles and beyond, the Bush administration still had not agreed to completely abandon the military option. Conservative forces in South Korea and many media outlets continued to question the state of the ROK-U.S. alliance. The business community wanted this summit to be a showcase of the solid state of the alliance; Roh, too, focused on confirming the traditional arrangement of friendly cooperation and putting aside differences in approaches to the North Korean nuclear problem.

President Roh's U.S. visit was a success; the press, for the most part, also rated it favorably. There were, however, several issues, all related to North Korea, that dimmed the achievements made during the visit. First, during a May 13 speech Roh gave at the invitation of the Korea Society, he said, "If the United States had not helped South Korea fifty-three years ago, I think that I might have ended up at a camp for political prisoners." This was too much praise for the United States and an unnecessary provocation of the North. The remark not unexpectedly fed a spike in critical public opinion and negatively influenced the South Korean public's evaluation of the achievements of the U.S. visit.

Another issue was in a joint statement from the summit, published on May 14. It proclaimed the intention to solve the North Korean nuclear problem "through peaceful means based on international cooperation." The problem was this sentence: "While noting that increased threats to peace and stability on the peninsula would require consideration of further steps, they [Bush and Roh] expressed confidence that a peaceful resolution could be achieved." The press focused on the definition of "further steps." Most experts and media outlets said that "further steps" implied pressuring the North, including through military measures, and condemned the South Korean government for what they saw as accommodation of the U.S. containment policy.

Seeing the media's reaction to the phrase "further steps" left me with an indescribable feeling of failure. It is convention that joint statements from summits between two allied nations first undergo discussions between officials and receive de facto approval before the summit is actually held. For the discussion on this summit statement, the government sent Deputy Foreign Minister Lee Soo-hyuk to Washington, and I asked Park Sun-won, a senior executive officer at the NSC Secretariat, to accompany Lee. During this discussion, the U.S. side expressed its desire to retain the option of a military attack on North Korea in the event of a crisis, and demanded that the phrase "all options are on the table"—a common euphemism that military measures are not excluded—be included in the joint statement. They were saying that there should be a display of will to use all means for solving the North Korean nuclear problem.

The South Korean NSC had ordered that the U.S. insistence on "all options" be rejected. When President Roh was briefed, he also agreed that the moment we accepted this wording, we were essentially giving the United States permission to decide whether to resort to military action against the North; he said it must be rejected, no matter how difficult. But the U.S. side would not yield, even asserting that they used these words only for negotiation purposes. Logically speaking, the American side had a point; but the reality was different. The work of moderating the joint statement came to a stalemate over the phrase "all options," while all other parts were finished. Even as the president's departure date approached, the United States refused to budge from its position. The situation became so dire that it was affecting the bilateral summit itself.

Just as I was walking up the stairs to the main hall of the Blue House to attend a meeting chaired by the president, Park Sun-won telephoned from Washington. He said that because the American position was so adamant, a consensus was difficult to reach; it might even have an impact on the publication of the joint statement as a whole. I thought to myself: "If there is no joint statement, the first bilateral summit between South Korea and the United States will be recorded as a failure. This will severely damage our government. But it is better than including 'all options' in the joint statement. And Washington, too, will also suffer from this, since it is the host. Let's hold out one more time. Isn't the United States already aware of President Roh's strong opposition to military sanctions against North Korea?"

I told Park, "Then just come back." He understood perfectly what I meant. He probably reminded the negotiating team of the government's strong stance yet again and leaked my directions—to return to South Korea empty-handed—to the American side. In the end, the United States abandoned the phrase, "all options are on the table," and the two nations instead agreed to use the phrase "further steps." Even this wording was followed by the emphasis on "confidence that a peaceful resolution can be achieved." We simply were not in a position to ignore the U.S. protest that, since North Korea had made the situation worse, further steps could not be ruled out. Our government had always said that the North Korean nuclear problem should be addressed rationally, and it was difficult to come up with a logic that would allow a rational answer to the U.S. question: "Will we consistently emphasize dialogue in the face of continued provocation by the North?" I am sure our negotiating team was in a rather difficult spot. If we had not accommodated even this much, Washington probably would have seen the Roh administration as a regime that only stubbornly and illogically whined.

Once I received the report that this agreement had been reached, I was finally able to sleep untroubled for the first time in a while. But several days later, when the text was released, public opinion was firmly negative, contrary to my expectations. Some experts even distorted the meaning of the agreement, saying that "further steps" were a precursor to a new phase of sanctions against the North under an agreement between South Korea and the United States. If you look at the development of the North Korean nuclear situation from then on, it is easy to see that this was untrue, but the misunderstanding continues to this day. Even now, certain expert-compiled timelines of the North Korean nuclear issue claim that "further steps" had a major influence on the development of the problem. The phrase elicited so many insults, but I still cannot think of any other way that I could have handled it.

When criticism against "further steps" continued, Roh personally explained the issue at a meeting of chief aides:

> "Further steps" was a compromise phrase that came out of the process of drafting the joint statement and rejecting the American demand to keep all options at its disposal . . . but since such proceedings cannot be explained blow by blow, "further steps" should be understood to be a kind of expression of the principle that should North Korea engage in measures that exceptionally and unprecedentedly worsen the situation, there simply has to be a response. . . . We insist on the principle of peaceful solution but only under the premise that North Korea will not worsen the situation and will sincerely engage in dialogue. Only then can a peaceful solution be possible.... But if the North makes the situation worse, can we really exclude measures that should be taken?

On the afternoon of May 19, 2003, President Roh, having returned from his first ROK-U.S. summit, summoned ranking NSC Secretariat officials down to the director level. But I took along even lower-level bureaucrats with the approval of the president's personal secretary.

Despite the demands of the full schedule of an overseas visit, the president still performed his morning work in the Blue House main hall and greeted us, dressed casually. "I called you because I wanted to share my opinions with you without higher-ups in the mix," he began.

"There seems to be positive feedback now that I have returned, but I also hear some negative takes. Please tell me your opinions about this." Reluctant to let this opportunity pass, I encouraged Kim Chang-soo, the senior executive officer in charge of handling civil society, to discuss the grassroots-level response. Kim said that civil society's reaction to the president's "camp for political prisoners" remark was not so good; the public opinion was that it did not help inter-Korean relations. The president sheepishly smiled. "It was a bit much, wasn't it? The atmosphere was convivial and I felt like I should say something concrete. But I clearly went overboard." He admitted his mistake. He also explained why he had behaved so amiably toward the Americans, to the point of seeming excessive.

> I expressed my gratitude and said nice things while meeting American figures because the U.S. side first made friendly remarks about us, so I returned the gesture. An American figure expressed gratitude for South Korea's support for the Iraq War and praised South Korea's breathtaking development. He also complimented the South Korean people's passion and potential, so I returned the compliment by saying, "It is thanks to the United States." My goal in going to the United States was to meet people who would invest in our economy and to foster a friendly climate and a hopeful atmosphere. I didn't go to the United States to fight; I went to create a friendly atmosphere and I made efforts to achieve this goal.

President Roh's path during the two and a half months between inauguration and the bilateral summit can be divided into two stages. In the beginning, he poured his heart and soul into proclaiming his opposition to war in the face of growing risks on the Korean Peninsula and into forcing the United States to give up its military option. Once he judged that this objective had been achieved to a certain extent, he focused on hastening his efforts toward bringing about a peaceful solution to the North Korean nuclear problem and stabilizing ROK-U.S. relations. But this two-stage action may appear paradoxical if seen purely in the context of the relationship with the United States, which led some to denounce Roh as flip-flopping between being pro- and anti-American. But President Roh was neither: he only sought to find a realistic way to put an end to the military tension on the Korean Peninsula and stabilize the domestic climate.

By proclaiming his opposition to war, President Roh faced trenchant criticism from conservative forces, while the deployment of soldiers to Iraq and "further steps" in the joint statement of the bilateral summit attracted denunciations from progressive forces. This illustrated how the path President Roh took was, from its beginning, narrow and riddled with thorns. What South Korean president would, from the very start of his presidency, want to say discomfiting things to the United States, a superpower and a close ally, no matter how much resolve he had? Conversely, would a president with the personality of President Roh so easily send his own soldiers to an unjustifiable war like the one in Iraq, even if it were waged by an ally? But Roh risked saying discomfiting things about the United States to block the path to war, and in the desperate situation of March 2003, he gave up on his much-cherished principles and deployed soldiers to Iraq, for the sake of peace on the Korean Peninsula. It was because he was no mere citizen; he was president.

The President's Anguish:
"What is the Point of Giving Such People a Few Men?"

Roh made it clear during his candidacy that as president, he would speak plainly to the United States. In his policymaking, he pursued an autonomous diplomacy and autonomous defense. But the threat of North Korean nuclear arms on the Korean Peninsula and the existing national security structure that depended on the United States frequently limited the scope of policy choices at the president's disposal, sometimes forcing him to make painful decisions. His anguish over such decisions reached its peak with the Iraq deployment.

Sunday, October 12, 2003: For the first time in a while, I had an early lunch at home and was taking a shower, when my wife furiously knocked on the bathroom door with a call from the Blue House. I was barely out of the shower when the president's voice emerged out of the phone. "What are you up to? Why don't we have lunch?" When I told him I had been in the shower after lunch, he invited me to tea, and I headed right over.

This was the first time since I had become the NSC deputy secretary-general that the president had summoned me at home on a day off. As I rushed to drive over to the Blue House, I wondered what it was about. Dressed like an off-duty middle-aged man, the president met me in the reception room, overlooking a garden that had begun to lose some of its green in the October weather. Normally, there would be a secretary in attendance for the purpose of recording, but there was none of that. The president usually was wary of one-on-one meetings because of the potential ill-effects, so it was almost unimaginable that no one else was sitting in on a meeting with a policy aide. But of course, meetings such as this would never lead to a policy decision or an actual presidential order.

"I just wanted to have a little chat." Given the president's tone it seemed that this was no urgent matter. But this was also a period marked by major foreign affairs and national security matters—the Iraq deployment, the USFK reduction, Pyongyang's nuclear development, the relocation of the Yongsan garrison, autonomous defense—all of which were scattered around the political landscape like mines. It was difficult to get a sense of why the president had summoned me.

The president took out a cigarette—despite having said he had quit—and held it between his lips. It was, of course, about Iraq. He must have been experiencing many mixed feelings; only two days earlier he had made an explosive remark that he would re-seek popular mandate from the electorate, given the ongoing controversy over the Millennium Democratic Party's secret presidential election fund.[2] So it was surprising that he would bring up the Iraq deployment now. Even a morning meeting on October 10 was focused entirely on the USFK reduction. Those outside the Blue House, including the media and political opponents, were probably thinking that the president was meeting with his aides and figures from the ruling faction to discuss how best to overcome the electoral fund scandal. But what preoccupied the president was not the issue of seeking renewed popular mandate, but the deployment of additional soldiers to Iraq—that was how great his concern was. In fact, outside the Blue House, the country was in an uproar over his asking for the electorate's trust all over again, but the president was remarkably calm.

The additional U.S. troop deployment to Iraq caused the president pain on several fronts. Roh himself was seeking answers to many fundamental questions over whether or not to deploy soldiers. His recognition of the reality that additional deployment was unavoidable simply went against his principles. While my own dilemma could in no way be compared to his, I still felt we were in the same boat. The path Roh ought to take as president of the Republic of Korea and his own character and philosophy were clearly in collision, plunging him into deep agony.

---

2   [Roh was a member of the Millennium Democratic Party (renamed simply as the Democratic party in 2005) when he sought the presidency. However, he renounced his membership after the inauguration, and his supporters in the National Assembly also left the Millennium Democratic Party to form a new one, called Uri, short for the Yeollin Uri Party.]

If freed from the harsh reality of international politics, Roh Moo-hyun the individual saw the Iraq War not as a war for world peace, nor a just war, but an invasion. That was why Iraq was no place for South Korean soldiers. The United States had attacked Iraq based on the argument that Saddam Hussein might be manufacturing weapons of mass destruction, but it found nothing; there simply was no rationale for the war. As noted above, during the first deployment in the spring his speech to the nation made no mention of the rationale for getting involved in the Iraq War. He had ordered that the relevant passage be deleted.

But that was all he could do. Inside the Blue House, Roh Moo-hyun the private citizen did not exist. He occupied that place as president of the Republic of Korea and he had to uphold the ROK-U.S. alliance. Half of all South Koreans believed that our national interests could be advanced by readily accepting requests from this ally, no matter what such requests were. It was also not possible to ignore the sentiment that additional deployment was a moral duty to the United States, which had sacrificed some fifty thousand young men of its own to protect our country. If only these factors were at play, it might have been possible to ask for understanding at times and resort to persuasion at others, all so that we could continue to work in accordance with our principles. But a bigger issue, the North Korean nuclear problem, lay before us.

The nuclear problem could not be solved without cooperating with the United States. With the Bush administration defining Pyongyang as part of the Axis of Evil and ready to punish it militarily, and North Korea provoking the United States in response, cooperating with the United States was essential if we were to prevent a collision between the two and create peace. We could not solve the nuclear problem on our own by independently persuading North Korea. If we deployed soldiers to Iraq, there was a possibility that we could strengthen, even a little, our right to voice opinions to the United States about peace on the Korean Peninsula. But what was truly frightening was the kind of tension that might result from our refusal to deploy troops. Given the Bush administration's character, it might become difficult to win respect for our determination to prevent military conflicts on the Korean Peninsula. It was very possible that the Bush administration would treat us like an invisible man during discussions over the North Korean nuclear issue, much less respect our opinions. The president was going through all these different scenarios in his head in a quest to reach the best possible decision.

But for Roh Moo-hyun the politician, additional deployment meant serious political damage; he would lose half of his support base, while the other half would only reluctantly agree because they trusted Roh, even though deployment went against their own beliefs. Polls already predicted this unfortunate outcome. According to a September 18 report from the office of the Blue House secretary in charge of gauging popular opinion, the breakdown between the "yes" and "no" camps was clearly different depending on the nature of the entity that conducted the poll. The progressive *Kyunghyang Ilbo*'s poll was evenly divided; according to the conservative *Chosun Ilbo*, 66.3 percent were for, while 33.7 percent were against additional deployment; and the leftist *Hankyoreh* showed the opposite, with 37.7 percent against and 62.3 percent for deployment. For the most part, supporters of President Roh were against additional deployment, while his political opposition supported the action.

On September 29, 2003, at a banquet commemorating the fiftieth anniversary of the ROK-U.S. alliance, President Roh talked frankly with U.S. ambassador Hubbard about the impact the Iraq deployment would have on his political standing:

> Most of the people who support me oppose the deployment. If I decide in favor of deployment, about fifty percent of them will pull their support for me on this basis alone. The other half will withdraw their opposition to deployment just for my sake. Meanwhile, those who support deployment are without exception all those who oppose me politically.

But the president did not take into consideration the problem of losing half his political base; he deemed that the deciding factor between accommodating and refusing the deployment request ought to be the North Korean nuclear problem. Roh thought that a change in the American position was essential to realizing peace on the Korean Peninsula, which was destabilized by the North Korean nuclear problem, and that we should proactively create a structure that allowed for cooperation with the United States. He therefore emphasized in several meetings that any additional deployment on our part should be predicated on the stabilization of the situation on the Korean Peninsula and on making progress in solving the North Korean nuclear problem.

After much deliberation, the president edged toward the view that additional deployment was inevitable. In fact, when the United States requested additional deployment, the president instinctively knew it would be difficult to refuse. I felt the same. There was a sentiment within conservative circles of our society, as well as in Washington, that our refusal to deploy soldiers would amount to destroying the alliance. There were still more difficult problems facing us in our management of the ROK-U.S. relationship, like the realignment and reduction of the USFK and stopping the North's construction of a light water reactor. We had to determine how to use the additional deployment to smooth the path toward solving the North Korean nuclear problem, and how to set the number and character of troops deployed to minimize loss of our soldiers' lives. The NSC Secretariat had already recommended that the president opt for a small-scale force of noncombat troops.

But within the government, practically no foreign affairs or national security advisors understood how painful it was for the president to decide in favor of deployment, against his own philosophy, at the price of seeing his own political base collapse. They mostly thought that the Iraq War was a justifiable war waged by the United States for world peace. Although they could never publicly criticize the president's take on the war, they considered it taboo even to rationally discuss the nature of this war, calling that action itself "anti-American." They argued that this was the perfect opportunity to engage in a large-scale troop deployment, strengthen the ROK-U.S. alliance, and secure economic rights in Iraq, which held large quantities of oil. Some within the military even said that this was a rare opportunity for the South Korean forces to experience military operations on the ground. More than anything, they thought that it was necessary to accommodate the American request and strengthen the alliance in the aftermath of the disagreement with the United States over publicly disclosing the USFK reduction negotiations. While there is no doubt that they made such arguments in the national interest, rare was the official who worried equally about the ROK-U.S. alliance, some economic interest that may or may not accrue, the bigger political principles at stake, and the potential sacrifices by our soldiers. The president's belief in dignified negotiations to further our national interests—even with an ally such as the United States—simply did not get through to most officials.

Even Foreign Minister Yoon Young-kwan, whom the president trusted very much, seemed to be taking a different path from what the president wished. Once Yoon made a gambit to emphasize to the president the need to accommodate the American request for combat troop deployment. At a banquet at the official residence that doubled as an unofficial meeting of foreign affairs and national security advisors, Yoon began to read aloud a diplomatic cable from the South Korean embassy in Washington, which allegedly showed the U.S. response to our government's attitude. The text, quotes of midlevel American officials, detailed the ROK government's mostly lukewarm response toward additional deployment, its efforts to link deployment to the North Korean nuclear problem, and its demand for a change in the Bush administration's approach to North Korean nuclear arms. The officials stated that the American government was greatly disappointed and expressed concerns over the future of the ROK-U.S. alliance. The cable was full of explicit criticism of the South Korean government and it lamented the future of the alliance, to the point of coming across as threatening. From my view, it was obviously a message demonstrating the American's secret intent to extract deployment at a level Washington desired and to tame the Roh administration.

But here was the issue: normally even those diplomatic cables that feature the remarks of another nation's highest leader are edited into a type of report before the president is briefed on them—and remarks from another nation's administrative-level figures are not even included in reports to the president, except under special circumstances. Reading such a diplomatic cable in its entirety in the president's presence is inconceivable; it is enough to be considered a breach in protocol. Yoon's move implied that he did not believe the president was in touch with reality. He apparently wanted to directly inform Roh of the American view of his administration's attitudes, to make him see the "truth" and come to the right decision. But the president had been regularly checking reactions from every part of Washington through the NSC Secretariat and knew the reality better than anyone. The reality, as seen by the foreign minister, was composed of only a single player—the United States—but the president was coolly seeking a solution amidst a far more complicated reality made up of the United States, the South Korean people, and our history.

When Yoon finished reading, the room fell silent. The president rubbed his face with one hand and shared his feelings in a grim voice. It appeared that the president felt he had been seriously insulted and the dignity of the nation wounded. Foreign Affairs Advisor Ban Ki-moon tried to downplay the meaning of the remarks by U.S. officials and advised the president not to take the cable seriously, but Roh's face was full of both rage and sadness. The president expressed his feelings about existing ROK-U.S. relations and said that they should not be allowed to continue in such a one-sided manner, and that he would fix this unequal relationship even if it meant putting his presidency at stake. Suppressing his anger, he said firmly, "If my efforts somehow break ROK-U.S. relations, the next president will be able to create a more balanced ROK-U.S. relationship."

The president's concerns deepened after several experiences like this. In my presence, he once sighed and said, "I struggle to believe that people like these could persuade the United States, regardless of how many soldiers I authorize for deployment." The president's lament echoed in my ears for a long time. As the person in charge of managing the practicalities of additional deployment, I felt my entire body shrink under the responsibility and I felt remorse in the face of the president's honesty, which bordered on despair. I mustered the courage to remind him of what I had told him already:

> Mr. President, please don't worry too much. The United States originally wanted three to five thousand light infantry soldiers. So even if we come up with something along the lines of three thousand, it is not outside the American demand and gives us room to negotiate. When it comes to the character of the force, the U.S. opposes our dispatching medical or engineering personnel, so there is nothing to be done about that. But I will come up with a way to create a non-combat force that is focused on assisting Iraqi reconstruction.

The American Request for Additional Forces and the NSC's Search for a "Korean Model"

On September 4, 2003, the U.S. government made an official request to the South Korean government for a division-sized combat force to maintain security in Iraq. Since in spring 2003 the ROK had already deployed two units—Seohee and Jema—consisting of some six hundred engineering and medical personnel, this was a second deployment request. In his request, U.S. deputy undersecretary of defense Lawless floated as an acceptable example the equivalent of a so-called Polish light infantry division, with a minimum of three to fifty thousand soldiers, and possessing a combat brigade. But this was an example of the least that Washington expected; if possible, they wanted far more soldiers to be deployed.

The request for additional deployment made the administration's management of national security extremely complicated and difficult. Already the South Korean government was wrestling with a mountain of major national security and diplomatic issues. Far from reaching a solution, the North Korean nuclear problem was worsening. The Yongsan garrison relocation alone was dividing national opinion and thrusting the country into a sense of crisis over the cost of relocation and its impact on national security. The problem of the proposed USFK reduction, too, was slowly surfacing. Under these circumstances, having to deal with a second deployment to Iraq, which would undoubtedly further divide the nation's opinion, was enough to make my stomach turn.

President Roh, however, ordered that existing national security matters and the additional deployment be handled separately—except in connection with the North Korean nuclear problem. All other matters would be handled regardless of the deployment issue, but he showed his resolve to make progress on the North Korean nuclear situation an important element of considering the deployment.

As expected, the additional deployment divided opinions within the government into several camps. The military leadership, rallying around the Defense Ministry, along with Foreign Ministry officials who had long dealt with the ROK-U.S. alliance, called unanimously for a swift acceptance of the American request. Some even argued that to further the alliance we should deploy even more soldiers than requested by Washington. And some said that since the structure of the bilateral alliance depended for the most part on the United States for security, it was impossible to refuse the American demand—but by proactively acceding to the demand we would move toward strengthening our position within the ROK-U.S. alliance and on the North Korean nuclear problem.

Of all the foreign affairs and national security apparatuses within the government, the only one offering a measured position on the American request was the NSC Secretariat, and at the center of this camp was the president. Considering the potential sacrifices by ROK soldiers and the possibility that the nation could be mired in the Iraq problem, Roh had to be careful. Public opinion, too, was divided. Even if we accommodated the deployment request, there was no guarantee that the United States would shift its position on the North Korean nuclear problem. From the president's perspective, it was necessary at the very least to consider all these fundamental issues. And this required more time.

The president did not reveal his intentions and proceeded measuredly. He leaned in the direction of consulting public opinion before deciding the government's position. He ordered advisors to research just what kind of danger we might be exposed to in sending combat forces and to seriously consider how deployment might affect diplomatic relations with Arab states. He cautioned against the tendency to link deployment to economic gains, stressing that any actual economic benefit would not be great, and that the government should not be using the lives of our soldiers as collateral to bargain for economic advantage. Roh emphasized that, above all, we must approach the deployment issue within the broader context of the East Asian political order, including the security of the Korean Peninsula. He said that he would carefully assess the situation and take all responsibility for the decision.

On September 15, 2003, President Roh summoned National Security Advisor Ra Jong-yil and me. "The rationale for us in deploying additional soldiers is increased peace on the Korean Peninsula in the context of the North Korean nuclear problem. So please study this point carefully," he ordered. "How can we persuade the public if there cannot be any optimistic outlook on resolving the North Korean nuclear problem? Surely we cannot create another source of anxiety in Iraq when the situation on the Korean Peninsula itself is worrisome?" The president judged that sending soldiers overseas would be difficult with South Korea's own sense of national security looking dire; the United States, as the party making the deployment request, must first make a sincere effort to calm the situation on the Korean Peninsula. This was the president's most urgent task—it was not appropriate to allow a single government entity such as the defense or foreign ministry to handle it. Both were already singing in sync that the American request for combat troops should be accommodated. While unprecedented, there was no choice but for the NSC Secretariat, which answered to the president, to oversee the whole affair, as it did the North Korean nuclear problem.

On September 26, at a national security meeting of relevant ministers chaired by the president, I presented "Strategic Factors to Consider in Relation to the Deployment Request," a report drafted by the NSC Secretariat. I argued that the deployment decision should be reviewed over a sufficiently long period, for several reasons: the uncertainty over the North Korean nuclear problem meant we lacked an optimistic outlook on peace and stability on the Korean Peninsula; the United States had not yet proposed a plan on how to reconstruct Iraq and no international consensus had formed; and there was still no clear national consensus on deployment. My assessment contained the president's resolve and was meant to overrule the strong opinion within and outside the government that the decision to deploy soldiers should be reached as early and quickly as possible. Prime Minister Goh Kun said,

If the UN Security Council approves the formation of a multi-national force in Iraq, the United States will obtain an international mandate, and from our position it will be difficult to refuse the repeated U.S. demands for an early decision on deployment.

Many in attendance expressed agreement. The president saw that the ROK-U.S. summit at the Asia-Pacific Economic Cooperation (APEC) meeting on October 20 would be the ideal time to decide on deployment. The president noted that if in the end the government was leaning against deployment, it might be appropriate to simply delay the decision.

In the event the decision was for additional deployment, I presented a pilot "Korean model" of support for Iraq, as envisioned by the NSC Secretariat. This model conceived of a reinforcement force that would take charge of interrelated goals such as humanitarian aid, economic assistance, and security assurance in a specific geographic area; it would take on the character of a postwar revitalization support force that would essentially improve the quality of life of Iraqi citizens and contribute to early stabilization. One part of the force would provide postwar revitalization support, consisting of a medical unit for humanitarian assistance, an engineering unit for postwar reconstruction support, and economic projects bringing state-level economic aid for Iraq; and the other part would provide security maintenance, mobilizing an appropriate number of light infantry troops for the purpose of protecting residents. The concept would prioritize postwar revitalization support, but still deploy some military personnel to handle security within an area.

This pilot model did not satisfy any one participant at the meeting. For those arguing for deploying combat personnel, the plan drew suspicion for only pretending to carry out the security maintenance the United States so badly wanted, given its emphasis on reconstruction assistance. And for the president and the NSC Secretariat that wanted to avoid deploying combat troops, there could be no escaping the criticism that we were doing just that. The model was immediately killed. But something was achieved: I had gained the confidence that I could come up with a noncombat troop deployment model, if I could somehow work out the question of security maintenance.

8

A Choice That Satisfied No One

The Initial Decision on October 18: Things Gained and Lost

On October 16, 2003, Foreign Minister Yoon Young-kwan briefed the president over breakfast. I was also present. The briefing covered the maneuverings within the United Nations (UN) over Iraq deployment, and the Republic of Korea (ROK)–U.S. summit scheduled for October 20. Yoon reported that the UN Security Council would on that day approve the decision to deploy a multinational force to Iraq. Yoon advised it was now time for the ROK government to decide on deployment; it was not feasible, in light of our alliance, to keep Washington waiting any longer. He stressed that there should be an early decision on deployment to bring about a change in the American position on the North Korean nuclear problem at the upcoming summit.

The UN Security Council did unanimously pass Resolution 1511 on that day; it approved "a multinational force under unified command to take all necessary measures to contribute to the maintenance of security and stability in Iraq" and urged UN member states "to contribute assistance . . . including military forces, to the multinational force." Of course, the passing of the resolution, pushed by the American side, did not mean an invasion had suddenly become a just war. But at least on paper, a UN member state could send soldiers to Iraq under the UN banner.

Domestic surveys had showed that 74 percent of South Koreans would support additional deployment if such a resolution for a multinational force were passed at the United Nations. Therefore, the president and the government paid keen attention to movements within the international community and the contents and direction of this resolution. We had expected the resolution to take a considerable amount of time to pass, given the difficulties surrounding the discussion at the United Nations. After deciding to formulate our position depending on the trajectory of the resolution, we thought that we could buy a certain amount of time to allow for a domestic discussion on additional deployment. But this resolution ended up being passed earlier than expected.

And there was yet more news. National Security Advisor Ra Jong-yil, visiting Washington as a special envoy carrying Roh's letter for President Bush, sent an optimistic report that the United States seemed on the verge of issuing a more accommodating stance toward the restart of the Six-Party Talks if we were to decide to deploy soldiers. Roh had already conveyed to the Americans, through Minister Yoon at the meeting of the ROK-U.S. foreign ministers in New York on September 25, that stabilization of the situation on the Korean Peninsula through progress on the North Korean nuclear problem was essential to us before reaching a decision on deployment.

But during this process, the U.S. State Department realized that we were trying to link the North Korean nuclear issue to deployment, with the goal of using additional deployment as a chance to influence U.S. North Korea policy. As is well known, Foreign Minister Yoon gave U.S. secretary of state Colin Powell a book criticizing the Bush administration's North Korea policy and arguing for a "great bargain."[1] Yoon's action prompted great American discontent; I do not understand why he did such a thing, since he had been opposed to linking the North Korean nuclear problem to the deployment.

American officials, unhappy, noted that South Korea's additional deployment to Iraq should not be tied to issues like the North Korean nuclear arms problem, and should be decided by itself, as something that would strengthen the alliance and the ROK's international role. Following this diplomatic incident, I could see where the Americans were coming from, but I also thought they were taking advantage of an opportunity

---

1   [The book was *Crisis on the Korean Peninsula*, written by Michael E. O'Hanlon and Mike M. Mochizuki, both senior fellows at the Brookings Institution.]

to tame the South Korean government. They were telling us to do as we were told, but given our own national interests, we could not.

At this point the South Korean government unambiguously informed the U.S. government that the North Korean nuclear problem and the decision to send additional soldiers were not linked. But we still had hope. Our position was that the issues were not linked, but we simultaneously sent a message of hope for progress in the Six-Party Talks. Even in the personal letter carried by Ra, President Roh clarified that deployment and the North Korean nuclear problem would be "separately handled." But he also wrote, "We can have a more concrete optimistic outlook on peace and stability on the Korean Peninsula if the Six-Party Talks are expeditiously held. . . . This development would be of big help to my management of state affairs." Roh added, "I hope that you will once again exercise your great leadership so that the national security condition on the Korean Peninsula, as caused by the North Korean nuclear problem, can be improved." In other words, he exercised courtesy by declaring a disconnect between North Korean nuclear arms and deployment, but emphasized that progress in resolving the North Korean nuclear problem was necessary even if it was just to smooth the decision to send extra soldiers. This shows how desperate we were to gain some progress toward solving the nuclear problem and reaching stability on the Korean Peninsula.

We believed that the United States would carefully listen to what President Roh wanted, even as it expressed its dissatisfaction. The situation on the Korean Peninsula was deteriorating. The North Korean foreign ministry announced on October 2, 2003, that Pyongyang had completed reprocessing more than eight thousand spent fuel rods for the purpose of using the resulting plutonium to strengthen its nuclear deterrent force. President Roh urgently wanted to the United States take a positive stance toward a peaceful solution to the North Korean nuclear problem.

There were many who judged the South Korean government's maneuvering on this matter as diplomatically immature. I accept that our method was rather blunt. But the outcome was significant. The United States may have expressed its unhappiness to South Korea, but it began to respond positively to our hope for progress in the Six-Party Talks. We received a report from Ra in Washington that U.S. national security advisor Condoleezza Rice said, "We are proactively trying to make the second Six-Party Talks take place as early as possible," and had even expressed interest in knowing "whether there can be deployment if

Six-Party Talks were held expeditiously and conditions were achieved at the talk allowing for progress in resolving substantial problems." Finally, we could anticipate that the bilateral summit at the Asia-Pacific Economic Cooperation (APEC) meeting could create an opening for progress in solving the North Korean nuclear problem.

With progress on these fronts, it was difficult to delay the decision on additional deployment any longer; the conditions proposed by the president had, to a degree, been satisfied. After receiving Minister Yoon's report President Roh calmly said, as though he had just reached his conclusion overnight, that he would decide on deployment by holding a National Security Council (NSC) meeting just before the APEC summit. Only the principle of deployment would be decided at this time; the more sensitive question of the size and character of the force would be determined later. The president would accommodate the U.S. demand for an early decision on additional deployment, but the more controversial issue of the troops' number and character would require additional discussion.

Advisors who had argued for an early decision on deployment were relieved even if not completely satisfied; I myself, who had been carrying out the president's will and arguing for a careful decision while moderating relevant event schedules, felt a bad headache coming on.

The president's two-step decision process regarding deployment was actually quite wise. But its timing made things rather difficult for me. I had deemed it necessary for Roh to consult civic organizations directly about additional deployment and had asked Kim Ki-sik—an official at the People's Solidarity for Participatory Democracy (PSPD), a prominent progressive NGO—to schedule an October 17 lunch where the president would attend a round-table discussion.[2] But on the morning of October 16 the president had already decided in favor of deployment; the NSC meeting that would formalize it as government policy was confirmed for October 18. With the president's preliminary decision made one day before and the official decision scheduled for one day after the round table, there was no way civic organizations would not rise up. They would most certainly express outrage at being used as mere window dressing, and fiercely oppose the government's decision. It was now going to be difficult to prevent hostile public reaction, even if progress were to be

2   [During the Roh administration, civic organizations—often dubbed "civil society"—referred to progressives NGOs that shared Roh's ideological leanings. They became a thorn in his side when he attempted to pursue more centrist policies.]

made on the North Korean nuclear problem. We were trapped with no way to move forward or backward.

The media environment was bad enough as it was; if civic organizations turned their backs, governance would become even more difficult. I considered canceling the round table, but that would simply be criticized as an outright insult to civil society. I wanted to ask the president, "What about the round table?" but I could not; I knew the anguish and thought that had gone into his decision. Even if I told him, there was no way to change his schedule: he was bound for Bangkok on October 19.

The scheduled NSC meeting was held on October 18 and the decision was reached to additionally deploy our soldiers to Iraq. As he announced this decision, the president said, "If the relevant ministries begin speculating on the character of the force to be deployed or other matters, it would be meaningless to divide the decision-making process into two steps." He warned, "There is a possibility of public misunderstanding, so be cautious not to engage in any kind of speculation."

At the ROK-U.S. summit in Bangkok on October 20, President Bush expressed his gratitude for the South Korean government's decision to send more soldiers to Iraq. President Roh explained the difficulties faced by the South Korean government and said, "We respect the American demand and needs as much as possible, but we seek to organize the deployed forces in a way that considers the situation in South Korea, so we beg for American understanding for our own position." President Bush replied, "It would be nice if you could send more troops, but I fully understand the pressures on you."

As anticipated, Bush brought up the North Korean nuclear problem: "We will consider the matter of providing North Korea with regime security and will put in writing a public mention of this." Although he expressed strong distrust of the North, Bush said, "Secretary Powell will draft, with the five parties including North Korea, a text that favorably expresses the provision of regime security, and he will consult other nations." In response to this change in position by Bush, Pyongyang also said through its Foreign Ministry spokesperson on October 25 that it was willing to consider a "promise of regime security in writing" from President Bush. This promising development led to the start of the second Six-Party Talks the following year, on February 25, 2004.

When the decision to deploy additional soldiers was announced, a public debate raged between opposing camps. Supporters of the president were greatly disappointed. The government's explanation that it had taken into consideration the ROK-U.S. alliance, peace on the peninsula, and national interest did not convince them. And when the government, which had claimed to approach the additional deployment question cautiously, suddenly appeared to decide in favor of additional deployment, it only served to provoke them further. This had been expected. The government said that it had decided only on additional deployment, and the important questions of the scale and character of that deployment remained open, but civic organizations took issue. Many claimed that the president had met with the representatives of various civil society organizations just for show. That was not the government's intention, of course, but as the person who had set up the round table, I had few excuses to offer.

Now a fierce public movement against deployment was all but certain. Up until this point, most civic organizations had drawn the line at opposing the deployment of a combat force, but now a more radical argument against deployment of any kind was bound to gain currency. Even if the government avoided deploying combat troops and sent soldiers only as part of a unit for peace-building, civic organizations would no doubt charge that such soldiers were still, in effect, combat troops since they carried weapons for personal protection.

All this was the fault of the government, and much of it my own fault since I had been aiding the president from the sidelines. I criticized myself harshly. But the decision had already been made, and the president would successfully use the summit with Bush to propel the discussion surrounding the North Korean nuclear problem. I spent the weekend in a foul mood but scheduled an appearance for Monday, October 20, on a news program anchored by well-known media personality Son Suk-hee, plunging myself into the task of persuading the public.

"Two to Three Thousand Troops are Appropriate"

Once the government decided in favor of sending soldiers, most media outlets and those in favor of sending combat troops moved to speak of a large-scale deployment as a settled fact. Even though the president clearly issued a gag order before his departure to Bangkok, as soon as the preliminary decision was announced the media reported—quoting unnamed foreign affairs and national security officials—that the size of deployment would be at least five to six thousand soldiers. This was a number that even I, the person in charge of the deployment matter, had never brought up. This number grew by one to two thousand every day the president spent abroad; by week's end, there was even a report that we were sending twelve thousand soldiers. Taking advantage of the president's absence, the government faction in favor of a large-scale deployment was finally speaking out, full of conviction and beyond compromise. At the Blue House, Defense Advisor Kim Hee-sang argued that an entire division with somewhere around eight thousand soldiers was appropriate.

One factor that fed this growing estimate was the hope of the Americans. As the United States began facing rejection from countries it had called on for deployment, its expectations of South Korea could only grow in proportion. To borrow a classical Chinese expression, "one dare not hope but still ardently desires." South Korea's conservative faction was scratching America's itch by strongly arguing for a large-scale deployment. And in a perverse development, that argument itself was reflected in U.S. policymaking and fed the American expectation that South Korea might approve a large-scale deployment.

Amidst this chaos, at lunch on Saturday, October 25, I briefed the president, who had just returned from the APEC summit. The president found it unfortunate that during his absence rampant rumors had inflated the scale of the deployment. In particular, Roh expressed his deep regret that some figures inside the government had promoted large-scale deployment. He asked me for a solution.

I answered, "I think it's time for me to put things in order."

"Let's do that."

"I will make it two to three thousand." That was the plan that the NSC Secretariat had drafted and informed the president of well before.

At noon on October 27, I snuck out of a meeting of chief aides chaired by the president and met reporter Cho Bok-rae, a member of the Blue House press corps from *Yonhap News*, at the Lotte Hotel Metropolitan. I had made this appointment the weekend before. I simply told him, "The government policy has not been finalized, but it would be rational to think of it [the size of deployment] as two to three thousand." I told him this on the condition that I would be named only as a "key government official." I made the remark knowing that people would understand that a force of such size would not be for combat purposes. From Cho's perspective, there was no reason not to report it immediately, since he had been handed an exclusive. But even if he granted me anonymity as a "key government official," only NSC officials could do something like this—to use a member of the Blue House press corps to crush rumors about the specific size of a combat force. As soon as the *Yonhap News* report went out, the press simply used my name instead of calling the source a "key government official."

Until then I never revealed my feelings about the deployment during meetings or conversations among foreign affairs and national security advisors. I personally opposed deployment without a rationale, but I believed that, realistically, it was unavoidable. My conclusion was reached with an eye to national interest, but my conception of national interest differed from those who advocated for combat soldiers. I looked for an approach that would allow us to deploy a relatively small number of non-combat troops and limit the sacrifice of our troops, while still maintaining a healthy ROK-U.S. alliance and a minimum status in the international community. But to those senior officials advocating a large-scale combat deployment, I was betraying an ally and endangering ROK-U.S. relations. They saw my position as tantamount to opposing deployment. Knowing this, I refrained from speaking out to avoid worsening the internal dispute.

The deployment issue was not easy to resolve through debate because it ultimately did not come down to who was right or wrong; it was a fight over hardened convictions between factions that had lived very different lives in pursuit of national interest and big principles. It was far more likely that debating the problem would lead to anger and personal attacks. I thought, in the end, that only the president's resolve could put an end to all this, so there was no reason for me to express my own opinion. Above all, I was in charge of overseeing the deployment from inside the government. I merely explained the NSC Secretariat's established plan and sought cooperation from the Blue House Secretariat and chief secretaries in charge of handling civil society and political figures.

My little media leak helped to calm the rumors about a large-scale combat force deployment. But I was condemned from every direction. The foreign and defense ministers and the foreign affairs advisor promptly gave media interviews characterizing my remarks as a private opinion; they tried to sow the idea that nothing had been decided yet. They probably thought my leak—which directly contravened their own argument for deploying a mass-scale combat force—more than a little unfortunate. But despite their denials, the media began to treat my remarks as established fact. There was no other way to see it: I was one of the president's closest aides and I had made my remark in spite of the presidential embargo.

The conservative faction showered me with criticism for making the case for a smaller than expected, noncombat force. Within the Foreign

Ministry, some even compared my approach to "offering ice cream when asked for rice cake." The opposition Grand National Party accused me of overstepping authority and demanded my resignation. Some media outlets charged that I was using the president's trust to wield unparalleled power and control various ministries through the NSC. One newspaper even ran a daily editorial to attack me and the NSC Secretariat. It was around this time that my colleagues and I at the NSC Secretariat were given the media nickname of the "Autonomy Faction." Some unconscionable diplomats criticized the NSC Secretariat employees as "anti-American" and even "Taliban" in front of U.S. officials in charge of Korean affairs. But if we had been truly guilty of such inclinations, we would have opposed the deployment outright.

Can a president of a country divided internally between progressives and conservatives, and externally into North and South, carry out diplomacy and national security policies according to his own ideological leanings? If he truly cared about national interests and the people, he would probably choose policies that did not isolate one side of the population, even while he aspired to stay true to his ideological convictions. Such decisions would be founded on common sense and rationality rather than ideology. But even that much is difficult to realize. That is why advisors must assist the president so that he can lead the country in the right direction without deviating from common sense and rationality. They should be too busy to pay attention to other things. That, at least, should be the norm.

The situation in Iraq deteriorated further after the government decided in favor of deploying additional South Korean soldiers. Terror attacks intensified in tandem with the commencement of Ramadan; resistance from the Saddam Hussein faction was not inconsiderable. It felt as though Iraq was falling into a large-scale anti-terror war rather than shifting to a stage of stabilization. Although the UN Security Council had approved the multinational force, those countries that the United States had asked to deploy soldiers were beginning to shy away.

Roh sought one more review of the situation in Iraq. Between late September and early October, he had dispatched a twelve-person joint civilian-official investigation team to the country, headed by a brigadier general from the Defense Ministry. The report that he received was too perfunctory, too sketchy to be of any use for policymaking. The Defense Ministry disclosed the report to the public, but the overwhelming opinion was that the report was simply deficient. The president judged that a more accurate and serious field report was necessary and ordered the NSC Secretariat to consider dispatching a second investigation team.

But the defense and foreign ministry officials felt it would suffice to decide the scale and character of deployment on the basis of the first report; they did not believe dispatching another team was necessary and worried that doing so would be seen by the United States as an excuse to further delay deployment. Some within the Defense Ministry started to leak to the press, from early October onward, a completely baseless story that the deployed South Korean forces would replace the U.S. 101st Airborne Division occupying northern Mosul. It was an attempt to influence the national mood.

But the president was firm. The second investigation team was created during the APEC summit. The Defense Ministry, already angered by the dispatch of another investigation team, made clear from the beginning that no one from its ranks would head the new team. I thought it should be headed by a Foreign Ministry official and received presidential approval for the idea. But when I asked the Foreign Ministry to name the team leader, their response was lukewarm, and they said an order from the foreign minister was necessary. They knew, however, that when the NSC Secretariat made a request, it was based on the president's will—so it was odd that they were bringing up this order. I had the feeling that Foreign Minister Yoon, who was attending a meeting in Madrid of foreign ministers from various nations to discuss support for the Iraq War, was vetoing the second investigation team, and immediately called him. Yoon was unexpectedly adamant. He said his ministry would not supply the team leader because a decision should be made based on the report from the first team. I emphasized that the president had ordered the Foreign Ministry to head the team, but he insisted that his ministry would not do it. I did not know whether it was because he was dissatisfied with the idea or because the Defense Ministry had been criticized after heading the first investigation. I was confounded and in a difficult situation.

Regardless of Minister Yoon's unhappiness with the president over additional deployment, his response, strictly speaking, was insubordination, and needed to be reported to the president, but there was still much time before the president's scheduled return. I convened an Iraq deployment task force at the NSC and sought opinions on who should head the second investigation team, in light of the Foreign Ministry's refusal. It was logical that a ministry overseen by a member of the NSC Standing Committee should provide the team leader, but given the nature of Iraq deployment, the Unification Ministry was automatically ruled out, and the National Intelligence Service (NIS) could not do it, given the nature of its work. In the end, it had to be either the Office for Government Policy Coordination or the NSC Secretariat. Following the discussion, I called the president, who was busy with summit diplomacy; I reported my phone conversation with the foreign minister and recommended either a senior official from the Office for Government Policy Coordination, or the NSC director of information management Kim Man-bok be the Iraq team leader. The president ordered that the NSC head the team, saying that entrusting the position to the Office for Government Policy Coordination would amount to avoidance of responsibility by the Blue House.

In a desperate measure, Kim Man-bok led a team of thirteen members to Iraq on October 31. The team did its best to get a sense of the local situation in Iraq and submitted a report that possessed a sufficient level of objectivity to satisfy civil society. The fact that during the investigation the team's hotel came under mortar fire as soon as they checked out served to show the public and the president the situation in Iraq even more vividly than did the contents of the report.

Dispatching the Consultation Team to the United States and Advice from President Musharraf

The president continued to be cautious in the run-up to his second-stage—and final—decision on additional deployment. High-ranking officials in foreign affairs and national security were unhappy that the president was taking so much time over something that could be quickly decided. When he dispatched a second investigation team and did not intervene in the aftermath of my October 27 remarks about a force of two or three thousand soldiers being appropriate, their dissatisfaction and suspicion grew. They were clearly worried that the president might decide in favor of a small-scale noncombat deployment and thought such a decision would complicate the ROK-U.S. alliance and plunge the nation into danger. They therefore tried their best to influence the president's decision until the end. Outside pressure to actively accept the U.S. demand also grew, led by the opposition and conservative media. Civil society, meanwhile, grew louder in its opposition to the deployment.

On October 30, Roh revealed to his aides a few very important decisions he had made. He ordered that, before the scale and character of the deployment was decided, there should first be a consultation with the United States; he made explicit, however, that this consultation was more about informing and persuading the Americans to see our situation than about clarifying the American request. About the deployment itself, he ordered that efforts be made to identify an approach that would help calm the local Iraqi sentiment, regardless of whether we would manage a region jointly with the United States or independently. He ordered that a deployment of two to three thousand soldiers be announced, principally made up of noncombat units, although this was by no means the final decision.

When the president proposed a noncombat force of that size, most in attendance were in shock and despair. What they had feared since the day I leaked information to the press had become a reality. Some tried to sway the outcome by suggesting, "Let's not tell the United States the scale and nature of the deployed force we have in mind. Let's first share information on the war against terror and confirm the U.S. intention and request before deciding on the scale and character." But the president was resolute. At last a big picture of the government's additional deployment—both of its scale and character—emerged. But this picture could hardly satisfy those foreign and defense ministers, along with foreign affairs and national security officials in the Blue House, who had argued for a combat force of at least five thousand soldiers.

In hindsight, no compromise was possible between the two opposing arguments within the government, even though both sides had at their foundation a desire to protect the national interest. Foreign affairs and national security officials might have thought that the additional deployment issue was something to be decided among the president and themselves. But the president was in a bind, caught between citizens who opposed the deployment itself and officials demanding a large combat force. The officials believed that deploying a smaller, noncombat force was the worst scenario. But for the president, trapped between these two factions, a noncombat force of two to three thousand soldiers was a compromise.

Of course, the president did not arrive at this compromise through cynical political calculation. It was a decision that had taken into consideration numerous factors including the greater right and wrong, the security situation on the Korean Peninsula, the ROK-U.S. alliance, and popular sentiment. From what I could see, the one thing he had not considered was his own political standing. What would naturally be the most important consideration for a politician—one's own personal support base—had been altogether excluded. As a result, Roh suffered the political sacrifice of losing half his supporters, as once prophesied to Ambassador Hubbard. And on the half who didn't rescind their support, he inflicted the pain of having to accept his decision on additional deployment under duress. Meanwhile, the political opposition still branded the Roh administration an "anti-American faction." And it was I who had come up with and executed a solution that demanded such incredible political sacrifice from the president—all for the sake of a national interest that neither side recognized.

The president's October 30 order set the NSC Secretariat into motion. First, we created a consultation team, headed by Deputy Foreign Minister Lee Soo-hyuk and including Seo Joo-seok, director of strategic planning at the NSC Secretariat. Lee was appointed the team leader because he was the only person among the high-level foreign and defense ministry officials who I knew had responded positively to the president's decision. Since I was the government figure in charge of the North Korean nuclear problem, I often met with Lee, our chief representative at the Six-Party Talks. Once, when I worried about consulting the United States, he said to me, "You deserve gratitude, no matter how many soldiers are deployed." His words made feel like I was backed by a great army of my own. Early in the presidency, very few senior diplomats shared the president's philosophy; I was willing to entrust work to anyone whose ability to perform duties and desire to work according to the president's direction in diplomacy were certain.

The consultation team went to the United States with the plan of deploying two to three thousand noncombat troops; there was, however, no guarantee that the team would explain our plan to the Americans persuasively and with a sense of duty. Because these people served as the right arms of the foreign and defense ministers, I worried that it would be impossible for them to not heed their direct superiors, or follow the trends within their ministries. The NSC had already learned a valuable lesson from observing the previous consultation team's dissatisfying performance over the reduction issue. This new team needed something concrete to give their ministers and those in their ministries. The NSC Secretariat drafted guidelines, hand-signed by the president, to be given to the team:

- Conduct the consultation with the United States sincerely and amicably, including the sharing of information.

- The deployed force is to consist of noncombat units (engineering, medical, and transportation) that will carry out the tasks of supporting peace and reconstruction.
- The deployed force will be independent brigade-class, and its size will be around 2,500 soldiers (fewer than three thousand, including the Seohee and Jema units).
- The team will be made up of Lee Soo-hyuk, deputy foreign minister; Cha Young-gu, director of policy, Defense Ministry; and Seo Joo-seok, director of strategic planning, NSC. Given the nature of the issue to be resolved through diplomatic negotiations, Deputy Minister Lee will be the chief representative.
- The consultation will commence during the first week of November.

When he was approving these guidelines, Roh personally drew another bullet point below the last sentence and wrote, "The government's plan has yet to be adopted, so pursue discussion at the level of prior information exchange and consultation for policymaking decisions." Then he signed the document. He meant that the team was not to unilaterally push the original plan and it should maintain flexibility in persuading the United States. In fact, carrying a plan that was advantageous to us meant that we were willing to display some flexibility. The president made this point explicit to give the consultation team some breathing room.

I did not feel reassured by the guidelines alone. I wanted to set up a face-to-face meeting between the president and Deputy Foreign Minister Lee to help Lee precisely understand and carry out the president's thinking on deployment. Ordinarily a meeting between a high-ranking ministerial official and the president called for the minister's attendance. But I did not have the confidence to invite Foreign Minister Yoon—who had called for an early decision to deploy combat troops at the risk of collision with the president—to a meeting that was intended to facilitate a clear understanding of the president's deployment philosophy; Yoon's presence would only make things even more uncomfortable and complicated. Yet the foreign minister could not be excluded. After much worry, I created an occasion for Lee to meet the president in an undisclosed, unofficial fashion. It was a plan of last resort. This was the only time during my tenure at the NSC when the president saw a high-ranking bureaucrat without a minister present.

The consultation team visited Washington between November 5 and 7, meeting with Condoleezza Rice, national security advisor; Stephen Hadley, deputy national security advisor; Richard Armitage, deputy secretary of state; Paul Wolfowitz, deputy secretary of defense; Richard Myers, chairman of the Joint Chiefs of Staff, and others. All were major figures who normally would not meet with deputy-ministerial-level representatives from South Korea. This proved that the United States was in desperate straits after most countries courted by the Americans had declined to deploy soldiers. The only country left, essentially, was South Korea. Thanks to President Roh's call for caution, we had more leverage to argue our position on deployment.

As expected, the Americans were disappointed in our plan. Once they heard our position, they said they had expected a division command, two to three infantry brigades, and at least one or two brigades that could take charge of a specified area and handle stabilization. National Security Advisor Rice personally asked that we review our plan. It was somewhat optimistic that, after hearing our position, Rice ordered her deputy Hadley to try and narrow the differences between the two sides.

But while the consultation team was in the United States, President Roh reaffirmed his conviction in the final deployment plan he had long developed in his mind. The impetus came from the ROK-Pakistan summit. President Roh held a dinner for Pakistani president Pervez Musharraf, who visited South Korea on November 6. Roh asked Musharraf for advice on the deployment, wondering how Muslim countries would react if South Korea were to decide in favor of it. Musharraf replied, "They will not care much. South Korea is respected by these countries, so in Arab states and even inside Iraq [the deployment] will be welcomed. What is unfortunate is that their feelings toward Western nations, especially the United States, have worsened." In response to the question of whether he thought it would be possible for the United States to overcome the difficulties in Iraq, Musharraf said it would be extremely difficult, since internal divisions within Iraq were presenting too many irreconcilable demands. The conversation continued:

ROH: If South Korea deployed troops, what kind of force should it be, and what kind of work could it do in Iraq?

MUSHARRAF: It must be for reconstructing Iraq and for winning the hearts of the Iraqi people. It should never be police work, particularly in problematic areas.

ROH: Do you think that the South Korean force could engage in activities like training the military and police?

MUSHARRAF: It should be able to, except that it should not offend locals by being seen in the streets like the American force. I hope you will perform behind-the-line activities such as helping with training. Iraqi people think of the U.S. military as an occupying force. The South Korean soldiers should not be thought of as an extension of this occupying force. It is best that the South Korean force play a role in service of reconstruction and welfare of the Iraqi people and training.

Musharraf advised that central Iraq was the most unstable and the southern Shi'ite region was not bad, but there was no predicting when and how Iran would act.

MUSHARRAF: The northern Kurdish region is the safest, so try to choose it as the area for deployment.

ROH: Are you saying that it is best for the South Korean force to independently manage a specific region rather than working together with the United States?

MUSHARRAF: Of course. Working together with the U.S. forces can give the impression that the South Korean force is an extension of the U.S. military. This can unnecessarily expose the South Korean force to danger.

At this point in the conversation, Musharraf asked, "Is the United States pressuring you to deploy soldiers?" He was not very aware of the situation between the United States and South Korea in connection to deployment to Iraq.

After listening to Musharraf, Roh gained confidence. A leader of an Islamic nation who understood Iraq all too well had told him that the decision he made—in opposition to foreign affairs and national security officials—regarding the size and nature of the force to be deployed to Iraq, had been the right one. Furthermore, Musharraf gave us confidence in our plan to independently manage an area. Roh was so grateful for the advice that he told the leader of an Islamic nation, "The Buddha must have sent you today, Mr. President, so that we could be guided in solving a very difficult problem."

Before then, I had thought of President Musharraf as an iron-fisted dictator who had gained power purely through a coup, but that was not the case at all. He had real insight and an objective view into the Iraq problem, and offered President Roh very frank advice based on these qualities. Roh later spoke highly of President Musharraf's insight and judgments concerning the Iraqi situation to advisors and was sincerely grateful for his advice.

The President's Final Instructions
and the White House's Reply: "Thank you"

Controversy continued within South Korea over the size and nature of the additional deployment, even as the consultation team continued its work in the United States. Adding to the chaos was the fact that some of their discussions were leaked to the media, accompanied by commentary from high-ranking American officials, even before the reports reached our government. As the news spread that the United States did not react positively, people within and outside the government once again argued that the government's plan, if left unchanged, would endanger the alliance. More calls for a large-scale combat force ensued.

Only the president's authority could control the situation now. Normally, President Roh's style was to reach a decision through several phases of discussion and negotiation, but in this case compromise was essentially impossible. Even those against deployment were not supporting him and called for vigorous opposition. There was no compromise that could satisfy two completely opposing arguments, but there was one that, while being criticized by both sides, would best serve national interests under the conditions, and this could only be decided through the president's own resolve. President Roh issued his last instructions in preparation for the final deployment plan.

On November 11, 2003, President Roh held a meeting of ministers concerned with national security, the fifth since the United States had first requested an additional deployment to Iraq. He ordered the Defense Ministry to keep the size of the force under three thousand and to structure it to be independent from the militaries of other countries. He ordered a study of two separate possibilities: our forces taking charge of a specific area, or mainly performing reconstruction support functions. Should our military independently oversee a single area, then a plan should be drafted in such a way that the local Iraqi military and police would handle security and we would guide their training.

So, the two-month-long controversy and chaos surrounding additional deployment finally came to an end. Although the president ordered preparation of two different plans, neither the United States nor the military would favor the plan focused on reconstruction support; naturally the plan calling for overseeing a region would be chosen. President Roh had confidence in this plan following his conversation with Musharraf. Even the United States, no matter how dissatisfied, would not be able to quibble over the nature or size of a South Korean force if we said that it would oversee an entire area and manage it independently, for better or for worse.

Blue House spokesperson Yoon Tae-young proclaimed on November 13 that the last instruction had been clearly conveyed to relevant ministries. His announcement was aimed at limiting any further miscommunications within the government, reducing speculative reports from the media, and influencing the U.S. negotiations.

But the official U.S. response to our plan did not come quickly. Many within the foreign affairs and national security circles predicted that the United States would reject it. The president, while always looking composed, might have felt he was walking on thin ice. I, too, felt nervous but could not show it. If they did not accept our plan, we could have a serious problem.

If that were to happen, the opposing faction in South Korea would assail the president for damaging the alliance. Public anxiety would reach new heights. Government officials who had argued for deploying combat troops would rage that the NSC Secretariat had brought about this predicament through its stubbornness, despite their many warnings. If we were to accept the U.S. demand and propose a revised plan, it would be a major diplomatic failure and a humiliation. The U.S. rejection of our proposal would turn our efforts into a strategic miscalculation. The president himself would be plunged into serious political danger. Supporters of the Roh administration would have their trust breached and we would be open to criticism that we were incompetent, inexperienced amateurs. With my imagination running wild, I felt weighed down with an incredible burden—like I was standing on the edge of a cliff, a step away from plunging into oblivion. This plan had been prepared with conviction, following several analyses and strategic evaluations of the situation, but I could not relax. For about a week I could barely sleep.

Then on November 12, a suicide attack against the Italian garrison in the southern Iraqi city of Nasiriyah killed nineteen Italian soldiers. I am well aware of how unethical it is to think of someone else's misfortune as my opportunity, but I anticipated that this event would help expedite the U.S. decision in the direction favored by the South Korean government. In fact, this event caused public opinion over participation in the Iraq war to worsen in various countries. It would make the United States that much more desperate and increase the symbolic significance of South

Korea's deployment. The situation in Iraq was unfolding in such a way that the mere fact of the South Korean military's deployment, not the size or character of the force, became important in and of itself.

U.S. secretary of defense Donald Rumsfeld was scheduled to visit the Blue House on November 17 after traveling to South Korea for the annual Security Consultative Meeting (SCM). Rumsfeld would at that time perhaps reveal the U.S. position on South Korea's proposal regarding additional deployment. Even if the White House had not finalized its position by then, Rumsfeld would reveal his private opinion, given his directness. He might make a strongly negative remark, and once again churn public opinion. Already the media's attention was focused on what words might come out of Rumsfeld's mouth.

I greeted the morning of Monday, November 17, with my worries and a hint of indigestion. I went up to the main hall of the Blue House to attend the 9:00 a.m. meeting of chief aides. As I was entering the conference room, someone tapped on my shoulder—it was Chief of Staff Moon Hee-sang. "Congratulations, Deputy Secretary-General Lee. Well done." I was confused, but Moon must have been congratulating me for something I had done, so I nodded and smiled at him. It turned out that, even before Rumsfeld's arrival in South Korea, the White House had accepted our additional deployment proposal, and had instructed the American embassy in Seoul to express its gratitude. Ambassador Hubbard had conveyed this to Foreign Affairs Advisor Ban Ki-moon over the weekend, and Ban had filled the president in before the chief aides' meeting was to begin. Moon had been present for this report, thus his congratulations. I felt relieved, as though a heavy weight had just been taken off my shoulders.

That afternoon at the Blue House, the president expressed his regrets to Secretary Rumsfeld for "not providing support to the satisfaction of the United States." Rumsfeld thanked the president and expressed respect for his decision: "I understand that this was a very difficult decision, given the circumstances."

The White House acceptance of and gratitude for South Korea's additional deployment plan implied that the domestic controversy over this issue and the diplomatic dispute between South Korea and the United States were coming to an end. But there were still unresolved issues. U.S. defense officials simply did not understand why the South Korean military was dispatching a peace-building force and not combat troops, even as we said we would take over a specific region in Iraq. In early December

2003, I met Deputy Secretary of Defense Paul Wolfowitz—the main power in the defense department and a key neocon figure—during my visit to the United States at the invitation of Deputy National Security Advisor Stephen Hadley at the White House.

When I introduced our deployment plan of dispatching a unit aimed at peace-building within an independent region, but not directly handling security, he asked, "Then how will you manage the region?" I answered, "For the time being we will use the local militia. And later as reconstruction of Iraq gets underway, we will train the police and military and support them in their role of maintaining security." He still had a look of confusion. For someone who thought that the military was only for military operations, this might have sounded strange, so I added, "If the United States entrusts us with a certain area, we will not need U.S. forces within that area. We will handle all matters as our responsibility." Only then did he express his understanding: "I get it. Then it's fine." In fact, a specific region had not yet been identified, but it was well understood even by the United States that our forces, if deployed, would be heading to the northern region inhabited by the Kurds. The South Korean NSC believed that the well-organized militia of the Kurdish region would make it possible for us to help with peace-building without getting involved in security or stabilization operations, as long as we made good use of these militia.

The plan of overseeing an independent area with a noncombat force was something incomprehensible not only to the United States, but also to the progressive faction within South Korea. When the government announced the plan that ROK forces would entrust local security to militia as our own way of winning the trust of the local population, the progressive faction interpreted this as a government ploy to conceal the deployment of soldiers for combat. A significant number of progressive figures believed the deployed soldiers were meant for combat, by the simple fact that they were armed members of the special forces. But the character of a military force is determined through its function and mission. There is no need for me to offer excuses: the Zaytun Division, which would later be deployed to Arbil, Iraq, was never mobilized for tracking down terrorists, never engaged in a battle, and never suffered a casualty. Its work in realizing regional security, assisting in local reconstruction, providing medical services, and training police and military is well documented. Even though this decision ended up being painful, dividing public opinion and alienating Roh's supporters, history proves that Roh kept his word to the nation that the government was deploying a force to assist with peace-building.

The Zaytun Division projected a very positive image in Iraq. As promised by President Roh, they were proud and courageous elite soldiers of the Republic of Korea who executed a South Korean–style civilian affairs operation. While they carried arms for their own protection, they were noncombat soldiers. Unfortunately, many people within the progressive faction that opposed additional deployment still want to call them a combat force. What do such people have to gain by this?

December 17: The Final Decision on Additional Deployment, and Its Aftermath

Following the U.S. acknowledgement of gratitude, President Roh held a meeting of ministers concerned with national security on December 17 and decided to send a division of less than three thousand soldiers in support of peace and reconstruction to Iraq for the additional deployment; the Zaytun Division, following government consultation with the United States, departed South Korea in August 2004 and arrived in Arbil, the chosen area of deployment. The issue of additional deployment to Iraq, which had divided government and society as no other issue in the history of the Roh administration's handling of unification, foreign affairs, and national security (UFN) matters, reached a definite conclusion. The issue prompted striking opposition and persuasion from ministers and Blue House officials within foreign affairs and national security circles, even after the president's intention was revealed to be clearly different from theirs. Ironically, the president's leadership style of respecting discussion and opinions different from his own made this opposition seem even greater. Even issues like the recalibration of the ROK-U.S. alliance did not reach this level of conflict and confrontation.

While my opinion was different from those of most high-level figures within foreign affairs and national security circles, I did not doubt their patriotism. Some thought of the ROK-U.S. alliance itself as the ultimate objective, while others called for deploying a combat force as a pragmatic approach to addressing the harsh reality of international politics. But not one person made his argument out of a desire to uphold anything but South Korea's own national interests. What I could not understand, however, was the idea that we should almost reflexively accept the U.S. request as soon as Washington issued it, or that the president's decision to deploy a smaller number of noncombat soldiers somehow endangered the country. Why should we unconditionally accept American requests? Adjusting the scale and character of deployment, or even declining an American request, does not mean that we want to be anti-American. Is it really so reckless to pursue balanced and healthy ROK-U.S. relations of mutual respect that allow for negotiation? These are questions that I still ask to this day.

Through this ordeal, the NSC Secretariat became an object of attention as the control tower over the Roh administration's UFN policies, and I became a target of attacks from the political opposition that had argued for deploying a large-scale combat force. It was entirely up to the NSC Secretariat to persuade politicians and civil society opposed to additional deployment; there was no way the Defense Ministry—itself not pleased with deploying a force for peace-building support—would persuade politicians, including lawmakers on the national assembly's defense committee. Yet I felt it would be too much to impose this work on the Office of Chief Secretary for Civil Society or the Office of Chief Secretary for Political Affairs, both of whom viewed the deployment itself in a negative light. The NSC Secretariat thus had to make every effort to persuade the public and facilitate the smooth deployment of additional soldiers once the final decision had been made.

Two days after returning from a twelve-day Latin American tour following the November 25, 2004, APEC summit, the president summoned me in the early morning. Despite his fatigue from the trip and a sore throat, he informed me he wished to stop in Arbil and cheer the soldiers of the Zaytun Division on his way back from the ASEAN + 3 summit and his eleven-day European tour. I was surprised, considering his extreme exhaustion from all these foreign tours.

It was no simple matter for the president to visit Zaytun. The project could succeed only if we could keep secret the flight plan from France—the last country the president was scheduled to visit—to Kuwait, and then the itinerary from Kuwait to Arbil. The president would have to transfer to the ROK Air Force's transportation plane in Kuwait and head to the Arbil airport; during landing and takeoff the plane had to risk the danger of flying in an evasive pattern in anticipation of anti-aircraft-gun attacks from terrorists. To make matters worse, the president only had three days remaining in South Korea before he left on his trip. I told him that, with so little preparation time, it might be difficult to arrange a visit on the way back home due to the local situation and security problems. But he maintained his strong resolve to visit Arbil: "If it's difficult now

because there isn't time, I will go during the Lunar New Year holidays."
The president spoke with much gratitude and sympathy for the Zaytun
Division. Once I sensed his resolve, I immediately set up a task force and
arranged, through close cooperation with relevant government offices, the
president's December 8 meeting with the soldiers of the Zaytun Division.

The president's Arbil visit boosted the morale of Division Commander
Hwang Eui-don and his soldiers; while the president was moving about,
one soldier jumped out from the assembled crowd and shouted, "Mr.
President! I want to give you a hug!" He embraced the president. Back in
his jeep, the president shed tears of joy and sympathy. Foreign Minister
Ban Ki-moon, observing him, said, "Mr. President, you appear to be in
a better mood than when you rode the golden carriage in England."[3]
The president had gone to offer comfort to the soldiers of the Zaytun
Division, but he himself was comforted, thanks to them.

On this day, Roh emphasized to our soldiers that their efforts toward
peace-building would transcend Iraq and become part of the Republic
of Korea's strength in the world: "It is painful work to try and build the
image of the South Korean military. But your sweat and effort will one
day become the Republic of Korea's right to speak. The sweat you shed
now will become the power of diplomacy, yet another kind of power,
for the Republic of Korea."

Looking Back

The additional deployment to Iraq was so painful and chaotic for a
simple reason: the Iraq War was an invasion without a mandate. President Roh had strong principles and valued justice. Many South Koreans
chose him because they supported his unwillingness to compromise on
injustice. If the United States had asked South Korea to deploy soldiers
to a just war, Roh would not have found it so painful. Unfortunately, he
was asked to participate in cleaning up after an unjust war, defined by
the international community as an American invasion of Iraq. South
Korea had to put its feet in this mud. That is why Roh did not fault those
who opposed additional deployment and assailed his administration. He
accepted that criticism. He was sensitive enough not to preach acceptance
of reality to those opposing deployment on principle.

In any case, the president abandoned his trademark principles and
chose additional deployment in consideration of peace on the Korean

---

3 [President Roh was the first South Korean leader to be ceremonially received
by Queen Elizabeth II at Buckingham Palace, in December 2004].

Peninsula. I, for one, tried with all my strength to assist him. I think the deployment of the Zaytun Division writes an entirely new history and shows that it is possible to deploy soldiers for peace—it is possible to go beyond the equations that anti-deployment equals peace, and pro-deployment is anti-peace.

In hindsight, Roh would have refused the additional deployment request if there had been no North Korean nuclear problem. He did not believe the threatening arguments that exaggerated the price of refusing additional deployment as the destruction of the ROK-U.S. alliance. And even if our relationship with the United States would suffer as a result, the president would have sought other ways of support that did not involve deploying our troops to this unjust war. But in 2003, Roh's stress over the North Korean nuclear problem was too great.

The United States requested additional deployment to Iraq in the same breath that they used to discuss ROK-U.S. relations and the existence of the U.S. Forces Korea (USFK). Washington did not refrain from threatening that it had no choice but to withdraw the USFK if South Korea did not deploy its own soldiers or if the scale of that deployment were too small. When our government said that the United States should shift its position on the North Korean nuclear problem to enable our deployment under stable conditions, Washington did not hesitate to express displeasure and hounded us, as though our behavior was inappropriate in the context of the alliance. We frequently found ourselves within this unequal structure of dialogue; the problem of protecting our national interests amidst the unilateralism of the world's superpower has not left my mind.

The Roh administration chose the narrow path between outright opposition and deployment of a large-scale combat force. I felt that the administration was pioneering the beginning of a long road toward horizontal ROK-U.S. relations. I never asked the president about this, but I am sure he would have agreed. The Roh administration's direction was dismissed or overlooked by both factions: the one that treated the ROK-U.S. alliance as a sacred object on par with ancestral tablets, and the faction that called for realization of complete autonomy. That is why the demand for the government's resignation came from both the opposition party and from civil society, which was diametrically opposed to the political opposition. The progressive faction ignored the noncombat character of the deployed force outright or simply dismissed the force as one secretly meant for combat operations. They emphasized the government's alleged "subservient nature toward the United States" and scorned it, with such statements as, "So you think sending five thousand is pro-alliance and sending three thousand is pro-autonomy?" Few tried to understand the president's pragmatic position of using his power to pursue autonomy and balance.

The Roh administration suffered a great deal of damage in the process of deciding in favor of this deployment. But if we were to turn the clock back to autumn 2003, could we find a better solution? I think not. While painful and dissatisfying, my choice would have been the same. I cannot speak for the president, but I believe—based on his rational character—that his, too, would have been no different.

President Roh was a progressive but he was also a leader who knew how to distinguish between being a politician and a ruler. He understood he was a ruler who had to lead a nation on behalf of all people before he was a politician who could act in accordance with his political convictions. For Roh the politician, the additional deployment to Iraq offered several choices, but for Roh the president, there was little room to maneuver. Whenever I think about President Roh's agony during the Iraq deployment period, I recall the letter he wrote to the nation on May 8, 2003, Parents' Day in South Korea:

> Before becoming president, I lived as a human rights lawyer, defending the weak in society. That is why I am someone to whom the voice of powerless citizens rings louder than that of powerful citizens. But as the president who governs the nation, I cannot lean one way or the other. I can only evaluate national interest from the center. Because the moment I lose balance, this country will succumb to a battle of strength between one group and another. Politics and governance are different. The position of a critic and that of a president are different. I will not be swayed by popularity. I will move ahead unshaken while holding on to the center, which is national interest.

IV

A Narrow Path
to Peace

9

The First Step toward Peace:
The Six-Party Talks and a Quest for Balance

No Special Envoy to the North–
Between the Nuclear Crisis and Inter-Korean Relations

I became National Security Council (NSC) deputy secretary-general in late March 2003. I was keen to observe how the investigation into money transfers[1] to the North would influence inter-Korean relations. It was around this time that Chief of Staff Moon Hee-sang sought me out. Moon had unexpected news: the National Intelligence Service (NIS) had made unofficial contact with the North and reached an agreement for us to send a special presidential envoy to Pyongyang. This was the first time Moon had called on me since I accompanied the Kim Dae-jung administration's special envoy to Pyongyang on behalf of then president-elect Roh. And here we were, speaking of another special envoy to the North. There were no special conditions attached to the envoy's visit, except that, as in previous years, Seoul would provide four hundred thousand tons of rice to the North on humanitarian grounds. Moon said that, given the nature of the situation, there was a strong possibility I would be the special envoy and the NSC Secretariat should

---

1   [First discussed in chapter 2.]

prepare accordingly. Since the discussion over sending a special envoy had begun before I joined the government, I did not know the details, but I suspected that the NIS's North Korea section had worked on this before and after the new administration took power.

I thought the timing of the visit was appropriate. I had been worried about inter-Korean relations due to the special investigation into the money transfers. This was a good opportunity, not only for the future of inter-Korean relations, but also for persuading the North to discuss the nuclear problem and finding a measure acceptable to Pyongyang and Washington. But I was also worried about Republic of Korea (ROK)–U.S. relations, which we were just beginning to stabilize after the issue of excluding a military option against the North. If the United States saw the special envoy's visit to the North in a negative light, it would create problems. The Bush administration even opposed the groundbreaking ceremony at the Kaesong Industrial Complex, so there was cause for worry.

And I was right. When Foreign Minister Yoon Young-kwan informed the American ambassador of the agreement to send a special envoy, Hubbard was not thrilled: "Isn't it too soon to trust North Korea?" Our Foreign Ministry was equally negative; it asserted that at the moment there was no special topic for a special envoy to discuss in person with the North, so the visit should be postponed until after the ROK-U.S. summit. But the Unification Ministry and the NSC Secretariat saw this as a valuable opportunity for improving inter-Korean relations and strongly argued that we should make it happen. If we delayed sending a special envoy until after the ROK-U.S. summit, the North would not agree, citing our violation of the agreement.

Even after agreeing to send an envoy, President Roh still had to face the ferocious opposition of the Foreign Ministry. To work through the problem, the president held a special high-level discussion with NSC Standing Committee members on Sunday, April 13, 2003. That day the Blue House grounds were filled with cherry blossoms under a clear blue sky. Invited to the official residence were the unification minister, the foreign minister, the defense minister, the NIS chief, the chief of staff, the national security advisor, the foreign affairs advisor, the national security advisor, and myself, along with spouses. The spouses went for a walk with First Lady Kwon Yang-sook. Everyone else followed the president to a cozy pavilion in the front yard of the official residence and sat on the wooden floor. The president noted that the pavilion had been built during former president Kim Dae-jung's tenure, but was never used, as Kim had a leg problem. "You are the first guests," Roh said. Everyone was in good humor and laughed.

But once the topic of the special envoy came up, the atmosphere immediately became serious. The president told the group to hold a free discussion and he listened the entire time. Opinions were divided into two groups, with neither side showing any sign of giving in.

Unification Minister Jeong Se-hyun and NIS chief Shin Geon forcefully argued in favor of sending a special envoy. I tried my best to help. I had thought we would easily conclude in favor of sending a special envoy; it had already been agreed upon at a meeting between the two Koreas, pre-approved by the president, and it would be a tragic loss if we canceled it just because the United States had a negative attitude.

But there was an unexpected variable. Foreign Minister Yoon reported that, while it might be premature for him to announce it, there had been news from U.S. secretary of state Colin Powell that the United States, North Korea, and China would soon hold a three-way talk in Beijing to address the nuclear problem. This was welcome news to Seoul, which had long argued for solving the nuclear crisis through dialogue; it could also be seen as a diplomatic victory for the ROK government, which had made every effort to bring about dialogue. Everyone was delighted. The opposition party and the press would no doubt criticize the government because this dialogue excluded South Korea, but this was a minor issue considering the more urgent goal of solving the nuclear problem itself.

Minister Yoon expressed concern that if we sent an envoy to the North just when such a talk had been arranged, with difficulty, we might get swept up in the North's strategy of sowing confusion. In that case, sending a special envoy might end up interfering with the three-party talk and could prevent a meaningful outcome. Yoon said, "This simply isn't the right time." I did not agree, but I could see how he might think this way after trying so hard to bring about a dialogue to solve the North Korean nuclear problem. Foreign Affairs Advisor Ban, Defense Minister Cho Young-kil, Defense Advisor Kim Hee-sang, and others supported Yoon's position.

The side in support of sending an envoy disputed the suggestion that the North might be trying to sow confusion. We argued that the North's strategy had already shifted, from one of engaging the United States and blocking the South, to one of either trying to improve its relations with both the United States and the South, or spurning both simultaneously.

We believed that the North consented to the three-party talk and agreed to host a special envoy at the same time to improve relations with both the United States and South Korea. Now, more than ever, it was time to go to Pyongyang, discuss the nuclear crisis with the North, and improve inter-Korean relations.

After a long discussion, President Roh concluded that Seoul would cancel the special envoy visit and focus its diplomatic efforts on ensuring the success of the three-party talk in the interests of solving the North Korean nuclear problem. He ordered that the four hundred thousand tons of rice promised to the North should still be sent, without attaching any conditions.

I therefore stopped all preparations for the special envoy's visit and decided not to object any further. The president's decision to cancel the visit had been reached after much thought and discussion; I would not object, but I still thought it was wrong. Given the nature of the North's international strategies, the three-party talk might influence inter-Korean relations, but it was unlikely for inter-Korean relations to influence the three-party talk; a negative influence was particularly unlikely. That is why I thought we should ask the United States for understanding and still send an envoy.

In hindsight, though, perhaps Roh saw a bigger picture than I had. After taking office, the president did his utmost to directly face the risks on the Korean Peninsula—risks that might increase the possibility of a military conflict—so that he could calm the situation. That is why, even up to the very moment of his election, he did not hesitate to publicly criticize the U.S. refusal to eliminate the possibility of a military strike against North Korea. In that vein, he proposed to the international community the principle of a peaceful solution to the North Korean nuclear problem and made every effort to create a framework for dialogue. His efforts were not in vain; the United States changed course toward finding a peaceful solution, and a three-party talk was now going forward. Since the situation was improving, the president felt hesitant to deploy an envoy to the North against American objections. Even though the president had demanded a change in the U.S. attitude to the point of risking tension in ROK-U.S. relations, he also felt it was his duty to reciprocate the U.S. change in attitude.

The Launch of the Six-Party Talks:
Washington's Intentions vs. Seoul's Vision

On April 23, 2003, a three-party talk between the United States, North Korea, and China took place in Beijing. It meant that the North Korean nuclear crisis, once again precipitated by the highly enriched uranium (HEU) problem in October 2002, had improved and it was possible to enter a negotiation phase. Representatives of North Korea and the United States sat across the table from each other, with China as mediator. The United States could justify the proceedings by claiming that it had avoided bilateral talks with the North—which the United States was not keen on—and the North saved face by being able to hold what was, in all reality, a bilateral talk with the United States, despite China's official presence as a third party. There was very little room for South Korea to intervene. The president believed that this three-party talk was bound to develop into a multiparty format that would include South Korea, and that we should not ruin the talk—organized with considerable difficulty—by our stubborn insistence that we had to participate here and now. Solving the North Korean nuclear problem was important, not the format of the talk.

But as expected, the opposition party and many media outlets assailed the government for its incompetence because of South Korea's exclusion. To this, the president replied, "What is important now is the contents, not the format." He was unshaken by the criticism and maintained his rational, pragmatic stance.

At the China-mediated talk, North Korea proposed a series of steps that Washington and Pyongyang should take to solve the nuclear problem. It suggested measures for the United States to take in exchange for measures by the North. The U.S. measures included promises of regime security and normalization of relations with Pyongyang; a guarantee that Washington would not disrupt economic cooperation between the two Koreas or between the North and Japan; compensation for loss of electric power due to delays in the construction of the light-water reactor at Sinpo; and the provision of a new light-water reactor. North Korean measures included restraint in nuclear weapons development and consent to the inspection of nuclear facilities; gradual dismantlement of the nuclear program; and a cessation of long-range missile launches and exports, to be implemented in sequence. Pyongyang was looking for a comprehensive solution that would address everything at once.

The NSC's North Korean nuclear task force saw the North's proposal and thought that it was worth a review, even though it contained some unrealistic points. Of special importance was how the proposal linked solving the nuclear problem to normalizing relations with Washington; its accommodation of the U.S. wish for irreversible and complete dismantlement of the nuclear program; and its inclusion of the end of missile development and export. Washington, too, expressed its intent to carefully review the North Korean proposal.

But at the dinner that followed, there was an incident. The North Korean delegation head, Lee Geun, suddenly called U.S. assistant secretary of state James A. Kelly aside. "We have nuclear weapons and cannot abandon them," he threatened, "Whether we disclose the fact that we have nuclear weapons, and whether we transfer or increase them, depends on the United States. We hope that the United States will carefully review our proposal. We do not expect a quick answer." After his blunt words, the U.S. delegation left immediately, and the three-party talk collapsed just one day after it began.

Hearing this, I thought that North Korea did not know the Bush administration well enough if it had resorted to threats. To make a reasonable proposal on one hand and then whisper threats into the ears of the chief American representative was an immature negotiation strategy. This behavior only served to provide the Bush administration, controlled by hardline neocons, with an excuse to be more hostile toward the North. But Kelly's attitude was equally problematic for a negotiator. While the North was certainly deserving of criticism for the kind of remarks it made, one does not have to be a North Korea specialist to know that their threats were mostly for the sake of negotiation. I could not understand how the U.S. delegation could immediately pack up and leave the talk just because the North had uttered threats, right after it presented a worthwhile proposal. My interpretation is that the United States, too, had little interest in negotiating with the North. Kelly was an experienced negotiator; he would not have left purely based on his own judgment. I thought that the neocons, filled with a distorted, medieval crusader-like religious conviction and determined to see North Korea as part of the Axis of Evil, were behind Kelly's departure.

While the three-party talk collapsed, it did yield some benefits. More than anything, it inaugurated the convention of multiparty talks for peacefully solving the North Korean nuclear problem. By demonstrating the limits of a three-party talk format, it led, ironically but also naturally, to a multiparty talk format that included South Korea. Furthermore, the West, including the United States, gained some understanding of the North's intentions after it presented a proposal worth reviewing. Seoul then presented the United States with our basic position based on three principles—sequential solution, simultaneous implementation, and comprehensive solution—and began an earnest consultation to solve the nuclear problem.

In the end, South Korea, Japan, and Russia would be added, forming the Six-Party Talks (SPTs) in summer 2003. From August 27 to 29, 2003, the first round of the SPTs was held in Beijing. This one was less than successful; in lieu of a joint statement, the top representative of China— the presiding nation—simply summarized and announced the results of the talk. The South Korean government sought to secure its position as facilitator from the very first talk and to invite the other five nations, including North Korea and the United States, to exchange their opinions on the issues of denuclearization and the guarantee of regime security. While success was limited due to the mistrust between Pyongyang and Washington, the first SPT did yield consensus on several basic points, such as peacefully solving the nuclear problem and deciding the dates of the next talk through diplomatic channels. In any event, it was a first step.

The real problem was that the main parties, the United States and North Korea, were dreaming different dreams while looking at the same problem. Neither side was interested in any potential outcome of the SPTs. North Korea was convinced that its security problem could be solved only through bilateral negotiations with the United States. Since the HEU incident in October 2002, Pyongyang had tried, whatever the cost, to hold bilateral talks with the United States; the United States, in turn, had pressed Pyongyang but avoided one-on-one talks with the North. This was the motivation for Pyongyang to join the three-party talk in Beijing in April. Pyongyang joined the SPTs only after Beijing said that it would be possible for the North to have one-on-one contact with the United States, while the United States indicated it would be possible to have a bilateral discussion with the North within the framework of a multiparty discussion.

The Roh administration believed that the future of the SPTs remained dark if the North insisted on talking only to the United States and refused to consider other options. Seoul, therefore, focused on making Pyongyang see, through various routes, that multiparty talks would be more effective than bilateral dialogue with the United States in helping the North reach its goals. Our logic was that agreements between two parties can be broken by one side, but agreements guaranteed by many parties are harder to break. We reminded the North of how the agreement signed with Clinton had been broken by the current U.S. president, Bush, and reiterated the weakness of a bilateral agreement. President Roh emphasized that the nuclear problem must be solved through multiparty talks; at a meeting of ministers concerned with national security on July 4, 2003, he said, "The problem will not be solved by a talk between the two main parties, North Korea and the United States, who could not distrust one another more. Considering the nature of the topic, we have no choice but to shift to a multiparty framework."

The United States, however, ignored the value of the SPTs for a completely different reason, even though it was Washington that had wanted them in the first place. As the 1994 Agreed Framework between North Korea and the United States shows, the North Korean nuclear crisis had been an issue between North Korea and the United States until October 2002, when the issue of HEU erupted. But after the HEU incident, the Bush administration sought to make the situation not about North Korea versus the United States, but about North Korea versus the peace-loving international community. That is why, in early 2003, you began to hear talk from Washington that North Korean nuclear arms were not merely a U.S. problem, but that China was also responsible for solving it. So the three-party talk was held under China's mediation, and this expanded into the SPTs.

What the Bush administration sought through the SPTs was not the resolution of the nuclear problem through bilateral concessions, but the creation of a five-to-one dynamic with the United States, China, South Korea, Japan, and Russia on one side, and North Korea on the other. It apparently was an American strategy of pressuring North Korea to solve the problem. At the ROK-U.S. summit on October 20, 2003, President Bush frankly revealed the U.S. thinking. Explaining to President Roh the importance of involving China in solving the problem, he said, "Kim Jong-il will be nervous about the Chinese role." He emphasized the current setup of the game was "not North Korea vs. the United States, but North Korea vs. surrounding nations," noting that "the five nations must unite and send a single message to North Korea." He brought up his mistrust of Kim Jong-il. President Roh replied, "We have a couple of proverbs: even a mouse will bite a cat when cornered, and you shouldn't chase a dog without giving it a way to flee." Bush said, "If there is only one cat, the mouse might bite. But if there are five cats, can it bite them all?" Roh replied, "The problem is that the first cat to be bitten might be us."

While the United States may have given birth to the SPTs, it did not get everything it wanted. When it came to the nuclear problem, the United States, South Korea, and China each had slightly different national interests. South Korea's foremost worry was the nuclear problem turning into a military conflict; China, while it participated in sanctions, did not wish to disrupt the North Korean system. Therefore, South Korea and China focused, from the beginning of the talks, on identifying the common desires of all six parties rather than pressuring North Korea. This complicated the U.S. intent to create a five-to-one dynamic at the talks.

Even though the SPTs had been created with different aims on the part of the participating nations, Seoul worked hard to find common ground within that framework. For those living under the direct threat of North Korea's nuclear program, the fact that we now had a way to directly express our opinions was welcome. Seoul actively proposed a three-stage road map of solutions to the problem even before the start of the first talk: (1) maintain the status quo (freeze the nuclear program), (2) return to the situation before the nuclear crisis, and (3) find a comprehensive solution. This road map took into consideration the basic U.S. position and the proposal North Korea had made at the three-party talk. The United States, meanwhile, shied away from presenting specific solutions.

At the talks, Seoul tried to exercise its right to speak as one of the six parties, but the United States had a different idea: it wanted to single-handedly write the strategy for dealing with North Korea and have other nations follow. The United States seemed to be trying to gain the undiluted support of its allies, South Korea and Japan, for its policy, and then to persuade China and Russia with the support of those allies. Despite the six-party format, the U.S. concept was that North Korea policy was about the United States vs. North Korea. At the beginning of the talks, the United States did not want to recognize any independent measures from South Korea. When the first talks ended, State Department officials argued that if South Korea shared the U.S. position, North Korea would have no place to lean and would return to the second round of talks. They were hoping that South Korea would not raise any objections against the United States.

Washington did not want Seoul to act as an honest broker between Pyongyang and the United States: it simply wanted Seoul to enthusiastically support and follow American leadership on the nuclear problem. Of course, seasoned American diplomats never once directly told the ROK government to "follow the United States." Their dismay at the South Korean government's objections to U.S. policy on North Korea and their description of our position as showing "division before the enemy" made their intent sufficiently clear. State Department officials would later openly argue that blaming the talks' lack of success on the United States was simply succumbing to North Korean tricks; their evaluation of the first SPT was that North Korea saw expected behavior from the United States and Japan, but was disappointed that Russia and China acted unexpectedly; and since South Korea had for the most part acted as expected, the North would use economic cooperation with the South to obtain benefits and then use those benefits to pressure the United States. It boiled down to the United States openly complaining that South Korea had aided the North at the talks. From the Bush administration's perspective, it was simply unacceptable to assert that, yes, North Korea was wrong, but the United States was wrong, too.

For the South Korean government to yield and silently follow the U.S. North Korea policy, that policy at the very least had to be rational. But as far as we could see, the Bush administration's solution would only lead the Korean Peninsula into a military conflict or provoke North Korea to hasten nuclear development. So, we thought it was better for us to create an independent measure and try to persuade the United States and North Korea.

The Bush administration found Seoul's initiative unpleasant. They did not try to understand the special circumstances facing the South Korean government: we needed to simultaneously solve inter-Korean relations and the nuclear problem. But if U.S. policy could not provide us with any hope for peace, we had no choice but to continually raise questions and pursue a more rational and peace-oriented solution. If the Bush administration rejected a peaceful solution till the end, then we had no choice but to align ourselves with China and persuade the United States.

Dispatching a Special Envoy to the North: Background

I remember the date as September 1, 2003, immediately after the first SPT ended and just before the United States notified us of the need for Iraq deployment. President Roh summoned me to say that he would send a special envoy to the North and that I should make necessary preparations.

The envoy would be the actor Moon Sung-keun. The president normally asked for my opinion but this time he had already decided the matter.

I wondered why the president wanted to send a special envoy at this juncture. If this had been done in April, the envoy would have met Chairman Kim Jong-il and we could have created an important opportunity to advance inter-Korean relations. But now it would be difficult to meet Chairman Kim or to achieve any discernible results. But I kept silent; I still thought that even in the current situation, sending a special envoy could strengthen our voice on the North Korean nuclear problem and improve inter-Korean relations.

Only when the president gave instructions for the direction his personal letter, addressed to Kim, should take did I begin to understand. He thought, with the talks ended without a meaningful outcome, he should step up and personally persuade the North; dispatching a special envoy to the North would demonstrate his sincerity in wanting peace and prosperity for both Koreas, and would be an opportunity to urge Chairman Kim to resolve the nuclear crisis and improve inter-Korean relations.

The envoy-designate, Moon Sung-keun, was Pastor Moon Ik-hwan's son and the president's special acquaintance, someone with a deep knowledge of and interest in unification. When support for the president declined during the presidential election and his situation was desperate, Moon Sung-keun made a historic speech calling for support for Roh while quoting the president's words, "A farmer does not blame the field." It could be said that Moon was the greatest contributor to the president's electoral success.

The NSC Secretariat handled the special envoy matter as top secret, in consultation with the NIS. Inside the government, only the unification minister and the foreign minister were informed in advance. We conveyed the news to National Security Advisor Condoleezza Rice through our own national security advisor, Ra Jong-yil, during the October 20 Asia-Pacific Economic Cooperation (APEC) summit. Ra explained to Rice the objective and rough contents of Roh's personal letter, and asked her to inform President Bush in absolute secrecy.

Moon's visit took place from November 12 to 15 after a working group meeting with the North. Moon was not able to meet with Chairman Kim Jong-il but met other relevant officials, conveyed the presidential letter, and returned with a message from Kim. For the first time, President Roh could, albeit indirectly, talk to Chairman Kim. In the letter, Roh urged Kim to make bold decisions on the nuclear issue. The longish

letter summarized everything President Roh wanted to say to the North
Korean leadership at the beginning of his tenure. Below I reproduce the
letter's important parts:

> Dear National Defense Chairman Kim Jong-il of the Democratic People's
> Republic of Korea,
>
> Hello. This is President Roh Moo-hyun of the Republic of Korea.
>
> I am very glad to make your acquaintance. My desire to meet you in
> person, sit face to face and heart to heart, and hold a conversation is
> great, but I still feel fortunate and am pleased to be able to send Special
> Envoy Moon Sung-keun, whom I trust, and convey my thoughts and
> intentions. . . . It has already been a half century since the division
> imposed by the Cold War began. And I am someone who is very embar-
> rassed that we have not been able to overcome it ourselves.
>
> While I respect Mr. Kim Gu,[2] who said "I would rather die while lying
> on the thirty-eighth parallel than see our nation divided," it hurts me
> deeply that this person we respect has to be a failed historical figure. . . .
>
> The Roh administration has proclaimed a policy to begin an era of
> peace and prosperity in Northeast Asia. This policy envisions establishing
> unwavering peace on the Korean Peninsula and pursuing the collective
> prosperity of South and North Korea so that we can create a foundation
> of peaceful unification and develop the Korean Peninsula into the center
> of Northeast Asia. . . .
>
> Mr. Chairman,
>
> This policy for peace and prosperity for South and North Korea,
> however, finds itself within a structure from which it cannot move even
> one step forward without first resolving the existing differences and
> tension between North Korea and the United States. . . .
>
> My administration and I have made every effort to reduce rising
> tensions and the danger of war on the Korean Peninsula, no matter the
> circumstance.
>
> Following suit, the United States started emphasizing a "peaceful
> solution through dialogue" to the nuclear problem starting this April,
> and President Bush went so far as to mention his willingness to "guar-
> antee security in writing" at the ROK-U.S. summit at the APEC meeting
> last October. . . .
>
> Of course, it is true that the first [six-party] talk did not yield any
> satisfactory results. But as they say, "The beginning is halfway." Given
> that the framework of dialogue is intact and each nation continues to

---

2   [Kim Gu (1876–1949), pen name Baekbeom, was a leader of the Korean independence movement and an activist for Korean reunification.]

make sincere efforts to solve the problem, I am confident that future talks will certainly proceed successfully. . . .

The heart of the matter is how quickly the nuclear problem will be resolved. Once the nuclear problem has been resolved, no nation can act militarily against the North without the consent of the South. Therefore, it is essential that more active efforts are made to see an early resolution to the issues of nuclear development and guarantee of regime security. . . .

The problem of guaranteeing security for the North is not just between the North and the United States. It is a problem that will ultimately be resolved within the framework of unwavering peace between South and North Korea, which share their destiny as a single collective.

With the resolve of both the Roh administration and myself, I am convinced that if the North can provide a turning point for solving the nuclear problem at the upcoming Six-Party Talks, the North will be able to solve the problem of security guarantee and pursue unprecedented economic development.

Given such significance, this Six-Party Talk, which began under difficult circumstances, is an unparalleled opportunity for our nation.

Mr. Chairman! Let us join hands on this occasion!

In the process of solving the nuclear problem and advancing inter-Korean relations, let us boldly, totally solve all without dividing issues into smaller pieces or pushing and tugging!

Mr. Chairman, let us make a breakthrough together! . . .

Our people and I await your visit to Seoul, which was mentioned in the 6.15 joint statement. If this does not suit you, then I sincerely wish that I can meet you in person anywhere on the Korean Peninsula as soon as possible so that we can discuss our yearning for peace on the Korean Peninsula and collective prosperity of the nation. . . .

Moon returned with a message from Kim Jong-il. Kim argued that the best way to solve the nuclear problem was to "make the United States cease its hostile policy toward us." About the inter-Korean summit, he replied, "I think that I could meet President Roh anytime and anywhere once a favorable environment and climate is prepared."

Kim Yong-sun, head of North Korea's United Front Department, had just died, so his deputy, Lim Dong-ok, took over the task of speaking to the special envoy regarding the impending second round of SPTs. Lim said,

Based on President Bush's remark during the APEC summit that he was willing to guarantee us regime security in writing, we have decided to join the Six-Party Talks on the condition that the United States is willing to peacefully coexist with us and accept a proposal for overall settlement founded on the principle of simultaneous action.

North Korea also informed us that it wished to hold the second round of talks in December; they had already informed the United States and China. In addition, they said that at the talk they would be willing to rephrase the expression "principle of simultaneous action," which the United States had difficulty accepting, so long as its content was upheld. To guarantee nonaggression, they were "willing to make adjustments in consideration of each other's face in a positive way." The special envoy had brought back a positive message.

Sending the special envoy showed results much faster than we had anticipated. In December, North Korea informed us through the NIS of matters related to its dialogue with the United States as well as its position (December 9) and the outcome of a consultation with China (December 29), conducted when Chinese vice minister Wang Yi visited the North from December 25 to 27 in connection with the SPTs. In early February of the following year, the North reiterated to China, the United States, and us that it was indeed going to participate in the second round of the SPTs.

Just like that, starting in late 2003, the North changed its position on discussions of the nuclear problem, and began actively consulting the South on the issue. We, too, conveyed our position in a sustained fashion through the channel of inter-Korean dialogue.

Looking back, I see that 2003 was a year South Korean diplomacy faced unprecedented challenges; I lived through that year feeling like a man trying to navigate a jungle. But, unlike me, President Roh tried to understand and manage every situation strategically. Even though he was not an expert on foreign affairs or national security, he utilized his exceptionally strategic mind in handling the nuclear crisis, ROK-U.S. relations, and inter-Korean relations from his inauguration to the end of 2003. He did not try to solve these difficult and complex problems by mixing them together; he devised stages to tackle the problems one after another. As I see it, Roh, in three phases, made strategic decisions to move from crisis to peace in 2003.

In the first phase, Roh shut down the possibility that the North Korean nuclear crisis might lead to war and established the principle of solving the problem peacefully through dialogue. In the process, the president ran into differences with the United States, which was unwilling to rule out the possibility of a military sanction. He brooked discomfort in ROK-U.S. relations and did not hesitate to make public remarks to block American military action in advance. The result was the establishment of a principle of peaceful solution to the North Korean nuclear problem through dialogue.

In the second phase, Roh concentrated on stabilizing ROK-U.S. relations, rocked during the first phase, and on creating a structure of dialogue for solving the North Korean nuclear problem. It was precisely during this phase when he gave up on the idea of sending a special envoy to the North—even after an agreement was reached with Pyongyang—out of respect for U.S. opinion during the three-party talk. Then, in an atmosphere of cooperation, he held the ROK-U.S. summit. Even as the opposition party and the media strongly condemned him for South Korea's exclusion from the three-party talk, he supported it, and sought to transform it into the SPTs, opening a chapter for us to justifiably play a role as a party to the North Korean nuclear problem.

In phase three, President Roh looked for a way to strengthen our voice before the United States and North Korea in relation to the nuclear problem and to reinvigorate inter-Korean relations. During this phase, the president put front and center progress on the nuclear problem as a precondition of additional troop deployment to Iraq, and he extricated from President Bush, at the ROK-U.S. summit during the APEC meeting in October, a written declaration of willingness to guarantee security to the North. On another front, he sent the special envoy and a clear message to the North emphasizing the necessity of giving up the nuclear program. Once he believed that the nuclear crisis had come to a turning point, he simultaneously sought to create an impetus for improving inter-Korean relations.

Roh always emphasized that it was necessary to show the North our determination to solve the nuclear problem. He wanted to send the North a message, besides an official warning, that could have a real effect on the North's provocative behavior. For example, at an October 10, 2003, meeting of ministers concerned with national security, the president expressed his strong displeasure at the North Korean Foreign Ministry's recent announcement (made on October 2, 2003) of the completion of spent nuclear fuel reprocessing:

> If things continue like this, the North will, in the end, simply leave negotiations altogether. . . . We must make them see that we will not simply do as the North demands. . . . We must demand a more advanced position than before from President Bush at the APEC, but it is difficult to demand unilateral concessions from the United States. To demand

American concessions, we need to issue stronger warnings against the North.

But to send necessary messages to the North and heighten their effectiveness, trust between the leaders of the two Koreas was essential. That is why the president sent Moon Sung-keun as his special envoy.

10

Inter-Korean Relations:
Accomplishments and Ordeals

The Inter-Korean Agreement on the Northern Limit Line:
The President's National Security Vision
vs. the Military's Understanding

The Roh administration's efforts to improve inter-Korean relations and peace never went smoothly. Within and outside South Korea, there were friction and obstacles on several occasions. It was partly because government figures held different understandings of and attitudes toward the North Korea issue. It was also due to the distance between the principle of reconciliation and the reality of division. For example, the stabilization of the Northern Limit Line (NLL) and the agreement to cease propaganda activities near the military demarcation line show both the Roh administration's accomplishments, as well as the conflicts and noise inside the government that accompanied them.

The Second Battle of the West Sea[1] occurred on June 29, 2002, just after President Roh became the Millennium Democratic Party's presidential candidate. An unprovoked North Korean military strike resulted in the

---

[1] [Also known as the Second Battle of Yeonpyeong, the island near the incident. The so-called First Battle was a dispute over the NLL in June 1999.]

death of six South Korean soldiers and the sinking of a *Chamsuri*-class patrol boat. As the candidate of the ruling party, Roh deeply felt this tragic incident, and vowed to throw himself into stabilizing the western NLL—an annual source of tension when the crab season approached—if he were to become president.

I knew of the president's special interest in the NLL, so as soon as I became National Security Council (NSC) deputy secretary-general, I ordered the Office for Policy Coordination at the NSC Secretariat to quickly create a plan that would prevent, manage, and fundamentally resolve this annual crisis. The report came eight days after I took my office. On May 13, 2003, I went on an inspection tour of the Second Naval Fleet command in charge of defending the NLL and the islands of Yeonpyeong and Baeknyeong, as well as the fishing grounds near Yeonpyeong Island that were close to the NLL. The naval commander responsible for protecting Yeonpyeong Island lamented that our fishermen could not go into the bountiful fishing grounds near the NLL during the crab season; he expressed hope for an inter-Korean agreement that would allow fishing vessels from South and North Korea to alternate fishing near the NLL every other day. Although my tour was brief, in early June I had the Office of Strategic Planning draft a report on how to set an NLL policy. On June 11, I also briefed the president on my personal feelings after the visit, as well as on the plight of the fishermen. When President Roh received my report, he lamented the reality of the NLL and said we should try to come up with a solution within a year, in consultation with the North.

On June 27, 2003, just before the anniversary of the Battle of the West Sea, the president visited the Second Naval Fleet command headquarters. He gave a special order to "negotiate with the North and create a system that, without fail, would establish peace in the West Sea." The NSC Secretariat made stabilization of the NLL its top priority in its handling of inter-Korean relations and contacted the North after consulting relevant ministries on a possible measure. But the wall of mistrust and tension was high: the militaries of the two Koreas had never once reached a detailed agreement to relax military tensions. The North usually insisted that it would talk to only the United States about military matters.

But its attitude began to change after the special envoy's visit in November 2003, which inspired Pyongyang to begin an inter-Korean dialogue on the nuclear problem. Based on this, I believed that it would be possible for the two Koreas to hold a talk on more salient military issues, beyond simply winning a military guarantee to enable the work of building railways and roads across the Korean Demilitarized Zone (DMZ). Moved by the president's special interest and the comprehensive situation assessment by the NSC Standing Committee, on February 12, 2004, the Defense Ministry proposed to the North "a general-level talk to discuss the issue of relieving military tensions, including the prevention of accidental physical conflict in the West Sea." The North said nothing for months, but at the May 4 inter-Korean ministerial talks in Pyongyang, it expressed its intention to immediately accommodate the general-level talk. On May 12, 2004, the North Korean military leadership proposed hosting an inter-Korean generals' talk in the North, at Mt. Kumgang. On May 20, the North proposed, in addition to the topic of "prevention of maritime collision in the West Sea," the "issue of ending propaganda activities and dismantling instruments of propaganda along the DMZ."

The Defense Ministry and the Joint Chiefs of Staff were lukewarm about the proposal. But the president ordered an active review of it, an order welcomed by the Unification Ministry and the National Intelligence Service (NIS). Ending mutual slander in the DMZ and removing the means of propagandizing were significant steps toward relaxing military tensions and a great opportunity for improving inter-Korean relations. That is why the second clause of the 7.4 inter-Korean statement,[2] issued thirty years ago during the Cold War era, called for the end of mutual slander, and why the inter-Korean Basic Agreement signed during the Roh administration also stipulated that "South and North Korea will not slander or defame one another using the media, leaflets, or other means."

The joint chiefs, however, opposed dismantling instruments of propaganda. With our superior equipment, like electronic display boards and speakers, we had the upper hand in psychological warfare over the North. It was reasonable that the organization responsible for psychological warfare would react this way, since dismantling tools of propaganda would shake the foundation of their existence. From the president's perspective, national security would be achieved through two angles: strengthening the capacity for national defense and advancing peace. If we continued to fight just because our propaganda tools were superior, there would never be room for efforts toward promoting peace. For the last several decades we had expressed our rage at the North's slander of the South and its dissemination of leaflets. Yet even today the two Koreas blasted their speakers at each other across the DMZ, and weren't our soldiers on the frontline unable to sleep well at night because of it?

---

2   [Also known as the July 4 South-North Joint Communiqué.]

The positions of the president and the NSC Standing Committee on this issue were clear, but the committee decided to proceed with the inter-Korean negotiation by determining that we would first cease the propaganda from both sides, but would not dismantle the equipment, in consideration of the opposition from the joint chiefs. If this half-measure proved unfeasible, we would strike a compromise by exchanging our proposal to stabilize the NLL for the North's proposal to end propaganda.

We appointed a naval admiral, not someone from the army, as the head of our delegation at the inter-Korean generals' talk, because our main interest was in preventing accidental conflicts in the West Sea. On May 21, I held a discussion with our delegation, headed by the navy's Rear Admiral Park Jeong-hwa. I stressed four points: (1) do not react emotionally to the other side's words and refuse to discuss matters beyond the topic of the talk by simply responding, "I don't know"; (2) achieving no outcome is acceptable, so do not plead with the other side just to produce results; (3) do not argue over minor issues—stick to the fundamentals; and (4) when the NSC Standing Committee affirms its guidelines, abide by them, no matter what.

On May 26, 2004, the historic first inter-Korean generals' talk took place at a guesthouse on Mt. Kumgang. There were great differences between the two Koreas over how to prevent accidental clashes in the West Sea. The North argued that we should first come to an agreement on a new maritime border. It demanded that ending propaganda activities in the DMZ and dismantling the equipment be done simultaneous to any decision on the West Sea issue. Their delegation was particularly interested in stopping propaganda and dismantling the equipment. They pressured the southern delegation by saying this could not be that difficult, when tensions had already been lowered to the point of allowing railway and roads to be built in the DMZ. They reminded us that there had already been a tentative agreement on this issue at the second inter-Korean ministerial talks in October 2002, at the end of Kim Dae-jung's term. Since we focused on the West Sea problem without mentioning the propaganda issue, the negotiations could not proceed and we decided to continue them in early June.

The NSC Standing Committee, out of respect for the Defense Ministry, had approved the strategy of delaying the dismantling of propaganda equipment, but the North's stubbornness was putting the entire negotiation in jeopardy. This had been entirely expected, so we needed to issue new negotiation guidelines.

Roh believed that delaying the removal of propaganda equipment appeared to offer no clear benefits, not to mention seeming entirely inappropriate in view of the president's comprehensive national security strategy. This issue was much less important than preventing conflict along the NLL, which had become the peninsula's powder keg. While the president had advised Kim Jong-il in his letter to "boldly, totally solve all without dividing issues into smaller pieces or pushing and tugging," the Defense Ministry's negotiation direction was making the president look like he was going against his own words, finely slicing issues for the sake of small gains.

The Defense Ministry created new negotiation guidelines that still focused on maintaining the propaganda equipment, but the NSC Standing Committee ordered the delegation to negotiate more actively. In response, the Defense Ministry proposed a way of removing the propaganda equipment in steps.

The second inter-Korean generals' talk took place in South Korea on Mt. Seorak from June 3 to 4. The two Koreas continued negotiations through the night to reach an agreement. To improve our negotiating power, the government linked this talk to the ninth inter-Korean economic cooperation committee's meeting, taking place simultaneously in Pyongyang. At that meeting, the government had planned to promise to ship four hundred thousand tons of rice to the North, as in the previous year. But now it made the rice shipments conditional on an agreement to establish a system to prevent accidental clashes on the West Sea. The inter-Korean economic cooperation committee delayed drafting its final agreement text, even though it had reached an agreement on all matters except the rice aid. They waited in Pyongyang for the outcome of the generals' talk.

The two Koreas finally came to an agreement on June 4 at 4:30 a.m. The military delegations simultaneously agreed on a series of measures to prevent accidental clashes on the West Sea and to dismantle propaganda equipment along the military demarcation line. In the resulting pact, the "Agreement Concerning the Prevention of Accidental Clashes in the West Sea and the Stoppage of Propaganda Activities and Removal of Propaganda Equipment in the Military Demarcation Line Area," the two Koreas agreed to establish a direct phone line between the militaries, to exchange information on illegal fishing routes, and to communicate via the International Maritime Very High Frequency (VHF) Radio (156.8 megahertz [MHz], 156.6 MHz) to prevent confrontations between ships (due to confusion during navigation) and eliminate misunderstandings. The decision was also made to cease propaganda activities in the area near the military demarcation line and remove propaganda equipment. At the same time, in Pyongyang, the heads of the two Korean delegations signed the agreement on the shipment of four hundred thousand tons of rice to the North in the form of a loan.

The agreement reached at the second inter-Korean generals' talk was the first ever between the militaries of the two Koreas aimed at relaxing military tensions. It also marked the realization of the goal, specified in the president's special order from a year earlier, to find a way to prevent military clashes along the NLL. The two Koreas also activated a system for ending all propaganda activities along the DMZ and gradually dismantling the propaganda equipment starting on June 15, 2004—the fourth anniversary of the 6.15 joint statement.

I feel this important agreement, a groundbreaking event for relaxing inter-Korean military tensions under the Roh administration, has not been properly appreciated. The absence of even a single clash along the NLL and the DMZ during the Roh administration's five-year tenure, not to mention the absence of even a single casualty—whether military or civilian, due to an inter-Korean clash—attests to its significance. This breakthrough agreement was behind this record, not to mention the efforts of the two Korean governments and their militaries to abide by it.

A Military Report Omission and a Troubling Act of Insubordination

On July 14, 2004, just after five o'clock in the afternoon, an emergency report that completely shattered the accomplishments of the inter-Korean NLL agreement came to the NSC situation room from an intelligence office to the Joint Chiefs of Staff. It said that a North Korean patrol ship had crossed the NLL into the South. A South Korean vessel broadcast a warning and, when there was no response, fired a warning shot. The North Korean vessel was repelled. It all started at 4:40 p.m. and lasted for about twenty minutes. The report unsettled me. More than anything, I was greatly disappointed that the North had not responded, even though we had broadcast a warning. Was the inter-Korean agreement for preventing accidental clashes along the NLL—accomplished with such incredible effort—only a piece of paper? Having spearheaded this agreement, I could not say anything before the public and certainly was too ashamed to see the president. I asked the joint chiefs to reconfirm the facts—the response was that the North had not answered our communications.

That evening, the joint chiefs' public relations office issued a press release: "A North Korean patrol ship invaded the NLL by 0.7 mile fifteen miles west of Yeonpyong-do while pursuing Chinese fishing vessels. Our naval vessel fired warning shots." This press release said that our naval vessel had used the International Maritime VHF Radio to broadcast a warning to the North Korean vessel in accordance with the inter-Korean agreement. When the reporters asked if the North had responded, the spokesperson replied, "The North didn't respond."

This incident, coming only forty days after the agreement at the inter-Korean generals' talk, attracted attention not because there had been warning shots, but over the question of whether there had been communication between the two sides. The president harbored the same question. The media began condemning and ridiculing us, calling the inter-Korean agreement a worthless document.

But the very next day a high-ranking NIS official came to my office with an alarmed look on his face. "Take a look—the North *did* reply to our warning yesterday." He showed me a special communications log that clearly recorded three replies from the North. The first reply had come after hearing our broadcast and before the warning shots: "What has veered off course is not our fishing vessel but a Chinese one! A Chinese fishing vessel!" The second reply came at about the same time as our warning shot: "Traveling south is a Chinese fishing vessel. You must sail south." The final message had been one minute after the warning shot: "You have violated the military demarcation line by one mile. Sail south."

If yesterday I had been unsettled, today I was in shock. According to this log, our military had lied to us and to the Blue House. Something was not right. There had essentially been two fraudulent reports: one, from the navy, which did not report the communication between the two sides to the superiors; the other, from the joint chiefs, who had been made aware of the communication by the intelligence office, but had intentionally deleted the North's response before sending the report to the NSC situation room.

This was a major issue. I summarized the facts and reported them to the president, together with National Security Advisor Kwon Jin-ho. The president took the matter very seriously and held an emergency meeting of the NSC Standing Committee.

The president's order was clear: he wanted an investigation into why the navy had concealed that the vessels from both sides had been in communication, and how the portion containing the North's replies had been deleted from the communications log. Roh did not take issue with the ground response of firing warning shots at the North Korean patrol ship. The navy had been within its rights to deem the North Korean military's reply as deceptive and fire warning shots on the spot—this was not a matter for the president or the NSC to determine. But the commander should have reported them. If he had not had the wits to report them in the moment, he should have made a report after the situation wound down. Furthermore, hadn't the Blue House asked whether there had been any reply from the North?

That evening, Major General Ahn Ik-san, the head of the North Korean delegation at the inter-Korean generals' talks, sent a message of protest to our delegation chief, charging that the North had "called your side three times and informed you of the movements of fishing vessels from a third nation." But the South had not replied, and instead had fired warning shots.

An emergency meeting of the NSC Standing Committee was held on the morning of July 16, 2004. After listening to the Defense Ministry's report, we decided to form a joint investigation team to uncover the whole truth of the situation, and announce the outcome of the meeting to the press. As we saw it, the failure to report the communication contents through the chain of command within the Defense Ministry was not a simple technical issue, but a serious problem with the command structure operation. The NSC Secretariat did not participate in the investigation; instead it watched the situation one step removed. If the navy had simply reported that the North had replied to our warning, but that we had fired warning shots after determining that they were being deceptive, there would have been no problem—the whole affair would have come to an end with the NSC and the military both contemplating the introduction of additional measures to guarantee the validity of the inter-Korean agreement. But instead the situation had unfolded in a strange direction.

The investigation team, made up of army generals, conducted its work quickly and reported its findings to the president on July 19. It revealed that the commander of the Second Naval Fleet had reported the North's communications to the operation commander of the navy, who had failed to report it to the joint chiefs; in addition, a relevant defense intelligence office that dealt with special intelligence (SI) had not reported the communications log recording the North's replies to his superiors. Therefore, the president and the NSC, not to mention the defense minister and the chairman of the joint chiefs, had not been informed.

However, the investigation report itself glossed over such facts, essentially ignoring the presidential order to ascertain what had happened, establish the responsibility for the omission, and seek a way to prevent recurrence. It only focused on arguing that our military had responded legitimately to the North's NLL violation. It gave the impression that the navy had not reported the North's replies because they were deceptive, and even seemed to be justifying the omission. But the reporting of deceptive communications is a routine matter. It is moreover unthinkable that a defense intelligence office should intentionally excise parts of a special communications log before reporting an incident. Everything about this felt wrong.

The president was disappointed that the result of the investigation appeared to be an attempt to cover up the omission in the original report by justifying the on-site response. He ordered another investigation on July 19 and made it clear, through the Blue House spokesperson, that "the focus of this investigation is not whether the conduct on the ground had been appropriate, but whether the situation had been properly reported at the time." He said, "While the issue of operations is determined by the commander-in-charge, reports to superiors must be accurate, no matter what."

But some inside the military bristled at the president's order of an additional investigation. Park Sung-choon, the head of intelligence under the joint chiefs and in charge of the intelligence office that had produced the problematic communications log, met with reporters from three media outlets who covered the Defense Ministry, and leaked special intelligence, including the contents of the communication with the North Korean vessel at the time of the incident, and the subsequent notification from the North. He distorted the substance of the matter in a strange direction and argued that the military's response had been justified. For the head of a military intelligence apparatus, this insubordination was unacceptable behavior. It created a crisis in which the conservative media and the opposition party led the public to think that the Blue House was unjustifiably persecuting the military. The July 20 conservative press editorials had such titles as "Silence on NLL Violation, Interested Only in Why?"; "Swayed by the North but Selling Out Our Military?"; and "First Investigate Why North Korean Patrol Vessel Crossed into South under Deception." They all tried to gloss over the issue at the heart of the problem.

The situation continued its strange evolution. Without even being able to evaluate the conduct of commanders who had violated military rules, the Blue House was suddenly at odds with the military. I witnessed the massive power of the media establishment, which could, in matters related to the North, distort a lie into a fact. To use the classical Chinese axiom, they could "point at a deer and turn it into a horse." I needed all my experience and cunning to fight against this power, which I was unable to counter even in my position managing state affairs.

The outcome of the investigation by the second team, on July 23, proved to be a complete letdown; it ascribed the problem to the "misjudgment and carelessness on the part of the commander." After dealing with national defense issues for three years as NSC deputy secretary-general, I had to conclude that the while the military may be a bulwark of national defense, it was also a massive special-interest group. The Roh administration had, as a show of respect to the military, allowed the investigation team to be made up from the military, an organization separate from civil society. It was a necessary move considering the possible impact on military morale. But this decision amounted to letting the cat guard the fish, and from the start the hope for an objective conclusion to the investigation seemed impossible. This was our limit.

We had to bring the affair to a conclusion; at the very least, I thought the commanders who made false reports, including the naval operations commander, should be severely punished as an example. But I could not give the president such advice. The conservative media giants, on the side of the military, were deliberately inciting a battle between the military and the Blue House. Severe punishment would only worsen the situation, and the president's ability to govern would be hindered. Yet if we did not correct the military's behavior, the administration's pursuit of autonomous defense might become more difficult.

I could neither move forward nor fall back. I often discussed the issue with National Security Advisor Kwon Jin-ho and National Defense Advisor Yoon Kwang-woong, who shared my concerns. Ultimately Yoon, who had once served as the navy's operations commander, advised the president to consider a light punishment. Yoon, who had attended the president's high school, had the ability to sway others. The president may have preferred a stronger punishment, but he accepted Yoon's recommendation.

The president found a way to restructure the military without getting embroiled in the conservative media's plot to sow division. On July 28, he fired Defense Minister Cho Young-kil and appointed National Defense Advisor Yoon Kwang-woong, who commanded the president's trust and the NSC's respect, as his successor.

Executing the State's Basic Obligations and Its Price: Inter-Korean Relations Gone Wrong

The Roh administration pursued dialogue and communication with the North, but the reality of division and confrontation remained.

In early summer 2004, Elder Park Yong-gil—the wife of late Pastor Moon Ik-hwan—and six people from Tongil Maji, a pro-unification organization, requested permission to visit the North. Their objective was not an ordinary exchange project but a condolence call at Kumsusan Memorial Palace, where the body of Kim Il-sung was enshrined. They wanted to pay their respects on the tenth anniversary of Kim Il-sung's death. The North invited them because of the special connection between Kim and Pastor Moon, who had visited the North in 1989 and discussed unification in person with the North Korean leader. To address this topic, a high-level strategic meeting was held, chaired by Unification Minister Chung Dong-young.

It was a difficult issue. If the government gave its permission, the opposition party and the media would assail the decision on ideological grounds, intensifying social division and disrupting the president's ability to govern; on the other hand, I wondered how long we should allow such a climate of confrontation to continue, which did not permit even those people with special personal connections to pay respect to the dead. I thought these issues needed to be overcome, one by one, for genuine inter-Korean reconciliation. But one question weighed on my mind: Pastor Moon Ik-hwan's son, Moon Sung-keun, had recently visited Pyongyang as a special secret envoy in November 2003. If Elder Park Yong-gil were to go to the North, it would certainly create a great controversy, and if as a result Moon Sung-keun's trip as special envoy became known, the problem would become very serious. Conspiracy theorists would link these two unrelated matters as one and spread slanderous criticism; there would be an incredible backlash.

I attended the meeting without having made up my mind, but everyone else was unanimous in opposition to the trip: "Given the current domestic situation and public sentiment, it is premature to permit condolence visits to the North." Most in attendance were enthusiastic supporters of the government's engagement policy, but were worried about the possible backlash from a visit and came to this decision even though they were unaware of Moon Sung-keun's visit to the North. It was thus easy for me to put aside my concerns, and the government officially rejected the application by Park's entourage to visit the North. As expected, the North strongly condemned the decision.

Not long after, a large-scale transfer of North Korean defectors in Vietnam further dampened inter-Korean relations. In spring 2004, the South Korean embassy in Vietnam had requested emergency assistance over a sudden spike in the number of North Korean defectors entering Vietnam and coming to the South Korean embassy. It was reportedly on the verge of becoming a diplomatic crisis. Until 1998, the Vietnam-ese government had allowed the transfer to South Korea of defectors who tried to reach the South Korean embassy via the so-called Ho Chi Minh route connecting Yunnan Province, China, to Vietnam. But in consideration of its relations with North Korea and over worries that Vietnam would become an established route for escaping the North, Hanoi stopped assisting the transfer of defectors to the South following a final case involving the South Korea–bound transfer of five defectors in August 1998. After that, any defector arrested by the Vietnamese police would be sent back to North Korea.

This did not reduce the number of defectors traveling into Vietnam—the number actually increased. In 2003 alone, some 40 percent of all defectors transported to South Korea had arrived via the Ho Chi Minh route. But the Vietnamese government did not know this. The Republic of Korea (ROK) embassy in Vietnam could not reject all the incoming defectors, since it was the state's duty to protect them. The number of defectors in Vietnam that the South Korean government could transport in secrecy to a third country for the ultimate purpose of bringing them to South Korea was around ten per week. But by 2004, the number that made it to the embassy had increased to many times what we were able to transport to a third country. As of June 24, 2004, 382 North Korean defectors were being housed in five different secret safe houses provided by our embassy around Ho Chi Minh City. As the time required to trans-port these defectors to the South grew longer and more people moved into the safe houses, problems began to occur. With many people packed in small spaces for a long time, violence and conflict became frequent.

Our embassy in Vietnam reported that it could no longer accommodate all the defectors who were coming; if the situation persisted, there was a strong possibility of discovery by the Vietnamese and a subsequent diplomatic incident. The NSC Standing Committee, deliberating the matter, was worried that if hundreds of defectors protected by the South Korean embassy were sent back to North Korea, it would not only be a serious humanitarian problem but also have a serious impact on inter-Korean relations, as well as on relations between South Korea and Vietnam. After some discussion, I proposed an idea: we should negotiate with the Vietnamese government and bring the defectors all at once to the South in secrecy. There was no other answer. If the situation became public, the Vietnamese government would also be in a tough position. The NSC Standing Committee chose my solution and reported it to the president, who, while not entirely happy, approved it as the only way.

On May 28, 2004, Foreign Minister Ban Ki-moon met with the Vietnamese ambassador in Seoul and officially requested cooperation in transporting the defectors in Ho Chi Minh City to South Korea. Vietnam, unaware of the large number of defectors in hiding, demanded a detailed accounting from our government. From then on, we contacted the Vietnamese government through a number of diplomatic channels in an effort to solve the crisis. During these negotiations, our intelligence apparatus, not to mention the Foreign Ministry, played a large role. In late June, the Vietnamese government agreed to the idea of using our charter planes to transport the defectors to South Korea, on the condition that utmost secrecy would be maintained. We agreed to carry out the operation over two days, July 27 and 28.

But just one day before the operation, it was leaked to the domestic press by the missionary organization that was helping the defectors in Vietnam. The government had repeatedly impressed on the organization the importance of security, but it was for naught. I regretted their refusal to respect national interests. Nonetheless, 468 of the North Korean defectors in Vietnam safely made it to South Korea.

The government had upheld its duty of protecting the North Korean defectors who sought refuge through our embassy, but we had paid a steep price. Inter-Korean relations came to a temporary halt—the North defined the incident as the kidnapping of its own citizens and fiercely condemned the South, canceling the inter-Korean ministerial talk scheduled for August. The Vietnamese government also expressed its strong regret in the domestic press and articulated its position that no further assistance of North Korean defectors was possible. We could not say anything in response, since we ultimately had not been able to keep our promise. Relations between North Korea and Vietnam also suffered. The North Korean Foreign Ministry issued a statement on August 4 condemning the Vietnamese government for the transportation of the defectors to the South. And on August 8, Pyongyang recalled Ambassador Park Eung-seob from Vietnam and dispatched in his place a *chargé d'affaires*, a position one rank lower than that of ambassador.

I had no excuse to offer the president—I had told him that I would take care of things quietly, but the result had been anything but. He had every right to reprimand me but did not. He only expressed his regret over this incident several times, until the resumption of dialogue between the two Koreas in May 2005.

Despite the unexpected media leak, I would still make the same choice if faced with the situation again. It had been the only way to safely transport to South Korea the hundreds of defectors who were housed in our embassy's safe houses in Vietnam, a country with friendly relations with North Korea. But this incident, along with the disallowance of the condolence call in July 2004, instantly froze inter-Korean relations, despite the recent historic agreement at the generals' talk.

Seven Ignored Messages, then Total Resumption of Dialogue

Such events led to the North's refusal of official inter-Korean dialogue in the second half of 2004, though civilian exchanges and economic cooperation continued. Amid the suspension of dialogue, the government still routinely processed the humanitarian food aid already promised to the North.

Even with inter-Korean dialogue at a standstill, the government worked to send a special envoy to the North in fall 2004. Originally, the NSC had decided to review a new way of solving the North Korean nuclear crisis if the third Six-Party Talks (June 23–26) were unproductive. And when those ended without any meaningful progress, the idea was raised to send a special envoy to coax a more favorable position from the North and propose a revolutionary conception of inter-Korean relations. The U.S. reaction was also positive. A special envoy, dispatched in consultation between the U.S. and ROK NSCs, could deliver not only President Roh's personal letter, but a U.S. message as well. Presidents Roh and Bush, during a phone call, came to an agreement on this. With even the United States in a rare positive mood about the special envoy, I was eager to make it a success. The timing of the visit was to be decided as early as possible, for any time beginning the fourth week of September.

But the North did not respond. Our refusal to allow the condolence call, on top of the large-scale transportation of North Korean defectors to the South, had already poisoned the well. Then, in early September, a series of tests on nuclear materials by the Korea Nuclear Power Research Center in 2000 was disclosed to the media, which provoked the North. This so-called nuclear materials incident, which raised suspicion that the ROK government had attempted to develop nuclear weapons, could prove useful to the North, which was in the middle of international negotiations over its nuclear program. Then talk began in the United States suggesting that Congress would pass the North Korean Human Rights Act under the Bush administration's leadership. The act was indeed passed, unanimously, in both houses of Congress in October 2004. All this served as an excuse for the North to shy away from our special envoy, worsening inter-Korean relations.

I realized then how difficult it was to shift the North Korea problem in another direction. As a North Korea specialist, I had long argued that it was important to send consistent messages to the North for policy to succeed. But this was not an easy feat. The matters of the condolence call and the defectors in Vietnam had not been offensive maneuvers against the North but unavoidable choices on our part, given domestic circumstances and state obligations, but the North still read them as negative messages counter to our previous policy. And what can be said about the combative U.S. North Korean Human Rights Act? In the end, the plan to send a special envoy to the North only took place on paper.

A new opportunity for dialogue came in January 2005. On January 13, as the spring planting season approached, the North sent a message in the name of the chairman of the North Korean Red Cross Society's central committee, addressed to the Korean Red Cross Society president, Han Wan-sang. They were requesting aid in the form of five hundred thousand tons of fertilizer. On January 18, the government, under the auspices of Unification Minister Chung Dong-Young, held a high-level strategic meeting on North Korea to discuss this matter. Fertilizer aid was a humanitarian matter and was ostensibly under the purview of the Korean Red Cross Society, but because the expenses were paid by the government, it was customary for the government to determine the feasibility, timing, and scale of the fertilizer aid provided annually and to propose in exchange another humanitarian matter: the reunion of divided families.

Things were different this time. Despite being a humanitarian matter officially handled by the Red Cross, the government could not respond to the request after the North had refused dialogue between Seoul and Pyongyang. We decided that our response to the North's fertilizer request would be that, first, official dialogue between the two Koreas had to take place.

I regretted the Red Cross would not be allowed to provide unconditional aid on humanitarian grounds, but the fertilizer was paid for with taxpayer money and the government had to maintain at least this much resolve.

At our request, the Korea Red Cross Society replied to its Northern counterpart that the government was reviewing the matter, without making any detailed promises about the aid. The North did not reply. On February 1, the North Korean Red Cross Society sent a second message, urging us to provide the fertilizer. The message implied that if the South provided fertilizer, inter-Korean dialogue could resume. In return, the government made a proposal in the name of the unification minister to hold a working group meeting to discuss current issues between the two Koreas, including the question of fertilizer. The North ignored us and sent its third message to the Korean Red Cross Society: "We regret that you have not sent a clear answer to our proposal." Then the Korean Red Cross Society sent another message to the North on February 15 at the government's behest, more clearly articulating our principle: "Fertilizer aid requires a significant budget and the public's consent. This is an issue that requires internal review and must be decided through an agreement between Seoul and Pyongyang." In other words, come to an official talk if you want your fertilizer.

At this juncture, the NSC Secretariat was in the process of reviewing an important proposal that it had drafted, to be presented to the North. The goal of this proposal was to further progress on the nuclear crisis. To present the North with this proposal—which I will discuss in greater detail below—inter-Korean dialogue had to resume and our special envoy had to meet with Chairman Kim Jong-il. It became even more important to resume inter-Korean dialogue by using the fertilizer aid as a catalyst.

But it is the nature of inter-Korean dialogue that the more we hurry, the more complicated things become, and the higher the costs. The North, which did not know what was on our minds, was probably feeling more pressured. I thought that to realize inter-Korean dialogue it was best to maintain our composure in the face of repeated messages from the North. After our latest response, the North sent its fourth message urging aid be sent, using rather coarse and threatening language:

> If you try to make the issue of fertilizer aid into official business between the two sides, to end even humanitarian cooperation, or to politicize the fertilizer issue and complicate the situation, it will have irreversible consequences, not only for the Red Cross, but for inter-Korean relations as a whole. The responsibility for this will be squarely on your Red Cross Society and your government.

This time we did not even bother to reply.

Then on February 24, the North sent a fifth message urging us to provide fertilizer. When we did not respond yet again, the North sent an emotion-filled sixth message on March 7:

> Not only has your side failed in the last two months to send a clear answer about providing fertilizer, it has not even sent any answer to the messages from our side after informing us that it was turning the fertilizer matter over to the government. . . . Such are the facts. Your side has failed to abide by the basic position of the Red Cross, politicized the issue of providing fertilizer, and even avoided answering our messages. This is extremely rude conduct that destroys the foundation of trust between the two sides' Red Cross organizations. We regret that this abnormal situation has been created by your side and express our concern over how this situation will develop.

On the afternoon of March 9, another high-level strategic meeting on North Korea took place under Minister Chung Dong-young's watch to discuss how to respond to the North's sixth message. One opinion was that we should put an end to the tug-of-war at this juncture and propose official dialogue. Some expressed worry that inter-Korean relations might deteriorate even further if we held out for too long. But I did not see it as the right time. We had already conveyed our position that official dialogue was necessary to enable fertilizer aid. The North should either respond by proposing dialogue, or be ready to immediately accept when we proposed official dialogue. But to get that far, the North had to feel a little more desperate and we had to hold out a little longer.

As the presidential advisor in charge of overseeing unification, foreign affairs, and national security, I always felt badly that the unification minister had not even had a chance to be at the forefront of inter-Korean dialogue since taking his post on July 1, 2004. So it weighed on me that I might be arguing for a choice that could further worsen inter-Korean relations if things went wrong. But I thought that we should maintain our position if we were to create proper conditions for inter-Korean dialogue on this occasion. I stuck to my guns at the meeting and won support.

When our side again sent a message reiterating our original position, the North Korean Red Cross Society sent its seventh message the very next day, full of threatening language that sounded like a farewell to the Korean Red Cross Society:

> Our position is clear: We recognize that it will be difficult from now on to solve basic humanitarian issues, much less pursue cooperative projects, together with your Red Cross Society, which has blindly refused our repeated requests for fertilizer from a compatriotic and humanitarian perspective, by insisting it is a matter for negotiation between authorities. The insincere and uncooperative attitude of your Red Cross Society, far from what should be its correct attitude, causes extreme regret and will certainly be taken into consideration in the future. All responsibility for the aftermath will be borne by your side.

I felt bad that the North Korean Red Cross Society had slandered its southern counterpart with the charge of being anti-humanitarian. But we still did not reply to the North's message.

Then an opportunity to restart the inter-Korean dialogue came in early May. On May 4, Red Cross president Han Wan-sang informed the North that in mid-May he wanted to visit Yongcheon, North Korea, where a large-scale explosion had taken place in April. The North Korea Red Cross Society promptly sent a proposal in a May 5 message: "If you first provide 200,000 tons of fertilizer and the first ship leaves port, followed by President Han's arrival in Pyongyang, we can negotiate over matters currently on the table between the two Koreas' Red Cross Societies." The North was desperate, and the government decided the time was ripe.

At last, the government decided to embark on an inter-Korean dialogue after a high-level strategic meeting. On May 10, we sent a message to the North in the name of the Red Cross president: "Our government will shortly deliver to the North its position on matters facing the two Koreas, including the issue of fertilizer." On the morning of May 11, North Korea used an unofficial communication channel to express its intent to hold inter-Korean dialogue, even as it assailed our behavior.

On the afternoon of May 11, the government proposed, in the name of Unification Minister Chung Dong-young, a working group meeting between the two sides as soon as possible. The North reacted immediately. The very next day, May 12, the North proposed that a working group meeting between vice-minister-level officials as chief representatives be held in Kaesong or at Mt. Kumgang as soon as the South floated its first ship carrying fertilizer.

Finally, the four-month-long tug-of-war between the two Koreas came to an end and a period of full-scale inter-Korean dialogue began. The transition from a boring battle of wills to dialogue was so short that it could literally be described as a "moment." Once the Korean Red Cross Society informed the Northern side on May 10 that our government was on its way to delivering its position, it took only three days for the North to propose a working group meeting between vice-minister-level officials. And on May 16, a three-night, four-day inter-Korean vice-ministers' talk began in Kaesong, and that same day, a ship carrying fertilizer to the North left our port. Things could proceed at lightning speed because the two Koreas had anticipated that dialogue would resume in May at the latest and had made sufficient preparations beforehand.

At the working group talk in Kaesong, it was decided that the "6.15 Unification Grand Celebration" would be held in Pyongyang, a South Korean delegation headed by a minister-rank official would be dispatched, and the fifteenth inter-Korean ministers' talk would be held in Seoul starting on June 21. The government also proposed through an official channel the idea of exchanging special envoys for a comprehensive consultation on inter-Korean matters, including the nuclear problem. The government revealed at the same time that the South's special envoy would carry a "proposal of great significance" and meet National Defense Chairman Kim Jong-il, revealing its contents only at that moment. Of course, we said absolutely nothing to the North about the contents of this proposal. In fact, even inside the government, few people knew about this proposal besides the president, Prime Minister Lee Hae-chan, and members of the NSC Standing Committee such as the unification, foreign, and defense ministers.

11

Toward the 9.19 Joint Statement

The North Korean Nuclear Crisis:
"Tell Washington to Let Us Handle It for One Year"

In autumn 2004, I believed that it was possible to make the North give up its nuclear program in exchange for regime security and financial compensation. No, we *had* to make it do so. Otherwise, the future of the state and the nation would be too bleak. If the nuclear problem could not be solved, then we had to accept the current security crisis and the inter-Korean confrontation as a constant, no matter what else we did. In that case, the Roh administration would have no opportunity to pursue its policy for peace on the Korean Peninsula or its vision of collective prosperity for the two Koreas. The president's five-year term would be a waste. I became conscious of the desperate nature of the crisis.

But objectively viewed, solving the nuclear problem appeared to be a distant reality. Rather than contemplating a mutually beneficial win-win solution, the United States was more interested in refusing bilateral dialogue and bringing the North to its knees through a five-to-one dynamic at the Six-Party Talks (SPTs). The North did not bend before the U.S. hardline policy, instead resorting to the risky approach of visibly strengthening its nuclear capability step by step. If Bush were reelected in November and his administration continued to implement its hardline policy under these circumstances, the likely outcome of this head-to-head conflict would be a continued North Korean nuclear program. That would mean the government could not seriously pursue a single item on its agenda, whether it be North Korea policy, autonomous defense, or balanced diplomacy. Therefore, we tried to send a special envoy to persuade the North, but could not do even that. Ultimately, we had no choice but to first persuade the United States.

With this in mind, I presented to the president on November 5, 2004, the "Plan to Make Progress in the North Korean Nuclear Crisis and Inter-Korean relations after the U.S. Presidential Election," a report the NSC Secretariat had drafted in consultation with various ministries. In evaluating the first two years of the Roh administration, I advised the president that the most important task now was "creating a watershed moment in the North Korean nuclear crisis and making qualitative progress in inter-Korean relations." I said it was necessary to actively persuade President Bush, who was expected to easily win reelection, and develop a proactive, aggressive vision that would help overcome the problems at hand—the delays in solving the North Korean nuclear crisis and the stagnation of inter-Korean relations. I proposed that to realize this, we had to move toward a policy of securing U.S. flexibility through consultation with Washington. Taking it one step further, we had to make an inter-Korean summit happen. I advised the president that it was necessary that he proclaim his strong determination regarding the North Korean nuclear problem and inter-Korean relations in his upcoming November 13 speech in Los Angeles. And, at the Republic of Korea (ROK)–U.S. summit scheduled for November 20 in Santiago, presidents Roh and Bush should reach common ground in recognizing the need for a flexible solution to the nuclear crisis.

After the briefing, the president must have felt incredibly frustrated. He asked his advisors, "How about I propose to the United States to let us handle the nuclear problem for the next year, in the spirit of alliance?" His thinking was that, although Seoul and Washington disagreed on how to solve the nuclear crisis, we had tried for the last two years to do things according to U.S. policy, but there had been no progress—so why not ask the Bush administration to let us take the initiative, even if only for 2005? If South Korea failed to make major progress on the nuclear issue within the SPT framework even after that, then Seoul would raise no further objection and agree to U.S. policy going forward. The idea was worth trying in theory, but there was no way the Bush administration would go for it. The United States was less than thrilled with the South Korean government, which did not silently follow Washington's own policy and argued about right and wrong at every turn; it was unimaginable that Washington would give Seoul the freedom to act on the North Korean nuclear issue based on its own judgment, even if it were for only a limited time. This kind of proposal itself could actually lead to a grave misunderstanding, so it was going to be hard enough just to raise it with Washington. But since the president had spoken, the NSC Secretariat prepared a way for Roh to bring up the proposal with Bush, just in case. But this plan was never executed—the president himself knew that the United States would never accept the proposal.

In any event, President Roh decided that in 2005 South Korea must lead in finding a way to break the impasse over the North Korean nuclear issue. He told his advisors how the government should behave in solving the nuclear problem:

> The United States has a wide range of choices concerning the North Korean nuclear problem. In comparison, we don't have much room. Despite this, we must ultimately create a balanced and rational plan, based on the knowledge that this is our job, and propose it to the North and the United States, while taking a leading role. It is necessary for us to move forward with the resolve to maintain our basic position and, at times, say uncomfortable things.

The NSC Secretariat accepted what the president said and prepared for the approaching year. We decided to lower the threshold for agreement at the SPTs by attempting to persuade Washington, and by asking Beijing to try to persuade the North, which was opposed to reopening the SPTs after their third round in June 2004. And we decided to restart inter-Korean dialogue and to send a special envoy to persuade the North.

President Roh's first step going into 2005 was in the form of a statement made during his conversation with members of the Korean American community in Los Angeles on November 13:

> The North argues that its nuclear program and missiles are a deterrence measure for protecting itself from external danger. Such words are generally difficult to believe, but I see that the North's argument concerning this problem has an element of logic, given various circumstances.

The president's remarks were sufficiently calculated. In a prior discussion, advisors, including myself, suggested to the president that, while we sufficiently understood his intentions, the statement should be toned down, given its possible effect on U.S. relations. But Roh rejected our concerns after long deliberation. The president was trying to send a clear message to everyone, including North Korea and the other participating nations of the SPTs. He wanted to put the brakes on a hardline approach to the North, which was being argued for in the United States after Bush's reelection. He wanted to signal that Seoul did not agree with the United States' unilateral arguments—that the North should first denuclearize or that Washington should avoid direct talks with Pyongyang—and that it sought to influence the direction of policy under the Bush administration in its second term. He also was indicating a certain understanding of the North's position, and asking the North to accept and respect South Korea's role as balancer during discussions on the nuclear problem. To China, which chaired the SPTs, as well as the other participating nations, this was a strong message that Seoul would take a more active role in solving the problem than it had in the past.

President Roh's efforts to lead progress in the nuclear crisis was on ample display at a ROK-U.S. summit that took place alongside the Asia-Pacific Economic Cooperation (APEC) meeting in Santiago after the Los Angeles event. Many people had been pessimistic about the prospects of this summit, following as it did the Los Angeles remarks, but the summit ended in success. President Roh was able to extract important concessions from President Bush regarding the nuclear problem. Bush, successfully reelected, in a rare mood showed much interest in peacefully solving the nuclear problem. But his understanding of the solution or of the North had not changed at all. As always, he wanted "the United States, South Korea, Japan, China, and Russia in a single voice" to pressure the North his way. He also refused bilateral talks with the North. And as he had done at each summit, he again expressed extreme mistrust of Kim Jong-il:

> I really don't trust Kim Jong-il. I will tell you why. He lied to my pre-decessor. We must be on guard for the sake of being vigilant because he can lie again. I don't trust anyone who starves his own people. Kim Jong-il is a tyrant and that's why I don't trust him. But I trust democratic leaders like myself and you, Mr. President.

When Bush stopped talking, Roh objected, expressing his own opinions in a display of determination. I copy verbatim this conversation, which remains a memorable scene in my mind.

ROH: I want to tell you clearly that I have a different opinion on this issue, Mr. President. About [Kim Jong-il] breaking promises or being difficult to trust, I also have had my own experiences, and our citizens and I share your feelings. But many successful negotiations in the past involved partners who could not trust one another. But they still held historic negotiations and yielded excellent results. That is why such success is even more precious. I think that there is no need to negotiate with someone you trust. Negotiation is a conversation with someone who is originally hard to trust.

BUSH: Absolutely. That's a very good point.

ROH: When negotiating, it is necessary to refrain at times from speaking the truth and to delay it until negotiation is over.

BUSH: A good point. I will not say that Kim Jong-il is a liar. I say this to you, Mr. President, only as your friend. You have offered me good advice.

ROH: Kim Jong-il appears to be more afraid of being called morally illegitimate than of being called untrustworthy.

BUSH: Yes.

ROH: The sense of danger can only be greater in someone who doesn't get any recognition for the legitimacy of his existence. And that person can only depend more greatly on nuclear arms.

BUSH: Yes.

ROH: You are the president of the United States, Mr. President. If you just wanted to, you can change the North Korean regime, even if it is a regime under Kim Jong-il's leadership. Together with the participating nations of the Six-Party Talks, you can change North Korea.

BUSH: I also want that. I want you to believe me. This is a problem that the American government considers to be its top priority. And I plan to see close cooperation between Seoul and Washington so that we can solve it peacefully. You can trust me on this point. If we can succeed, this will be a great achievement for both nations.

ROH: This problem is objectively the most important issue for Korea. The United States must have other important tasks, but now that you have been reelected, I hope that by cooperating, tackling the issue together, and making this problem the U.S. number one priority, you will send a message of peace and hope to the Korean Peninsula, the participating nations of the Six-Party Talks, and people worldwide.

BUSH: I completely agree. You've got a deal!

ROH: Let me say one more thing. It is important to show everyone the strong will to solve the problem through the Six-Party Talks. It is important to say your precise and honest thoughts about Kim Jong-il so that writers will not suggest methods besides dialogue.

BUSH: I will try.

As this conversation shows, President Bush promised two things to President Roh. One, he would treat the North Korean nuclear problem as the top priority of U.S. North Korea policy. Two, he would cease insulting Kim Jong-il. To interpret it more broadly, he was saying that he would not call Kim Jong-il such names as "tyrant," "liar," or "someone who starves his own people," for the sake of the SPTs, and that he would not denounce the North Korean regime using extreme language such as the "Axis of Evil." Roh logically explained the importance of negotiating with an enemy and won great empathy from Bush, who did not care for direct contact between North Korea and the United States. Later on, this became important grounds for the South Korean government to argue for the necessity of bilateral negotiations between North Korea and the United States. Immediately after this summit, on November 30, the United States contacted the North in New York and officially informed the North that it was "willing to make bilateral contact within the 'framework of the Six-Party Talks.'"[1]

On December 2, 2004, President Roh visited Britain and spent most of the time at the summit discussing the North Korean nuclear problem with British prime minister Tony Blair. At the time, the South Korean government believed that the only foreign leader who could persuade President Bush regarding the nuclear issue was Blair. "President Bush places importance on morally judging North Korea and ultimately denies the legitimacy of North Korea itself because of this," Roh told Blair, "We must strive so that President Bush realistically solves the problem rather than rendering any moral judgment." The president hoped that Blair would persuade Bush to see this.

On another front, in December 2004 President Roh dispatched Unification Minister Chung Dong-young as a special presidential envoy to China. Chung met with Wu Bangguo, the chairman of the standing committee at

[1]   President Bush did not keep his promise very long, however. At a press conference on April 29, 2005, he called Chairman Kim Jong-il a "tyrant" and the North, in turn, engaged in colorful slander, calling Bush an "ill-tempered lout" and "morally immature." At the fourth round of the SPTs, the United States showed relative enthusiasm, and the 9.19 Joint Statement was born. But at the same time, Bush prompted the Banco Delta Asia incident and placed financial sanctions on North Korea, breaking his own promise to make North Korea's nuclear development the number one priority of his North Korea policy.

the National Assembly of People's Representatives, and delivered Roh's personal letter for President Hu Jintao. In it, Roh frankly explained South Korea's predicament at the time and asked for cooperation:

> It is an urgent matter at this point to meet with National Defense Chairman Kim Jong-il, explain to him so that he can understand the current situation, and urge him to quickly solve the problem. But North Korea is shunning any in-depth discussion with our side on international matters such as the nuclear issue, and inter-Korean relations are not smooth, either. Therefore, it is unavoidable that you, Mr. President, have to persuade Chairman Kim. I believe that it is very important for you or a high-level figure ordered by you to visit North Korea sometime early next year and persuade Chairman Kim in person. I hope that you will carefully review this point.

On December 28, Beijing sent word through Kim Ha-jung, the South Korean ambassador to China, expressing admiration for the efforts President Roh was making domestically and abroad to solve the North Korean nuclear issue. In addition, it notified us that, while the issue of dispatching a special envoy from the Chinese government—as requested by the South Korean side—required some time, it was in the process of reviewing when and how to send a special envoy, and whom it should be. Beijing explained that any attempt to persuade the North would not have much effect until after the Bush administration began its second term, and that it planned to actively embark on persuading the North starting late January 2005.

In late December 2004, President Roh—believing that the time was approaching when conditions would be right for peacefully resolving the nuclear problem—ordered that a message be sent to the North. The message, sent through an unofficial channel at the NIS, given that inter-Korean dialogue was in a state of suspension, was that "North Korea should utilize the current atmosphere and make the decision to take advantage of this opportunity and answer the call to the Six-Party Talks as soon as possible." In this message he was also saying that to solve the problem, the North itself had to come to a rational decision of its own.

Once 2005 began, a new lineup of figures for U.S. North Korea policy was announced. For the incoming secretary of state, National Security Advisor Rice was chosen, and U.S. ambassador Christopher Hill in Seoul was chosen for the post of assistant secretary for East Asia and Pacific Affairs at the State Department, a position that included serving as the U.S. delegation's chief representative at the Six-Party Talks. The

South Korean government was greatly encouraged by Ambassador Hill's appointment—he possessed diplomatic flexibility and knew how to deploy creative strategies, and his posting was fortuitous for South Korea, which had been busy since fall 2004 in trying to concoct some kind of agreement for 2005. Furthermore, when he was ambassador to Poland, he had become acquainted with South Korea's chief representative at the SPTs, Deputy Foreign Minister Song Min-soon.

President Roh thought highly of Hill and wanted to have an unofficial and frank conversation with him about the nuclear issue before he assumed his new position. On January 17, 2005, the president invited Hill to his official residence and held a conversation over dinner. Besides the interpreter, I was the only one to attend. The president said,

> Once I almost fooled myself into thinking, while listening to Washington and Pyongyang talk, that everything could be solved in theory. But once seated at the negotiating table, I saw how positions in principle were positions in principle only and we could not get even one step closer. It is truly remarkable, this thing called diplomacy.

Ambassador Hill explained in detail his own personal vision, while issuing the disclaimer that he had not yet discussed it with anyone. He was, as expected, rational, strategic, and systematic. He explained that once the fourth round of the SPTs began, he wanted to first create an agreement text that was no more than one page long, containing basic principles such as denuclearizing the Korean Peninsula (the ultimate goal of the SPTs), normalizing diplomatic relations, and providing financial assistance. Afterwards, he wanted to lead the talk through the process of finding a way to act on those principles in agreement.

He said that, "while I have not discussed this with the administration," he would try to "visit not capitals of four nations, but of all five nations, and hold consultations." He would take this opportunity to explain to the governments of the five other nations the basic concepts of the principles to be agreed on at the fourth round of the SPTs. This was the right direction. It was common sense for the U.S. representative to visit the other participating nations of the talks during recess and discuss the matters under consideration. But until then, the U.S. representative had refused bilateral dialogue with the North and had never once visited North Korea.

"When I listen to you, I get the impression that you are holding the key, Mr. Ambassador," President Roh delightedly remarked, "There is always a strategy to what you say." The president expressed his hope: "Strictly speaking, reaching an agreement on the North Korean nuclear problem is a form of salvation for the Korean people." But he was still concerned that the American leadership's hardline policy would frustrate Ambassador Hill: "If the American president delegated complete authority to you and said you should give it a try with your talent, it appears that the problem would be easily solved. But I wonder if the president would actually do that."

Roh made a special request of Hill:

> After solving the North Korean nuclear problem through the Six-Party Talks, please build on that momentum and try to establish a multiparty framework in Northeast Asia. I think that it would be very good if the United States introduced a fundamental change to its policy and made the creation of this kind of a multiparty collective framework its new diplomatic strategy.

Hill replied, "It's an excellent idea. I agree. I will mention it as a long-term objective at my confirmation hearing at the Senate. I can do so next month."

North Korea's Declaration as a Nuclear Power and the President's Rage

On January 18, 2005, the U.S. Congress held confirmation hearings on the nomination of Condoleezza Rice as secretary of state. Our government was worried about what Rice would say at the hearing, and more than anything, hoped that she would be mindful of how North Korea considered criticisms of Chairman Kim Jong-il and his regime as key indicators of a hostile policy. In early January, National Security Advisor Kwon Jin-ho sent a letter to Rice respectfully requesting that she refrain from criticisms of North Korea at the confirmation hearings. Kwon emphasized, "At a moment as sensitive and significant as now, any public message we send to the North will have a very important meaning. There should be careful consideration." The South Korean embassy in Washington also made a request to the U.S. authorities that they contribute to breaking the impasse at the SPTs with positive statements in President Bush's second inauguration speech and at Rice's confirmation hearing. Beijing made similar efforts. On January 10, the South Korean embassy in Beijing reported that the Chinese government had asked that Bush's inauguration speech, his State of the Union address, and Rice's confirmation hearing exclude content that might provoke North Korea and Kim Jong-il.

But these efforts came to naught when Rice pointed to North Korea as an "outpost of tyranny." I could not understand why she unnecessarily provoked North Korea when she had been present at the ROK-U.S. summit in Santiago in November and knew full well that President Bush had expressed his complete agreement with President Roh, who said, "When negotiating, it is necessary at times to refrain from speaking the truth or to delay it until after the negotiation is over." We had hoped that the Americans, if they indeed recognized North Korea as a partner in negotiations, would not influence the situation with words outside of the negotiation setting. But things rarely worked according to our wishes.

In the end, North Korea made a shocking declaration that shook the foundation of the Six-Party Talks and worsened the situation. On February 10, 2005—the very last day of the long Lunar New Year holidays—Pyongyang declared that it was indefinitely suspending its participation in the SPTs, and that it was in possession of nuclear arms. It justified the announcement by arguing that it was completely clear the second-term Bush administration plotted to treat the North as an enemy, and to even isolate and crush the North by terming it a "post of tyranny," denying its legitimacy, and taking other steps. Although the North clarified that neither "the fundamental position in favor of dialogue and negotiation, nor the ultimate goal of denuclearizing the Korean Peninsula, has changed," the shock was very great.

The North's conduct enraged President Roh. He had been trying since fall 2004 to restart the SPTs: he had made his remarks in Los Angeles in spite of criticisms internal and external, had persuaded President Bush with all his energy, and had sent a personal letter to President Hu Jintao. But the North's answer to all this was that it did not care to play. Until then, the president had tried to persuade the United States and had voiced differing opinions at the risk of disharmony. And he had told his advisors, "Now the North must show sincerity. If it doesn't, we can no longer say anything to the United States," instructing them to send messages to the North urging a change in attitude. But now he thought that all his and the government's efforts to solve the nuclear problem had been rendered a failure by this declaration. I sensed that the president's patience for North Korea was about to run out.

On Sunday, February 13, 2005, a meeting was held at the presidential residence for a situation report and discussion, with top officials like Prime

Minister Lee Hae-chan, Unification Minister Chung Dong-young, and others in attendance. Roh strongly condemned the North for wanting to only deal with the United States and acting as though it thought nothing of the South's efforts, and said, "If I could change North Korea's policy by firing Deputy Secretary-General Lee, I would."[2] He used strong language to float the idea of changing policies. I knew full well that the president was very angry, but I could not just sit and listen, and said:

> If the president's words are executed verbatim, that just might bring about a shift in the cornerstone of our North Korea policy. But now is not yet the time to change our principles. The president speaks this way simply because he is too disappointed, but this is not the end. The game is not yet over.

Once I reached this conclusion in my mind, I began to boldly offer my opinions each time the president expressed doubt about the existing North Korea policy, almost as if I were countering each sentence he spoke. The scene that day, full of the president's terribly emotional words and my audacious responses, is shown in this transcript.

ROH: I must inform the North of our principled position. The North must understand our clear position—we cannot allow nuclear weapons—and that the true threat to North Korea is not an American invasion but economic devastation. We must send a clear message to the North and let it predict our actions. Do not bring up anything like a special envoy until the North says it first. Do not link the fertilizer issue to the special envoy but make it an issue to be discussed between the authorities, in other words at the inter-Korean ministers' talk. How will we explain the link between progress in the Kaesong Industrial Complex and the nuclear situation, and the paradox that Kaesong continues to proceed but the North acquires nuclear weapons? If we view the nuclear problem as a long-term issue and the North actually tries to acquire nuclear weapons, what should we do? How should we change our position that we cannot allow the North to go nuclear?

LEE: It might be better to talk in the abstract about the position of disallowing the North's nuclear capability. You say that we must be clear in our position on this, but it might be wise to not make our position on this any more detailed.

ROH: The South Korean government cannot get dragged around by the North without having a position. We must send a clear message to the

---

2   [To be clear, here "Deputy Secretary-General Lee" is the author, Lee Jong-seok.]

North so it can predict what we will do. We must make it clearly know where we will go if this game is over. The South Korean government must come to a decision.

LEE: We cannot say this is the end. The nuclear problem has dragged on for fourteen years. I believe that it is a matter of time. We must stay the course until the end of the year. If there is no progress in the nuclear problem until then, we will have to make a decision. Even the North is continuing the dialogue with relinquishing nuclear arms as a condition.

ROH: If the declaration that it possesses nuclear arms proves true, what is to be done about the Kaesong Industrial Complex? Can we live together with a nuclear North Korea?

LEE: Our society and economy are structurally vulnerable to heightening tensions, in comparison to that of the North. We must review which elements have influence on the North Korean nuclear problem. What is the influence the nuclear problem has on international politics, ROK-U.S. relations, and inter-Korean relations, not to mention the domestic economy? What will be the influence on our economy and society if inter-Korean relations were to freeze due to our principle-based position? What will be the influence on the international community? How will it influence our leverage within the international community? And how will domestic supporters react? We must examine these questions.

ROH: We must decide how we can live alongside nuclear North Korea. If we want to live [that way], then we must persuade the public. If we don't think we can persuade them, shouldn't we sternly deliver our position? And we must decide.

LEE: It's not the end of the world. There has been deviation in the negotiation process. We might be nearing the end but it's not the end of the world yet. It's enough that we talk about not allowing the North to have nuclear arms. There is no need to say anything more.

ROH: The biggest threat to the North is an economic crisis, not the United States. The security of the North Korean regime depends on the economy, not nuclear weapons. Nuclear weapons do not help the North in any way. If we provide economic assistance to the North, which is developing nuclear weapons, will it be possible to obtain authorization from the Uri Party?[3] What will happen if we severed all economic assistance to the North?

---

3 [The progressive Uri Party consisted of members of the Millennium Democratic Party who broke with it to show their loyalty to Roh; the party existed for only a few years, from 2003 to 2007.]

LEE: A sanction without China's participation will not have much of an effect. How effective will our own independent sanctions be? Shouldn't we consult with China? Otherwise, it will not have an effect and it will be difficult to restore inter-Korean relations. Cooperation with China is essential.

ROH: We can get dragged around just because the North is developing nuclear arms. Now it is tough to add new projects to inter-Korean exchanges. What if we convey to China our position that South Korea has no choice but to possess nuclear arms if North Korea develops nuclear arms?

LEE: If South Korea hypothetically develops nuclear weapons, it will not have much effect on North Korea. But it will have a large impact on China or the United States.

ROH: In any case, clarify our position in principle and refine our message to the North. Review the Kaesong Industrial Complex project in relation to the nuclear crisis. Even the Mt. Kumgang tourism project will be difficult to expand. Surely we cannot expand the Kaesong project with the nuclear problem in our sights? New things cannot be permitted.

LEE: During the first nuclear crisis, the Kim Young-sam administration said it would not shake hands with someone in possession of nuclear arms, and linked it to inter-Korean relations. But when negotiations between Pyongyang and Washington later began, we had no direct participation and were completely excluded. Inter-Korean relations never recovered during the whole term. There are many times we have wanted to scream over inter-Korean relations, but we have held back because we have more at stake in comparison to the North. There are two types of military tension on the Korean Peninsula: one involves the North's nuclear problem; the other is traditional tension. The latter has been greatly reduced at present because of the Kaesong Industrial Complex and the Mt. Kumgang tourism project.

Later, when the North conducted a nuclear test, the president did not rage as he had done this day. I think that this was the moment the Roh administration's North Korea policy was at a crossroads. But, even when he was engulfed by anger, the president did not block me from offering my insolent advice. He was furious over the North's conduct, but still showed self-restraint in carefully listening to an advisor opposed to his orders. And his conclusion was reached not based on his original instructions, but reflecting my advice.

On February 16, a meeting of ministers concerned with national security was held under the president's auspices to address the North's 2.10 declaration. At this meeting, the government decided to establish its basic response strategy based on international government discussions and the president's orders on February 13. A decision was also made to send a strongly worded message of warning to the North through an unofficial communication channel, and to establish a plan of action for an early restart of the SPTs. Our basic response strategy came down to three things. One, solving the North Korean nuclear problem had involved repeated shifts between volatile confrontation and reversal over a prolonged process. We must respond with patience to changes in the situation. Two, inter-Korean dialogue was utilized as a path to maintaining stability in inter-Korean relations and solving the nuclear problem. Maintaining the stability of inter-Korean relations played an important role as our lever in managing domestic social and economic situations, in ROK-U.S. relations and at the SPTs. However, while inter-Korean dialogue should be sought out and developed, the speed of assistance to the North and economic cooperation should be adjusted depending on how the situation unfolded. Three, if North Korea crossed the line (a nuclear test or weapons-grade nuclear material proliferation) or if it became clear that the North's position was to not abandon nuclear arms, then an exceptional measure would be considered. The ultimate decision was to confirm that the South Korean government's patience over the nuclear problem had not yet been exhausted, and the government would do its best to once again solve the problem according to the principles of its existing policy.

After this meeting ended, I drafted a resignation letter to the president. Although he had spoken in the hypothetical—"If North Korea's policy could change"—I felt it only right that I submit a letter of resignation, given that he had mentioned replacing me. Of course, the North would not blink, much less change its policy, even if the president replaced me. But when I thought about the disappointment the president must have felt during this crisis, guilt and a heavy sense of responsibility weighed on my shoulders.

On Monday, February 21, I went to work and pulled out the letter of resignation I had drafted over the weekend.

> I have tried to serve you, Mr. President, with the same mind as in the beginning, and to work hard in the realm of foreign affairs and national security. But there have been too many shortcomings on my part during

this time. Especially as we face the recent deterioration of the North Korean nuclear crisis, I fully recognize my responsibility as the person in charge of the matter. There is no way to shed my feelings of guilt before you, someone who threw himself into solving the problem. I bear the responsibility and offer you this letter of resignation.

I called the president's personal secretary, Yoon Tae-young, to send the letter to the Office of the President. Yoon sounded dumbfounded: "Mr. Deputy Secretary-General, don't you really know what the president meant? He meant that his regrets about North Korea were that great. What is this talk of a resignation letter?"

In the end, I could not even submit my carefully written letter. It went back into my desk drawer.

The Birth of a "Proposal of Great Significance" and Special Envoy Chung Dong-young's meeting with Kim Jong-il

The president was enraged by the North's declaration of itself as a nuclear power, and a chill descended on the already troubled inter-Korean relations. The North Korean nuclear problem really seemed impossible to solve and the crisis on the Korean Peninsula grew in weight. But an idea that might just lead to a breakthrough was the "proposal of great significance." Its birth predated the North's declaration by about two weeks.

In January 2005, the South was under American pressure to permanently terminate the construction of a light-water reactor (LWR) at Sinpo, then under construction in accordance with the Geneva Agreed Framework between Pyongyang and Washington. The construction had already been in a state of temporary suspension since December 2003, following the October 2002 highly enriched uranium (HEU) crisis. The Bush administration demanded that construction be halted since North Korea had broken the terms of the agreement, and the project indeed stopped.

Back in 1994, the United States had promised to build two 100,000 kilowatt (kW) LWRs for the North in return for the freezing of the North's nuclear program. Washington did not shoulder the cost, instead passing it on to South Korea, Japan, and the European Union. At the time President Kim Young-sam promised that the ROK government would shoulder 70 percent of the construction cost, in response to a request from President Clinton. Thanks to that promise, the Kim Dae-jung and

Roh Moo-hyun administrations had to annually spend incredible sums on the construction of these LWRs in the North.

The United States began arguing in 2003 that the construction must be halted and then permanently terminated, but the South Korean government opposed the idea. Terminating the construction now would mean pronouncing the official death of the Geneva Agreed Framework; our government was concerned about shredding the agreement before another had been reached to replace it. And there was a strong possibility that the North would oppose the termination of the LWR construction and the situation would deteriorate in a new way.

Another problem was the amount we had already spent on this project. By January 2005, the LWR construction had been 34.5 percent completed, and South Korea had already spent $1.12 billion. We could not simply waste the staggering sum of more than $1 billion of taxpayer money just because the United States demanded it.

But the U.S. demands were unceasing. In November 2004, the Roh administration cast its vote to extend the term of construction suspension by one year at the meeting of the Korean Peninsula Energy Development Organization's (KEDO's) executive committee, going against the Bush administration, which argued for the permanent termination of the LWR construction. But Japan and the European Union had already yielded under U.S. pressure, so it was difficult for us to stand our ground alone. It had reached the point where we might have to terminate the construction, but we did not know how we would explain it to the public.

In late January 2005, I was sitting at my desk, worrying about the rationale under which we could safely terminate the LWR project. I stared at the reactor report on my desk. Suddenly I noticed another report just next to it, about the North Korean nuclear problem. At the time, I was filled with regret that, despite intense government efforts over the nuclear problem, in reality there were not many suitable ways we could effectively involve ourselves in the situation. But when I noticed this report, I was inspired. "Yes, let's create a new plan that links the termination of the LWR project to the North Korean nuclear problem!" This was the moment the "proposal of great significance" was born.

If the reactor construction were to continue, the ROK government would have to incur an additional $2.4 billion in costs. On top of that, the United States would demand at the time of the reactors' completion that we also bear a substantial portion of the construction costs for sending the electricity from Sinpo to Pyongyang. So, even if the Agreed Framework were put into action and the construction proceeded smoothly, the South Korean government would be obligated to pay billions of dollars from then on as the price for freezing North Korea's nuclear program.

I wondered, "What if we said we would use this amount to directly send electricity to the North, thereby solving the issue of financially compensating the North for giving up the nuclear program?" Different ideas on how to link the method of solving the nuclear problem to the termination of the LWR project raced through my head. Right now, the North was demanding a guarantee of regime security and financial compensation in exchange for giving up its nuclear program. If the South Korean government were to say that it would solve the problem by directly supplying the 200,000 kW of electricity that had been promised to the North through the LWR, it would simplify the solution to the nuclear problem and also expand and elevate the South Korean government's role and standing at the SPTs. Moreover, if this proposal were realized, then a significant portion of the North's electricity supply would depend on the South's transmission, making inter-Korean war practically impossible, and opening the door to more active inter-Korean cooperation. A proposal with this level of benefits would lessen the regret the government felt about terminating the LWR construction, and the North would not oppose it, either. The North had already mentioned once before that it wanted us to send electricity to them, so it could not easily reject the proposal—even if it did, we had nothing to lose.

I discussed the idea with relevant NSC officials, including Director of Strategic Planning Seo Joo-seok and Senior Executive Officer Park Sun-won. Everyone's face lit up. I explained the vision to National Security Advisor Kwon Jin-ho and Unification Minister Chung Dong-young and they were most pleased. As it required top-level secrecy, Chung proposed that we call the idea "Project Ahn Jung-geun"—after the name of Korea's famed independence fighter, so that was its name for some time.

I refined the proposal and, on February 19, briefed the president. In my report, "Plan for Exchanging Light-Water Reactors for Electricity Support to the North," the NSC Secretariat defined the plan as "completely terminating the now-suspended LWR construction and instead using the remaining construction budget to supply 200,000 kW of electricity to the North via transmission, if the North abandons its nuclear program." We summarized the plan's four objectives and expected effects:

One, it provides a watershed moment at the SPTs on the North Korean nuclear problem and allows us to take charge. It creates a stepping stone for us to play an active role during the restructuring of the geopolitical order in Northeast Asia after the North Korean nuclear crisis is solved.

Two, it provides the foundation for the two Koreas' common prosperity. It serves as a turning point for improving inter-Korean relations.

Three, it provides a safety valve for the issue of constructing the Kaesong Industrial Complex.

Four, it solves the problem of the light-water reactors, mired in chaos, while allowing us to claim justification and real benefits.

President Roh gave high points to the plan and approved it. With presidential approval, the NSC Secretariat discussed the plan in utmost secrecy with relevant officials and continued to develop it further. In fact, the plan made great contributions to restarting the SPTs a few months later and drawing out the 9.19 Joint Statement. Ultimately, while the plan was never realized, it helped to elevate the South Korean government's role and standing. It also had a positive effect on the stable termination of the LWR project at Sinpo. There probably has not been another case in the history of South Korea diplomacy that proclaimed policy determination without any additional expenditure and achieved this level of diplomatic accomplishment.

The situation on the Korean Peninsula, having rapidly chilled over the North's declaration as a nuclear power, soon showed signs of improving. Wang Jiarui, head of external communications in the Chinese Communist Party (CCP), visited North Korea as President Hu Jintao's special envoy on February 19. Wang met with Chairman Kim Jong-il and urged a return to the SPTs. On March 2, the North Korean Foreign Ministry expressed its position: "If conditions are met, we can participate in the Six-Party Talks." Of course, "conditions" could always fluctuate, and it was difficult to expect a change right away, but it certainly confirmed that the North was open to returning to the SPTs.

Our government was researching, in consultation with Assistant Undersecretary Hill, a plan for him to visit North Korea and hold a bilateral talk between Washington and Pyongyang, if the North would make clear its intention to return to the SPTs. But to succeed, someone had to persuade the North to do just that. With inter-Korean dialogue suspended, the only country that could play this role was China. The NSC decided to try this plan on the occasion of incoming U.S. secretary of state Rice's three-nation tour to South Korea, China, and Japan, scheduled to begin on March 18. To discuss this issue, I traveled unofficially to China on March 11 and met with Foreign Minister Li Zhaoxing, the

CCP head of external communications Wang Jiarui, and Vice Foreign Minister Wu Dawei.

The Chinese figures who heard our plan said it was a good idea and readily offered their agreement. But the problem was that the mistrust between Pyongyang and Washington was too great. If China were to be able to persuade North Korea in the current climate, it would be necessary for Secretary Rice to express some flexibility about North Korea. Wang Jiarui, after returning from his meeting with Kim Jong-il, said that the North was unhappy about the label "post of tyranny." Even if Secretary Rice did not apologize, it would help greatly if she said it was her own personal view and not the official U.S. position, and end the matter by saying that the official U.S. position was to solve the North Korean nuclear problem through peaceful means, as expressed in Bush's State of the Union address. When I saw that the party secretary of external communications, and not even the foreign minister in charge of the North Korean nuclear issue, was proposing such detailed phrases with this level of persuasiveness, I sensed the Chinese government's determination to solve the nuclear problem. This plan, agreed upon by South Korea and China, could not be realized because of the lack of cooperation from the two main parties to the problem.

As they say, there can be hardship but there can be no despair. The Roh administration did not give up, even after trial and error. No, it could not give up—if it did, the future of the Korean Peninsula would fall under darkness. This time, we decided to try and drag the North to the SPTs through inter-Korean relations. The government decided to send to the 6.15 Unification Grand Celebration in Pyongyang a delegation, headed by Unification Minister Chung Dong-young, and to entrust him with the task of being a special envoy. He would meet Chairman Kim Jong-il and convey our "proposal of great significance." He would also urge the North to return to the SPTs and would propose an inter-Korean summit.

The NSC Standing Committee believed that with the Roh administration nearly at its midpoint, it would be difficult to delay the inter-Korean summit any longer. The problem was how to make Minister Chung Dong-young's meeting with Kim Jong-il happen. I believed that Kim would meet with Chung, even if it was only to learn the contents of our "proposal of great significance."

And at the ROK-U.S. summit, held on June 10, President Roh provided the decisive cover fire to support special envoy Chung Dong-young. At Roh's suggestion, President Bush added the prefix "Mr." to Kim

Jong-il's name at the press conference. The North Korean leadership had reacted with sensitivity to the various terms like "tyrant," "Axis of Evil," and "post of tyranny"; when President Bush addressed Kim Jong-il as "Mister," it sent a very positive signal. And this incident served as a reminder to Kim Jong-il that Roh had the power to move Bush in a direction helpful to Kim.[4]

In the end, Chung Dong-young was able to meet with Chairman Kim Jong-il in Pyongyang on June 17 as President Roh's special envoy. During the two-and-a-half-hour-long discussion, many important topics that would later lead to watershed moments for the nuclear problem and inter-Korean relations were addressed. Chung's first task was to extract, through the "proposal of great significance," a promise that the fourth SPTs would restart, and to lead Chairman Kim to agree on resolving the nuclear crisis. Chung's second task was to convey President Roh's proposal for an inter-Korean summit and to receive a reply. Of course, there were no secret offerings to sway the North toward agreeing to a summit. As per the Roh administration's character, the plan was to address the problem head on.

Minister Chung did not tremble at all before Chairman Kim; he persuaded him by using precise logic. He did his best to get Kim to agree to resume the SPTs. Chung was a talented negotiator. Regarding the U.S. guarantee of regime security so coveted by the North, he persuasively explained that a multiparty guarantee of security was far stronger than a bilateral one. And he emphasized that the SPTs were actually an opportunity for the North.

---

4   President Bush, however, thought that the event was a "useless deed" that he had only reluctantly performed at President Roh's request. He told Roh, "I called Kim Jong-il 'Mr.' at the press conference earlier. If this is truly effective, then I could even receive the Nobel Peace Prize." President Roh replied to Bush's regretful words, "The title 'Mr.' could be the key to opening new peace in Northeast Asia."

Many American officials did not try to understand just how sensitive North Korea was to the way Chairman Kim Jong-il was addressed and to negative evaluations of the regime, and how this actually had a great influence on their American policy. When President Bush called Kim Jong-il "Mr." for the first time on May 31, 2005, the North Korean Foreign Ministry issued a statement that "American President Bush has respectfully addressed our supreme leadership as 'Mr.'. . . . We are mindful of this." U.S. officials should have paid attention this fact and analyzed its significance.

But Kim shied away from giving a firm answer. He expressed his displeasure that the United States did not recognize North Korea, but rather condemned both him and his regime.

"I had made up my mind to be friendly, even with the Bush administration, but I changed my mind when it called me a thug from the beginning," he said, "The 'post of tyranny' comment showed that it wanted to deal with Kim Jong-il like Saddam Hussein." But Kim was undoubtedly intent on returning to the SPTs. When Chung urged a July return to the SPTs, Kim replied,

> Our Foreign Ministry is on standby and it could even go right now. But about the "post of tyranny" comment, the United States should contact us, if not publicly, then at least below the surface. It should explain, for example, that it had been a mistake, or a practical misunderstanding. That is why we are waiting.

Kim Jong-il was looking for only the slightest pretext to return to the talks.

Minister Chung noted that President Roh had urged President Bush to use honorifics to address Chairman Kim Jong-il, and suggested that Kim Jong-il also use honorifics, such as "Mr. President," to refer to President Bush. Kim quickly expressed his willingness, "Is it enough if I call President Bush 'Mr. President'? There is no reason I can't." And once again he expressed his desire for a new relationship with the United States. "If I should call President Bush 'Mr. President,' then that is what I will do."

After this meeting, Chung announced that the North had expressed its intent to return to the SPTs in July (if the United States were to recognize and show respect to North Korea). And a high-level figure at the North Korean mission at the United Nations (UN) suggested the minimum pretext for a return to the talks: "Even if the United States does not retract its comment about the 'post of tyranny,' we could see it as sort of retraction if they refrained from further provocative comments." But the Americans simply could not hold themselves back, even during that time. On June 19, Secretary of State Rice expressed her cynicism regarding the outcome of the meeting between Kim Jong-il and Chung Dong-young. She said in an interview, "North Korea likes to create excuses not to return to the Six-Party Talks." On June 20, Undersecretary of State Dobriansky labeled four nations, including North Korea, as "posts of tyranny." What on earth were they thinking? All we wanted was that they refrain from criticizing the North Korean regime for one month, just to create a rationale for North Korea to return to dialogue. It cost neither money nor pride. It was difficult to understand why the United States was acting like this, and it was all the more regrettable when you consider that U.S. leaders knew how hard the South Korean government was working to remedy the situation stemming from verbal attacks on North Korea.

On June 20, President Roh issued a strong order to mobilize maximum diplomatic capability to urge the United States to speak more thoughtfully. The NSC Secretariat drafted "Guidelines on Urging the United States to Exercise Prudence in Speech," which pointed out problematic American comments. It was delivered to the Foreign Ministry, whose minister and deputy minister both stepped up to request that U.S. figures speak with restraint. Foreign Minister Ban Ki-moon expressed his regret at the U.S. "post of tyranny" comment at a press conference. It was a desperate measure that was intended to make sure the North would not once again take a step back by using the American comments as an excuse.

After all these turns and twists, the North Korean media announced on July 9, 2005, that North Korean vice foreign minister Kim Kye-gwan and U.S. assistant secretary Hill had met in Beijing and "the two sides agreed that the fourth Six-Party Talk would be held in the week beginning July 25, 2005."

Once the SPTs looked set to restart, the South Korean government revealed the contents of the so-called proposal of great significance to the public, for the sake of ensuring the transparency of its North Korea policy. Immediately after we explained the proposal to the North, we revealed the contents to the other nations participating in the SPTs, who evaluated the proposal positively. Regarding the United States, I personally explained the detailed contents to Assistant Secretary Hill on June 15, before Minister Chung met with Chairman Kim. I had already told Hill back in March that the South Korean government was preparing an idea in hopes of making groundbreaking progress at the SPTs. I asked him to understand that we could not reveal the proposal then, but I assured him that it would be helpful to Washington and that we would share its details at the same time that we made the proposal to the North. When Hill heard the contents of the proposal, he expressed his delight. Secretary Rice, who visited South Korea on July 12, heard Ban Ki-moon's explanation of the proposal and evaluated it as "a creative plan that is useful for solving the North Korean nuclear problem." U.S. diplomats welcomed the proposal of great significance on the grounds that it would help advance the discussion over the nuclear crisis and make the permanent termination of the LWR construction at Sinpo— over which the United States and South Korea had shown differences in opinion—as a precondition.

The First-Phase Conference at the Fourth Six-Party Talks and the Path of a Facilitator

The first-phase conference of the fourth SPT—the longest in the history of the talks—took place in Beijing from July 26 to August 7, 2005. We sent a delegation headed by Deputy Foreign Minister Song Min-soon, with the head of the North Korean nuclear planning team, Cho Tae-yong, as his deputy. The NSC Secretariat also supplied Senior Executive Officer Park Sun-won and Lee Yeo-jin, a department head, to the delegation to provide smooth assistance. Fortunately, the American position, which had been so firm, showed a degree of flexibility at the fourth SPT. Above all, the phrase that symbolized the Americans' hardline policy—complete, verifiable, irreversible dismantlement (CVID)—disappeared from their representatives' remarks. It looked like the U.S. State Department was using the occasion of Secretary Rice's appointment to go head-to-head against the diplomacy of pressure advocated by Vice President Cheney and Secretary of Defense Rumsfeld, and to pursue a diplomatic approach oriented toward negotiation. Assistant Secretary Hill, who had the political skills and rational judgment to convince his superiors, must have had great influence on this change. More than anything, President Bush had agreed on most of President Roh's points at the ROK-U.S. summits (November 2004 and June 2005), so South Korea's voice had grown louder in discussions between it and the United States on the North Korean nuclear issue.

The South Korean government thought that, with the situation improved, it was imperative we make progress on the nuclear problem. On July 20 the NSC held a high-level strategic meeting attended by the foreign minister, a deputy chief of the NIS, the NSC deputy secretary-general, and other important relevant figures, under the auspices of the NSC Standing Committee chairman and Unification Minister Chung Dong-young. At the meeting, it was decided that the goal of the fourth SPT was the "adoption of a joint text regarding the solution to the North Korean nuclear issue and the objective" and the "creation of a foundation for arriving at an agreement on action." The joint text should be based on the tentative agreement reached between South Korea, the United States, and Japan in mid-July, but efforts were to be made to strike a balance between the U.S. principles on how to solve the North Korean nuclear problem and the North's demands. Simultaneously, the proposal of great significance was to be strategically utilized in order to urge every side to shift its position.

But the draft of the agreement that the United States brought to the SPT was far more retrogressive and disappointing than the tentative draft produced as a result of the agreement at the three-party talk. It appeared that Assistant Secretary Hill had taken to Washington the tentative text produced by the SPT representatives of South Korea, the United States, and Japan, but it became a rigid, hardline proposal after it was circulated between the U.S. NSC and Vice President Cheney's office. If things stood like this, the SPTs would be in peril, and we could not just stand by and watch while that happened. The South Korean NSC decided to clearly show the United States our position. We calculated that the South Korean government could also give Hill greater room to maneuver at the negotiations with the North by demonstrating its determination. On July 26, an NSC high-level strategic meeting instructed our delegation to forcefully deliver to the United States the following policy:

> If the United States adheres to the revised proposal, the ROK-U.S. joint statement will be difficult to realize. When each nation presents its own statements, we will clearly reveal our position. If necessary, we will publicly point out those elements devoid of rationality in arguments from both the North and the United States.

After receiving these instructions, the South Korean delegation demanded further revisions, pointing out to the American delegation, "The U.S. revised statement contains contents that the North Korean delegation dare not report to Pyongyang." The American delegation reported South Korea's position to Washington and received a newly revised proposal, but it did not appear much improved from the South Korean perspective. Therefore, our delegation made clear that it would be impossible to jointly present an agreement draft as the United States desired. By not making a joint proposal with the United States, we were gaining that much more freedom to act. When Hill asked, "Do you think that it's difficult for South Korea to accommodate the American proposal?" Song Min-soon responded, "It's not important whether South Korea can accommodate it or not. The question is how to increase the possibility that North Korea will accept it." I do not know how much effect our resolute position had, but from then on the United States embarked on negotiations with a far more flexible attitude than at past talks.

The NSC high-level strategic meeting sent our delegation a special order to simplify the topic into solving the North Korean nuclear problem. It meant that the objective in this phase of the SPTs was to make North Korea give up its nuclear program and that this issue must take precedence over any other problems. That is why we strongly opposed the North's call for arms-reduction talks and why we worried that the United States or Japan would try to make North Korean human rights or the kidnapping of Japanese citizens a main topic within the SPT framework. Ultimately, the North did not bring up arms reduction, and the United States and Japan did not make their interests a prerequisite to the discussion, even if they did mention them intermittently.

All participating nations—with the exception of North Korea— welcomed our proposal of great significance. The North assumed a reserved position. In principle, the North showed appreciation for our government's efforts and intention, but it expressed the position that the measure first required the North to give up its nuclear program, and so could not be easily accommodated in its existing form. This reaction had been expected to some degree. The South Korean NSC did not imagine the North would be compelled to accept the proposal in its original form. It was not hard to predict that, no matter how desperate the North was for electricity, they would not put control of their power entirely in the hands of the South. But we believed that the proposal was too tempting to easily refuse.

And we believed that all the countries, excluding the United States, would want to equally participate in offering economic compensation to the North in consideration of the potential influence they could yield after the nuclear program was dismantled. The North would naturally prefer that its dependence be shared among different nations, so as not to rely exclusively on the South. Given such facts, we believed that a revised draft of the proposal of great significance would emerge when an agreement was reached at the SPTs on how to solve the North Korean nuclear problem and a subsequent discussion of how to put that agreement into action began. Therefore, the South Korean government thought that it would be sufficient in the current phase if the SPT agreement text specified that proposal, which would serve the role of a safety valve in the matter of supplying economic compensation in return for giving up the nuclear program.

The first-phase conference of the fourth SPT recorded dozens of different meetings, including contact between the North and the United States, within the six-party framework. It lasted for thirteen days. Each nation's delegation tenaciously participated in the arduous negotiation process, which demanded long hours of high-level concentration and patience. Unexpectedly, the North Korean delegation sincerely embarked on the negotiations. Assistant Secretary Hill, very much the experienced diplomat, always maintained a flexible attitude in negotiations with the North, even as he safeguarded U.S. principles. He gave the North Korean delegation a feeling of reassurance that the United States was engaging in negotiations while firmly recognizing the North's existence, and played a significant role in preventing their exit.

China gave each nation sufficient time to moderate its position, using a number of approaches, including bilateral meetings, and then invited every nation to submit contents it wished to see included in the joint text. On that basis, China offered a draft of the agreement that subsequently underwent three rounds of revision. When the fourth draft was created, five nations, excluding North Korea, agreed on its overall framework.

The North expressed satisfaction with all the clauses, but rejected article 1, clause 2, which read, "North Korea gives up all its nuclear weapons and nuclear programs in a verifiable manner, and promises to return to the safety measures of the NPT and IAEA as soon as possible, in order to acquire the rights and duties under the NPT." The North objected to the phrase "all nuclear weapons and programs" to describe the target of nuclear disarmament, on the grounds that abiding by this phrase would force the North to give up not only programs related to nuclear weapons, but all programs related to nuclear power, essentially depriving it of the right to use nuclear power for peaceful purposes. To reduce the differences between the North and the United States, a three-way meeting among South Korea, North Korea, and the United States was held on August 4 at South Korea's behest. At this meeting, Deputy Minister Song Min-soon asked why the North could not return to the non-proliferation treaty (NPT) and accept the International Atomic Energy Agency's (IAEA's) safety measures before gaining the right to use nuclear power peacefully in the future. North Korea's vice foreign minister, Kim Kye-gwan, sternly replied, "We could have it in the future, but we cannot have it until the future, so we cannot accept." Ultimately, even as all other matters fell into place, the disagreement between Pyongyang and Washington over the right to the peaceful use of nuclear power revealed itself to be the ultimate problem. North Korea proposed replacing the problematic phrase with "all nuclear weapons and nuclear programs leading to producing nuclear weapons," but the United States refused the change. The United States in turn suggested giving up "all nuclear weapons and existing nuclear programs," but this time the North refused.

The North was adamant. On August 3, Chinese foreign minister Li Zhaoxing called North Korean vice foreign minister Kim Kye-gwan and asked him to send a message to Pyongyang, written in the name of China's supreme leadership, urging the North Korean supreme leadership to accept the fourth draft. But it did not change the North's mind. If anything, because of this phrase in the fourth draft, the North hinted at its desire to mention the issue of providing an LWR—something the North had demanded throughout the first phase of the talks—in the agreement text. At the inter-Korean meeting on August 6, Vice Minister Kim Kye-gwan said, "The differences in policy between North Korea and the United States has reached the point where creative and ambiguous language cannot cover it up." He said the agreement text had to specifically mention the LWR. Ultimately the SPT's participating nations left the issues of the scope of North Korea's nuclear disarmament and of providing an LWR unresolved. They broke for recess after deciding to resume the talks in the week beginning on August 29. Fortunately, China, South Korea, the United States, Japan, and Russia shared the understanding that when the talks resumed, they should start from discussion of the fourth draft and the final agreement should be reached on that basis. North Korea did not express any opposition to this plan.

As I watched the first-phase conference of the fourth SPT, I was deeply impressed with China's ability as mediator. The Chinese delegation developed the draft of the agreement text while reflecting contents under discussion at a multitude of meetings. From the beginning, China did not propose a single idea. Its skill at accepting different nations' proposals, creating a single draft, creating a space for free diplomatic maneuvers among interested parties, and coordinating the whole thing was remarkable. In particular, Cui Tiankai, the deputy head of the Chinese delegation—he was the Foreign Ministry's Asia director—was a genius at creating appropriate sentences in the agreement text. Each time he wrote a revised draft of the agreement text, I marveled at his ability to distill the extremely complicated understandings of various nations into an agreement draft of only a few pages.

But from what I could see, it was the South Korean delegation that played the role of facilitator and advanced the discussion from the first-phase conference onward by moving more dynamically than anyone else. The South Korean delegation was everywhere, trying to facilitate discussion, holding sixteen bilateral meetings with the United States, ten with the North, ten with China, three with Russia, one with Japan, and one with both the United States and Japan. There was even a three-way talk among South Korea, North Korea, and the United States. The South Korean delegation utilized its initiative, elevated by the proposal of great significance, by working hard to close the gap between the United States and North Korea, and by consulting with China (with whom a relationship of cooperation was maintained) in the process of drafting and moderating sentences that would go into the draft of the final agreement.

The first-phase conference of the talks did not go so far as to produce an agreement text, but it reached a new milestone in the history of the SPTs. Participating nations exercised, for the first time, wisdom in reducing points of contention and built a firm ground for future agreement in the shape of the fourth draft. North Korea and the United States engaged in the negotiations with more sincerity than ever before, and the effectiveness of the talks increased as many different forms of contact took place within a single framework. Starting with the first-phase conference, it became routine for the two Koreas to consult one another at the talks, and the significance of this consultation as an important means for facilitating overall discussion was confirmed.

Movements within Silence for the Sake of Consultation

The recess before the second-phase conference of the talks was no break by any means—a more apt description would be "movement within silence." Internally, the South Korean government prepared measures for the second phase, while externally, it quietly consulted with the other participating nations. The NSC Standing Committee issued guidelines on how to handle external consultations during the recess: first, reconfirm that the fourth draft remains valid; and second, clearly convey to every side our position on the unresolved point of contention—article 1, clause 2 (concerning North Korea's nuclear disarmament and peaceful use of nuclear power).

In fact, our government had already established its position on the North's right to the peaceful use of nuclear power, on the basis of an earlier presidential instruction. When briefed on the status of the negotiations during the first-phase conference, President Roh asked, in reference to the North's peaceful use of nuclear power, "Once the proper process has been satisfied, isn't it only appropriate to have such rights?" He issued the standard that "as long as the North clearly accepts nuclear disarmament, the issue of peaceful use can be solved by negotiation." The president ordered that it be "clearly made known to the U.S. government that South Korea might say something ill-tempered" if the talks broke down over the issue of restricting the North's peaceful use of nuclear power. He also told Kim Jong-il, via a secret inter-Korean channel, that the South was interested in the North's right to peacefully use nuclear power, and urged a decision for the sake of reaching a settlement.

The NSC Standing Committee decided to dispatch high-level government figures to the United States, China, Japan, and Russia, and to consult with the North through inter-Korean channels in order to strengthen cooperation over points of contention expected at the second-phase conference. Foreign Minister Ban Ki-moon was to handle the United States and China, and I would take Russia and Japan. For the North, Unification Minister Chung Dong-young was to consult with First Deputy Director of the United Front Department Lim Dong-ok, who was visiting Seoul to attend the 8.15 National Grand Celebration.[5]

The NSC Standing Committee separately advised President Roh to convey a relevant message to Chairman Kim Jong-il when the North Korean delegation visited the Blue House. Accordingly, President Roh asked the Worker's Party of Korea secretary, Kim Ki-nam, Lim Dong-ok, and others on their visit to the Blue House on August 17 to convey a message regarding the North's peaceful use of nuclear power to Chairman Kim Jong-il: "Even if your principle on this question is clear, I hope you will respond with flexibility." Roh added, "The main issue should be settled through dialogue between the North and the United States. It will not be resolved just because we take the North's side," and "making dialogue between the North and the United States flexible, normalizing relations, and solving the issue through cooperation is most realistic."

The countries I was to visit—Russia and Japan—had not made their presence felt at the first-phase conference. Japan, in particular, took its cues from the American position for the most part and was shunned

---

5 August 15 marks Korea's independence from Japan in 1945.

by the North. Like a sack of wheat in a corner, it did not play much of a role. But things would be different at the second-phase conference, where the remaining points of contention had to be resolved and a joint agreement text drafted. Russia and Japan both clearly had roles to play. First of all, Russia was a country with a certain amount of influence over the North and the United States. I thought that a settlement would become much easier if Russia clearly expressed its position, based on common sense and rationality, regarding the contentious clause. On the other hand, I thought Japan's role was a little different. Japan did not possess a lever that would greatly help in moving the discussion at the SPTs forward. But it was my judgement that Japan's position on the fifth draft, which China would create at the second-phase conference, would have a tremendous impact on whether or not we would be able to arrive at the text of a joint agreement.

China discarded the phrase proposed by the North for the clause in dispute and added the phrase desired by the United States in the fourth draft. The result was welcomed by the United States but strongly opposed by the North. China, however, inwardly understood why the North was against the U.S. position that it should not have the right to use nuclear power peacefully until it discarded all nuclear weapons and nuclear programs. Therefore, I could somewhat guess that China's revision at the second-phase conference would probably leave intact the scope of North Korea's disarmament as desired by the United States—"all nuclear weapons and nuclear programs" or "all nuclear weapons and existing nuclear programs"—but would add a phrase or clause that clearly recognized the North's right to the peaceful use of nuclear power, in order to introduce balance. To Foreign Minister Ban Ki-moon, who visited China from August 11 to 13, the Chinese side had already expressed its view that "if the United States wants to keep its position that 'all nuclear weapons and nuclear programs' must be abandoned, then it will be necessary for North Korea to see a substantial countermeasure beyond the current level."

But if the fifth draft were to include a clause showing consideration for the North's position, the United States would certainly object, and persistent U.S. objections would surely result in the collapse of the talks. To prevent this scenario, one most feared by the ROK government, it might be necessary to create a five-to-one dynamic with South Korea, China, Japan, Russia, and North Korea pressuring the United States, in a departure from the discussion of the fourth draft. If the North were to face such a situation it could quit the talks, but the United States—the main actor behind the launch of the SPTs and the world's greatest superpower—would not be able to do the same because it would lose face. To create this dynamic against the United States, it was critical for us to secure Japan's cooperation at the second-phase conference; if Japan took the U.S. side, then the collapse of the talks would be less of a burden on the United States.

On August 21, I visited Moscow and met with Vice Foreign Minister Alexander Alexeyev and National Security Committee vice secretary Nikolai Spassky. The Russian side had a rather pessimistic outlook on the resumption of the talks, saying that the United States was not changing its position on the North's right to the peaceful use of nuclear power and there was no possibility the North would readily agree under such conditions. And yet Russia showed flexibility by agreeing that the North's right to the peaceful use of nuclear power, including the construction of LWRs, should be recognized if the North returned to the NPT and cooperated with the IAEA. I asked the Russians to continue to engage in the upcoming conference with the same keenness and then I left for Tokyo on August 23.

I frankly did not want to visit Japan. I will say more on this later, but I had unpleasant memories of making secret visits to Japan and tasting failure in December 2004. And the relations between South Korea and Japan were not great due to Dokdo[6] and the history issue.[7] Furthermore, it had not been that long since an opposition lawmaker had placed the South Korean government in a difficult predicament by leaking to the press the false story that the United States was sharing military and nuclear intelligence with Japan, but not with South Korea because it mistrusted the ROK government. The apparent source of the false leak was Japanese vice foreign minister Yachi Shotaro, who was going to be my main dialogue partner during this visit. But solving the North Korean nuclear problem was the priority—dwelling on other matters was a luxury I could not afford.

My visit was welcomed by the Japanese government, which expressed its hopes for strengthened cooperation between our two nations at the

6   [South Korea and Japan both assert territorial claim over Dokdo (Takeshima in Japanese), a group of rocky islets in the Sea of Japan (known as the East Sea in both Koreas).]

7   [Japan has been accused by other Asian countries, in particular China and South Korea, of whitewashing its own war crimes during the Pacific War and of teaching revisionist history to its students.]

SPTs from then on. Government officials told me that, while they in theory agreed with our position on allowing the North the peaceful use of nuclear power, the Japanese government thought that sticking to its principle for the time being might be more effective in persuading the North. This approach would allow participating nations to take up different roles in the negotiation; ultimately, Japan would be willing to show more flexibility in the final phase of the negotiations. Vice Foreign Minister Yachi expressed discontent that the North Korean delegation had shied away from consulting with Japan, only once having brief contact with the Japanese delegation at the end of the first-phase conference. He was also unhappy that there had not been sufficient consultation between South Korea and Japan. I promised that at the second-phase conference we would strengthen cooperation with Japan and sway the North so that consultation between the North and Japan could take place normally. I emphasized, however, that in return, South Korea and Japan had to take joint steps so that the second-phase conference could yield a joint agreement text. The Japanese side was positive about my proposal. They probably appreciated, to some extent, President Roh's decision to send his closest advisor to Japan to discuss the North Korean nuclear issue, despite the extremely uncomfortable relations between South Korea and Japan. On my way back to Seoul, I thought that the visit had created a foundation for cooperation that could stop Japan from siding with the United States. It was certainly successful when compared to my December 2004 visit to Japan.

While I was visiting Russia and Japan, Ban Ki-moon had gone to the United States and met with Secretary of State Rice and Secretary of Defense Rumsfeld for the sake of laying a foundation for smooth proceedings at the second-phase conference. Ban specifically asked Rice if the United States would show some flexibility regarding the North's peaceful use of nuclear power. Rice replied, "The United States will exercise flexibility under certain conditions."

On August 15 in South Korea, there was a late-night discussion between Unification Minister Chung Dong-young and Lim Dong-ok, first deputy director of the United Front Department of the North Korean Worker's Party. I was also present. Lim Dong-ok explained the North's position on article 1, clause 2. We emphasized to them the meaning of the "proposal of great significance" and asked that the North respond flexibly to the problematic clause.

Then the South Korean government had a chance to hear about the North's strategy in joining the second-phase conference from Chinese vice foreign minister Wu Dawei, who had visited North Korea in late August. According to Wu, the centerpiece of the North's strategy was that giving up all of its current nuclear programs would require a reciprocal measure, and the North would demand an LWR as compensation. The North had told Wu, "The light-water reactor we demand is not the one from 1994. It is a light-water reactor that several nations can jointly manage. The nuclear materials imported into the North can also be jointly managed by the international community." They argued, "If the three words 'light-water reactor' are not included in the joint text, then North Korea cannot sign any text." Wu Dawei conveyed this information to our ambassador to China, Kim Ha-jung, and expressed his view that it was necessary to consider whether it was worth exchanging the LWR for the North's denuclearization. And he added, strictly as his private opinion, that if necessary China could supply the funds to provide the North with an LWR, and if the five participating nations in the SPTs collectively provided funds, it would be possible to provide the North with an LWR.

He asked South Korea to persuade the United States regarding the LWR. His take was that since the Americans thought China was speaking from the North's position, China was unable to persuade the United States. He regretted that Japan–North Korea relations were not great at that time, because Japan was the party in the best position to persuade the United States.

China's strategy at the second-phase conference seemed clear. China had been confronted by North Korea's strong opposition during the first-phase conference because it had appeared to agree with the North on the matter of article 1, clause 2, only to adopt the desired U.S. expression in the final process of drafting the fourth draft. China had no room to ask the North to yield during the second-phase conference. As expected, China was contemplating how to keep the main phrase of article 1, clause 2 intact—per U.S. wishes—but in return include in the agreement text the LWR as an incentive to the North, without stretching the agreement so far that it broke.

Frankly, we had no reason to oppose the idea of having five nations provide an LWR to the North in exchange for denuclearization—it was just U.S. opposition to the idea that prevented South Korea from saying so. Since South Korea had to live with the threat of the North's nuclear weapons every day, this was a worthy trade from our point of view. In the 1994 Agreed Framework, the United States did decide to provide an LWR to the North, on the grounds that electricity production using an LWR was not likely to allow the production of plutonium, enabling the production of nuclear weapons, while nuclear-power-based production of electricity using a graphite-moderated reactor could yield plutonium. That was why the construction at Sinpo had started. But if now the United States was claiming to oppose an LWR because it might be used for nuclear weapons production, the logic was simply too flimsy. And if the future LWR came with safety mechanisms, including joint management by provider nations as the North had indicated, then it was not something the United States should outright oppose. But the neocon-controlled Bush administration was allergic to the mere phrase "light-water reactor."

The Formation of a Reverse Five-to-One Dynamic and the Birth of the 9.19 Joint Statement

The second-phase conference of the fourth SPT opened in Beijing two weeks behind schedule, on September 13. The North had delayed the resumption over South Korea's Eulji military drill, which concluded on September 2, and the U.S. appointment of a special envoy on North Korean human rights.

On September 12, the South Korean government held a high-level strategic meeting on the North Korean nuclear issue and confirmed our position on the contentious article 1, clause 2: "If the North gives up all its nuclear weapons and nuclear programs, returns to the NPT, and executes IAEA safety measures, then it can exercise the rights to use nuclear power peacefully." To the United States, the government would advise being flexible on the exact phrasing of the peaceful use of nuclear power. To the North, we would advise adopting a more cooperative stance on various points of contention that would arise in the fourth draft; in return we would recognize the North's interest in acquiring rights to the peaceful use of nuclear power.

Regarding the North's demand for an LWR, the government would seek a compromise at the level of giving North Korea "possession of rights."

It became clear on the very first day of the resumed talks that the fate of the second-phase conference would depend on whether the LWR issue could be mentioned in the agreement text. At the bilateral consultation between South Korea and China on September 13, the Chinese side made it clear that if the United States did not accept the North's demand for an LWR, then the United States would simply have to give up the expression "giving up all nuclear programs"—which meant that this time the talks would center on resolving the LWR issue. When our side proposed first reaching an agreement on principles in this phase and delaying the discussion of specific issues, the Chinese side showed clear determination to explicitly mention the LWR in the text, pointing out, "What you are doing is ignoring reality and saying we should not discuss the light-water reactor."

At the inter-Korean consultation that followed, the North's vice foreign minister, Kim Kye-gwan, consistently emphasized to our deputy minister, Song Min-soon, that at issue was the provision of the LWR: "The question of the light-water reactor is fundamentally a matter of political will; if that will can be confirmed, we can be flexible on the timing of the provision."

On the morning of September 14, a bilateral consultation was held between South Korea and Russia. The Russian position was as clear as the Chinese one. The Russian delegation head, Vice Minister Alexeyev, asked, "Why is it said that a sovereign nation has no right to use nuclear power peacefully? Explain to me the American logic on this." When Song said, "The American position is not like that," Alexeyev rebutted, "Exactly a half day ago, Assistant Secretary Hill clearly told me that the North did not have such rights." When Song replied, "The biggest problem is that the North declared on February 10 that it possessed nuclear weapons," Alexeyev retorted,

> So what? Any country can announce as early as tomorrow that it has nuclear arms. But the important thing is, the North has expressed its intention to completely destroy its nuclear infrastructure, says it has made such a strategic decision, and has agreed to put it in writing. As far as I can see, we are not taking advantage of this historic opportunity. We are saying that we should come to an agreement on principles. We are not saying we should review each and every possibility that the agreement might fail. A detailed review is a matter for discussion in a different setting later.

As a matter of fact, the Russian position was not very different from South Korea's. It was just that the South Korean delegation had strategically taken a relatively passive position during the first bilateral consultation, because we had to deal with the task of later persuading the United States. Once I received reports on the clear positions of the Chinese and Russian delegations, I thought that the possibility of arriving at a joint agreement was high. Even as a superpower, with its diplomacy controlled by neocons, it would be difficult for the United States to easily brush aside the opinions of other major powers at the SPTs. Since China and Russia, which had until then shied away from taking a clear position because of the United States, were now clearly expressing opposition to the United States on the matter of article 1, clause 2, I thought it would now be that much easier for the South Korean government to persuade the United States.

The problem was Japan. If only Japan could recognize the North's right to the peaceful use of nuclear power, including having an LWR, then the United States would be facing opposition to its flawed argument from five nations, and would have no choice but to change its original position.

Perhaps it was telepathy. Soon after the consultation between South Korea and Russia, Deputy Minister Song Min-soon deployed the strategy of coaxing a new position from Japan at the consultation between South Korea and Japan. Director Sasae Kenichiro, the Japanese delegation head, expressed his gratitude to the South Korean delegation for arranging a consultation between Japan and North Korea, a meeting that had lasted more than an hour. Sasae told Song,

> I think it will be possible for North Korea to have the right to the peaceful use of nuclear power if its position on giving up nuclear weapons and programs is clear. It is difficult to talk now about discussing the matter of whether to include LWRs in this. But our position is that it's possible to exercise flexibility.

When Song explained the quid-pro-quo arrangement—that the North would promise to completely denuclearize and the other nations would express their position that the North has the right to the peaceful use of nuclear power, including LWRs—Sasae said, "I understand," and then: "Japan's final conclusion is that this quid-pro-quo formulation is within the scope of our draft submission." In this way, our delegation partly blocked Japan's ability to stand by the United States. I expressed my admiration for Song's negotiation skills and asked that the delegation continue to pay attention to cooperation between South Korea and Japan so that Japan would not change its position under American pressure.

The only party left to persuade was the United States. At the bilateral consultation between the North and the United States on the afternoon of September 14, the Americans firmly rejected the North's demand for an LWR, saying it was "100 percent impossible."

I dispatched Senior Executive Officer Park Sun-won and Department Head Lee Yeo-jin of the NSC Secretariat so that they could meet daily with the North Korean side, prevent them from exiting negotiations, and make the contents of the meetings with the North known to the American NSC. In fact, they met regularly with American NSC figures during the second-phase conference and held seven working group meetings with the North Korean side. On the evening of September 14, Park and Lee met with Victor Cha and Bill Toby of the American NSC and explained the various countries' positions, noting that all five nations besides the United States had agreed on providing an LWR. Park explained,

> We have held bilateral meetings from yesterday until today, and it has been confirmed that China, Russia, and South Korea have all expressed positions in favor of adding the phrase "the right to peaceful use of nuclear power including light-water reactors" to article 1, clause 2. And now even Japan has joined in.

He drew a diagram of the five-to-one dynamic and said, "Five participating nations besides the United States take the position that this phrase must be in the agreement text, and Japan, too, has confirmed during a bilateral meeting that it shares this position." The U.S. figures reacted as though they did not believe the explanation; they said that during an unofficial conversation at the U.S.-China summit on September 13, just before this conference, President Bush had told President Hu Jintao that it was not possible to provide an LWR. They emphasized that the American position had not changed. Then Lee Yeo-jin weighed in and said that the Russian delegation, in particular, had strongly condemned the South Korean delegation during conversation for assuming a passive position on the issue of LWRs. Lee revealed that the Russians had even argued for South Korea to persuade the United States on the issue. Park showed a table that summarized the fourteen demands made by the North from the first talk to the fourth talk. He urged the United States to change its attitude: "Besides the light-water reactor, all demands have been satisfied. If we can provide a certain amount of satisfaction on the issue of the light-water reactor that the North wants, then we believe it will be possible to arrive at an agreement text."

Three tasks remained. First, China had to create a fifth draft that revised article 1, clause 2 in a rational and balanced way; second, South Korea and China had to persuade the United States; and third, we had to ensure that no unexpected crisis took place, for example, during a meeting between the North and the United States, that might prompt North Korea to suddenly exit the talks.

President Roh personally took action on the third task. He visited New York to attend the UN General Assembly and argued during his September 16 speech at the Korea Society that normalizing relations between Pyongyang and Washington had to be seriously reviewed in an effort to fundamentally resolve the hostility and mistrust between the two nations that had stemmed from the Cold War. The argument could not have thrilled the United States, but his raising of the possibility of normalization was founded on objective facts. More important, Roh's words could encourage the North, which desperately wanted to be recognized by the United States. By showing South Korea's balanced position, the president wanted to plant the idea that it was far more beneficial to the North to stick with the talks than to storm out. In fact, immediately after the speech at the Korea Society, Han Seong-ryeol from the North Korean delegation to the SPT told Park Sun-won, NSC senior executive officer, that he had heard the president's speech, and expressed his gratitude.

At the inter-Korean ministers' conference held in Pyongyang from September 13 to 16, Unification Minister Chung Dong-young urged the North to make a strategic decision enabling the birth of a joint agreement at the talks in Beijing. Chung also delivered Japan's message expressing the desire to resume dialogue between North Korea and Japan, and urged the North to do more to improve its relations with Tokyo. Even though relations between Japan and South Korea were uncomfortable at the time, the South Korean government stepped up as a mediator to improve relations between Tokyo and Pyongyang, because this was essential for peace on the Korean Peninsula.

After a very complicated consultation process, China revealed on September 16 a fifth draft, one that included the LWR issue, and requested that each nation send word as to its acceptance by 3:00 p.m. on September 17, at which point the plenary session would be held. This fifth draft, which became the backbone of the 9.19 Joint Statement, kept article 1, clause 2 as the United States wanted, but added an additional article 1, clause 6, separating the issue of the peaceful use of nuclear power and including the issue of providing an LWR. The changes looked like this:

- The Democratic People's Republic of Korea promises to give up all nuclear weapons and existing nuclear programs and return to the NPT and IAEA safety measures as soon as possible. (article 1, clause 2)

- The Democratic People's Republic of Korea declares that it has the right to the peaceful use of nuclear power. All other concerned nations expressed their respect on this matter, and agreed to discuss at an appropriate time the issue of providing a light-water reactor to the Democratic People's Republic of Korea. (article 1, clause 6, newly added)

Everyone except the American delegation agreed on the fifth draft. Japan, for the most part positive, was mindful of the American opposition. Then Foreign Minister Ban Ki-moon met with Japanese foreign minister Machimura Nobutaka on a visit to New York, where they were attending the UN General Assembly. Ban asked the Japanese government to agree on the fifth draft and to join South Korea in persuading the United States. Minister Machimura expressed his intent to cooperate as much as possible with the South Korean position.

But, as expected, the U.S. reaction was negative—they wanted China to delete the three words "light-water reactor" from the fifth draft. If that were impossible, they requested that the phrase "after North Korea has executed its obligations" be added in front of "at an appropriate time" in article 1, clause 6, in order to prevent any discussion of the provision of an LWR before the North had completely denuclearized. Assistant Secretary Hill told Deputy Minister Song the same thing. Song replied,

> While we are also not completely satisfied with the fifth draft, we believe that the draft does reflect that the objective of this talk is to arrive at an agreement on objectives in principle with regard to denuclearization of the Korean Peninsula and the North's denuclearization.

He made it clear that the South Korean government could not publicly support the American position: "We are concerned that the United States will sacrifice the good that is realistically possible in order to choose the perfect, which does not appear to be possible." Our opposition was not because we did not want to accommodate the American position, but because if we tried to revise the phrase, then the North would object and the problem would become more complicated.

When arriving at an agreement text seemed impossible due to American objections, the Chinese side considered calling for recess. But it could not end here. The consensus over the current draft was already past the 90 percent mark. If we broke for recess now, there was no guarantee something might not happen in the interval. The possibility of recess also put pressure on the United States, because it alone was objecting in a situation of five against one. Our delegation persuaded China to once again hold a meeting of delegate heads on September 18.

We hung our hopes on the ROK-U.S. foreign ministers' conference scheduled for September 17. We trusted the negotiating skill of Ban Ki-moon, whom the international community considered one of its foremost diplomats. Minister Ban did not let us down. Over two phone calls, one official meeting, and one more round of conversation at a reception, the ROK-U.S. foreign ministers' conference dramatically yielded an agreement. Secretary Rice proposed that the United States, South Korea, Japan, and Russia remark at the plenary meeting that the meaning of "an appropriate time" for providing an LWR should be understood as being after North Korea's return to the NPT, the return of trust following the execution of IAEA safety measures, and denuclearization. Then the United States would accept the fifth draft in its entirety. Ban accepted the proposal. This was a marvelous idea that would allow the United States to at least maintain its face while still producing an agreement.

I do not understand why the Bush administration, in its approach to North Korea policy, met every turn with suspicion and failed to arrive at bold decisions by adopting a broad perspective. They thought they could handle North Korea in this way, but their method didn't work, not even once. Even if discussions of the LWR to be provided to the North began immediately, they would be so lengthy that it would be impossible to begin constructing the LWR before the North had denuclearized. And only when the North had executed its return to the NPT, adopted IAEA safety measures, and denuclearized, could other participating nations at the SPTs hand over the keys to the LWR. And, if the North violated its promise to denuclearize in the course of the construction, then this LWR risked ending up very much like the one in Sinpo. But North Korea's denuclearization was such a major issue that South Korea, China, Japan, and Russia—which had no choice but to pay for the reactor—agreed to accommodate the U.S. request for the phrase "at an appropriate time," even though it increased this risk; and somehow it was the United States, which had announced it would not pay a cent toward the reactor, who undercut everyone. In all honesty, I doubted the sincerity of the Bush administration's intent to make the North's denuclearization a reality.

Still, at the closing ceremony of the fourth SPT, both South Korea and Japan briefly discussed the timing of providing an LWR, as requested by the United States, with only a slight difference in their approaches. Russia did not mention it at all. But the United States mentioned the issue at length, and in strong language, earning the ire of the North. While I was not thrilled, I thought it was acceptable to have this degree of ambiguity in major agreements that forecasted a seismic shift in Northeast Asia's Cold War–era order. This shift, I hoped, would include not only a solution to the North Korean nuclear problem, but also the normalization of relations between Pyongyang and Washington, and between Pyongyang and Tokyo, as well as the establishment of a peace regime on the Korean Peninsula. Some, of course, worry that the devil is in the details. But I thought these could be resolved down the road, as creative solutions were proposed in the course of execution, and trust between Pyongyang and Washington grew.

Only one more phrase required revision after this. On the morning of September 18, 2005, Assistant Secretary Hill met with Deputy Minister Song Min-soon and told him that an order had come from Washington to revise the fifth draft in light of a discussion between Ban Ki-moon and Condoleezza Rice. The United States said that a phrase in article 2, clause 2, which defined the resolution of hostility and normalization of relations between the United States and the North—"coexist peacefully"—was reminiscent of the concept of peaceful coexistence advocated by Soviet premier Nikita Khrushchev during the Cold War. Washington wanted it changed to "exist peacefully together." The order must have come from Secretary Rice, who had specialized in Russia as a scholar. Finally, after a long negotiation, the historic 9.19 joint statement was born. I summarize it in the table below.

The "proposal of great significance" made by the South Korean government earned a mention in article 3, clause 4, of the joint statement, as South Korea reaffirmed its commitment to supplying electricity to the North. In this way, the proposal, while not replacing financial compensation or aid to the North, was able to facilitate the subsequent execution of the 9.19 joint statement and function as a kind of safety valve for controversial matters, such as the provision of a light-water reactor. I believe that the proposal played the following roles in our eventual arrival at the 9.19 joint statement.

First, it served to facilitate the SPTs and thus functioned as the foundation for the birth of the 9.19 joint statement. The basic formula for solving the nuclear problem, shared by the six parties, was to exchange the North's denuclearization for economic compensation. Because the proposal stated that the South Korean government would shoulder economic compensation, it simplified discussion by allowing focus on the

ARTICLE 1   Denuclearization (Denuclearization by North Korea/ Resolution of North Korea's Concern over Security)
• North Korea gives up all nuclear weapons and existing nuclear programs, and returns to NPT and IAEA safety measures. • The United States renounces its intention to attack North Korea using nuclear or conventional weapons. • South Korea reaffirms its promise not to have nuclear weapons in the South and not to accept or proliferate nuclear weapons. • The two Koreas adhere to and execute the Korean Peninsula Denuclearization Joint Declaration. • North Korea retains the right to the peaceful use of nuclear energy. Other nations respect that right and agree to discuss at an appropriate time the issue of providing a light-water reactor.
ARTICLE 2   Normalization of Relations
• Respect the UN charter and international norms in mutual relations. • North Korea and the United States will respect one another's sovereignty and exist peacefully together. Measures to be taken to normalize relations. • Measures to be taken to normalize relations between North Korea and Japan.
ARTICLE 3   International Assistance to North Korea
• Increase economic cooperation in energy, trade, and investment sectors. • Express willingness to provide energy assistance to North Korea. • South Korea reaffirms its proposal to supply 200 million kW of electricity.
ARTICLE 4   (Peace Regime) Vision of Peace on the Korean Peninsula
• Relevant nations to hold negotiations on a peace regime on the Korean Peninsula at a separate forum. • Contemplate ways to increase security cooperation in Northeast Asia.
ARTICLE 5   Principle of Execution
• Principle of "promise for promise," "action for action"; measures to be mutually modulated over stages.
ARTICLE 6   Next Talk
• Early November in Beijing.

issue of promising regime security to the North and gave the other parties more room to maneuver to reach an agreement. While the economic compensation issue did not unfold as the proposal laid it out, it still acted as a safety valve.

Second, once the South Korean government made the selfless decision to bear a significant portion of the cost to solve the nuclear problem, it made other participating nations' conditions for negotiations more flexible and served as a strong stimulant to more enthusiastically engage in negotiations.

Third, the proposal strengthened South Korea's position and elevated its standing at the SPTs, from a facilitator to also a balancer.

Thus was born the historic 9.19 joint statement, containing the vision for transforming the Korean Peninsula—mired in confrontation and conflict—into a land of peace and cooperation. It had been eleven months since the South Korean NSC had informed the president—on November 5, 2004—that it would "make a breakthrough in the North Korean nuclear problem in 2005." The 9.19 joint statement was an incredible agreement that changed the security map, not only of the Korean Peninsula, but of the whole of Northeast Asia. If this statement had been properly executed, the Korean Peninsula would now be in the midst of establishing a peace regime, and a multiparty security cooperative system would have been activated in Northeast Asia. Inter-Korean economic cooperation would have intensified, allowing us to open a new economic era on the Korean Peninsula and to make new leaps and bounds.

The Roh administration did not passively await this great agreement, nor did it follow a specific faction's lead. It overcame many difficulties and showed the international community that the South Korean government had the ability to play a leading role in dismantling the Cold War structure and overcoming division on the Korean Peninsula.

I never imagined that this precious agreement, realized through long efforts of the participating governments, would be so easily destroyed by one powerful nation's unilateralism.

IV

Unfinished Tasks,
Unfinished Times

12

A Fragile Dream of Peace

The Banco Delta Asia Incident:
An Assault on the 9.19 Joint Statement

On September 17, 2005, the pain of birthing the 9.19 joint statement reached its peak. A brief diplomatic cable arrived from the South Korean embassy in Washington. Our representative, Wi Sung-rak, had, through an official at the U.S. National Security Council (NSC), confirmed that

> The U.S. Treasury Department has designated as "objects of concern over money-laundering" banks in Hong Kong and Macau that have been laundering money for North Korean companies in disguise. Hundreds of people who had savings at such banks have gathered to withdraw money.

The news left me feeling uneasy.

We were about to come to a grand agreement at the Six-Party Talks (SPTs). Success would mean that the United States would end all measures against North Korea and normalize relations with Pyongyang in exchange for the dismantling of the North's nuclear program. But if Washington were to take issue with the North's illegal financial transactions and impose financial sanctions, it was certain to threaten the SPTs. The concern was at the back of my mind, but I felt that if the talks reached an agreement, Washington would find a way to facilitate it. At the time, I had no idea this problem would grow into a monster and threaten the 9.19 joint statement.

In the immediate aftermath of the 9.19 joint statement, Seoul threw itself into drafting a plan to execute it, to be submitted at the fifth SPT. We were keen on finding a way to provide a light-water reactor (LWR) to the North. This issue had the potential to come up at any time, given Washington's unease with the idea. We considered the possibility of constructing the reactor within the Korean Demilitarized Zone (DMZ), near the east coast, and transmitting electricity to the North from there.

But even as the South Korean government diligently prepared for the fifth SPT, the U.S. Department of the Treasury designated the Chinese bank Banco Delta Asia (BDA) in Macau as an entity of suspicion over money laundering. This move—using the Patriot Act enacted after 9/11 to shut down terrorist funding sources—essentially forbade U.S. financial institutions from engaging in direct or indirect financial transactions with BDA. The Treasury Department provided background: BDA had been providing financial services to Pyongyang for more than twenty years, as well as to various North Korean companies. More importantly, BDA executives had been cooperating with North Korean officials to provide services, including wire transfers to North Korean companies that were suspected of circulating large amounts of cash that included counterfeit U.S. dollars. When Washington's measure became public, BDA customers began withdrawing their savings. On September 28, the government of Macau sent its officials to BDA in order to stabilize the financial market; Macau authorities also froze most of the $25 million in accounts that were linked to North Korea.

As time passed, the situation became more difficult. Hopes that the Bush administration would lift or relax the financial sanctions against BDA in consideration of the 9.19 joint statement were dashed. Pyongyang was certain to react angrily, but there was no way to predict the scale of that anger since the North was likely still analyzing how the BDA sanctions would impact it. Even if the United States were not going to unfreeze the BDA's North Korean accounts, at the least we wanted to minimize the impact of the case on the North Korean nuclear problem and bring this latest incident to a speedy conclusion. But since the investigation itself would take many months, there was no easy solution in sight.

When the North finally issued a response on October 18, its North Korean Foreign Ministry was livid: "The U.S. sanctions against BDA are an indirect attack intended to bring about the dismantling of the nuclear program." And on October 24, the ministry added that, while Pyongyang would return to the fifth SPT scheduled for early November, at the talks it would "quibble over and tabulate" the United States' responsibility.

I was dejected. Why was the United States raising the BDA issue now? Seoul was aware that some North Korean diplomats were engaging in illegal activities abroad, including the circulation of drugs and occasionally counterfeit U.S. dollars. But this was supposed to be a significant moment marking new relations between Washington and Pyongyang, not to mention the North's dismantling of its nuclear program. Seoul had long argued that while the so-called North Korea problem encompassed a slew of issues that included human rights violations and illegal transactions, looking at these now would only obstruct solving the nuclear problem, which was our absolute priority. President Bush himself had promised President Roh at the Republic of Korea (ROK)–U.S. summit in Santiago in November 2004 that he would focus on the nuclear issue as a priority.

We soon learned the reason for the United States' behavior: it believed North Korea was counterfeiting U.S. dollars, a serious matter if true. Despite the imperative of solving the nuclear problem, we could understand the U.S. position if the sanctions had been targeted at Pyongyang's production of counterfeit dollars. Yet if the BDA incident had been precipitated by counterfeiting, there was almost no room for any third country, such as South Korea, to get involved. In that case, the 9.19 Joint Statement was in danger.

The evidence the United States presented was weak. North Korea had purchased color-changing ink for currency production; this hinted at the possibility of counterfeiting, but was not firm proof. The Americans requested cooperation from our government on several occasions to prove the North's counterfeiting activities. It seemed that they had only circumstantial evidence. In my experience, even when the North was presented with incontrovertible evidence, the regime was highly likely to deny everything. An accusation based on flimsy evidence would only worsen the situation on the Korean Peninsula.

In the quest for facts, to form a clear stance on this issue, our government conducted its own investigation, headed by the NSC Secretariat. The conclusion was that North Korea was certainly circulating counterfeit U.S. dollars, but it was difficult to prove that it was counterfeiting them itself.

The first phase of the fifth SPT was held in Beijing from November 9 to 11. As foretold by Pyongyang, it proceeded grimly. The North's Kim

Kye-gwan, vice foreign minister, clarified Pyongyang's position at the inter-Korean consultation just before the opening of the talks:

> These financial sanctions against North Korea by the United States are aimed at making our system collapse and making us first abandon the nuclear program. We are at these talks to discuss this. As long as this issue is not solved, there will not be a single step toward progress.

At the keynote speech marking the opening of the talks, Kim assailed the United States for circulating rumors about Pyongyang's alleged illegal transactions, like drug trade. He called it an "American conspiracy to denigrate the republic, much like earlier talk of the 'Axis of Evil,'" and said, "This has exposed the secret intention of the highest U.S. leader to categorically reject the spirit of the joint statement before the fifth Six-Party Talks open."

On November 10 Kim declared, "I have the impression that other nations do not understand the seriousness of the financial sanctions or are deliberately downplaying it." He said that discussions over ending the nuclear program could not continue until the BDA issue was solved. This is how the first phase of the fifth SPT ended on November 11, even before the main discussion could begin.

In response to the North's protest, at the main conference Assistant Secretary Christopher Hill argued,

> The financial sanctions are beyond the scope of the joint statement. The American sanctions in regard to North Korea's illegal activities fundamentally are measures taken by the U.S. judicial authorities and have nothing to do with the Six-Party Talks.

The American representatives told the South Korean delegation,

> The measures currently taken by the financial and judicial authorities have been put in to place purely as part of law enforcement. The law blocks the White House from knowing the details of the investigation, given the possibility of political influence. It is even more impossible for the administration to have a say over the contents or outcome of the investigation.

As I reviewed a report on the progress of the talks, I thought North Korea pathetic for giving the U.S. Treasury Department an excuse to impose sanctions at this important juncture. But I also thought the American government quite illogical for arguing that the BDA incident and the SPTs had nothing to do with each other. This was pretending to shake someone's hand while slapping him in the face. Of course, the BDA incident was not under Hill's purview and the SPTs were not part of the U.S. Treasury Department's responsibilities. But what about President Bush? Weren't both matters under his authority? Frankly, it looked like a dirty trick to pretend as though these two branches of the U.S. government were as divided as two countries and unable to interfere with each other. It would have been far easier to solve the problem—and would have reflected better on the United States—if Washington had simply declared, "You North Koreans are counterfeiting U.S. dollars and that's far more important to us than the Six-Party Talks."

The hawks among the American delegation at the fifth SPT could barely conceal their smiles at the strong protest from the North Korean delegation. This, to them, revealed that the U.S. financial sanctions were having an effect on Pyongyang. Seeing their reaction, I feared the sanctions might become even more onerous. Indeed, the American position became increasingly confrontational. At the meeting between the U.S. and South Korean NSCs, the American side even criticized South Korea's policy toward North Korea. A report reached me that one U.S. NSC official had said the Kaesong Industrial Complex was "complete nonsense" and was "without any persuasiveness, economically speaking." He criticized the complex:

> The salary is not going to North Korean workers and for the most part is being siphoned off by the North Korean regime. Finished products and packaging materials are being transported from South Korea and all Kaesong does is packaging. What kind of economic effect can this have and what social impact will it have inside North Korea?

Without first resolving the BDA incident, there was little hope for progress at the talks. President Roh wanted to put the 9.19 joint statement into action and decided to raise the BDA issue at the U.S.–South Korean bilateral summit scheduled for November 17, 2005, in Gyeongju, South Korea. I briefed the president on the NSC Secretariat findings regarding the alleged North Korean counterfeiting; I was worried that, if Roh were to ask Bush to deal with BDA in a low-key manner, Bush would claim, without solid evidence, that the North was counterfeiting U.S. dollars, and put Roh in a difficult position. The only way to prevent Roh from pressing the issue would be if I were to exaggerate the NSC findings and confirm the accusation of counterfeiting. But I could not distort the

NSC findings, even though I was not sure whether the NSC's judgment was ultimately correct.

As expected, the BDA incident came up at the Gyeongju summit. "We are doing what we can to stop Kim Jong-il from counterfeiting our currency," President Bush told President Roh, "We will stop him from funneling funds around the world in the course of illegal drug trade."

President Roh objected:

> I feel that on this issue the United States and South Korea are not cooperating efficiently. It's not that officials are having difficulty coordinating their actions. It's actually between you, Mr. President, and me. The question I want to ask is this: We are about to sit down at the table for the Six-Party Talks, but will North Korea come to the table and trust us if we shut the doors on the funds that they have been using until now and threaten the North's survival? The message North Korea gets from this action is "Ah, America wants to destroy our regime after all."

Roh's remark frankly expressed his sense of despair in the face of this impasse to solving the North Korean nuclear problem. President Bush grew serious:

> Kim Jong-il is producing more fake U.S. dollars than anyone else in the world. What do you expect me to do as the president? I cannot sit idly and let him counterfeit our currency. Mr. President, you, too, would not simply watch North Korea produce fake South Korean bills.

Roh was inwardly shaken by Bush's answer. It was as I had feared: Roh had been briefed by the NSC that the counterfeiting charge was possible, but not certain, yet here was President Bush arguing matter-of-factly that South Korea would react similarly if their currency were at stake. Roh, unable to counter the argument, must have felt trapped.

But Roh did not give up; he countered by asking whether it was pure coincidence that the BDA incident emerged in the immediate aftermath of the 9.19 joint statement. And, even if it were a coincidence, he asked that the United States lift the measures imposed on the BDA, so detrimental to the SPTs, as long as this would not inflict any immediate and major damage on the United States.

President Roh waged this difficult fight against an American president because the Republic of Korea's security situation was so tied to the issue of North Korea's nuclear program that its people trembled in fear over where things were headed. He wanted to prevent the SPTs from failing over the BDA incident just at the moment when a solution was on the horizon.

But Bush was every bit a neocon president, bogged down by unilateralism and hegemonism; he was deaf to a small allied nation's leader who worried about and sought understanding for his country's fate. From my perspective, Bush had no intention of keeping his words in the 9.19 joint statement—that the United States and North Korea would "respect each other's sovereignty and exist peacefully together." He could not accept Kim Jong-il (who "starved his own people") as a partner for dialogue and cooperation. The next bit of conversation clearly shows that Bush was emotionally overcome by his hatred for Kim Jong-il and that this hatred influenced U.S. policy toward North Korea.

ROH: If I am to understand what you are saying, Mr. President, you seem to base your words about Chairman Kim Jong-il on your philosophical judgment of him as bad rather than any strategic or tactical judgment.

BUSH: That's right. You are correct.

ROH: To solve the problem peacefully, you have to acknowledge the regime and coax it to open up but, Mr. President, you seem to really hate acknowledging him, from a philosophical point of view.

BUSH: I acknowledge him, but I cannot stand the fact that he is starving his own people. That precisely is the problem for me—I am someone who will say I hate what I hate. I will not kindly view a dictator who starves his own people. That is my honest feeling.

Roh genuinely wondered whether it would make any difference to preach the importance of diplomatic negotiations based on compromise to a leader who saw North Korea from a black-and-white religious perspective. Bush seemed to have completely forgotten that only a year earlier he had accepted President Roh's plea: that he refrain from calling Kim Jong-il a liar for the sake of negotiations. Our president could be equally stubborn, but I felt sorry that he could not reveal his stubbornness in the context of diplomacy. If we had somehow overcome the confrontational relationship between the two Koreas, there would have been no need for the president to endure the kind of bitter pain he experienced on that day, or to preach to deaf ears all while maintaining decorum, just to keep a shred of hope alive.

The discussions at the bilateral summit nudged the NSC Secretariat, with the assistance of other government offices, to again look into the possibility that Pyongyang was counterfeiting dollars. Our conclusion, however, did not deviate much from the original assessment; we decided to emphasize "concern" in the government's official wording, for the sake of ROK-U.S. relations, and therefore wrote, "Our government is seriously concerned about the issue of North Korea's counterfeit currency production."

On December 13, 2005, the South Korean embassy in Beijing sent a report about the Chinese government's BDA investigation, based on information provided by Chinese authorities. Beijing had received a report from Macau's autonomous government on its own investigation and had concluded,

> We did not discover anything in connection to North Korea's money laundering, but confirmed a history of transactions that do not conform to regulations, including withdrawals of large amounts of cash on several occasions. . . . The investigation revealed nothing illegal and showed only a history of transactions that somewhat violated regulations. It remains unclear how the U.S. can pressure North Korea with only this.

I read the report and wondered how Bush had been able to look Roh in the eye and accuse North Korea of counterfeiting U.S. currency. Did he have any proof? The United States did not accept the Macau government's findings and insisted on carrying out its own investigation, taking away several truckloads of BDA-related documents. Meanwhile the discussion of North Korea's nuclear problem walked an ever-deteriorating path, rendering the 9.19 joint statement more hollow by the day.

Washington also intensified its sanctions against North Korea, going into areas beyond finance. The Bush administration boasted, "The BDA sanctions are founded on firm proof of North Korea's production and circulation of counterfeit currency." But the outcome was Pyongyang's nuclear experiment. And only after paying such a heavy price did Washington return to the 9.19 joint statement and finally reach the 2.13 agreement with Pyongyang in February 2007. The Bush administration failed to present proof of North Korea's counterfeit currency production, despite its conviction and assurances. In June 2007, Washington unfroze $24 million of North Korean funds kept at BDA and returned the amount to Pyongyang.

In hindsight, the BDA incident may have been beyond the U.S. State Department's control, but could have been resolved at the presidential level and by the U.S. NSC. The Bush administration invoked the Patriot Act in introducing sanctions against BDA, but ultimately lifted the same sanctions in a political decision; it was a self-contradicting act. I still cannot understand why the Bush administration made such a big deal of the BDA incident, only to dismiss it, or why it went to such lengths at the risk of destroying the precious 9.19 joint declaration.

The repercussions of the BDA incident on the North Korean nuclear problem did not end there. The incident once again shifted the framing of the issue to that of confrontation between Washington and Pyongyang. There was nothing that the SPTs could achieve while North Korea bristled at U.S. financial sanctions; in the context of the BDA controversy, there was no room for China or South Korea to play their erstwhile roles as mediator and expeditor. Perhaps the U.S. neocons deliberately fueled the BDA incident because of their dissatisfaction with the final agreement at the SPTs, which saw Washington outnumbered five to one. But the U.S. actions resulted in Pyongyang's nuclear test, and the nuclear problem once again became an issue between Washington and Pyongyang—no matter how much Washington hated the idea of bilateral engagement with North Korea. The fact that the agreement of February 13, 2007, was based on a secret understanding reached between Assistant Secretary Hill and Vice Foreign Minister Kim Kye-gwan in January of that year attests to this.

The Inter-Korean Summit Aborted in the Aftermath of the BDA Incident

The BDA incident not only undermined the 9.19 joint statement—it also led to the cancellation of the second inter-Korean summit, which was tentatively scheduled for fall 2005. Unification Minister Chung Dong-young visited Pyongyang as a special presidential envoy in June 2005 and conveyed to Chairman Kim our president's desire for a second inter-Korean summit. Chung proposed holding the summit in mid-September, with no preference for location, and Chairman Kim responded positively.

Aware that he had never visited Seoul as promised to Kim Dae-jung at the first inter-Korean summit in Pyongyang, Kim Jong-il said, "I have never opposed paying a visit to Seoul. But the circumstances clearly aren't favorable, so what could be achieved by the visit?" The mood in Seoul was such that he would not be very welcome. Still, he floated several ideas for locations, and he seemed to have already given a great deal of thought to the inter-Korean summit. Kim told Minister Chung, who was pushing for an agreement on holding a summit in September, "I am glad to hear President Roh suggests a summit. We can notify you of the location in the near future. As for timing, how about September?" But Minister Chung again urged Kim to make a firm commitment, "The decision must be made by July if it is to be in September." Kim replied, "Then I will send my answer by mid-July." But North Korea did not bring up the summit timing in July—they appeared to be waiting for the results of the fourth SPT before giving us a concrete answer.

On August 15, 2005, a North Korean delegation headed by the Democratic People's Republic of Korea (DPRK) Worker's Party secretary, Kim Ki-nam, visited Seoul to attend the sixtieth anniversary of Korea's independence from Japan. The group made an unprecedented gesture of reconciliation by paying respects at the National Cemetery, and then on August 17 paid a courtesy call to President Roh at the Blue House. The delegation expressed its admiration for Roh's actions and his commitment to improving inter-Korean relations. Roh, in turn, emphasized the necessity of improving relations, "We must consider how people fifty years later will judge today's history and how we will be appraised if we fail to create a new history that sees progress in reconciliation and cooperation between the two Koreas."

But on this occasion, President Roh also directly criticized the North's clichéd argument that it was developing nuclear weapons to preserve its autonomy.

> The North may argue that it is developing nuclear weapons to defend itself from American threats, but it is the nuclear problem that actually brings about American interference. . . . The failure to resolve the nuclear problem is only bringing about interference at the international level. . . . Realistically speaking, Washington's standing to speak about the Korean Peninsula situation has only strengthened after the North's nuclear problem came into being.
>
> If the nuclear problem is quickly resolved, the United States will no longer be able to say this or that about the Korean Peninsula. Our government will then be able to possess greater freedom to improve inter-Korean relations, so the North must take this fact into consideration.

The Northern delegation responded nervously to President Roh's frank articulation of the problem. Delegation leader Kim Ki-nam said, "As long as the United States pursues its hostile policies, giving up nuclear arms amounts to making ourselves vulnerable." Roh had a succinct response:

> I did say, during a speech in Los Angeles last year, that there is a certain logic to the North's argument. But there is another side to the situation. Ultimately, I would like the North to understand that the United States

cannot exercise its military might on the Korean Peninsula under any circumstances if Seoul does not give its consent.

The Northern delegation must have reported the rather charged atmosphere at the discussion that day in its entirety to Kim Jong-il. Kim might have learned that President Roh was not always accommodating of North Korea, even as Roh pursued improvement in inter-Korean relations and national autonomy. Roh's leadership style was to distinguish between right and wrong, in every matter based on common sense and logic. It would not change in his stance toward North Korea. He was simply more embracing of weak Pyongyang, given his tendency to be strong before the powerful and weak before the powerless.

At lunch following the official reception, Roh was intentionally frank as he recalled the North's declaration as a nuclear power six months earlier:

> When the North declared it possessed nuclear arms, my immediate worry was over the Kaesong Industrial Complex. I wondered whether the project could properly continue under the circumstances. So I ordered that everything be put on hold. But the deputy minister of unification and the NSC deputy secretary-general opposed me and pushed forward as planned. Frankly, I was extremely disappointed at the time at the North's attitude.

Everyone smiled broadly while listening to the president's recollection. But the North Korean figures must have understood that behind Roh's frankness was criticism of the North's unilateral attitude. This meeting with the Northern delegation served as a kind of indirect summit that allowed the two sides to get a sense of each other just as the prospect of an actual summit faced the two heads of state.

In the late hours of August 15, before the Northern delegation's meeting with the president, Unification Minister Chung Dong-young and Lim Dong-ok, first deputy director of the United Front Department, discussed possible dates for the inter-Korean summit. I was also present. The Northern side, while expressing openness to the summit, could not commit to specific dates: "We can tell you with certainty that we will provide a very hopeful answer in the near future," as it was "an already decided matter." They asked us for a little more time to watch the current situation, and inquired, "Should the summit take place simultaneously with the Six-Party Talks, or should it proceed once the talks reach a certain conclusion?" Also, since we had earlier indicated that we would accommodate their choice of location, they suggested that the summit might have to take place in a third country. We replied, "We must, by holding a summit, create a decisive foundation on which to proactively solve the nuclear issue and radically improve inter-Korean relations before the end of the Roh administration's term." We proposed once again that the summit be held "as soon as possible after early September." We confirmed our position on the location: "We hope it will be in the South but we respect the North's position, as we indicated before." But we made clear to them that we had not yet reviewed the possibility of hosting the summit outside of North or South Korea. Two days later, we proposed to the delegation Mt. Kumgang as the summit location—we excluded Kaesong from the potential list because it lacked the facilities to accommodate such an event.

On August 18, Seo Dae-won, an NIS deputy chief, sought me out with important information: the Russian government had secretly contacted us through intelligence channels to say that President Putin was willing to provide support if the inter-Korean summit were held in Russia. According to Seo, North Korea had already tentatively agreed and Russia had proposed that the summit be held in Russia's far eastern region in early September. Moscow said it would act as an honest broker and would send out the invitation if Seoul agreed. The government convened a high-level strategic meeting to review the Russian proposal. We would have accepted if the summit discussion between the two Koreas had not progressed as it had. It appeared that Russia had made its proposal without knowledge of the August 15 discussion we had with the North Korean delegation:

> We express our regret that we must decline the Russian proposal. We have already communicated our position concerning the inter-Korean summit to the North Korean delegation on August 15. Given the progress currently in the making in inter-Korean relations, it would be ideal to hold the inter-Korean summit on the Korean Peninsula. About this matter the two Koreas are currently communicating directly with one other.

We believed that an inter-Korean summit was well within reach once a joint agreement was signed at the SPTs, given Pyongyang's attitude and the political conditions. We were almost certain that an inter-Korean summit would take place in fall 2005, the same time that the 9.19 joint statement would be announced. But things began to unravel once the BDA incident erupted. When the incident became a major point of contention and the talks stalled, North Korea began to express much less enthusiasm for the summit. During the inter-Korean consultation over the summit in fall 2005, North Korea said, "Please wait." And it repeated the same words thereafter. Ultimately it was the BDA incident that sabotaged the summit.

At the ROK-China summit in Busan on November 16, 2005, President Roh and the Chinese president, Hu Jintao, were briefly left alone in the waiting room just before the start of the official dinner. Hu said to Roh,

> There is something I want to tell you privately. When I visited North Korea, Chairman Kim Jong-il told me to convey his regards to you, Mr. President, and that he wanted to meet at a time of mutual convenience. I am not obligated to tell you other things, but I wanted to say this much for sure.

It was welcome news, but still no different from "please wait." Roh replied,

> It would be wonderful if North and South Korea could meet and talk for the purpose of improving mutual trust, but there are difficulties due to North Korea's nuclear problem. If North Korea gave up its nuclear program and the United States still tried to exercise its might even after the North Korean nuclear problem had been resolved, South Korea would certainly stop Washington. But Pyongyang doesn't seem to trust us on this.

As I said earlier, the NSC Secretariat had received presidential approval a year earlier, in November 2004, to pursue two main goals for 2005: to resolve the nuclear problem and to hold an inter-Korean summit. And for that whole year, President Roh and many others had single-mindedly worked together to achieve those goals. The result was the 9.19 joint statement and a tentative agreement to hold an inter-Korean summit. It was a remarkable achievement. But those precious fruits of our efforts were laid to waste because of the Bush administration's maneuver against BDA.

President Roh did not allow himself to be disappointed and returned to a waiting mode. But I could not. Even at the end of 2005, I did not give up hope and tried to feel out the North's intentions. Even after becoming unification minister in February 2006, I continued to try to make an inter-Korean summit a reality, even as problems grew in conjunction with the North's nuclear development. But each time Pyongyang told me to wait. It wounded my pride to admit it, but Pyongyang had no intention of participating in an inter-Korean summit amid a worsening confrontation with Washington over the nuclear situation. I thought that an inter-Korean summit would be possible only when the situation involving the United States thawed to a certain degree.

President Roh was a leader who understood the necessity of an inter-Korean summit better than anyone else, but at his core he was also a pragmatist, and a cold rationalist. He thought it would be very difficult to hold an inter-Korean summit even as North Korea and the United States continued to quarrel. That is why, though he approved my attempts to try and hold the summit, at the same time he told me, "Don't try so hard to achieve what is difficult." Ultimately, as the president had judged, the second inter-Korean summit could take place in October 2007, only after progress was made on the North Korean nuclear problem following the 2.13 agreement and the conclusion of the BDA incident.

A Seed that Failed to Sprout:
Discussing a Peace Regime on the Korean Peninsula

Apart from the agreement over North Korea's abandonment of its nuclear program, the 9.19 joint statement had a special clause on the establishment of a peace regime on the Korean Peninsula. Article 4, clause 1 read:

> The six parties have pledged to join efforts for lasting peace and stability in Northeast Asia. The directly related parties will negotiate a permanent peace regime on the Korean Peninsula at an appropriate separate forum.

This clause held great significance for the destiny of the Korean Peninsula: it declared that negotiations would begin to transition the ceasefire, created by the July 27, 1953, armistice agreement, into a permanent peace regime.

President Roh saw peace as the leading principle behind his unification, foreign affairs, and national security policies, and from its beginning, his administration worked to realize this principle, seeing as its central task the ending of the unstable ceasefire and the formation of a peace regime on the peninsula. Efforts stalled after the North Korean nuclear problem arose, but on July 12, 2005, just before the start of the fourth SPT, Secretary of State Rice informed South Korea at a meeting of ROK-U.S. foreign ministers in Seoul of her intention to discuss in detail the question of establishing a peace regime on the peninsula; its precondition was North Korea's abandonment of nuclear arms. The South Korean government immediately welcomed the U.S. proposal and suggested in return the start of bilateral consultations.

Discussing the peace regime at the SPTs presented both an opportunity and a risk. It was certainly meaningful to start an international discussion on how to go beyond the state of ceasefire that had oppressed Koreans for fifty years. Frankly I had long thought that the DPRK-U.S. peace negotiations that Pyongyang demanded, and the ROK-DPRK peace negotiations that Seoul had called for, both ignored history and reality. The historical parties to the ceasefire were the United Nations (UN) forces, the North Korean military, and the Chinese military. Even in 2005, as the forces of the two Koreas continued to face off, the U.S. military was stationed in South Korea as part of the forces against North Korea. While Chinese soldiers completely withdrew from North Korea in 1958, the military alliance between North Korea and China remained intact and China's influence on the security of the peninsula remained considerable. Therefore, I thought it logical to sign a peace treaty among four parties: South Korea, North Korea, the United States, and China. Establishing a peace regime on the Korean Peninsula required an international discussion.

But there were potential dangers in discussing this matter at the SPTs. More than anything, I worried that North Korea had long argued for a DPRK-U.S. peace treaty, refusing to recognize South Korea as party to negotiations. If Pyongyang were to maintain its established position of excluding Seoul, then the talks would hardly be the starting point of a healthy international discussion, but rather become an ugly scene of acrimonious disagreement between the two Koreas. Another possibility was that Russia or Japan—hardly parties to the problem—would become involved in the Korean Peninsula question.

Our NSC Standing Committee recognized both the opportunity and the danger, and dispatched appropriate guidelines to our delegation, about to depart for the fourth SPT, in case the peace regime question were to be raised:

> Should there be a proposal to transition from the armistice regime toward a peace regime, involving parties such as the two Koreas and the United States, we are willing to enter discussion. But while this discussion could take place alongside the Six-Party Talks, we wish that it proceed separately from the Six-Party Talks.

When the ROK delegation arrived at the talks and contacted the other delegations, there indeed was a possibility that the issue of the peace regime on the Korean Peninsula might be proposed. But an emergency

report arrived from Park Sun-won, a senior officer of the NSC Secretariat
and a member of the delegation: the South Korean delegation, composed
of mostly foreign ministry officials, was responding very passively to
the issue. Maybe it was because our delegation was still mindful of the
concern over internationalizing the Korean Peninsula issue and of the
argument from previous administrations for signing a peace treaty solely
between the two Koreas. The government in Seoul immediately held a
high-level NSC strategic meeting. On July 26, the opening day of the
fourth SPT, a new set of detailed guidelines concerning the discussion
of a peace regime was speedily drafted and delivered to the delegation:

> Should a discussion of the peace regime be mentioned at the fourth
> Six-Party Talks, express shared conviction in its necessity but lead the
> detailed discussion away from the six-party framework and toward
> a separate framework of discussion among relevant parties (the two
> Koreas, as well as the United States and China).

There were two additional factors for the delegation to take into
consideration: first, discussion of a U.S. Forces Korea (USFK) withdrawal
must be excluded from negotiations—the presence of the USFK in South
Korea is fundamentally an issue between South Korea and the United
States. Second, the existing DMZ line, which would become the border
between the two Koreas following a peace treaty, must be managed
jointly by the two Koreas.

In accordance with the guidelines, our delegation proactively led the
peace regime discussion at the talks. Fortunately, North Korea articulated its position that it did "not object to South Korea's participation
in the peace treaty." Through this process, article 4, clause 1 of the 9.19
joint statement was approved early in the first phase of the fourth SPT,
at our suggestion.

A discussion of a peace regime on the peninsula was also conducted
between South Korea and the United States, separate from the SPTs,
through the end of 2005. At a meeting of the ROK-U.S. foreign ministers
in Washington on August 23, 2005, Secretary of State Rice reaffirmed the
American government's interest in the Korean Peninsula's peace regime:

> Once the goal of denuclearization is reached at the Six-Party Talks,
> we are conceptualizing how to ultimately realize peace and security in
> Northeast Asia by establishing a peace regime through a transition from
> the armistice to a peace treaty and progress in inter-Korean relations.

And on September 17, 2005, Foreign Minister Ban Ki-moon conveyed to Secretary Rice, at a meeting of the ROK-U.S. foreign ministers in New York, a concept paper that contained our government's vision of the peace regime:

- Replace the armistice with a peace treaty and hold negotiations under the banner of "signing a peace treaty and establishing trust" with the participation of South Korea, North Korea, the United States (and China).

- After the issuance of a joint statement on the North Korean nuclear situation, propose to the North negotiations on the peace structure after consultation between South Korea and the United States on basic matters.

- Complete the basic agreement among the two Koreas, the United States (and China) as the final product of the negotiations. If necessary, bring to completion auxiliary bilateral agreements, such as those between the two Koreas, or between North Korea and the United States.

- Ensure that none of this damages the ROK-U.S. alliance or has an impact on the USFK. The disbandment of the UN Command or any change to the command structure of the ROK-U.S. Combined Forces Command is to be proposed to the North only after consultation between South Korea and the United States.

I believed that the U.S. State Department was interested in a peace regime because Eastern Europe specialists who dominated the state department—including Secretary Rice—had concluded that long-term regime change was more realistic than a replacement or collapse of the North Korean regime. But that view did not lead to concrete policy, as we were still embroiled in the BDA incident. It also failed to move President Bush and change U.S. strategy toward the Korean Peninsula.

Still, Seoul had to proactively pursue discussion while the United States still showed an interest in a Korean peace regime. The government decided to set up a pan-governmental task force managed by Kim Sook, the North American affairs bureau director-general at the Foreign Ministry. Kim was also appointed as the government's representative at the bilateral working group. Director-general Kim contacted high-level figures on the U.S. side and expanded the ground for understanding between the two countries, moving the discussion of a peace regime forward. It reached a point where the two sides agreed on the necessity of involving China as one of the directly involved parties in the negotiation of a peace regime. On this basis, the first working group meeting on the Korean Peninsula's peace regime was held in Seoul on December 8, 2005. A variety of topics in relation to the peace regime were discussed at this conference.

This was the extent of my involvement in the peace regime discussions under the Roh administration; in 2006, I became unification minister and Director-General Kim also left his position. I am unaware of further discussions, but considering the effect of the BDA incident on the SPTs, I suspect that discussions were halted; at best, holding them would have been difficult.

The Roh administration's efforts to create a peace regime progressed several steps further after I left the government, not in the least thanks to Roh himself, who yearned for it the most. The other major party in this matter was North Korea. Roh spoke at length about the necessity of building peace on the peninsula to Chairman Kim Jong-il at the second inter-Korean summit in October 2007, which resulted in a bilateral agreement. This achievement, which made it an official task for the two Koreas to build a peace regime, was contained in the October 4 inter-Korean summit statement:

> South and North Korea share an understanding that the current armistice structure must be brought to an end and a lasting peace structure be built. They have agreed to cooperate in order to pursue the matter of declaring an end to war, through a meeting in the Korean Peninsula region of three or four heads of state who are directly concerned.

Here, "three" was a reference to the two Koreas and the United States, while "four" added China to the list. One day, when the situation improves, we will hold peace regime discussions with the concerned nations. There will be no need to restart the discussion from the very beginning; I think it will be rational to proceed to the next step on the basis of the existing 9.19 joint statement and the agreements between South Korea and the United States, and those between the two Koreas. The steps should be progressive, much as the nations in the SPTs arrived at the 9.19 joint statement on the basis of the fourth draft produced at the first-level conference, which then led to the second-level conference of the fourth SPT. I am still proud that, during the Roh administration, all discussion of a peace regime on the Korean Peninsula moved in the direction led by South Korea.

13

The Will toward Balance, and Obstacles

Balanced Diplomacy and the Failure
of the "Balancer of Northeast Asia" Theory

While the official name of the Roh administration's foreign policy was "balanced and practical diplomacy," its actual nature was simply balance. There was a reason for the difference between name and substance, much as "autonomous defense" was actually written as "cooperative autonomous defense." Those who controlled the media thought of the ROK-U.S. alliance as the be-all, end-all of South Korean foreign policy; "balanced diplomacy" had the potential to be misconstrued by them as another name for anti-Americanism. The phrase "balanced and practical diplomacy" was sufficiently diluted. Just as President Roh derided "cooperative autonomous defense" as lame autonomous defense, "balanced and practical diplomacy" was also lame balanced diplomacy, named so by the Roh administration in acknowledgement of the realities of the day. "Peace, Prosperity and National Security,"[1] the administration's national security strategy guidelines, defined "balanced and practical diplomacy" as

---

1 [The National Security Council published this set of national security guidelines in March 2004.]

maintaining balance, in our external relations, in handling objectives
and demands that differ or contradict one another, but that we must
simultaneously realize; and exercising diplomatic flexibility to achieve
set goals.

Balanced diplomacy was defined as "achieving balance and harmony
between 'principles and national interests,' 'alliances and multi-party
cooperation,' 'globalization and national identity,' and 'state and state.'"

The Grand National Party, the opposition at the time, and conservative media giants dismissed balanced diplomacy as anti-American, but
when we spoke of balance, we did not have only the United States in
mind. Our original vision was to pursue in diplomacy a balance founded
on national interests and rationalism. It was about playing the role of
balancer in matters related to the Korean Peninsula—our home—and
pursuing peace and autonomy for the Republic of Korea. In this vein,
President Roh advocated the "Northeast Asia balancer theory." This
was in the spring of 2005.

To understand the theory, it is necessary to consider the situation
that faced South Korea's foreign and national security policies. In spring
2005, the Roh administration was busily pursuing a way to overcome the
impasse in solving the North Korean nuclear problem. The government
was also deeply worried about issues such as CONPLAN 5029 and strategic flexibility, as well as how to assert national sovereignty and expand
peace in Northeast Asia. Then the relations between South Korea and
Japan chilled over the Dokdo issue, and there was still room for dispute
with China over Beijing's pursuit of the Northeast Asia Project in 2004.[2]
Our relations with neighboring countries were sufficiently worrisome.
Domestically, the autonomous defense program was about to go into
full operation and preparations were underway, at the president's special order, to formally request retrieval of wartime military operational
control from the U.S. Department of Defense (DOD). It was in the midst
of these critical developments that President Roh articulated his determination, in a number of speeches, for South Korea to play the role of
balancer in Northeast Asia:

> At present, the goal for our military is to guard peace and prosperity,
> not just on the Korean Peninsula, but in Northeast Asia. We will firmly
> defend peace in this region as a balancer of Northeast Asia. For this

2 [The Northeast Project was a study by the Chinese Academy of Social Sci-
ences that stirred up controversy in 2004 when it made certain claims regarding
ancient Korean kingdoms.]

goal, we will aspire to build a security cooperation model in Northeast Asia and further strengthen our close cooperation with neighboring countries against the backdrop of the ROK-U.S. alliance.[3]

The Republic of Korea has traditionally been a force for peace in Northeast Asia. In its history, it has never invaded a neighboring country or harmed anyone. I believe that we have the qualifications to speak forthrightly of peace. From now on, we will play the role of balancer for peace and prosperity, not only on the Korean Peninsula, but also in Northeast Asia. I intend to argue what ought to be argued and cooperate when cooperation is called for, all while exercising our given rights and shouldering our responsibilities as a sovereign nation. The balance of power in Northeast Asia will change from now on, depending on the choices we make.[4]

Do we have power? We do. If we can offer our counsel to the United States and make proposals to Russia, it can be said that we do. We have the world's tenth-largest economic might and military power. Just as even a political party with ten seats in the National Assembly is still important, we, too, can be a player, even though China and Japan are stronger. It is a contradiction to see the Israeli military as our model but think that we have no power. I sincerely ask you not to underestimate yourselves.[5]

As these excerpts reveal, President Roh thought that the Republic of Korea (ROK) should act in accordance with changing circumstances and national capabilities: Korea should play the role of balancer for the sake of the peace and collective prosperity so necessary in Northeast Asia. Of course, he did not mean that the Republic of Korea, a relatively weak and small nation among powerhouses like the United States, Japan, China, and Russia, should be a balancer in every aspect. He meant that South Korea should play a central role in resolving disputes among powerful nations, and in fostering cooperation and peace for the Korean Peninsula, our home. We would be at the center maintaining balance among different parties, but within the limits of our capabilities.

But the balancer theory was mainly about setting an appropriately future-oriented policy direction. It was about things we could achieve then and things we wished to gradually achieve in the future. We were not trying to set specific policies based on detailed plans; we merely proposed

---

3   Speech given at the graduation ceremony of the Korean Air Force Academy, March 8, 2005.
4   Congratulatory speech at the No. 3 Korean Army Academy, March 22, 2005.
5   Remarks made during a Defense Ministry briefing, April 2005.

a direction and a vision for diplomacy and national security policy. The phrase "Northeast Asia balancer" did not telegraph complexity, but that did not prevent the opposition party, most media outlets, and intellectuals from issuing strong criticism, like, "The number one axis of South Korea's diplomacy and national security policy is the ROK-U.S. alliance. Are you saying that this should be discarded?" or "What abilities does South Korea have to enable it to become a balancer between the United States and China?"

I thought it natural that our country should aspire to be a balancer, for our own survival and for regional peace, even if we lacked certain capacities. Korea had long been located at a crossroads in Northeast Asia and had suffered very painful foreign invasions. This aspiration of ours should not have been derided or considered dangerous. To be honest, I thought that President Roh's balancer theory was far-sighted and pointed to issues that we would inevitably have to address.

Roh's vision focused on finding the balance in the conflict between China and Japan. In April 2005, the daily newspaper *Joongang Ilbo* interviewed me at length about the balancer theory, as embraced by President Roh. After seeing the article online, the president sent me an internal email on April 20 that he personally wrote, expressing his feelings:

> It was a pleasure to read. Thank you for your hard work. . . . The parties to the future conflict in Northeast Asia are the Korean Peninsula, China, and Japan. I described this as a predestined relationship. The United States and Russia are one step removed [from the situation]. I described this as a relationship of strategic understanding. History teaches us that South Korea must possess the power to play balancer when China and Japan enter into a conflict. Only then can we preserve our autonomy, independence, and peace. Yet to someone who believes the confrontational relationship between the United States and China will never change, the balancer theory prompts concern over the ROK-U.S. alliance. I think that to those who want only to depend on others—to those who think South Korea doesn't matter while the United States and China do—the theory is seen as delusions of grandeur.

Back then, some media outlets and the opposition party resorted to labeling the Roh administration "pro-China, anti-American," for proposing the balancer theory. But seven years later in 2012, Park Geun-hye, presidential candidate of the Saenuri Party—the latest incarnation of the Grand National Party—announced "balanced diplomacy" as a campaign pledge. While this surely differed from Roh's version, I was both surprised and glad to see such a promise from those who, on ideological grounds, had criticized Roh's own quest for balance. Their wording was shameless, yes, but their willingness to copy it proved the idea was not an ideological issue, and that took some of the sting away. The South Korean government could adopt a balanced approach to the ROK-U.S. alliance and to ROK-Chinese relations, to create a structure of cooperation for peace and shared prosperity. Still, after the Park Geun-hye administration launched, I would joke to scholars who had advised candidate Park Geun-hye: "Use it, but pay royalties first."

Conservative media giants, interpreting the balancer theory as a signal that the government was deviating from the ROK-U.S. alliance—contrary to Roh's intentions—printed article after article making that charge. While the United States had initially not paid attention to the balancer theory, our domestic fuss naturally influenced their understanding of it, and they took a negative view. An absurd protest from Richard Lawless revealed the full extent of that negative misunderstanding.

When I visited Washington on April 28, Lawless told me the United States felt "wounded and hurt" by the balancer theory, "not because this is South Korea's long-term strategy," but

> because when President Roh said it, and the Blue House spokesperson and you explained the concept, it was said to represent a shift by South Korea from the southern trilateral alliance toward the northern trilateral alliance. Because what this implies is that the ROK-U.S. alliance—or ROK-U.S. relations—for the last sixty years were losing business for South Korea and that the ROK-U.S. alliance limited or ignored South Korea's sovereignty. If we extend this logic, this must represent an argument that the Roh administration's task is to right this structure and that the ROK-U.S. alliance must be dismantled, because it was something unilaterally imposed by the United States regardless of South Korea's intentions or interests.

I was shocked by this preposterous statement.

Neither the president, nor I, nor the Blue House spokesperson had ever said any of this, much less appeared in the news as saying such. But here was Lawless, acting like we had and making up a story. The Roh administration's understanding did not even contain the concept of a northern or southern trilateral alliance. In Northeast Asian dynamics, there were bilateral alliances—such as the ROK-U.S. alliance and the Japan-U.S. alliance—but there were no multilateral alliances. The same held true moving northward. China and the Soviet Union had fought against each other as late as in 1969, so what trilateral alliance could exist? There could only be a bilateral alliance between North Korea and China, and friendly relations between North Korea and Russia.

I learned that Washington had come to this perception thanks to an article in South Korea's largest daily, *Chosun Ilbo*, which cited an anonymous high-level official as saying "We cannot remain trapped in the southern trilateral alliance (South Korea, the United States, and Japan)." This allegedly was the background to the presidential speeches about playing balancer in Northeast Asia. Some used this as an opportunity to shift the discourse on the balancer theory and insist that Seoul was looking to leave the ROK-U.S. alliance. The *Chosun Ilbo* article had made Washington think that the president and I were saying such nonsense; I do not know who the source was behind this story, but the negative impact on ROK-U.S. relations was immense.

In spring 2005, the Roh administration was losing the debate over the balancer theory. Facing relentless external criticism on top of the U.S. misunderstanding, the government turned defensive: it shied away from any mention of a balancer role between the United States and other Northeast Asian nations and ceased to publicly discuss the theory. Professor Moon Chung-in, the greatest theorist in the field of unification, diplomacy, and national security inside the Roh administration, tried his hardest to safeguard the balancer theory, but even his efforts failed.

In hindsight, the National Security Council (NSC) Secretariat, in charge of disseminating the theory, should have paved the way to further simplifying the debate and pushed it till the end without hesitation. Even though assaults from critics were merciless, we should have clearly articulated the true meaning and value of the balancer in Northeast Asia theory and responded resolutely.

The more time passes, the more I regret not having been able to properly respond to such attacks; after all, I had been in charge of systemizing President Roh's theory and impressing it on people's hearts. I fault myself most because when Roh presented the theory, we were already playing balancer in several important areas and the international community recognized our role as such. I am referring to many diplomatic achievements: the role South Korea played in the process of giving birth to the 9.19 joint statement; the early resolution of the nuclear material incident that threatened South Korea's diplomacy and national security; and the appointment of Ban Ki-moon as the United Nations Secretary General. These diplomatic achievements were made possible not because the Roh administration conducted its diplomacy with a one-sided reliance on its U.S. ally, but because the administration went beyond the ROK-U.S. alliance and pursued balanced diplomacy.

In the process of producing the 9.19 joint statement, Seoul clearly showed both domestic and foreign audiences that, by closely cooperating with China, it was often playing the role of balancer, beyond that of catalyzer, in matters related to the North Korean nuclear program. Frankly, it is very difficult to bring about an agreement in Northeast Asia, where interests of big nations collide and Pyongyang and Washington continue to be mired in disagreement. Under the circumstances, the Roh administration still overcame the Bush administration's hegemonic unilateralism and Pyongyang's brinkmanship. Seoul moderated between different nations' interests and played balancer in creating a path toward solving the North Korean nuclear problem.

Of course, the ROK government had not volunteered to be a balancer in the Six-Party Talks (SPTs) from the very beginning. Had the Bush administration possessed the rationality of the Clinton administration, Seoul would have tried to solve the problem through closer cooperation with the United States, rather than walking the path of balancer between Pyongyang and Washington at the risk of inviting charges of being pro-North and anti-American. But the Roh administration achieved something even more difficult than playing balancer between Beijing and Washington: it successfully played balancer between Pyongyang and Washington. But even after such achievements we still could not safeguard our balancer theory. Isn't this as true a sign as any of my incompetence as the advisor in charge of the matter?

A Wall that Even the President Could Not Climb: ROK-Japanese Relations

Balanced diplomacy is an approach that is mostly pursued in diplomatic realms when interests of three or more parties are in conflict. But as I said earlier, pursuing balance and harmony between principles and national interests, or between nations, is also balanced diplomacy. In the second case, balance can be a basic principle for handling bilateral relations. But some problems in bilateral relations are too difficult to solve this way. Northeast Asia's unresolved history issues are a good example. Of these, the conflict between South Korea and Japan was the hardest to resolve. The Roh administration tried to overcome it by "moving toward the future while looking history in the eye." But it ultimately failed.

Throughout its tenure, the administration could not find a point of diplomatic balance with Japan over the history issue. Each time history became a topic, ROK-Japanese relations lurched.

During my time at the NSC Secretariat, I visited Japan three times. Only one was an official visit; the other two were unofficial visits to discuss urgent matters. One such matter was the history issue, and the other, as described earlier, was the North Korean nuclear problem, during the recess of the fourth SPT.

From February 11 to 14, 2004, I was in Tokyo at the invitation of the Japanese government. I had a rather interesting experience during this visit. I was scheduled to meet Chief Cabinet Secretary Fukuda Yasuo on the afternoon of February 12, but Deputy Chief Cabinet Secretary Hosoda Hiroyuki asked to meet me, even if only for thirty minutes, since his office was in the same building as Fukuda's. I agreed, though I did not know what he wanted to meet me about.

It turned out he wanted to criticize South Korean policies and provoke me over the Dokdo problem. Though we had never met, he began by lecturing me on South Korean policies toward Pyongyang and Washington. He expressed his distrust of North Korea by citing the kidnappings of Japanese citizens and the North Korean nuclear problem. And he said, with dissatisfaction, that the South Korean government was too conciliatory toward North Korea. All this was still within reason. The problem came next.

He said that South Korea's policies toward North Korea offered little benefits, even in the context of domestic politics: "Even though the [Japanese economy] is not doing well and many factors are politically unfavorable, Prime Minister Koizumi still enjoys an approval rating of 50 percent, thanks to the kidnapping and the North Korean nuclear problems." Hosoda meant that Koizumi was still popular because he was strong on North Korea, even though his domestic policies were not good. Hosoda's tone was patronizing; he was implying that we did not understand the simple principle of how Koizumi's criticisms of the North could be beneficial for domestic politics. He added a few comments about ROK-U.S. relations. He said that the U.S. demand for the "complete, verifiable, irreversible dismantlement" of North Korea's nuclear program was firm, and Japan had no intention of asking or persuading the United States to compromise with North Korea. He emphasized that the ROK government should not take a position that contravened American thinking. He spoke as if he were worried for South Korea as

Seoul, seemingly without recognizing the strength of the United States, dared to express different opinions and withhold cooperation. He raised his voice to chide me that we should get along with and never fight with a country that was the world's greatest superpower and a leader in technical innovation.

I was flabbergasted and felt conflicted. Even if Japan were a parliamentary system, how could someone so rude be a deputy chief cabinet secretary? I could not tell whether he was being genuinely honest in his attempts to convince me with such simplistic and one-sided logic and direct talk, or whether he was just insulting me. I forced myself to respond but the whole time I felt uncomfortable; still, I stayed in my seat as an invited guest. I had met many Japanese people before this and had several longtime Japanese friends, but never had I met one like Hosoda.

Even up until the moment of parting, he continued to act in complete breach of diplomatic protocol. As the conversation wound down, he placed a small book in front of me. Kim Won-jin, who had accompanied me as the political attaché at the South Korean embassy in Tokyo, stiffened and flashed his eyes at me. Hosoda said, "My hometown is Shimane Prefecture; there is a small island called Takeshima in the distant sea. This book contains research about that island. I offer it to you as a present." I declined, "Despite our having different policy positions, I think I could bring myself to consult a research volume such as this. But if you have a present to give me, please send it via our embassy." It greatly concerned me that this man, who tried at an official meeting to give an advisor to the president of the Republic of Korea a Japanese book about Dokdo—one of the most potent points of contention between South Korea and Japan—was Japan's deputy chief cabinet secretary.

My intuition proved right; my ill-fated connection with Hosoda did not end there. Later he was promoted to chief cabinet secretary and I met him again in December 2004 to discuss the future of ROK-Japanese relations.

It began with the ROK-Japan summit. In Seoul in June 2004, I came to an agreement with Yachi Shotaro, advisor to the chief cabinet secretary, to pursue a "shuttle summit" between the leaders of South Korea and Japan. We divided the year into two halves and planned to have the leader of each country visit the other once during a six-month period to foster friendship, for a total of two summits. Yachi and I were in agreement: "It's necessary to create a practical setting where the two leaders can meet as though they were friends, without concern for protocol. It should not be an official and ceremonious visit as in the past." The result was the two summit meetings, one in Jeju in July 2004 and again in December that same year in the Japanese resort town of Ibusuki. But I soon found out that in our ambition to advance ROK-Japanese relations, this shuttle summit plan had greatly underestimated a real barrier.

At a joint press conference immediately after the July 21 summit, a reporter for the Japanese newspaper *Asahi Shimbun* asked President Roh how he would deal with problems like the disagreements over history between South Korea and Japan. The president quoted the Korean proverb, "One does not talk of a funeral on a wedding day." He gave a rather long reply in a positive tone, "On a good day one is supposed to say only good things." But while giving a positive answer the president committed a grave verbal gaffe that the nation would have a hard time swallowing. Regarding history, he said that Seoul "will try not to mention it as an official topic or a point of contention during my term, since it is difficult for the two governments to make any decisions or to come to any agreement." As soon as I heard his words, I knew this was trouble. The president had gone too far.

When President Roh said that Seoul would not be the first to raise a question about history, he certainly did not mean that he would not respond to the Japanese government's acts of provocation. The South Korean government cannot simply stand idle if Japan acts in a way that violates the principles set out in the 1995 Murayama Statement, in which Japan apologized for colonial rule. The president meant that, as long as Japan acted in a way that conformed to its previous apology, we would not raise new questions or create stumbling blocks for ROK-Japanese relations. In other words, he was saying that the Japanese government must resolve to accept the truthful version of history and end provocative acts. But that meaning came across only when the remark was interpreted benevolently; his words also left sufficient room for distortion. The media, frankly, do not parse such comments so finely.

It was certain that many news reports would claim that the president had agreed to never discuss the shared history of South Korea and Japan. And if the ROK government were to raise the history issue—say, in response to the Japanese government's distortions of history, or its indifference to other Japanese efforts to distort the past—the Japanese media would surely criticize us for raising the history issue after the president said he would not. The Roh administration would be condemned for flip-flopping in its Japan policy. To evade this criticism and have the presidential remark accepted as it was meant, we had to seek a favorable reply from the Japanese leadership. But this was as easy as trying to pluck fish from a tree. No matter how it was viewed, the president's comment had been an unforced error and it was my fault for not taking the pains to review his answers in anticipation of the press conference.

As feared, the situation took a turn for the worse. In fall 2004 there were several negative developments over the history issue. On October 2, the Shimane Prefectural Assembly reportedly decided to hold a meeting of the "alliance of assemblymen for consolidating the territorial rights over Takeshima" and to consider a proposal that would designate February 22, 2005—the centennial anniversary of the annexation of Dokdo by Japan as part of Shimane Prefecture—as "Takeshima Day."

There was more. The assembly then decided to exhort Tokyo to declare a "Day of Takeshima" at the national level. It had been only eight months since Hosoda had tried to give me the book about Dokdo.

Seoul was deeply worried that Japan, which a century earlier had forcibly robbed us of Dokdo, was shamefully exerting territorial rights over the island. Adding salt to the wound, 2005 was the centennial of the Eulsa Treaty, which Japan forced the Joseon Dynasty—the last Korean dynasty before colonization—to sign so that it could steal the dynasty of its diplomatic rights. Roh was enraged: was Japan trying to obscure its history of invasion and reclaim Dokdo? From the South Korean government's point of view, Japan's discussion of an event that took place over a hundred years ago and its argument for the rights to Dokdo amounted to denying the history of our nation's liberation. The president immediately ordered that an appropriate measure be found. It so happened, in response to a presidential directive in February 2, 2004, that the NSC had been operating a special task force to prepare for possible Japanese provocations over Dokdo. We had already completed an analysis of the situation and were formulating a response.

In November, we received a report that a right-wing Japanese history textbook was currently being reviewed by the Japanese government for use in schools. It seemed that the new textbook, for which the publisher was in the process of requesting the Japanese government to review and approve, contained even more problems than a highly controversial Japanese middle-school history textbook from 2001, produced by the right-wing organization Association for New History Textbooks and obtained and analyzed by the South Korean embassy in Japan. The Japanese Education Ministry was going to perform its initial review of this new textbook some time in December and request revisions for its final review, the result of which was to be announced in April 2005.

The South Korean government expressed its concerns over these issues to the Japanese government, but the reaction was very passive. Prime Minister Koizumi's annual visit to the Yasukuni Shrine, where the spirit tablets for fourteen A-Class World War II war criminals are enshrined, also presented major problems for ROK-Japanese relations, and was the greatest issue undermining trust between the two leaders. Each time I met high-level officials or politicians from Japan, I asked that they persuade the prime minister not to worship at the shrine. But they would respond that while they too were worried, Koizumi was doing this out of his personal convictions, and they were unable to overcome his stubbornness. Frankly, I was confident that I could create a basic foundation on which to pursue progress in ROK-Japanese relations, if only Koizumi would not visit Yasukuni Shrine. So I carried with me a series of talking points that explained why we could not help but see visits to Yasukuni Shrine by Japanese political leaders as a legitimation of the history of invasion. I brought this up whenever I met with high-ranking Japanese figures:

> No matter which region or city I visit in Japan, I cannot see any sign that Japan aspires to militarism or worships war. Japan is pacifist to the point that it might be said to despise war and militarism. But at Yasukuni Shrine there are spirit tablets of war criminals. And at the memorial hall of Yasukuni Shrine are displayed weapons used during the Second World War. It gives an impression of legitimating the Japanese imperial era and idealizing militarism and war. In pacifist Japan, this is an exceptional place that conveys longing for the history of aggression. And the fact that political leaders who represent Japan visit Yasukuni Shrine makes victims, such as Koreans, and people who love peace around the world, doubt Japan's intentions toward peace. We are not asking that ordinary Japanese refrain from worshiping at Yasukuni, which enshrines 2.6 million souls. We are saying only that political leaders, including Prime Minister Koizumi, should not worship there.

Beginning in early 2005, it appeared that ROK-Japanese relations would severely deteriorate over the history issue if things were to continue as they were. There was no predicting what other issues might arise. Thus, I felt anxious about the shuttle summit and President Roh's visit to Japan in December. If anything were to happen to aggravate the situation, it would be worse than holding no summit at all. I regretted making the shuttle summit possible.

As worries mounted, I thought that to avoid the problem we should at least reach a basic agreement at the Ibusuki summit between the two leaders, along the lines of, "The two nations are especially mindful that the history issue should not be raised in 2005." The Foreign Ministry thought the same. But if Koizumi were to agree to this statement, he would essentially be declaring that he would no longer worship at Yasukuni, and that was not likely. But we decided to try tackling the problem head on.

I had dinner with the Japanese ambassador, Takano Toshiyuki, on November 22. At this meeting, I emphasized the importance of 2005 for ROK-Japanese relations:

> What most interests us in the ROK-Japanese relationship is history. As you may be aware, Mr. Ambassador, next year is the Year of ROK-Japanese Friendship, marking the fortieth anniversary of the normalization of ties. But it is also the centennial of the Eulsa Treaty that led to Japanese rule over Korea, and the sixtieth anniversary of independence. What the South Korean government wishes for and aspires to is to see 2005 as an occasion to commemorate the normalization of ties forty years ago, rather than to reinforce the memory of what transpired between Korea and Japan one hundred years ago or the significance of history sixty years ago.

I emphasized that Seoul and Tokyo should work together to commemorate 2005 as the fortieth anniversary of the ROK-Japan talks and the year of friendship between Korea and Japan, rather than as the hundredth year since the start of colonial rule.

President Roh was also worried about 2005. On November 29, he met Prime Minister Koizumi at the Association of Southeast Asian Nations (ASEAN) + 3 meeting in Laos and asked Japan to exercise restraint in handling the history issue: "My footsteps are heavy in the run-up to the Japan visit, and I ask you, Mr. Prime Minister, to share the burden." To this Koizumi replied, "Let's discuss the problem when you come to Japan."

The NSC created a preliminary draft of what could be presented as a joint statement from the two leaders at the Ibusuki summit. There was a consultation with the Japanese government, and the final text came to be this: "The two leaders shared the awareness that they both should refrain from comments that evoke the unfortunate past." I asked the Asian and Pacific Affairs Bureau of the Foreign Ministry to first conduct working group discussions with Japan. But the bureau director-general, Park Joon-woo, came to see me. "I don't think this is something that can be solved through a working group. I think the NSC should directly consult with high-level Japanese leadership about this." He was correct.

Before the Ibusuki summit was to take place from December 17 to 18, 2004, I made a top-secret visit to Japan from December 13 to 14 and met with Chief Cabinet Secretary Hosoda, Advisor Yachi, and high-level figures of the Liberal Democratic Party. I thought that it would be useless to meet with Hosoda if he were still the same person from ten months prior, but since he was the secretary in charge on the Japanese side, I had to meet with him. Perhaps because he had been promoted to full secretary, however, he would exercise a far more flexible and diplomatic mode of speech than in the past. I explained to him the significance of 2005 for Seoul and proposed that there be an official agreement at the Ibusuki summit to "refrain from comments that evoke the unfortunate past." But Hosoda replied, "The Yasukuni issue is not something that even the chief cabinet secretary can control, and presently we are waiting for the prime minister to himself come to an understanding and mention [the Yasukuni matter] of his own accord."

"Our government is of the position that Prime Minister Koizumi should not worship at Yasukuni, but we have not made an official demand until now." I continued,

> As you must be aware, the approval rating among voters will rise if our president publicly questions Prime Minister Koizumi's Yasukuni visit. But the president believes that a leader should not engage in such politics and must look to the future even if the public opinion is against him in the short run.

Secretary Hosoda frankly answered that it was difficult for the prime minister to publicly pledge not to worship at the shrine, given the domestic political situation. Yachi had said the same thing the previous day. Ultimately, the talk with Hosoda was a failure, as the Japanese side could not accommodate even the short one-sentence statement we proposed. But they spoke with some confidence that Koizumi would not be visiting Yasukuni Shrine on January 1, 2005, given the opposition in South Korea and China. I knew it was hopeless, but I still met with a few more people before returning home. Even as I made my way back to Seoul, I could not abandon all hope, so I made NSC senior executive officer Park Sun-won, who had accompanied me, stay back in Tokyo. Park would be joined by our representative in Japan, Chu Gyu-ho, and meet with

Yabunaka Mitoji, the director of Asia-Pacific issues, to try to broker an agreement right up until the start of the summit.

As we had feared, instead of a "Year of ROK-Japanese friendship," 2005 became a year of misfortune haunted by ghosts of the colonial past. That misfortune began when Shimane Prefecture announced that it was declaring February 22 as Takeshima Day. The Japanese government did not care to know how South Koreans viewed Japan's annexation of Dokdo one hundred years earlier, when the Japanese military conquered Joseon and trampled our sovereignty. As far as I could tell, the Japanese government had overlooked an important fact: the prefecture's declaration of Takeshima Day and the Japanese government's abetting of it was seen by South Koreans as more than just an issue of territorial claims—it was seen as a denial of the history of Korea's liberation from their rule.

President Roh addressed this in his March 1, 2005, commemorative speech[6]:

> I once declared that I would not make a diplomatic issue out of history, in favor of making progress in bilateral relations. And my thinking has not changed to this day, because halting exchanges and cooperative relationships and heightening tensions between the two countries each time history is invoked does not help our future. But this is not something that can be solved only through our one-sided efforts—to improve relations between the two countries, the sincere efforts of the Japanese government and its people are necessary.

He was declaring that, from that moment on, he would publicly and proactively deal with Japan over history. This speech marked a turning point in the Roh administration's policies toward Japan. ROK-Japanese relations quickly chilled.

On March 28, 2005, former foreign minister Kawaguchi Yoriko, now the foreign affairs advisor to Prime Minister Koizumi, visited South Korea and asked me for a meeting. At our unofficial meeting, Kawaguchi conveyed an oral message from Koizumi to our government: he "wished to build a future-oriented relationship against the backdrop of history, while atoning for things to be atoned for and valuing the relationship of friendship and cooperation between Korea and Japan." I explained to her in detail why we had had no choice but to change the tone of our policies toward Japan. I told her that we had proposed to the Japanese government not to engage in improper conduct that evoked the past and

6 [March 1 is a South Korean national holiday marking the demonstrations by Koreans to protest Japanese colonial rule on March 1, 1919.]

to move toward a future-oriented relationship, but what we saw in return were disappointing government actions that stirred up the unfortunate past over the issues of Dokdo and history textbooks. Kawaguchi appeared not to have been aware of my December visit to Japan and asked me what proposals I had made. I read to her words from President Roh and asked that she convey them to the prime minister: "I am not trying to obtain anything from Japanese leaders in the short run. What interests us is just what exactly Japanese leaders are trying to plant in the hearts of the Japanese people."

In 2005 President Roh took up an active role in directing overall strategy toward Japan, including revamping our policy direction on Dokdo. Although his language toward Japan was firm, his actual policies remained pragmatic. The president distinguished between things that required a firm response and those that demanded sustained cooperation. He told the NSC Standing Committee in charge of Japan policymaking, "Do not resort to emotionally driven overreactions. Formulate a strategy and respond cautiously and proactively." When the media began to play fortune teller and predicted the recall of our ambassador from Tokyo over deteriorating relations, he drew a clear line, "There will be no recall of the ambassador." He also ordered the NSC Secretariat and Foreign Ministry to distinguish between politics and normal exchange and cooperation. Responses were to be limited only to the political sphere. Therefore, even as ROK-Japanese relations worsened, essential diplomatic exchanges between the two countries continued normally. Not only officials in charge of practical affairs, but even the foreign minister, who possessed political stature, was allowed to go to Japan, depending on the agenda. Goodwill exchanges with Japanese politicians were also to proceed normally, the president advised, as long as those who worshiped at Yasukuni Shrine were excluded.

Regarding the dispute over how to refer to the East Sea, the president said both sides were engaged in a useless and unwinnable fight. He felt that ultimately the government should draw the line at simultaneously writing the "East Sea/Sea of Japan," or "the Sea of Japan/East Sea." He knew that this kind of compromise would run into domestic opposition, but said, "There may be domestic political risks for us, but this decision is within our power to make." Even when the Japanese maritime police captured an ROK fishing vessel on June 2, 2005, he ordered a measured response from the Korean maritime police chief: "We should solve this rationally, while respecting each other's sovereignty and interests." About the issue of Japan's apology over the colonial past, the president said, "I am making an issue of [Japanese] actions that contradict the significance of the apology, even after apologizing twice." He added, "If one apologizes, one should act as the apology demands. Then there is no reason for anyone to ask for yet another apology."

Many Japanese media outlets took the view that President Roh had "shifted to a stronger stance over Japan in order to salvage his plummeting popularity in the domestic sphere." But this was not true. The Roh administration made multiple efforts to prevent ROK-Japanese relations from worsening in 2005. Also, President Roh's approval rating had been on a consistent upswing once 2005 began. Above all, Roh was not a leader who decided his foreign and national security policies based on whether they would benefit him politically. Otherwise, he would not have deployed troops to Iraq, fully aware that he would lose the support of half his base. And he would have pursued strong measures against North Korea, as Hosoda had advised.

While I was assisting President Roh at the NSC, I wanted to open a new era of cooperation between South Korea and Japan. There were some accomplishments but far more failures—I had not thought deeply enough about the heaviness and depth of national feelings over history, feelings that even the president could not easily overcome. There were just some things in ROK-Japanese relations that could not be verbalized or touched upon. Afterwards, I realized that there is very little that a political leader can do in the realm of ROK-Japanese relations. We are still living in a time when all our citizens are victims of the Japanese empire. Therefore, I came to recognize that there was no room for a future-oriented ROK policy toward Japan as long as Japan constantly tried to legitimate its history of aggression. Ultimately, I came to harbor the concern that the roller-coaster ride of ROK-Japanese relations would continue so long as there was no systemic mechanism in place to prevent historical provocations between South Korea and Japan.

14

Ambitious Plans that Did Not Reach Fruition: When I Was Unification Minister

Opening a New Chapter in Inter-Korean Relations

On the afternoon of Sunday, December 18, 2005, President Roh called me to his office for "a cup of tea." He had returned from an overseas tour only two days earlier. One-on-one presidential meetings were rare, so I assumed he just wanted to chat. As we sat, he asked me, "Haven't you heard anything from the prime minister or the minister?" I said I had not. "Prime Minister Lee Hae-chan and Minister Chung Dong-young have recommended you as the new unification minister. I intend to accept the recommendation." I was surprised by the unexpected news but at the same time felt happy, and thanked him.

By late 2005, I had already decided to leave the Blue House, and started preparing to do so. As I entered my third year as the NSC deputy secretary-general I began to feel the limits of my abilities. I was tired, and also thought that I was beginning to feel dominated by the president's charismatic leadership; it was increasingly difficult to serve the president while still remaining true to myself. As cooperation between the foreign and defense ministries seemed to be going well, and many important national security matters were resolved or heading toward stabilization, I decided to resign at the end of 2005 and resume in the fall my old hobby of fishing on Sundays—putting on a straw hat and seeking out good, but not too crowded, fishing spots.

But President Roh had no intention of letting me go. He had tried once, in 2004, to improve my weak standing as NSC deputy secretary-general by changing—while the Uri Party was in power in the National Assembly—the NSC Act so that he could promote me as the NSC secretary-general, even though the national security advisor was meant to assume this role. When the opposition party made this difficult, he tried to outright promote me to national security advisor and have me oversee the NSC. When in fall 2005, the national security advisor system was on the verge of being abolished, he tried to make me the director of unification, foreign affairs, and national security policy at the Presidential Secretariat, a minister-rank post. Aware of Roh's determination in such matters, I was at a loss to find the right way to tell him I wanted to resign.

This appointment came about because the current unification minister, Chung Dong-young, was returning to the National Assembly. I could not be more grateful that Roh chose me, liberating me from assisting him—a role in which I was beginning to feel my limitations—and allowing me to oversee inter-Korean relations, my academic expertise. But it was an unexpected appointment; I had heard in early December that although Chung had recommended me as his successor, the president wished to make me the director of national security policy. Prime Minister Lee, however, had apparently strongly urged the president to appoint me as unification minister, since there were many important future tasks that concerned inter-Korean relations. I was deeply grateful to Lee for his trust and high evaluation of me, and suspected the advice had crucial influence on the president, who himself changed his mind because he felt regret that I had suffered for three years at the NSC.

On February 10, 2006, I became the unification minister, following a confirmation hearing before the cabinet, a practice that was being tried for the first time. All scholars who study North Korea or inter-Korean relations hope to become unification ministers, even if they are opposed to taking up other government positions. President Roh unexpectedly made this dream possible for me.

During my term, I wanted to upgrade inter-Korean relations in two ways. The first was to come up with a model of inter-Korean cooperation that would be a win-win for both South and North Korea—one that would prove inter-Korean economic cooperation was the future of the

South Korean economy, opening new economic opportunities for South Korea, and would not just satisfy the traditional objectives of "relaxing military tensions on the Korean Peninsula and achieving national reconciliation." I wanted to form a national consensus that realizing prosperity for both Koreas was not some cliché, but ought instead to be an urgent strategy for the Republic of Korea (ROK).

My other plan was to ensure that the state carry out its basic obligations in the handling of inter-Korean relations. "Basic state obligations" refers to the responsibility the government must assume for citizens who suffer in their sacrifices for the country, or who are abandoned. For example, the state must rescue prisoners of war (POWs) taken captive and held in North Korea since the Korean War; it must also recover our citizens kidnapped by the North through various routes, and must find a way to allow separated families on opposite sides of the 38th parallel to reunite freely. I wanted to boldly solve these problems, even if it meant paying an economic price to Pyongyang.

Once in office, I tried to approach these objectives from a new angle. I ordered the ministry to develop a way to expand and develop the existing Kaesong Industrial Complex; to install an inter-Korean resource development special zone in Dancheon, North Hamgyeong Province; and to allow for joint use of the mouth of the Han River. This all boiled down to proposing a large-scale inter-Korean economic cooperation project to Pyongyang.

Dancheon was a world-class production base for noniron metals, with the largest magnesite deposit in the world (an estimated 3.6 billion tons at the Yonggwang Mine) and the biggest zinc deposit in North Korea (an estimated 300 million tons at the Geomdeok Mine). But as the North Korean economy declined, activities such as mining, power production, and smelting had been halted or were continuing very inefficiently. If the two Koreas could develop the area together, both South Korea, which imported 100 percent of its magnesite and zinc supplies, and North Korea, suffering from an economic crisis, would benefit enormously.

The plan to jointly use the mouth of the Han River involved harvesting the available one billion square meters of aggregates[1] and sharing the profit, an unprecedented opportunity to reduce military tensions. As NSC deputy secretary-general, I had visited the site with officials from the Ministry of Construction and Transportation to review this idea.

1　[Aggregates are minerals like sand and gravel that have a variety of industrial applications.]

In December 2005, the ministry reported that harvesting aggregates at the mouths of the Han and the Imjin rivers would cost an estimated 8.2 trillion won, while the profit would be an estimated 13 trillion won. I thought that these figures would be sufficient to win Pyongyang's agreement if we were to propose a joint venture. In hindsight, this was an idea that was likely to be criticized for being too focused on the relaxation of military tension and improvement of economic cooperation between the two Koreas, while ignoring the environmental impact. But, back in 2006, I did not pay attention to such concerns and believed that project would be a lever to propel inter-Korean relations forward and reduce military tensions.

At the 18th inter-Korean ministers' meeting in Pyongyang, held from April 21 to 24, 2006, I proposed these two economic cooperative ventures to the North. Pyongyang reacted positively; they agreed to add in the fifth clause of the joint press statement following the meeting that the inter-Korean economic cooperation committee would "review the issues of harvesting aggregates at the mouth of the Han River and jointly developing resources." If the North Korean nuclear problem had not worsened and inter-Korean relations had developed normally, these projects would have moved forward within a few years.

Following my appointment, the Unification Ministry began to make multidimensional efforts to free POWs and kidnapping victims held in North Korea. Making the exercise of the "state's basic obligations" central to the ministry's policy direction and putting my strength behind it was done in recognition of President Roh's determination to support those excluded from the state's care in every area of society—Roh would always lament that those who had sacrificed themselves for the state, or those who had been sacrificed because the state had not protected them, were left to help themselves. That is why the president tried hard to save victims, in all areas of society, excluded from the state's care. Within the areas of unification, foreign affairs, and national security, freeing POWs and kidnapping victims fell within my purview.

My efforts to find ways to solve these problems involved finding a bolder way to pay an economic price to the North. The Unification Ministry conceived an offer for the North, but as it would exact a significant cost, we needed to secure public understanding before the offer was made. I told the press, "Realizing this goal is very important, so I will try to solve the matter even if there is an economic price, all while trying not to wound the North's pride." To determine the whereabouts of POWs and kidnapping victims, I invited officials from the police, defense ministry, and the National Intelligence Service (NIS) to create a temporary investigation team, active from April 1 to May 30, 2006, at the Unification Ministry.

I was especially interested in bringing home POWs. It was the state's basic obligation to ensure their return—if they had fought during the Korean War but were captured by the enemy on the front, their return was promised by the armistice agreement. In fact, I pursued this even when I was at the NSC, at the special order of the president. But at the time, conditions for beginning return negotiations with the North were not suitable, so we had to consider the rather extraordinary method of bringing the prisoners back through a third nation. Using this approach, over a period of three years we were able to bring home thirty prisoners and their families by the end of 2005. By comparison, only twenty-eight prisoners had been returned in all the years prior to the Roh administration.

While I had already been working on various methods to bring back POWs, from the time my term as minister began I contemplated bolder approaches to solving this problem at the governmental level. Since the North's basic position was that there were no South Korean POWs, bringing them home was not a simple problem.

On June 18, 1953, then president Syngman Rhee opposed the June 8 prisoner exchange agreement and unilaterally freed twenty-seven thousand North Korean prisoners (who expressed opposition to communism) held in the South in violation of the agreement signed between the United Nations (UN) and the communist side. The two sides had agreed to exchange prisoners, with the ones who did not want to return home to be sent to a third nation. But President Rhee ignored this and independently freed those prisoners with anti-communist sentiments. The North reacted strongly—it wanted the South to jail them again. Ultimately, the prisoner exchange took place, but only with the prisoners who remained.

When we would argue that the North was violating the armistice agreement and refusing to send our soldiers home, our history of freeing anti-communist POWs from the North always became an obstacle. The North would counter by claiming that Rhee had violated the armistice agreement and that we should return all the freed prisoners to the North. Considering this, I thought that we had to first set a scope for the prisoners that we could ask the North to return if we were to make this POW return a reality. With this problem in mind, I wracked my brain to find a new approach.

We looked into when exactly those already-returned fifty-eight South Korean POWs had originally been captured, and discovered something startling: 60 percent had been captured after June 1953, with the signing of the armistice agreement on the horizon. We investigated further and found that most of them had been taken prisoner at the Battle of Geumseong, at the center of the front where South Korean forces and the Chinese military had engaged in a fierce battle up to the very moment the armistice agreement was signed. Our conclusion was that they were very likely to have been completely excluded from the prisoner exchange list submitted at the time of the agreement. If my theory was right, we had a new rationale for demanding the return of POWs. I asked the investigation team to draft a list of South Korean soldiers who were suspected to have been captured by the communist forces after June 1953 and we requested additional research on ROK POWs from a Korean War expert.

The kidnapping issue was a little more complex. There had been many routes by which South Koreans had been kidnapped by the North, but most victims had been fishing near the Northern Limit Line (NLL) when they were abducted by the North Korean navy. President Roh had already issued an order to get the kidnapping victims back: "This is a shameful example of how the state failed to protect and abandoned its own people." During my time at the NSC I began to come up with a solution. In particular, Roh wanted to address reports that some kidnapping victims had returned to the South, only to be tortured by the ROK intelligence apparatus. Their families had been destroyed in the ordeal.

The January 2006 report to the president from the NSC Secretariat showed that, since the Korean War, 3,794 South Koreans had been abducted to the North; of these, 3,305 had returned, but 489 remained. Pyongyang outright refused to discuss the issue of kidnapping and claimed, "There is not one person who is staying in the North against his will." It was true that some South Koreans had voluntarily gone to the North, but as the government in Seoul had no way to distinguish them, it considered all ROK citizens in the North to be kidnapped.

The Unification Ministry created negotiation guidelines on bringing home POWs and kidnapping victims. They were approved by the president and presented to the North at the 18th inter-Korean ministers' meeting. I told the Northern delegation, "Already thousands of North Korean defectors are living in South Korea—the return home of POWs and kidnapping victims will not inflict any damage on the North Korean regime." I persuaded them, "We have no intention to use this politically and want to solve the problem without wounding either side's pride." By defining the POWs we wanted returned as "people who did not fit within the framework of the armistice agreement around the end of the war," we offered a rationale that Pyongyang could accept. And we clarified that we were willing to pay an economic price. We were explicit:

> If we can confirm whether they are living or dead and letters can be exchanged, we are willing to build a heart disease center in Pyongyang. If a reunion takes place, we will build a food factory or housing in the North. If they make it home, we will consider funding North Korea's social overhead capital (SOC). For example, we could modernize Nampo Harbor or pay to repair the highway between Kaesong and Pyongyang.

I did not, however, specify to the North how much each project might cost. We believed that building a heart disease center might amount to $36 million, and SOC support in the event of the victims' homecoming would be somewhere between $88 million and 300 million. The plan was to ask for a combined return of approximately one thousand South Korean POWs and kidnapping victims.

The North expressed great surprise at my proposal—the delegation did not immediately show a positive response, but it also did not reject it outright. With this kind of reaction, I thought a good outcome would be possible if we were tenacious in persuading them. We believed the problem could not be solved in one or two meetings, so with a long-term conversation in mind, we suggested that we carry out the discussions not through the Red Cross but unofficially between the two governments. The North, however, insisted that it take place through the Red Cross. In the end, a compromise was reached. Between the South, which wanted an unofficial conversation and the North, which insisted on using the Red Cross as the channel, the agreement read, "The South and North have decided to agree to substantively solve the matter of people whose whereabouts became unknown during and after the war period." It was the first step in a long journey.

Another basic obligation of the state was to resolve the divided families' issue. Since the launch of the Roh administration, the number of families who were reunited had greatly increased; although we were building a permanent reunion facility on Mt. Kumgang, it was insufficient for the ninety thousand reunion applicants on our side. Many of these applicants were advanced in age, so waiting was not an option. I recalled that, back when I was a scholar, there was a businessman who privately pursued internet reunions for divided families, so I took my cue from that—I decided to first attempt a mass virtual reunion via internet. I had first proposed it at the high-level strategizing session on North Korea policy, chaired by then unification minister Chung Dong-young, and the Unification Ministry had creatively developed it into a video-chatting reunion for divided families and held it for the first time in August 2005.

The indirect video reunion took into consideration the fact that Pyongyang was not keen on large-scale reunions or hometown visits. Our proposal went like this:

> Once the two Koreas confirm that divided families seeking reunion are alive on both sides, everyone who has been confirmed as living will produce a roughly thirty-minute video using a camcorder. In this video people will introduce themselves, their family, personal histories, and the whereabouts of family or relatives.

To show the North what we had in mind, we presented them with a sample featuring a few divided family members living in the South. In proposing the exchange to the North, we attached the following condition:

> All expenses and equipment necessary for exchanging letters and videos between divided families will be provided by the South. We will pay $100 for each letter and $500–$1,000 for each video to cover administrative and personnel costs.

This meant that if the North provided us with videos for the ninety thousand divided family members, Pyongyang could make up to $90 million. The North was interested in this proposal—one that would help it financially but not threaten the regime—but it did not appear ready to give us an immediate answer. We decided to continue to pursue it over time.

The projects pursued by the Unification Ministry under me in 2006 aimed to find a solution to existing problems by linking cooperative ventures that would allow the state to execute its basic obligations and both Koreas to claim victory. In my opinion, all these projects were possible, given enough time and sustained efforts. But the North's long-range missile launch and nuclear test was the catastrophe that severely curtailed the space for inter-Korean conversations, and I had to resign from my position as unification minister. All the ideas that I had conceived and even proposed to the North went into dormancy. Fortunately, at least some of them were revived at the second inter-Korean summit in October 2007 and saw agreement at the summit level. The joint resource development, the joint use of the mouth of the Han River, and the exchange of videos of divided families were mentioned in the October 4 summit statement. But the project I had pursued most ambitiously—bringing home POWs and kidnapping victims—was not revived, even after inter-Korean relations improved. Both were very sensitive problems that required long-term efforts and detailed strategies, and the remaining tenure of the Roh administration was too short. This is something I regret to this day.

Finding Solutions through Secrecy: Settling the Issue of the Light-Water Reactor and Reuniting Kim Young-nam and His Mother

While I handled North Korea policy, we always looked for novel strategic thinking and ways to effectively persuade others, but it was rare that things worked exactly as we had planned. Our approach reflected our national interests, so even our best ideas had to be adjusted in the process of negotiation with others, given the competitive nature of international relations and conflict-ridden inter-Korean relations.

Still, several times during my time as unification minister, I resolved some important issues by deploying secret strategies. One was while settling the issue of the light-water reactor (LWR), and another was in pursuing a reunion between Kim Young-nam, the husband of a Japanese woman named Yokota Megumi—whom North Korea had kidnapped—and Kim's mother.

First, let's talk about the light-water reactor. The executive member-states of the Korean Peninsula Energy Development Organization (KEDO) agreed in November 2005 to put an end to the LWR operations pursuant to the Geneva Basic Agreement. Even the South Korean government, which had opposed ending this project until then, agreed after a major proposal of the South Korean government was reflected in the 9.19 joint statement.

But the process of terminating the project was complicated and difficult. Compensating the losses of subcontractors alone was estimated at $150 million, so the costs were significant. The ROK government had already paid more than $1.1 billion to construct the LWR, so it had no intention of shouldering the cost of ending the project. To put it plainly, if we did pay, we would look like total pushovers. Our government believed it was only right that the United States—which had demanded an end to the project—shoulder the cost, and argued this point. But the United States made its position very clear: it would not pay a cent. Japan likewise did not want to pay for it. The Japanese government seemed willing to say yes, however reluctantly, if the KEDO executive member-states shouldered the cost equally, but anything more was out of the question. And the European Union, which had made minor contributions to the LWR construction, was certainly not going to cover the costs, either. Ultimately it looked as though South Korea was on the hook for everything. That would mean our government, which had covered 70 percent of the construction expenses, would also have to pay 70 percent of the costs of ending the project. In fall 2005, I began to look for a way to avoid this unacceptable and unreasonable outcome.

Then one day, Senior Executive Officer Cheon Hae-seong, who was handling the LWR issue at the NSC Secretariat, brought by a senior executive from the Korea Electric Power Corporation (KEPCO), the Korean state enterprise that had overseen the Sinpo LWR construction. Cheon had important information to share: according to him, the Sinpo LWR construction process, carried out based on a contract between KEDO and KEPCO, had been delayed, leaving $200 million still in the account. KEDO was unaware of this balance, an unavoidable by-product of the repeated project delays.

This, I thought, was a breakthrough. With these funds, KEPCO would not have to spend an additional dime on terminating the LWR project; no country would have to pay any additional expenses. But if KEDO or one of its member states were to discover the $200 million surplus, they would immediately try to reclaim it from KEPCO. Adding that issue to the problem of disposing of machinery and materials would mean the project termination process would become even more complicated and protecting South Korea's national interests that much harder. Thus, I asked those in charge to maintain complete secrecy and asked KEPCO to treat the leftover funds as top secret.

I looked for a way to use this amount for the project termination—once we entered the termination phase, the leftover funds would become an issue between KEDO and KEPCO, but for the time being only South Korea knew of their existence. I held several internal meetings and created a secret strategy, reporting it to the NSC Standing Committee.

The LWR termination would cost around $150 million, coverable by the $200 million still in KEPCO's accounts; and machinery and materials that could be reused or resold were worth $700 million. Therefore,

KEPCO would incur no loss if it used the funds still in its account, took responsibility for terminating the project, and took possession of the existing equipment. KEPCO's assuming complete responsibility for the project's termination would maximize benefits to the South, but for this to work, we could not reveal that KEPCO had surplus funds—otherwise, other KEDO executive member-states would demand their return, or argue that the funds be used to pay for the termination costs, and KEDO would try to dispose of the equipment by itself. The lawyer retained by KEPCO advised that, because the surplus stemmed from KEDO's termination of the project, there was no duty to return the money. But if a controversy erupted, there were no guarantees.

We would need to deploy a two-pronged strategy to ensure that KEPCO would oversee the entire termination process. First, we would withdraw our argument that the United States shoulder the termination costs; then, in cooperation with Japan, we would propose that all KEDO executive member-states, including the United States, equally shoulder the burden. This proposal was sure to fail, as the Bush administration neocons would certainly refuse equal burden sharing. Once it failed, we would propose that KEPCO shoulder all termination costs but in return acquire the right to possess and dispose of machinery and materials. To minimize KEPCO's burden, we would limit the scope of responsibility handed over by KEDO to KEPCO as "bearing the costs of termination" and the right being given as "possession of machinery and materials." All nations would ultimately accept this proposal to reduce their own financial burdens.

This proposal passed at the NSC Standing Committee and was applied verbatim in the process of terminating the KEDO LWR project. The process unfolded as we had anticipated. However, while Japan and the European Union agreed on having one party oversee the termination, they objected that KEPCO might receive excessive benefits by taking charge. We replied that, although the machinery and materials were worth $700 million, their recycled/resale value was significantly less, but if Japan and the European Union thought otherwise, they should oversee the overall termination and South Korea would back out. But they raised their objection without any intention of handling the termination. Ultimately, the KEDO executive committee decided on May 31, 2006, that it accepted the South Korean proposal and decided to officially end the LWR project.

The South Korean state enterprise KEPCO was thus able to use the $200 million surplus to pay for termination, estimated at $150 million, and take possession of equipment worth around $700 million on top of that. The ROK government lost an astronomical sum due to the LWR termination, but thanks to this secret strategy, it was for once not the international community's pushover and struck the diplomatic coup of obtaining KEPCO's right to dispose of machinery and materials.

We were also able to reunite Kim Young-nam and his mother through use of a secret strategy. In 1979 Kim had been kidnapped by North Korea on the island of Seonyu-do, part of the city of Gunsan in North Jeolla Province, when he was still in high school. For a long time, our government did not know whether he was alive or dead. Then confirmation came that he was alive, following an incident involving his Japanese wife, Yokota Megumi.

North Korea's kidnapping of Japanese citizens was acknowledged by Chairman Kim at the September 2002 North Korea–Japan summit, where the remains of kidnap victims were returned to Japan. Among those returned were what was said to be Yokota's remains, but a DNA test revealed otherwise, prompting a diplomatic incident. In the process, the argument was raised that her husband was none other than Kim Young-nam, believed to have been kidnapped from Seonyu-do. We also believed that Yokota's husband was highly likely to be Kim, given various circumstances, but we had no firm proof.

I decided to directly ask the North about this problem at the 18th inter-Korean ministers' meeting, though I did not expect Pyongyang to readily confirm Kim's existence, as it would be an admission of kidnapping. Still, at this meeting I was planning to propose my large-scale project for ascertaining the status of POWs and kidnapping victims and retrieving them, so I thought it was worth trying to mention Kim in this context. At the meeting, I carefully brought up to the Northern delegation head the possibility of their looking into the matter of "Kim Young-nam, who went missing in the South and is believed to be the husband of the Japanese woman Yokota Megumi." He replied, "The relevant office is currently investigating." I had worried that the North would vehemently deny the entire affair, so this was a surprising answer. The fact they were "investigating" meant Kim Young-nam was indeed Yokota's husband, and was still alive. It also meant that one day they would be willing to officially confirm it, if conditions were met.

But we could not delay for long: there was much interest in Kim in both South Korea and Japan, and from our government's perspective, the North had essentially admitted it had kidnapped a South Korean citizen, so we had to actively address the matter. But if we asked why they kidnapped him twenty-eight years ago, Pyongyang was sure to deny his existence, rendering all discussion moot. The Unification Ministry had already offered to financially compensate the North and not wound its pride if it meant being able to confirm and repatriate POWs and kidnapping victims.

The ministry decided to adopt a pragmatic approach. As part of the ceremony commemorating the June 15 joint statement, we decided to try and reunite Kim Young-nam and his mother, living in the South, at the special divided families' reunion at Mt. Kumgang, taking place from June 28 to 30. The two Koreas had agreed to each choose two hundred divided families and reunite them at the event; it was also decided to exchange, on May 10, information about four hundred people on each side, double the number of reunion slots.

Our concern was that, if we included Kim on this list, the North would respond by saying it was "unable to trace" Kim. Normally, when asked for information on specific individuals, the North would claim to be unable to find 30 percent of them, a reasonable number since we ourselves usually could not locate about 20 percent of those the North asked us about. If we included Kim and were told he could not be located, then the issue would forever remain a mystery; if we pushed the North too hard and too soon, they might hide Kim forever.

Even within the ministry, some urged caution. I decided to send to the North on May 10 a list of 399 names that excluded Kim, and ordered that a message be sent through the communication channel at Panmunjom that "our list for status confirmation includes 399 names," while the remaining one name "would be explained separately to your side." This was our so-called Operation 399 + 1. I felt that if we informed the North, through a separate channel, that the last name on the list was Kim and asked to include him in the reunion, we would be free to include his name on the *next* reunion list even if the North could not confirm his status this time around.

When the South sent its list, the North began to show interest in the missing name. I decided to reveal that it was Kim, and to persuade Pyongyang through two channels. One was through Red Cross president Han Wan-sang. I asked Han, who would be in Pyongyang from May 16, to meet the North Korean person in charge and make a case for reuniting Kim Young-nam with his mother. I sent Hong Yong-jae, an official in the Conference Bureau of the Unification Ministry, to assist him. On May 18, Han met with Choi Seung-chul, deputy director of the United Front Department in the DPRK Worker's Party, and asked for his help in uniting

Kim Young-nam, along with his daughter Kim Hye-gyeong (also known as Kim Eun-gyeong), with his mother. The second channel was through our delegation, scheduled to meet with its Northern counterpart at Mt. Kumgang from May 16 to negotiate former president Kim Dae-jung's visit to the North. All the participants were in a position where they were able to convey the other side's intentions to their own superiors, so I asked our delegation head to tell the Northern side, "If the investigation is complete and conditions are good, it would be nice to hold the meeting [between Kim and his mother] at the divided families' reunion taking place as part of the June 15 commemoration." I also emphasized that it should be explained at length to the North that right now was a good opportunity for this reunion and that it would also help the North.

While pushing for Kim's reunion with his mother, the Unification Ministry also conducted DNA tests on the blood of Kim Hye-gyeong (provided by Japan), Kim Young-nam's mother (Choi Gye-wol), and his sister. In late May, the testing institution informed us that Kim Hye-gyeong and Kim Young-nam's mother were clearly granddaughter and paternal grandmother. It confirmed that Yokota's husband was Kim Young-nam, who had been kidnapped on Seonyu-do. Once this fact had been confirmed, it became even more important for the Unification Ministry to confirm Kim's status and realize his reunion with his mother. It was the state's basic obligation. There was also hope that if mother and son could meet, we might be able to confirm Yokota's fate, central to North Korean–Japanese relations.

As reuniting Kim with his mother became increasingly important, the ministry sent the DNA results to the North through Panmunjom, without attaching any documents or explanation—they would understand its meaning. But after receiving the results, the North simply sent them back in the form of returned mail. We did not react to their move—it was hard to ascertain if they were displeased or if they also understood—but what was certain was that we had shown them our firm proof.

On June 5, the two sides exchanged the outcome of their investigations into the lists of names. Because Kim was not on our list, the North, as expected, did not mention him. But on the morning of June 8, the North sent an additional letter addressed to the unification minister: it acknowledged that Kim was alive and that he would be participating in the reunion.

There must have been many reasons why the North decided to allow this, but I believe the primary one was their conviction that we would not entrap them with it, or use it politically. In its letter, the North insisted, "The [Southern] government must take responsibility to ensure that nothing will happen to create difficulties." It showed that Pyongyang felt particularly burdened in letting this mother-son reunion proceed. We did our best to ensure nothing untoward would happen, however unexpectedly, during the reunion.

On June 16, 2006, DPRK Worker's Party deputy director Choi Seung-chul was in Gwangju for the inter-Korean joint event commemorating June 15; I asked him to allow Japanese reporters to visit Mt. Kumgang for the reunion and interview Kim Young-nam and his daughter Kim Hye-gyeong. I said that this would allow the Japanese press to directly report on the truth about Yokota Megumi's status, at the heart of the dispute between North Korea and Japan. Would it not be good for North Korea? Choi replied, "You just gave me a good idea." He added that, while it was impossible to allow the Japanese press to cover this reunion, he would try to create another opportunity. As to whether Kim Hye-gyeong could accompany her father, he responded positively, saying he would discuss it with the relevant North Korean government offices.

Ultimately, through Operation 399 +1, in late June 2006 at Mt. Kumgang, Choi Gye-wol finally met her son Kim Young-nam and her granddaughter Kim Eun-gyeong (Kim Hye-gyeong) after twenty-eight years. The Japanese press could not enter Mt. Kumgang but they were able to visit Pyongyang that July and interview Kim Young-nam. This press conference in Pyongyang was the idea that Choi Seung-chul had claimed to have thought of after hearing my proposal. But it did not garner much attention because it coincided with the North's long-range missile launch.

Although I could relatively easily resolve this and a few other difficult problems through secrecy, far more situations did not allow even this approach. One example was the proposed visit by former president Kim Dae-jung to the North, a plan that was being pursued around the same time as the Kim Young-nam reunion. The North had invited former president Kim on three separate occasions, between June 2004 and August 2005. After the inter-Korean summit tentatively planned for fall 2005 was delayed because of the Banco Delta Asia (BDA) incident, the Roh administration also asked former president Kim to consider visiting the North in the interest of making progress on the nuclear problem and improving relations. Accommodating the wishes of both Korean governments, Kim Dae-jung decided in January 2006 that he would try to visit the North in late April, despite his advanced age of eighty-two years, and asked the government to help make it a reality. The government welcomed the former president's plan, informed the North, and began making preparations to support the visit. But the North never replied. With the BDA incident worsening and tensions between Pyongyang and Washington growing over the nuclear problem, it seemed that North Korea was having second thoughts about the visit.

When, in mid-January, there was still no reply from the North, former president Kim decided to delay the visit until June, after the local elections on May 31, to avoid political controversy. Still, at the inter-Korean ministers' meeting in Pyongyang that began on April 21, I forcefully raised this issue with the North. I told their delegation head that Kim had said, "I accepted the invitation from the North, made on three occasions, and asked the government to convey my feelings, but there has been no news after two months. Perhaps Minister Lee should demand a reply in person?" I urged them to give a positive answer. The North avoided a clear answer, but finally said, on the very last day of the meeting, that it was accepting, at my insistence, the former president's plan to visit the North in June. Pyongyang and Seoul then decided to hold a discussion on the visit's itinerary, scale, and protocol.

On May 16, the two Koreas held their first meeting at Mt. Kumgang devoted to discussing the visit and came to an agreement that the former president's entourage would travel by land, using railway or roads. But suddenly, the North attached a condition to the visit that Kim Dae-jung make a stop at Kumsusan Memorial Palace, where the body of Chairman Kim Il-sung was enshrined. At the second meeting in Kaesong on May 29, the North asked us outright to decide about this condition and simply avoided negotiating other matters; it was clear that Kim's visit would be impossible without settling the matter of Kumsusan. But at this point in 2006, a stop by Kim Dae-jung at Kumsusan would invite a violent reaction from the opposition and conservative media. Even if the visit were to prove to be a success, any accomplishments would be sidelined and the country would plunge into chaos over ideological differences.

For the Unification Ministry, which had championed Kim's visit to the North, the change in the North's attitude was befuddling, but the situation was clear: the Kumsusan demand was simply an excuse and the North was clearly uninterested in the visit, for the same reason they were avoiding an inter-Korean summit. The mood on the Korean Peninsula, worsened by the BDA incident, was already heading in an extreme direction, to the point that there was intense speculation over whether the North was going to launch long-range missiles. Kim Dae-jung and the Roh administration believed that this made a visit to the North that much more necessary, but with the North engaging in a protest against the United States and raising tensions, there was no way it could accommodate a visit by the former president, who would then urge Pyongyang to decide in favor of peace. Under the circumstances, I felt that it would be impossible to get the North to commit to peace, even if we agreed to Pyongyang's every demand. The only outcome of the visit would be a terrible political aftershock in the South. Former unification ministers Lim Dong-won and Jeong Se-hyun, both close associates of former president Kim, were of the same opinion.

Ultimately, the Unification Ministry and other figures close to former president Kim in the unification field concluded that the visit to the North had to be aborted. As the government's person in charge, I had to make the final recommendation to Kim Dae-jung that the visit was going to be difficult. I had to destroy the hopes of the former president, who sought, in the last stages of his life, to sacrifice himself for peace on the Korean Peninsula and for the nation's unification and prosperity. When I told him, "It appears that visiting the North now will be difficult," I could see he was crestfallen, and I felt a deep pain and guilt that I could not help him carry out his patriotic aspirations.

"Peace Is Also a Human Right"

In the early hours of July 5, 2006, from Daepo-dong, in North Hamgyeong Province's Hwadae County, North Korea launched the Daepodong-II (a long-range missile) and several Scud missiles, along with Rodong-class missiles, into the East Sea. It was a signal that Pyongyang was done negotiating the issue of U.S. financial sanctions precipitated by the BDA incident—it was going to settle the matter instead through a form of military protest. Uncertainty was gone and the situation continued to worsen. The only way to prevent things deteriorating further would be to reopen the Six-Party Talks (SPTs) but that seemed impossible. North Korea was adamant that it would not join the SPTs unless the BDA sanctions were lifted, while Washington refused to deal with North Korea and demanded that the North unconditionally return to the talks, insisting that BDA sanctions were separate from the talks. The result was Pyongyang's protest, in the form of a long-range missile launch.

This missile launch had already been foreseen at the Northeast Asia Cooperation Dialogue (NEACD) held in Tokyo the previous April, when Vice Foreign Minister Kim Kye-gwan was refused bilateral talks with the United States, represented by Assistant Secretary Hill. The NEACD, sponsored by a civic organization, brought together chief representatives of the SPTs for the first time since the first-phase meeting of the fifth SPT in November 2005. At that time, it seemed that Kim had come to Tokyo to settle matters once and for all with Hill. South Korea, deeply worried about restarting the talks, closely cooperated with China to find a mode of dialogue that would serve as a compromise between North Korea, which wanted a bilateral dialogue with Washington, and the United States, which refused any such thing. We decided that the Chinese vice foreign minister, Wu Dawei, would invite both Hill and Kim for a three-way meeting, then slip away from the venue to leave the North and the United States to talk. In fact, Wu was able to arrange this three-way meeting. I was hanging on to a thread of hope that this dialogue would yield some result. But the three-way talk was a failure: I received a report that Hill, on the way to meet Kim, received a call from Secretary Rice and turned his car around. After this incident, Pyongyang's strategy turned 180 degrees and became confrontational—it provoked the United States through military displays of long-range missiles and nuclear capabilities.

On June 1, 2006, North Korea sent its final signal to the United States in a statement made by a foreign ministry spokesperson. It took one step back from its previous position requiring the lifting of U.S. BDA sanctions before the SPTs could proceed:

> If the United States has truly made the political decision to execute the joint statement, we once again invite the American representative at the Six-Party Talks to come to Pyongyang and directly explain [Washington's position] to us.

But the proposal was immediately rejected; White House spokesperson Tony Snow said, "It is the U.S. policy not to accommodate a bilateral negotiation with North Korea."
But in its statement, North Korea said,

> If the United States continues to treat us as an enemy and puts greater pressure, we will have no choice but to resort to extreme measures in order to safeguard our survival and autonomy.

It declared that it would lodge a military protest if a bilateral dialogue with the United States did not take place. Since signs were detected that the North was preparing to launch missiles when this remark was made, there was a strong possibility it would lead to action. The only way to prevent the North's increasingly and explicitly provocative moves was a bilateral dialogue between the North and the United States, or the North's return to the SPTs—but these were both beyond the capability of the South Korean government.

The launch also put Seoul—which had ceaselessly proposed creative measures to solve the nuclear problem and sway Pyongyang and Washington—in a bind. The Roh administration expected that the United States and the opposition would demand an end to our engagement policy with the North and ask us to try to pressure the North should Pyongyang launch long-range missiles. Domestic opinion would not allow the government to continue with business as usual. But using the Kaesong Industrial Complex or the Mt. Kumgang tourism initiative to pressure the North was a dangerous step that would ruin inter-Korean relations. I decided instead to end the rice supply to the North. It would not be an unconditional suspension; if the North returned to the SPTs, shipments would immediately resume.

Beginning in May 2006 the South Korean government tried, through several channels, to persuade the North not to launch missiles. On June 16, I told the deputy director of the United Front Department, Choi Seung-chul,

> If the North launches long-range missiles, it is a threat to peace for the people of the South. It cannot be tolerated. Under the circumstances, rice shipments to the North will not be possible given public opinion. It would not matter if I had ten lives to spare.

I asked him to convey this message to his superiors, but I knew there was no way the North would buckle under my threats. Our government was trying to do what was within its powers, but we did not expect that this would change the North's attitude.

As the North's movements became clearer, the Bush administration conveyed to us a list of requests, in the form of a nonpaper,[2] that addressed scenarios following a long-range missile launch by the North:

> If the North pushes ahead with the launch, we urge Seoul to reconsider certain aspects of its engagement policy. To be specific, South Korea could consider canceling former president Kim Dae-jung's visit to the North,

---

2   [A nonpaper is an unofficial document used to convey opinions that might be too burdensome to communicate via official diplomatic documents.]

halting the expansion of the Kaesong Industrial Complex and canceling
inter-Korean meetings in regard to scheduled construction, canceling
the meeting of the inter-Korean economic cooperation committee, or
canceling the inter-Korean ministers' conference. We also urge Seoul to
approve all principles of the U.S. Proliferation Security Initiative (PSI)
and participate in training aimed at stopping WMD shipments and their
transportation means.

The United States also proposed an emergency three-way talk among
South Korea, the United States, and Japan, and demanded that we "consider strengthening the missile defense (MD) within the region." In a
nutshell, they were demanding that we give up our engagement policy,
officially join PSI, and accept the American MD system, if the North
were to launch long-range missiles.

It was interesting that this nonpaper did not mention the less-drastic
options of pressuring the North—ending fertilizer and rice shipments, or
the Mt. Kumgang tourism initiative. It seemed that U.S. officials had jotted
down whatever came to their minds, and simply forgot the less-radical
options. It was unthinkable that Washington did not mention them when
it was pushing for much stronger measures. That was common sense.

When I looked at the list of demands made in the Bush administration's
nonpaper, I wondered whether it was the North that Washington wanted to
pressure, or the South Korean government—given our engagement policy
and Seoul's lack of cooperation with the United States thus far. It was
deeply unpleasant that Washington was putting excessive pressure on us
without reflecting on its own faults, when in fact the United States shared
responsibility with the North for destroying the 9.19 joint statement by
causing the BDA incident, playing a game of chicken with Pyongyang, and
leading all of us into this situation. I wondered why we should change our
policy because of the North's long-range missile launch? I could not openly
express my discontent, as I was only a minister of a weak nation, and the
mood both in and outside South Korea was leaning toward confrontation.
But the intention of the Bush administration to use this opportunity to
torpedo our engagement policy and force us to join the MD system and
PSI—which we much opposed—seemed just shallow.

This nonpaper showed that the Bush administration was pressuring
Seoul with a strategy that presented no viable exit. But if South Korea
gave up its all-important relations with the North as per U.S. wishes, more
extreme conflicts would take place with greater frequency on the Korean
Peninsula, and in the end the situation would only worsen. Based on this

judgment, the Roh administration did not accept the U.S. demands. But it did suspend rice shipments after the North's missile launch. Besides former president Kim's already-canceled visit to the North, everything would proceed without great change.

The 19th inter-Korean ministers' conference, which I would attend as the South's chief representative, would also be held according to plan. There were objections from within the administration but I strongly argued that it should take place as scheduled. I had my own concerns; it was clear that the conference would not yield any productive outcomes. But if a regularly scheduled conference, established with great difficulty, did not proceed simply due to unfavorable circumstances, it would break continuity. Even though the North routinely acted this way, the right thing for us was to maintain continuity, no matter how difficult things became. This would help our North Korea policy in the long run. It was not right for us to argue that the North return to the SPTs and that all issues be resolved through dialogue, and yet avoid holding conferences. The Roh administration itself had called for a bilateral conference between the North and the United States, making the argument to the Bush administration that a conference did not equal a reward. It was according to this rationale that I decided the Unification Ministry's position: "We will embark on the conference and do our best."

As expected, the conference did not go smoothly. I had already announced beforehand that there would be no large-scale rice shipments to the North unless they returned to the SPTs. The Northern delegation would not allow the conference to proceed smoothly unless it secured a promise of rice shipments. When they found that our decision was firm, they refused to engage on all other topics and demanded an early end to the conference. We accepted the request without any regret. The conference ended one day earlier than scheduled, without any joint press statement. This, as expected, led to the suspension of official dialogue between the two Koreas.

I received much criticism because the ministers' conference collapsed. But the actual suspension of inter-Korean relations was limited to only that of the official channel via the Unification Ministry—exchanges of opinions in the military arena and the unofficial channels continued to operate as before. Economic cooperation and social and cultural exchanges in the civilian sector also proceeded without great change.

Although the failure of this inter-Korean ministers' conference was unavoidable, I wanted the incident to send a message to both the North and the United States. I wanted to show the North that the Roh administration keeps its word. I had made clear to the Northern officials that we could not send rice shipments—paid with taxpayer money—if the North launched long-range missiles. We clearly need to show that this was no empty threat if we were to ensure the healthy development of future inter-Korean relations.

I dealt out the rice shipment suspension card because I judged it allowed us some maneuverability in reaction to changes in the North's attitude, while at the same time its negative effects on inter-Korean relations were more limited than other forms of punishment that the United States demanded. I also took into consideration how difficult the Roh administration's position would become due to ferocious criticism from both in and outside the country if we were to continue to send rice while confronting the North over its nuclear test.

But before this strategic calculation, I thought that when the North committed actions that we clearly defined as errors, it would be inappropriate to refrain from responding. That would imply we had no influence over the North. Put another way, it would imply that any progress in inter-Korean relations had to depend entirely on the North's largess. I thought that we would not do our people justice if we continued to help the North while facing this kind of situation.

On the other hand, I wanted to show Washington that inter-Korean meetings—which the Bush administration found so distasteful—not only concerned matters between the two Koreas, but also addressed the North Korean nuclear problem. In fact, Washington saw how Seoul demanded the North's return to the SPTs and torpedoed the conference. And while we rejected the contents of the U.S. nonpaper, we also made large-scale rice shipments conditional on the North's returning to the SPTs. It showed that we were participating in the UN sanctions against the North in our own way. I wanted to ensure that the Bush administration would never again consider sending us a nonpaper that recklessly demanded a suspension of inter-Korean relations that would only worsen the nuclear problem.

However, I received considerable criticism for suspending rice shipments in response to the North's long-range missile launch. Some said the Roh administration's North Korea policy was inconsistent. Others asked, "How can you play games with food?" But the Roh administration was not inconsistent, nor was it playing with food for political reasons. This action was the least the government could do to try to reduce the risk of things heading toward a nuclear test. The rice shipments were partly humanitarian, but traditionally they were used between the two Koreas as a form of reward for the North's change in attitude. That is why the shipments were never offered for free, but took the form of a loan. On the other hand, fertilizer was clearly defined as a humanitarian item between the two Koreas. Therefore, the Unification Ministry continued to send tens of thousands of tons of fertilizer that we had promised to ship, even after the North's missile launch. I was severely criticized in the National Assembly by the Grand National Party lawmakers for the fertilizer shipment, but I could not break a promise made on purely humanitarian grounds.

I frankly believe that peace is also a human right, especially when our people feel severe anxiety and the nation's peace is threatened. When our people's peace was at risk, I believed that it was appropriate to suspend rice shipments to the North, so that South Koreans could enjoy their right to live in peace.

The North's Nuclear Test: My Return to the Life of a Scholar

On October 9, 2006, the North carried out its nuclear test. I should have been shocked, but I just felt drained, perhaps because it had been expected. Like everyone else, I had prayed that this day would not come. I tried till the last minute to stop it, even though I knew well that my ability to stop the North from carrying it out was only too limited.

As early as August 2006, signs possibly connected to a nuclear experiment were detected in Punggye-ri, Gilju County, North Hamgyeong Province. In late August, we concluded there was a strong possibility the North would carry out a nuclear test in the near future. The Roh administration started to prepare a measure with the Blue House's Office of National Security Policy at the helm. Of course, there was not much possibility that the ROK government could find a solution, considering that distrust and hostility between Pyongyang and Washington had reached its height. But the government could not resign itself to simply wait for the fateful day.

To prevent the North from carrying out its nuclear test, the ROK government made efforts to persuade both the North and the United States. We tried, starting in August 2006, to hold an inter-Korean summit and set up one last negotiation between President Roh and Chairman Kim. Even amid the deteriorating inter-Korean relations, we sent to a third country our premier veteran of negotiations with the North, Suh Hoon at the NIS, so that he could make unofficial contact with the North, but they only sent an empty reply: "We will report it to our superiors." Given the nature of the North Korean state, we understood there was only a very small possibility the North would agree to an inter-Korean summit at a time when confrontation with Washington was at its peak. But we could not sit on our hands. We kept on reminding the North of Chairman Kim Jong-il's promise, made in July 2005, to hold an inter-Korean summit, but our efforts ended in failure.

The attempts to persuade the United States were spearheaded by Song Min-soon, the director of UFN policy (from January to December 2006) at the Blue House. But this, too, proved difficult. Song's office drafted a "method for a joint comprehensive approach" and pressed the United States in the hopes of a breakthrough in the North Korean nuclear situation. And it further tried to bring about an agreement at the ROK-U.S. summit in Washington on September 14, 2006.

At the summit, President Roh suggested "creating between South Korea and the United States a way to restart dialogue and creating a momentum toward the resumption of dialogue while consulting nations who were party to the Six-Party Talks." And President Bush agreed, "That is what I wanted." We did reach an agreement at that summit to create a method for joint and comprehensive approach, but detailed methods were not agreed on or discussed. It was agreed that the method would be developed by advisors on both sides. But it was a difficult task to refine the method for a joint and comprehensive approach that the Korean government envisioned in such a way that the final product would satisfy the American neocons but still tempt the North Korean leadership. We knew this but had no choice but to do our best.

Worse still, very little time remained. On September 11, I told Assistant Secretary Hill during his visit to the Unification Ministry, "We have to make every effort as we face the prospect of a nuclear test by the North. There should be no exceptions to the efforts we make." I asked him to reconsider the North's June 1 invitation to him to visit. But Hill replied,

> I understand your words, but in Washington the feeling prevails that there is no need to meet with the North when it is not giving up its nuclear program and only using us. And the prevailing opinion is that the North will ultimately proceed with its nuclear test.

For a creative negotiator such as Hill to be heard in Washington, the North had to show greater flexibility, but the reality was heading in the opposite direction. Hill confessed his own worries: "The problem is that the North is not giving me anything to work with. It is also not giving me anything that I can use to refute the pessimistic perspective in Washington."

On October 1, Wu Dawei, the Chinese delegation's chief representative at the SPTs, came to see me; he was in South Korea to discuss President Roh's upcoming October 13 China visit and the possibility of restarting the SPTs. Wu was very interested to hear about the late September visit to the United States of our own SPT chief representative, Chun Young-woo, who held a detailed discussion over methods for a joint and comprehensive approach. Wu said that if the ROK-U.S. discussion had produced a suitable proposal to the North, he would immediately go to Pyongyang and use it to persuade the North Korean leadership. However, Chun's visit yielded virtually no results, and given the atmosphere in Washington, the outcome would have been the same no matter who had gone. Wu Dawei regretted that South Korea and the United States had not been able to draft an agreement, but still expressed his trust in the Korean government. "I publicly expressed my support for the U.S. and South Korean negotiations. This carries a certain political risk to me. Because nothing has been confirmed, [the substance of] what I am supporting has not been confirmed either. But I can do what I did because I completely trust my South Korean friends."

Yet all efforts were in vain and we ended up witnessing the North's nuclear test. Amid heightened tensions I kept a worried eye on the stock market. We had commissioned analyses of the possible effects of a North Korean nuclear test on the economy, and some had predicted that the market would fall by 30 to 40 percent. If the predictions came true, the South Korean economy was all but finished. Fortunately, the market did not crash. As I let out a sigh of relief, it occurred to me that the stock market had reacted better than the media, which were causing a ruckus that seemed to be worsening people's fears.

I had been greatly worried about the North's nuclear experiment, but after it happened, I did not believe that everything ended there. In a bid to prevent the test, we had established it as a kind of "red line" that, if crossed, would bring about a host of measures that signaled a shift in our policy toward the North. But once confronted with the nuclear test, we did not actually execute those measures, because they might have only worsened the situation and endangered the economy. The United States also spoke of having a red line, but after the test took place, it did not make any special mention of that line.

The nuclear test posed serious challenges to the ROK engagement policy. Following the BDA incident, as tensions between the North and the United States worsened, the South Korean government tried very hard to turn the situation toward execution of the 9.19 joint statement. But our efforts were not enough. What had brought about North Korea's nuclear test was not the Roh administration's engagement policy, but the Bush administration's hawkish policies. Nevertheless, the opposition party and the media giants put the blame squarely on the engagement policy and led a campaign demanding an end to the Kaesong Industrial Complex and the Mt. Kumgang tourism initiative. Unfortunately, this sort of irrational criticism worked in South Korean society, where North Korean policy is a politicized issue.

As unification minister, I was resolved to protect the engagement policy, as the foundation of government policy, as well as the Kaesong Industrial Complex and the tourism initiative. Fortunately, the engagement policy was not too difficult to safeguard. At the press conference following the October 9 ROK-Japan summit, President Roh said, "The North's nuclear experiment is a serious event that threatens peace and stability on the Korean Peninsula and in Northeast Asia. The government cannot simply insist on an engagement policy in light of this situation." The media interpreted this comment as Roh wanting to revisit his policy. I heard about this as I was on my way to Yeouido to attend a meeting of the National Assembly Standing Committee. I immediately called the Blue House and asked Secretary Yoon Tae-young to confirm the president's true intentions. Yoon said that the president thought some adjustments needed to be made, given the changing circumstances—including the nuclear test—but the president was not in any way thinking of moving away from the policy of engagement. Yoon confirmed that I could use this language to explain everything to the press and the public. After that phone call, I made it clear that while some adjustments could be made, there would be no change to the policy's basic principles.

On October 11, former president Kim Dae-jung called President Roh and lambasted the opposition party's and media's efforts to pin the blame for the nuclear test on our engagement policy. Kim asked, rhetorically, "What is the engagement policy guilty of?" He lent much strength to the government in safeguarding the engagement policy under what were very difficult circumstances.

In fact, if Roh had announced that he was reviewing the principles of the engagement policy, I would have immediately offered my resignation, despite my respect for him and my standing as one of his closest advisors. I could not discard my philosophy without a rational reason. But the president only said he would make strategic adjustments to the policy as he faced the terrible situation of the nuclear test, taking into consideration international dynamics, our expression of commitment to the North Korean issue, and domestic and international opinions. I also believed that, not unlike how we had suspended the rice shipments in response to the North's long-range missile launch, engagement policy should include a mechanism that could contain the North at a rational level in response to any undesirable actions.

Opinions were divided between the Unification Ministry and other ministries in foreign affairs and national security over what to do with the industrial complex and the tourism initiative. Roh himself concluded that the newly passed resolution at the UN Security Council did not concern these projects. After the nuclear test, there were strong opinions within the government that at least the Mt. Kumgang project, if not the Kaesong project, should be suspended. During debates, I felt like an island: public opinion was that we should accommodate the U.S. request for additional sanctions, and within the government the majority thought at least the Mt. Kumgang project should be suspended. But the president was clear in his position: "This is extremely dangerous and strategically undesirable. We cannot touch Mt. Kumgang." It put an end to the matter.

This time—unlike in the aftermath of the North's long-range missile launch—the Bush administration did not present our government with a wish list of sanctions. But it conveyed, through several channels, its position that the tourism project at Mt. Kumgang should not continue. On October 18, Assistant Secretary Hill visited me. While he said that the United States could not make any specific demands on the South Korean government over which sanctions to apply, but he made a pessimistic remark about the Mt. Kumgang venture. I explained to him, in detail, the chronology and significance of the tourism project and emphasized that it should continue.

HILL: The Kaesong Industrial Complex is easier to understand than the tourism project at Mt. Kumgang. The Kaesong Industrial Complex can offer North Koreans a chance to experience a better future. I do not know Mt. Kumgang well enough, but it seems to have different characteristics. But I am not in any way trying to impose a particular determination. . . . It appears that South Korea is not sending the kind of strong signal that we are all expecting. I am not telling you what to do, but it is my thinking that something should be done. . .

LEE: You make it sound like the South Korean government is doing nothing. Then I would like to hear from you what it is that you hope we will do.

HILL: I would like to be able to tell the press, without feeling any burden on my conscience, that I did not tell South Korea to do this or that. [Laughter.]

LEE: Aid to North Korea at the state level has stopped and economic cooperation between the two Koreas has also come to a halt. Immediately after the missile launch, we stopped shipping rice as well as providing materials for connecting the railways. There was an inter-Korean agreement that we would provide raw materials worth $80 million for light industries and receive in return underground resources from the North. But this, too, has stopped. There is not a cent of assistance at the government level any longer. What that leaves is the civilian sector, but because of the sustained confrontation between the two Koreas on the Korean Peninsula, there are very strong restrictions, including controls imposed on strategic goods. . . . The amount the South agreed to provide in 2006 was $350 million and that was all in goods and never in cash. . .

HILL: When you say, "additional military tension is rising," do you mean that [the North] will level military threats at tourists at Mt. Kumgang?

LEE: Tourists travel to Mt. Kumgang via a road that goes through the barbed-wire fence along the military demarcation line. What I mean is that if this path is shut off, tensions will rise and there will be negative effects on the economy. . . . When you leave this room, the waiting journalists will ask questions about tourism at Mt. Kumgang. It would be nice if you could say then that you respected the South Korean government's judgment.

HILL: I will do so. But I will not say I am going to Mt. Kumgang. [Laughter.]

LEE: It is important for you to understand that following the missile launch and the nuclear test the South Korean government has put a stop to far more things in its relationship with the North than the United States thinks.

HILL: If Secretary Rice asks me about the total amount of trade and aid that has been suspended due to the North's provocation, how should I answer?

LEE: The size of the governmental assistance and cooperative projects that have been halted amounts to $350 million.

HILL: Is this in cash?

LEE: No. Since President Roh took office four years ago, the government has never given the North a single cent in cash.

After this meeting, I gave an order for a list to be compiled (in English) of the South Korean projects that had provided assistance to the North but had been halted since the launch of long-range missiles. The list contained both names and scales (amounts) of the projects. It showed that we paid the North for the Mt. Kumgang tourism initiative and the Kaesong Industrial Complex—which the United States saw as so important—a total of only $20 million. That was only about 6 percent of the $350 million that the government had suspended in aid and economic cooperation ventures. I conveyed these data to Hill, who in turn reported them to Secretary Rice. This document played an important role in preventing Washington from placing demands on Seoul for additional sanctions. At that time, I would tell visiting American officials that we had always imposed a significant level of restrictions on the North due to the competitive nature of inter-Korean relations, and that we, more than anyone else, had imposed economically significant sanctions on the North since the missile launch.

As soon as I received the report that the North had carried out its nuclear test, I made the decision to resign from my post as unification minister. I saw my role in the Roh administration as lasting only up to that point. In fact, as the nuclear crisis headed toward the point of no return in the summer of 2006, I had already begun considering my resignation in the event of a nuclear test. It was not that, as unification minister or chairman of the NSC Standing Committee, I bore great responsibility for the test. Logically speaking, this was a provocation by the North, and I was not responsible for a misfortune caused by the Bush administration's ignorant hardline policy. And strictly speaking, it was the foreign ministry that held responsibility for the North Korean nuclear problem, and the overall responsibility lay with the director of national security policy at the Blue House. My responsibility for the event as the chairman of the NSC standing committee was only in a formal sense. But I thought that if anyone within the government should take responsibility for the North's shocking nuclear test, it should definitely be me. The opposition party and the press regarded me mainly as someone who had overseen the handling of the North Korean nuclear problem for the last three years at the NSC, and less as the leader of the Unification Ministry for the past year. I had no intention of trying to avoid that evaluation and criticism from the press.

But here are the real reasons I decided to resign. First, I thought it was the responsibility of the unification minister to create an opportunity for the president to have one final round of negotiations with Chairman Kim before the North went ahead with its nuclear test; in this regard, I tried and failed, and always felt guilty before the president for this failure. Second, the ridiculous assertions by the opposition party and the conservative media that held me responsible for the nuclear test, and their endless political attacks, led me to believe that I could no longer play a meaningful role as unification minister and was no longer able to devote myself to my duties with the same powers as before.

Third, considering the opposition's intensified attacks on the president after the nuclear test, and the fact that much of their criticism was directed at me, by resigning I thought that I would reduce the president's political burden. Finally, I was tired to my bones. The situation on the Korean Peninsula was already moving in a direction that made it difficult for me realize my vision, no matter how much longer I continued to lead the Unification Ministry. I wanted to return to my life as a scholar.

After U.S. secretary of state Rice visited South Korea, I called Yoon Tae-young, the secretary closet to the president, and asked him to schedule a meeting with the president so that I could express my desire to resign. But Yoon would have none of it, saying that the president's personnel plans did not include replacing me. The next day I called again and once more clarified my intention to resign: "Please tell the president. It is time I stepped down." Only then did I hear from the secretariat that the president wished to have lunch with me on October 24. It meant he had decided to accept my resignation. On that day, I ate with the president at the official residence and thanked him from the bottom of my heart for trusting me over the past four years, despite all my shortcomings. I also told him, in person, how sorry I was for my inability to bring about a meeting between him and Chairman Kim Jong-il before the nuclear test.

On October 25, I personally announced my resignation to the press corps at the Unification Ministry:

> I have always believed that it was important for a public figure to rec-
> ognize when to step down and to act when that day comes. I have felt
> limitless remorse before the nation and the president while facing the
> crisis over the North's nuclear test. I have already stated at the National

Assembly that I would not evade my responsibility. Yesterday, I saw the president and expressed my desire to step down from the post of unification minister. I do not believe that I have committed major errors while executing policies concerning the North in my capacity as unification minister. I also feel certainty about the accomplishments made by the engagement policy. But the nuclear test has subjected to scrutiny all the efforts and precious achievements of the past years for peace and stability on the Korean Peninsula, as well as inter-Korean reconciliation. And political strife is worsening. I thought that in this situation it would be best that someone more capable than me step up and overcome this problem. This is time for the ruling and opposition parties, as well as civil society, to come together and engage in discussion about North Korea policy, rather than succumbing to extreme confrontation. Our policy for peace and prosperity, as well as the engagement policy toward the North, will continue to work flexibly in response to changing circumstances and will further improve in the future.

Lastly, I revealed my personal feelings to the press corps:

I sincerely wish that I will be the last member of the nation's cabinet to suffer unbearable attacks based on ideological biases, attacks which have cast doubt on my patriotism and besmirched my character.

Not long after I expressed my intent to resign, the Bush administration abandoned its hardline policy toward the North and sought changes. The impetus came from the Republican Party's total defeat in the midterm election. On November 18, immediately after the electoral defeat, President Bush sacked Secretary of Defense Rumsfeld, an icon of the neoconservative movement, and sought changes in foreign policy, including the policy toward Iraq. U.S. North Korean policy also saw a complete turnabout in the process. The United States suddenly embarked on dialogue—which it had so distanced itself from—and began implementing a policy that suddenly prioritized the nuclear problem among all the issues connected to North Korea. And at the ROK-U.S. summit in Hanoi, Vietnam, on November 18, 2006, President Roh met, for the first time in four years, a new President Bush, one who was willing to sincerely engage over the North Korean nuclear problem:

ROH: This problem will be difficult to solve just based on negotiation tactics that go this way and that way while addressing a complex set of situations. To solve this problem, we must focus on eliminating the North's nuclear program. The nuclear problem is difficult to solve if we try to reach objectives besides the nuclear issue, such as human rights, democracy, and the authoritarian regime.

BUSH: We agree completely. That is our goal, and if you have received an impression to the contrary, it is not true at all. We must completely and wholly concentrate on eliminating the nuclear program. If anyone says otherwise to you, that is not true. Our position is clear.

This shift in U.S. policy toward North Korea ultimately led to the 2.13 agreement in February 2007. As I prepared for my resignation, I felt belated relief. But on the other hand, a sigh of sorrow escaped my mouth at the Bush administration's foolishness in changing its existing position only after the North had conducted a nuclear test. In Korean this is called "fixing the barn after losing an ox."

I went to Mt. Kumgang on December 5 and 6 and on Friday, December 8, finished my last official duty by visiting the Kaesong Industrial Complex, the signature symbol of inter-Korean cooperation. On December 11, I participated in an official departure ceremony and said goodbye to the Unification Ministry employees I had grown so fond of. As I left the ministry, I was full of remorse that I might have in vain filled our Unification Ministry staff with passion; they had believed me so much and worked so hard to formulate and execute strategies and visions that would upgrade inter-Korean relations.

The day after the ceremony, at nine o'clock in the morning, I donned my shabby jacket—which I had longed to wear for so long—in lieu of a suit and headed to my office at the Sejong Institute. It was my return after four years, since I was first appointed to the transition committee on January 1, 2003. That afternoon, after lunch, I reclined on my office sofa for a nap that I had wanted to take for a very long time. It was as if all those unfinished tasks and the dark future of the Korean Peninsula had nothing at all to do with me anymore.

Index

The authorized representative in the EU for product safety and compliance is:
Mare Nostrum Group
B.V Doelen 72
4831 GR Breda
The Netherlands

www.ingramcontent.com/pod-product-compliance
Lightning Source LLC
Chambersburg PA
CBHW020333270326
41926CB00007B/157